Love and Virtue in a Secular Age

THE BEGINNING AND THE BEYOND OF POLITICS

Series editors: James R. Stoner and David Walsh

The series is in continuity with the grand tradition of political philosophy that was revitalized by the scholars who, after the Second World War, taught us to return to the past as a means of understanding the present. We are convinced that legal and constitutional issues cannot be addressed without acknowledging the metaphysical dimensions that underpin them. Questions of order arise within a cosmos that invites us to wonder about its beginning and its end, while drawing out the consequences for the way we order our lives together. God and man, world and society are the abiding partners within the community of being in which we find ourselves. Without limiting authors to any particular framework we welcome all who wish to investigate politics in the widest possible horizon.

LOVE *and* VIRTUE *in a* SECULAR AGE

Christianity, Modernity, and the Human Good

RALPH C. HANCOCK

University of Notre Dame Press
Notre Dame, Indiana

University of Notre Dame Press
Notre Dame, Indiana 46556
undpress.nd.edu

All Rights Reserved

Copyright © 2026 by the University of Notre Dame

Published in the United States of America

Library of Congress Control Number: 2025948065

ISBN: 978-0-268-21086-1 (Hardback)
ISBN: 978-0-268-21087-8 (Paperback)
ISBN: 978-0-268-21089-2 (WebPDF)
ISBN: 978-0-268-21088-5 (Epub3)

GPSR Compliance Inquiries:
Lightning Source France, 1 Av. Johannes Gutenberg, 78310 Maurepas, France
compliance@lightningsource.fr | Phone: +33 1 30 49 23 42

To
PETER AUGUSTINE LAWLER
(1951–2017),

as we await and prepare for the resumption of our conversation. "What infinite delight would there be in conversing with them and asking them questions."

Moralists are constantly complaining that the favorite vice of our age is pride. There is a certain sense in which that is true: everyone indeed thinks himself better than his neighbor and declines to obey his superior. But . . . the same man . . . has so poor an opinion of himself that he thinks he is made for nothing but the enjoyment of vulgar pleasures. He freely limits himself to paltry desires and dares not undertake anything lofty, which he can hardly imagine.

Thus, far from thinking that we should counsel humility to our contemporaries, we should strive to give them a vaster idea of themselves and of humanity. Humility is far from healthy for them; what they lack most . . . is pride. I would gladly give up many of our little virtues for this vice.

—Tocqueville, *Democracy in America*

Jesus Christ had to come to earth in order to make it understood that all members of the human species were naturally similar and equal.

—Tocqueville, *Democracy in America*

CONTENTS

Preface   ix

Introduction   1

Part 1   23

ONE   The Failures of Theory and Theology   25
TWO   Manent: Toward the Truth of Practice   41
THREE   From the Politics of Fear to the Religion of Humanity   51
FOUR   Christianity and the Progress of Liberalism   61
FIVE   Strauss's Response to the Victory of Universalism: *On Tyranny*   76

Part 2   93

SIX   Liberty within a Christian (or Post-Christian) Horizon   95
SEVEN   Pierre Manent's Christian Aristotelianism   119
EIGHT   The Grammar of Action and Its Eternal Resonance   138

	Part 3	153
NINE	The Same and the Other: Western Configurations of Transcendence	155
TEN	The Claims of Subjectivity and the Limits of Politics	176
ELEVEN	Analogy, Virtue, and Politics	198
TWELVE	Christianity and the Truth about Man	226
Conclusion		244

Notes 259
Bibliography 291
Index 299

PREFACE

The contemporary ideology of "woke" victimhood reveals the complicity of the ethic of the "same" and that of the "other," of the expressive self and pure, formal altruism. An alternative to this vacuous complicity must include acceptance of the good as mediated by tradition and by political life.

I suffer, therefore I am. I *am* as victim. I am that I am a victim. This is the implicit fundamental creed of late Western humanity, the last feeble cry of modern (post-Christian) humanity's search for meaning.

In politics, we confront this cry in the first-personal plural: *We* are made to suffer, and therefore we are: we are insofar as we are oppressed, oppressed by the others. We exist insofar as we are victims for whom no action is yet possible except the act of blaming our oppressors. If we cannot convince ourselves and the ruling victims that we belong by some primordial right with them on the side of the "oppressed," then we cannot fully exist, we cannot stand forth, we cannot present ourselves as what we are, as positively existing or having the right to exist. There is nothing to stand up for, it seems, but the right of victimhood.

No doubt, the vogue of the rhetoric of victimhood will ebb as well as flow as we undergo the travails of late modernity. And there are, to be sure, apart from the problem of victimhood, any number of plausible ways of naming corrosive tendencies that have recently gathered force in our society and our politics. One can certainly describe and explain much, for example, by reference to the rising power of "expressive individualism."[1] Leo Strauss's tracing of the crisis of modernity's third wave to the very origins of the "modern project" of the rational mastery of nature remains pertinent, as does Eric Voegelin's discernment of a "Gnostic" temptation to the "immanentization of the eschaton" as endemic in Christian civilization.[2] The account of the contemporary ethos and ideology of victimhood that I propose to address here surely intersects with such diagnoses of the modern distemper at various points and can be read largely as a complement to them. But I submit that it is the protest against civilizational order expressed in terms of the cry of the victim that we find *hardest to answer* and thus most *disarming*, that it is in the perspective and rhetoric of victimhood that we can most precisely identify the challenge to moral and political responsibility in our times. Knowing how to respond to the perspective of the victim as a fundamental standpoint of ethics is for us the most urgent and indeed the deepest problem for responsible thinking, philosophical and theological. Until we can confidently answer the self-described victim's claim to a privileged moral status, we cannot articulate a defense of our civilization.

What lies behind our late modern obsession with victimhood? How might one trace the understanding of what it means to be human that underlies this obsession? And how might one answer the ideology of victimhood at the deep level at which it challenges our very understanding of our humanity?

I begin with two anecdotes, candid expressions of the heart that define a kind of axis for an understanding of the late modern—no doubt the terminally modern—soul. (Let me be clear that there is no question here of blaming or condemning the individual persons concerned in these stories; I consider them as representatives—even victims!—of vast social and psychological forces of which they are in no way the authors.) These two cris de coeur appear to be opposed, but they are joined fast together as the two poles of a magnetic field. To examine and evaluate these movements of the soul will require considerable abstraction in our discourse and, therefore, some patience from readers less practiced in philosophy. This abstraction is required by the radical character of today's morality and ideology. Our actual moral and political universe is increasingly driven by and framed by claims and concepts radically removed from common sense and from ordinary, practical experience.

But the abstractions, though unfamiliar, are finally quite simple in the movements of the soul they express, although, again, their implications are far removed from practice. The reader who is normally impatient with abstractions will find his or her patience in following my philosophical analysis rewarded by a vindication of prudent common sense. Practical wisdom must today arm itself with a knowing critique of the abstractions that have invaded, that are invading, our practical world.

As an example of the first expression, I will use the well-known outburst from a Yale University student in 2016. The details of the controversy (which concerned allegedly offensive Halloween costumes) need not detain us here. Let us recall only that a professor and residence "master" found himself trying to explain the intellectual mission of the university to a very agitated group of students, some calling for his firing. One student, at least, utterly rejected all such intellectual talk: "It is not about creating an intellectual space," she shrieked. "It is not. Do you understand that? It is about creating a *home* here." The Yale student's cry demands, at bottom, a kind of return to some imagined womb of pure self-identity or to the untroubled innocence of Rousseau's mythical and precivilized "state of nature." The pure embrace of who I am, of sameness with my "secret self,"[3] implies hatred of all actual institutions and conventions, simply because they allow some degree of inequality, and thus competition and alienation from the imagined purity and transparency of the aboriginal self are inherent in social reality.

The second expression is perhaps less vivid, but it too comes from a deep and powerful place in the late modern soul. My example comes from a private exchange with a student of mine. As a discussion in a small, seminar-style class I was teaching that concerned the place of sexual ethics in Christianity came to an end, a young student came to my office to pursue our discussion further. He spoke of a conversation with a male friend of his who is actively homosexual and troubled by his exclusion as such from full standing in our church. My student proposed to me that the sum and substance of a Christian ethical response to this problem is simply to listen, to be accepting, and to affirm without reserve the legitimacy of the views and the feelings of "the other"—in this case, of his friend. The truly Christian and the truly ethical response—the truly Christian *because* the truly ethical response—my student proposed, is always to set aside, to bracket, if necessary to negate, one's own convictions, "Christian" or otherwise, in order to be absolutely open to the perspective and the claims of the other person. On this view, the highest, most sublime ethical position and most truly Christian response to another person, in particular to one who feels him- or herself to be a victim, is identified with whatever is furthest from what seems normal or familiar "to us"—to people with *our* beliefs and sympathies. The student believed this moral attitude to have the deepest religious justification: just as Christ "emptied himself"[4] of divinity by taking upon himself our humanity, the summit of Christianity and of morality consists for us in voiding whatever moral feelings or convictions we may hold in order to embrace another's standpoint. The right thing, on this view, is defined essentially by the readiness to sacrifice what one otherwise believes is the right thing for "the other" to the one who sees himself as a victim.

Consider the bearing of each of these examples. On the one hand, the late modern soul demands a "home"; it claims the right to be "at home," to be just what one is, to be safely identical with oneself, to be purely immanent. The soul demands *the same*. On the other hand, the soul of late modernity longs for a kind of absolute transcendence, a repudiation of one's own good in favor not of some other understanding of the good but for the sake of "the other" pure and simple. The good is sublimated into the sacrifice of one's own good for the sake of the other. The good is nothing but the humble, self-emptying sacrifice of "the good."

The demand of the same and the offering to the other would appear to be opposites, but we immediately feel, and we can see upon examination, that they are, in fact, two sides of the same ethical or existential coin, or, to return to my earlier metaphor, two poles in one and the same magnetic field. Most evidently, my sacrifice to the other has no content and is utterly devoid of concrete, practical meaning unless some purpose, some claim, or some manner of being is attributed to the other. And since the claim of any substantive higher good has been voided in advance by my self-emptying openness to the other, how can I respect or serve the other? How can I express my absolute openness to the other, holding nothing back in the name of some allegedly "higher" good dear to me, except by validating the other's sameness with himself or herself, or, I suppose one must say, with themself or itself? The movement from the standpoint of the same to the other is perhaps less obvious. But if the demand of the same is to have any ethical content, indeed any properly human content at all, if it is not to be merely a mute movement of purely physical inertia, a brute expression of a natural *conatus*, the tendency of a being to be what it is and to preserve itself as what it is, a force that drives human behavior as it drives everything in nature, then the claim of the self as same, of the self-identity of the self, must implicitly situate itself within some human and moral horizon. And the only moral horizon compatible with the absolute claim of self-identity is surely, however paradoxically, the ethic of the self-emptying of the good for the other. The apparently opposite claims of the self and the other, absolute self-identity and absolute self-emptying for the other, are strict practical correlates.

The self's demand to be allowed and enabled to be just what it is appeals to the moral claim of otherness. And the moral claim of otherness, of the sacrifice of the good to the other, embraces the self's demand as its only possible content. Again, the abstractness of the claim of self-identity and of the sacrifice of the good are hard to grasp. In fact, I happily grant that they are impossible to grasp as practically coherent motives but only graspable as magnetic poles of the very abstract ethical framework advanced, more or less explicitly, by those today who believe themselves to be the most ethically radical and thus most ethically advanced, enlightened, or "woke." To grasp more concretely what is at stake in this radically enlightened or woke sensibility, we must look at what is denied or *negated* by each of the poles. This is what the ethical demands of sameness and otherness have in common, and this is where they engage the actual practical world, the moral, religious, and political world in which we live: in a word, the same and the other are both sworn enemies of *the good*.

"The good"—another outrageous abstraction? The reader would be in good company in finding the lofty, Platonic notion of a singular, transcendent "good" unhelpful, since Plato's illustrious student Aristotle already objected to its impracticality. And in a sense, our late-modern radicals are extreme followers of Plato, or of a certain Platonism, in their (misguided) longing for a kind of purity; they represent the complicit poles of a pure, transparent expression of the self and its mirror image, the pure sacrifice of one's own for the other. In their longing for some meaning purified of the stain of actual life, with its competition, its prejudices, its borders, and its limits, the woke may be said to be seeking a kind of absolute transcendence. When we say, then, that the devotees of the same and the other, our new Puritans, are sworn enemies of "the good," we mean that they disdain the actual *goods* inscribed in the concrete institutions and ways of life of any real society, any actual moral and political order. We mean that by rejecting all understandings of what is good that are *mediated* by particular, finite, and imperfect institutions, all norms that reflect the influence of human beings, past or present (that is, all actual effective norms), our immanent Platonists or secular Puritans are in fact rejecting *the good*, precisely because we have no access to any intrinsic goodness that is not in any way or to any degree contaminated by human mediation, moral, political, and religious. Pure sacrifice and the pure sanctity of the self come to the same thing: the pure negation of all socially inscribed goods—which is to say, of all goods. The same and the other are mobilized in a pincer movement against the mediated good. This is the practical meaning, the only really determinate meaning, of the great awakening of the same and the other.

VICTIMHOOD: HUMANITY'S LAST CRY?

Today's victims—that is, those radical critics of existing norms and institutions who understand humanity mainly under the category of victimhood—see themselves as victims of the human condition as a *mediated* condition. For the victim, mediation is oppression. From the repudiation of all civilized (unequal, alienated) mediation arises the creed or the cry of our woke radicals: I am a victim with my fellow victims; my common victimhood, my participation in victimhood, my communion with the oppressed, is my very humanity, my essential being.

I am as victim—here is the answer of the most intensely moral—in a way, the most spiritual—of the rising, or already risen, generation (and not only them), it seems, to the question of questions, the question of the meaning of life. However small a minority they may be, these adepts of purity from the mediated good represent the intense and hardened core of the new ethic. And, although the passion for victimhood appears to common sense as destructive, even mad, and though many stand ready to oppose various particular actions or claims of the fellowship of ontological victims, this answer to the question of life's meaning stands substantially unopposed, since no adequate or convincing or authoritative alternative seems to be available; no understanding of our humanity that addresses the radicality of the alliance between absolute self-identity and absolute sacrifice to the other seems to have been adequately transmitted from an earlier generation. Of course, there is often great risk, both material and spiritual—let us just say, then, there is an existential risk—in contradicting the claim of ontological victimhood, since doing so will almost surely mark one as a member of the only other category of humanity—that is, that of oppressor. Those of us who cannot plausibly produce credentials of victimhood may, at least for a time, avoid being named oppressor and thus cling to a kind of second-best shadow-existence by renouncing the original, inexpungeable sin of our caste and begging acceptance as allies of the authentic victims. Without a confident, substantial answer to the complicit polarity of the same and the other, resistance to the awakening of victimhood is circumstantial, merely pragmatic, and, finally, half-hearted.

To be sure, the blessed category of "minority" is more than ever a moving target. Discerning observers have pointed out the instability of the categories of victimhood and the inherent vulnerability of its privilege to another wave of radicalization. The only reliable logic of victimhood is a logic of negation. What Pierre Manent wrote, decades before the vocable "woke" became current, of the "pantheist dream" of democratic humanity now well describes the essential dynamic of victimhood politics, ethics, and religion: The victim "alone believes himself conscious and awake among an ignorant and sleepwalking humanity. . . . He maintains equilibrium by crushing all that is free, all that is happy, all that has a human shape."[5]

As I write this little capsule of the *fons et origo* of what one might call our Western "postmodern"—that is, our decadent, very late-modern—moral, political, and spiritual consciousness, optimists among us detect signs that this publicly ascendent ethic of sacred and aggressive victimhood, of predatory humility, is beginning to unravel, that there are straws in the wind that portend a storm of reaction against the compulsive and, for those who play the sinister game most adroitly, nicely remunerative cult that I have evoked. May it be so! May the counterwinds blast the ramparts of the victim-lords! But even if these counterwoke winds have become a hurricane by the time these words are published, even if we have learned to question the motives and the claims of those who have learned very quickly how to make victimhood pay socially, emotionally, and financially, the spiritual cry that fuels the clamor for victimhood status will not have been answered. The critical issue for those who would contribute to the articulate and confident defense of a decent and stable liberal-democratic order is not the beliefs or the psychology of those invested in or actively promoting the victimhood ideology and sensibility. What is critical is the capacity of those Tocqueville called "legislators for democracy," Christian and post-Christian, to understand the intellectual and spiritual dynamic at work in the ascendancy of victimhood and to respond to it constructively.

The spiritual anxiety, the soul's unrest, that lies beneath the attractions of victimhood will not be answered until we confront its deepest source. At the source of the West is a God who gave himself as a victim of and for humanity. We thought we had long ago dismissed this God or relegated him to a merely "private" realm. But he still rules. And until we learn again—or, perhaps, in an important sense, learn for the first time, learn radically—how to stand in, and therefore to stand up for, our humanity, even while confessing a God who descended below all things (Ephesians 4) to offer himself as the victim, we will not have supplied an alternative to the cult of victimhood.[6]

Let me add a couple of notes to clarify for the reader what kind of book this is intended to be.

First, this book is both very ambitious and, in other respects, necessarily modest. Some may find it excessively so on both counts. It is ambitious in that it respects no limits in attempting to think through the problem of love and virtue to its greatest depths. In addressing the secularization of Christian love as a new and "singular cause of discord in the city" (Marsilius of Padua), it is necessary to go beyond political theory and even beyond the conventional limits of ethical discourse to consider the meaning of being human and the necessary orientation of the human being to a whole or a ground that is beyond our ken and yet not utterly unknown to us. Thus, my response to the exhaustion of liberalism in a flattened and vacuous ethic of "love" or humanitarian compassion necessarily considers questions metaphysical, ontological, and theological (pick whichever you take to lie deepest!) and offers propositions that bear on these realms of discourse. I trust the reader not to fault me for failing to offer a complete and comprehensive vision concerning such ultimate matters. In fact, a main purpose of my argument is to moderate somewhat our hopes for a complete and systematic vision in such domains of theory by showing how ethical-political practice must remain a touchstone of theory—and one whose authority should not be sacrificed to the ambitions of specialists in theoretical systems. Emmanuel Levinas proposed "ethics as first philosophy."[7] I propose a more practical ethics, attentive to the enduring structure of active virtue or moral agency and reconciled to the necessity of the mediation of tradition and politics as a kind of first philosophy and theology—an insuperable precondition of philosophical theology. And I include in this bargain the suggestion that philosophy and theology, reason and faith, are insuperably bound up together for the most rigorous and self-aware thinker. (This suggestion was prepared by my *The Responsibility of Reason: Theory and Practice in a Liberal-Democratic Age*.) Such is the outsized ambition I have found myself assuming, or, let us say, such is the shape of the quest for moral, spiritual, and rational clarity that I have not been able to resist.

The modest part is this: I can hardly expect to have succeeded in any final way in pursuing such a quest. Most obviously, I have engaged some theological texts, but I in no way claim authority with respect to theological debates among theologians, Thomistic or otherwise. I write from the standpoint of my training in political philosophy and its history, and I hope only to have illuminated some intersections of this philosophical discipline with theological thought. I find some consolation in Thomas Aquinas's beautiful dictum, surely the best motto for those of us who have difficulty setting bounds to our thinking: a little knowledge of the highest things is better than perfect knowledge of the ordinary.[8]

My style and approach include some rather freehand observations and speculations, sometimes based on personal experience. But my favored method, the reader will find, is to select interlocutors who have something to teach me. I advance my argument dialectically, both by borrowing insights from authors I respect and by exploring, even pressing, disagreements. Here, I should explain my use (and I hope not abuse) of the author whom I engage at the greatest length: my friend, the great French political philosopher Pierre Manent. Indeed, I present and engage Manent's work in no fewer than five of my chapters. Still, it would be a mistake to approach my work as a summary of and commentary on Manent. While I am happy to introduce Manent's indispensable work to English-speaking readers who may not know of him, I cannot claim that the very ample discussions of his work in these pages are necessarily the best introduction. Mine is not a work of intellectual history in which I present Manent's work in a balanced and dispassionate overview. His ideas interest me too vitally to permit such a conventional scholarly presentation. In other words, Manent is not, for me, what we scholars call a "secondary source," a supporting reference in the development of some scholarly argument. Rather, I approach Manent's work as a "primary source," an original thinker with whom I am privileged to converse on the fundamental questions, a political philosopher in his own right, and along with whom I am developing a philosophical possibility. I engage Manent, that is, as I do, say, Tocqueville.

Such an engagement presents a certain temptation—namely, that of a "strong" interpretation that carries the argument beyond what was intended in the source text and thus risks bending the original a bit in order to access certain new possibilities. I cannot promise fully to have resisted this temptation; I have presented Manent's project with respect and, indeed, much admiration, but I am not sure I have not diverged in some ways from his intention. If I have so diverged, I'm not sure an apology to Pierre or to the reader is called for since my purpose is, finally, not to produce a faithful summary but to seek out the truth to the best of my abilities. I am not very troubled, you can see, by the fact that, in the end, having engaged Manent's text in all candor and seriousness, I am not always sure just where his argument ends and mine begins. It is worth noting in this connection that Pierre has sometimes averred to me that I may "theologize" his work more than he himself might judge best to do. The eminent French political philosopher tends, in the end, no doubt a little more than I, to separate the questions of political philosophy from those of Christian belief—as can be seen, for example, in the very different bearings of two of his recent books: *Pascal et la proposition chrétienne* and the book I rely on most here, *Natural Law and Human Rights*. Again, I have not been able to resist the temptation, as Tocqueville says, to "harmonize heaven and earth" or, at least, to coordinate the eternal and the temporal.

An early version of the argument of this book was presented to a group of colleagues at Brigham Young University's Neal A. Maxwell Institute in 2018 under the title "The Noble and the Just: Natural Preconditions of Christian Charity." Later, in 2018, I presented on the same theme for a colloquium in La Roche sur Yon, France; this French presentation was later published as "Le noble et le juste." I thank my hosts, J. Spencer Fluhman and Philippe Bénéton, and participants in both discussions for these opportunities to gather and present my ideas and for helpful questions and comments. I have benefited immensely, in particular, from conversations with my friend Philippe on this and related themes over a number of decades.

Chapters on Manent draw, sometimes very liberally, from my previously published works:

- Portions of chapters 1, 7, and 8 were previously published in "Thinking, Acting, Flourishing: The Audacious Modesty of Pierre Manent's Practical Natural Law," *Perspectives on Political Science* 49, no. 4 (2020): 209–20, https://www.tandfonline.com/doi/full/10.1080/10457097.2020.1807842. Portions of chapter 1 also appear in my translator's introduction to Pierre Manent, *Natural Law and Human Rights* (University of Notre Dame Press, 2020).
- Much of chapter 5 was previously published as "Leo Strauss's Profound and Fragile Critique of Christianity," in *Leo Strauss and His Catholic Readers*, ed. Geoffrey M. Vaughan (Catholic University of America Press, 2018).
- Portions of chapter 7 were previously published in "Conservatism, Aesthetic and Active: Reflections on Roger Scruton and Pierre Manent," *Perspectives on Political Science* 45, no. 4 (2016): 272–80, https://www.tandfonline.com/doi/full/10.1080/10457097.2016.1221692.

- My engagement with Peter Lawler on Pascal was anticipated in my "Restless Virtue: Greatness in Lawler, Tocqueville, Pascal," *Perspectives on Political Science* 51, no. 3 (2022): 123–32, https://www.tandfonline.com/doi/full/10.1080/10457097.2022.2085978. See also "Stuck with Pride: Belated Reflections on Peter Lawler's Tocquevillean Greatness," *Perspectives on Political Science* 47, no. 1 (2018): 19–20, https://www.tandfonline.com/doi/full/10.1080/10457097.2017.1399016.
- Much of chapter 10 was previously published as "The Claims of Subjectivity and the Limits of Politics," in *Subjectivity, Ancient and Modern*, ed. R. J. Snell and Steven F. McGuire (Lexington Books, 2016); all rights reserved.

The anonymous readers solicited by University of Notre Dame Press raised valuable questions, including some fruitful objections, concerning my arguments, and the press's editorial staff contributed much to polishing the manuscript and saved me from many errors.

I thank Brigham Young University and its College of Family, Home, and Social Sciences as well as the Department of Political Science for generous and continuous research support, including conference travel, over the long gestation of this book.

Thanking students, friends, and colleagues without whom this book would not have been possible is at once the most pleasant task of these acknowledgments and also the most difficult, since work on this project has been integral to my teaching and scholarship for more than a decade. I was working on this book long before I realized I was working on it more than eight years ago, and so my debts are many, far more than I can name here. Since 2017, I have regularly taught at BYU a small class called Reason, Revelation, and Politics. I owe much to the patient, earnest, and receptive students in these classes; in the largely unprogrammed discussions that emerged in this setting I discovered much that I never would have found in the study of the written word alone. As Plato wrote in his Seventh Letter, only after intensive and disciplined discussions of the highest things with people truly desirous of what is good can we hope for truth to blaze up in the midst of our spiritual and intellectual communion. Alas, I cannot name all the students who have shared these blazes with me.

I cannot fail to thank, however, two admirable young men and students who have aided me in the final stages of this blessed labor: Jacob Christensen and Luke Lyman. Jacob has served as a most reliable and competent last presubmission reader of this work and has given valuable advice on style and content while efficiently fixing mistakes. Apart from his contributions to class discussions from which some of these pages derive, Luke devoted countless hours to pondering my sometimes inchoate ideas and to conversations with me (which he then transcribed!) that were essential moments in the distillation of my central theses. The companionship of good and talented students such as these, wise beyond their years, is a priceless blessing of my teaching career. And there have been many others whose questions and suggestions have become part of the very tissue of my understanding of truth, rational and revealed.

The same can be said for my conversations with the best of friends and colleagues over the years. Philippe Bénéton first hosted me (in every sense) as a visiting professor at the University of Rennes more than thirty years ago. He opened the door for me in countless ways to what is best in the French tradition. More recently he gave indispensable advice and encouragement in the early stages of this work. Paul Seaton, both a thorough master on all things concerning Pierre Manent and well acquainted with the world of Roman Catholic theology, has been an indispensable interlocutor, generous both in guidance and in encouragement. Giulio De Ligio, a penetrating thinker and earnest seeker of truth political, philosophical, and theological, has bolstered and informed me in his own indispensable work on Manent and the political-theological problem and has engaged my work with rare seriousness and generosity. Pierre Manent himself has been marvelously indulgent toward my exploitation of his ideas and generous in responding to my propositions.

These friends are precious contributors to the overlapping conversations from which the thesis of this book has emerged. Along with them, I must give special thanks to our mutual friend, Daniel J. Mahoney, without whose friendly encouragement, advice, and sponsorship the completion of this work would have been quite impossible. Dan, as is evident to all who know him, is a steady font of wise and engaging essays that bring insights of the greatest authors of the Western tradition to bear on the most urgent of contemporary concerns, a great contributor to manifold worthy endeavors, political (in the highest sense) and philosophical, and the steadiest and most pleasant of friends. It is utterly mysterious to me how, in the midst of all his important occupations, he has found the time and energy to offer advice and encouragement on my projects so constantly over the years. It is without a trace of exaggeration that I gladly state the obvious: I could not have done this without you, Dan.

To Peter Augustine Lawler, to whom this book is dedicated, let me say: In writing these pages, I have often longed to share them with you. This is a continuation of a conversation that had already extended over years, but that still was just getting started when you suddenly took your leave. I am steadfastly hopeful of pursuing our talks further in person.

These acknowledgments, while still too short, have already gone on too long. I must conclude by thanking once again my dear Julie, whose companionship enhances the intimations of eternal felicity in our daily works and prayers as it softens the sting of our worldly trials.

———

Each of the three parts of this book is prefaced with a brief abstract of the argument of that part's chapters. While these very concise synopses may not be perfectly clear to the reader as freestanding statements, they will help to prepare him or her to follow the reasoning of the ensuing chapters by prefiguring the overall contours of the argument and will serve as very compressed summaries for review.

Introduction

Contemporary worship of "the idol of our age," a secularized and purely horizontal humanitarianism that necessarily devolves into Tocqueville's nightmare of "pantheism," can be challenged only by a renewal of "virtue-religion," in which transcendence does not exclude the real goodness of practical virtue, or, in Thomas Aquinas's terms, in which grace does not destroy but perfects nature.

The prestige and the attraction of the idea or notion of human individuality or subjectivity as essential victimhood is the deepest source of contemporary identity politics. The idea of victimhood springs from the suppression or the oblivion of the (necessarily mediated) goodness of human action in favor of a sense of the dignity of human passion, passivity, or suffering.

To act is to aim at some good. Such a good always has a public dimension, a meaning shared with some community of practical relevance, a community for whom one can *act* so as to make things better or worse. To act is to propose, promote, and stand up for some good, or against some evil, for and before some public. One cannot act without, in some way, proposing oneself and one's own character as a standard of action, however imperfect. To propose and stand up for some good implies that the person proposing and standing up comprehends and, therefore, in some way and to some degree embodies, reflects, or represents that good. Without claiming at least some minimal experience in the good to be proposed, how can I stand up for it?

The question is not, finally, one that concerns the sincerity or hypocrisy, the vanity or the material interests, of those who claim victimhood, although these may well be fair concerns. The question is rather one of simple logical, or let us say existential, consistency or coherence. Just from what positive standpoint, in view of what possible concrete improvement of our community, does a self-proclaimed victim claim social and political authority? Victimhood adopts a purely negative standpoint; it claims to name an oppressor without taking responsibility for defining what a common existence without "oppression" would look like. The standpoint of pure Sameness and of its accomplice, pure Otherness, is one that absolutely transcends or claims exemption from the practical problem of constructive action in the world, action for a practical good.

In the last decade, the pincer movement of the Same and the Other against the goods of mediation has adopted a plainly Christian or post-Christian rhetoric. Christianity teaches that God is love and that charity never faileth, and now woke radicalism frames its vision or its impulse in the language of love as the absolute ethical and political principle. "Love Wins"—you recognize the slogan that became viral in the summer of 2015 among those celebrating the U.S. Supreme Court decision *Obergefell v. Hodges*, which held that homosexual marriage is a fundamental right under the Constitution. A similar sensibility is conveyed in the "Love Has No Labels" propaganda campaign on television and the internet. More recently, the sensibility has been distilled in the shameless pleonasm: "Love is love."

What is the thrust of these appeals? What they imply is that there is no difficult question of constitutional law or political philosophy to examine, nothing to debate regarding the moral and social purposes of the natural family or the ethical principles that underlie our social compact: the simple word "love," and the feeling it is supposed to evoke, is held to have settled all such questions. If you are not against love, then you cannot oppose the indefinite expansion of "rights" protecting sexual expression and affirming "diverse lifestyles." And who can be against love?

Progressive liberalism claims the authority of reason and of openness to a "diversity" of views and ways of life. But the Love Wins mantra reveals the sacred dogma that underlies the pose of open-minded rationalism: "Love," understood as boundless acceptance and empathy, excluding all moral judgment, is the new, unquestioned standard of moral judgment. And the prestige of this secular love, impatient with all boundaries and standards, is clearly a residue (however distorted and misapplied) of the very Christianity that secularism must overcome. Secularism is the secularized residue *of Christianity*. And this residue, in the form of the ideology of "love," wields amazing dogmatic authority in our supposedly freethinking secular age. Question every authority, progressive liberalism entices us, but do not even think about questioning "love," understood as absolute acceptance and nonjudgmental empathy, as the sole standard of human goodness. Never in the darkest of Christian "Dark Ages" did an ideological authority envision such a total domination over the human mind and heart as that asserted by the post-Christian humanistic religion of "love."

The idea that exerts the greatest power over an age is invisible to that age; it defines its horizon and implicitly grounds its judgments. The ruling idea is necessarily sacred and unspeakable in itself, though its moral and intellectual ramifications are on everyone's lips, and its effects pervade our individual and collective lives. Our indignant refusal of the notion of a sacred ground of action and understanding is by no means evidence of its absence; on the contrary, our flattering self-understanding as infinitely open to other ideas and other ways, as defined by nothing but our freedom from definition, seals our sacred truth in a holy of holies more hidden and more secure than the sacred places of any earlier religion.

Almost forty years ago, Allan Bloom, author of *The Closing of the American Mind*, secured his status as an academic pariah[1] by pointing out the moral and intellectual trap of "openness" as "our virtue." No one is more closed, he argued, than a professor or intellectual who brandishes "openness" as his chief virtue—no one except, perhaps, the student or follower who basks in its borrowed glory. Professor Bloom's analysis still rings largely true today, but the banner of "openness" has yielded much to the cause of "social justice." Social justice has, for many, become a religious mission. Bloom was addressing a world in which traditional religious belief still stood as an obstacle to the total sway of the virtue of "openness." The virtuous elites targeted by Bloom's critique despised biblical belief too much to address an argument to it, except for the all-purpose formula of "openness." To be sure, Bloom despised claims of divine revelation only slightly less than his relativist adversaries; he preferred to see biblical religion and the moral traditions deriving from it as a useful sparring partner for his post-Nietzschean philosopher. "One has to have the experience of really believing before one can have the thrill of liberation."[2] Dialectical philosophers, he knew, must have some raw material to work with, after all, some authoritative propositions regarding the good and the just to engage and ultimately to deconstruct. He seemed not to realize that a sparring partner whom one has to hold up on his feet cannot provide much real exercise for the soul's higher faculties.

Bloom's critique of relativistic "openness" was addressed mainly to a secular intellectual elite for whom Christianity and its moral teaching still represented, not, to be sure, a respected spiritual rival, but still a substantial political force that had to be reckoned with in America, and one that thus provided a reliable foil to reason's rule, whether one conceived as reason more classically and aristocratically, with Bloom, or more progressively and democratically, with the mainstream academic targets of his critique. For the mainstream, the progressive left, as well as for Bloom's tiny but philosophically powerful High-Straussian[3] right, religion was understood to be inherently a friend of "traditional morality." The phony "openness" that held sway in the late twentieth century thus still encountered a limit in reason's grudging recognition of the residual existence of its once great rival and former partner, biblical religion. A little gap still remained in the vast enclosure of relativistic "openness"; the secular religion of progress was still aware of its Other, of the possibility of appeal to divine revelation in support of a traditional vision of morality and politics.

A generation later, we can see this gap vanishing; the mirrored dome of a secular age is closing over our heads, a vast ceiling without gaps or openings that returns every natural impulse of vertical transcendence back upon a horizontal field of meaning. Under the mirrored dome, all virtue, all substantive claims to the good, dissolve into the complicity of the Same and the Other, the Self and the Victim. We can feel the total sway of secular progress as the appeal of relativistic "openness" yields to the authority of the egalitarian "social justice" it has always served. The natural Other of egalitarian justice, the alliance of morality and revealed religion—traditional virtue as supported by transcendence, or transcendence understood as the concomitant of traditional virtue—has not disappeared, but it seems on the verge of losing its voice. The religion of virtue, or virtuous religion, can no longer speak its name, can no longer stand up for itself. Let us designate this forgotten other "virtue-religion"; the term sounds faintly ridiculous and invites many a familiar critique, but a clear and frank term for a discredited standpoint and sensibility must no doubt bear the weight of inevitable ridicule. For—and this is the sum and substance of this book's argument—there is, in fact, no alternative to this alliance of religion and virtue but the secular religion of social justice or purely humanitarian compassion.

Now that we see the face of God herself in the mirrored dome that arcs over our heads, we are less fond of talk of "openness." We remain "open," to be sure, but only to everything "equal" (or to the endless work of equalization) and global-humanitarian, everything that denies intrinsic elevation or superiority; we are resolutely closed to any concrete, particular claims of effective access to transcendence—that is, access that would show up in any real and therefore particular worldly hierarchy, any rank-ordering effective in an actual way of life. We are definitively closed to anything that might stand up for itself.

NIHILISTIC "PANTHEISM"

In the first volume of *Democracy in America* (1835), Tocqueville provided a largely optimistic perspective on his subject matter, emphasizing how the practical experience, decentralized politics, and religious beliefs of Americans served to check the worst tendencies of modern, secular democracy. But already he began in this work to diagnose the dark possibilities inherent in American egalitarianism, the emergence of a "tyranny of the majority" that was far stronger than any traditional despotism based on physical power, a dominion that bypassed the body and operated directly on the human soul. A fully democratized people would not even dare to think of any authoritative good or norm, any measure of goodness or excellence higher than the people's collective social and moral power. This majoritarian power was held in check or disrupted in Tocqueville's day by various inherited, broadly "aristocratic" features of American society, including reverence for the founders and the traditional formalism of the legal profession. But clearly the main check on the power of the majority was the continuing influence of Christianity. Even though Christianity's authority was already hard to distinguish from the authority of a democratic society—it was already hard to say whether Americans confessed Christianity because they believed in a divine truth or because they acceded to the opinion of the vast majority—enough genuine traditional and biblical content remained effective in American life to inform and limit democratic passions and ideals.

In the second volume of *Democracy in America* (1840), Tocqueville discerned a still more radical danger on democracy's horizon. "Pantheism" is Tocqueville's name for the condition in which democracy becomes its own God, in which it tends to occlude all transcendence by converting it into idealized or spiritualized immanence. This is precisely the condition of the "mirrored dome" I have evoked above. Tocqueville argues that approaching the end of the democratic dispensation, the mind becomes obsessed with unity; all true diversity, all heterogeneity and rank order—which necessarily appeal to some reality beyond the self-enclosed humanistic system—and, therefore, all true individualism must be laid low; there must be no permanent, authoritative pillars of order, no mediating representations between the all-too-human and the divine. All that exists is swallowed up in "an immense being which alone remains eternal in the midst of the continual change and incessant transformation of all that composes it."[4]

"Pantheism," as understood by Tocqueville, represents a dark, even mysterious possibility, and the idea is not easy to grasp. It is best understood negatively, in opposition to mediation, as mediation's relentless foe or solvent. And what do we intend by "mediation"? Mediating institutions are those "little platoons" that Burke famously opposed to the abstract and inhuman rationalism of the atheistic Enlightenment, and such institutions play a critical role in Tocqueville's resistance to the self-hollowing of democracy. They are ordered associations such as families, churches, voluntary associations, and organs of local self-government. Such little platoons or self-ordered clusters of human activity stand in between the naked individual and the impersonal state, and they represent vital concerns and authoritative ends excluded by the mutually reinforcing poles of amoral individualism and collective security/welfare. The emerging horizon of global humanity extends this polarity between the individual and the collective beyond Tocqueville's mild despotism of the democratic state to the limit of imagination, and "pantheism" is an apt term to evoke the exhaustion of actual human meaning at this limit of collusion between the radically individual and the universal.

An institution "mediates" when it provides moral content that resists the corrosive action of the abstractly individual and general. Healthy families enact every day, virtually every minute, the need for authority as well as mutual regard and the inseparable connection between caring feelings and the discipline of the passions. Healthy churches reinforce both love and the disciplining virtues from a perspective of eternity. Associations, public and private, promote mutual respect as they give scope to ambitions of excellence. All mediating institutions help to define human meaning as they solicit moral action without some bounded field; to define positive, livable meaning is inseparable from the acceptance, even the embrace, of finitude. Without mediation, Tocqueville writes in a chapter titled "Some Sources of Poetry in Democratic Nations" (II.i.17), reminding us of Pascal, we are left without any foothold between "two abysses," nothingness and infinity.[5]

THE IDOL OF OUR AGE

Hostility to the mediation of moral truths through the actual, concrete institutions that necessarily order human existence is inherent in the increasingly dominant framework of thought and feeling that Daniel J. Mahoney has recently exposed. Mahoney has put his finger on our all-powerful ruling idea, a sacred ground of justification that operates without the need for a rational account or defense. He aptly names the still point, the unspoken center of our contemporary sacred, in the title of his book *The Idol of Our Age: How the Religion of Humanity Subverts Christianity*. It is this emerging idolatry, the subversion of Christianity by the religion of humanity, that finally seals our closure from authentic transcendence and best marks our progress from relativistic openness to the resolute immanence of "social justice" as the absolute horizon of meaning. A review of and engagement with Mahoney's book, which lucidly documents the collapse of the residual tension that until recently still existed between secular openness and its other—namely, biblical religion—will serve me well here in launching my argument.

The collapse documented by Mahoney portends a world in which any truth beyond the domed mirror of egalitarian social justice has become quite unthinkable; any upward intimations of a meaning transcending the endless project of humanitarian equalization are reflected back to glorify the piecemeal revolution of immanence; all vertical aspirations to nobility or virtue are converted into fuel for the leveling of real moral differences. Divinity has no meaning other than humanity, and so humanity can mean nothing but the complex of (1) material necessity, (2) trivialized, empty freedom, and (3) spirituality converted into warfare serving (1) and (2)—that is, warfare for a "justice" that is pervasively, exclusively, "social."

The "idol" of "humanity" presented by Mahoney exposes us precisely to the powerful collusion, already discerned by Tocqueville, of meaningless individuality and monstrous universality. "Humanity," as the idol of our age, is understood at once according to the figure of Tocqueville's unthinkably "immense being," a being beyond all truly human proportion, and at the same time as what is subject to "continual change and incessant transformation." When the "immense being" of humanity fills the whole space of transcendence, when all vertical orientation—the orientation of the old virtue-religion and associated mediating institutions—has been abolished, then human beings can enact transcendence only on a purely horizontal vector, a plane with no truly humane thickness, no upward élan or effective moral grit; the fumes of spirituality can only be converted into the end-less transformation of humanity itself, the "hideous strength" of the on-going "abolition of man" (C. S. Lewis). Are we not witnessing daily the encroachment of the hideous strength of this two-front war against concrete humanity, the paralyzing spiritual power of the elusive notion of global humanity straining to complete its fusion with boundless individualism, the bottomless quest for equal and irresponsible freedom and passive security? How else are we to understand, for example, the rage that swept over our society practically the moment the right of same-sex "marriage" was conceded on our behalf by a sovereign court—that is, the rage to explore and to promote every possible insult to the natural human division and complementarity between male and female? Adolescents are putting into action our adult flirtation with the abolition of humanity, and our youth find themselves, it seems, in too many cases, with no meaningful action to undertake but the rejection of their bodies, a forlorn pursuit of self-creation in self-mutilation. Grownups who should know something more about responsible and limited human existence either find themselves at a loss to answer this rage for mutilation or actually connive in and promote the hopelessly destructive quest for an impossible meaning, a meaning that would triumph over nature. Tocqueville's "immense being" is the dark spirit that orders this destructive disorder, and we offer our children, reduced to subjects of "continual change and transformation," to this idol.

Tocqueville concludes his chapter on pantheism with this appeal: "All who remain enamored of the genuine greatness of man should unite and do combat against it."[6] This book would join this combat for true humanity, for the indispensable mediation of morality, and therefore of politics rightly understood. The only alternative to humanitarian pantheism, to the idol of our age, is a return to the honor of "intermediate things." The only way to fall in love again with "the genuine greatness of man" is to understand the essential truth of the old virtue-religion. The human virtues must look up to the divine, and divinity must be understood in the light of, or in continuity with the light of, knowable human virtue. If we would not succumb to the perpetual self-hollowing of pantheism, to the confinement of humanity to a mirrored dome of its own construction, then we must learn to articulate and embrace this human-divine and divine-human continuity; we must understand and love the feedback loops between what is virtuous and what is holy. There is no humanity without an awareness of sacred transcendence, without an orientation to an order of reality beyond our ken. But there is also no effective transcendence, no transcendence secure from the mirrored dome of pantheism, that does not admit of analogy with concrete human virtue. This shall be my argument: there is no alternative to secular humanitarianism, with its intrinsic vulnerability to nihilistic pantheism, but virtue-religion—that is, religion that supports and grounds natural virtue in its intrinsic nobility and virtue that is open to a personal divinity beyond human measure.

We have seen that, already 180 years ago, Alexis de Tocqueville evoked, in his original meditation on the ancient idea of "pantheism," the essence, or the essential abyss, of our age's humanitarian idolatry as limned by Daniel J. Mahoney. A God who transcends transcendence itself, who is absolutely beyond all practical human measure and so no longer can appear as the fulfillment of what is eternally "higher," can be identified only with the boundless process of change itself and thus, effectively, with the perpetual, insatiable laying low of all hierarchical claims, all honor or nobility associated with tradition or authoritative institutions.

Mahoney's examination of both representatives and critics of humanitarian ideology—Comte, Brownson, Pope Francis, Soloviev, Solzhenitsyn, Kolnai—reveals the features of a humanitarian worldview, in forms explicitly post-Christian or still nominally or ambiguously Christian, whose premises Tocqueville shows to culminate in the "pantheist" dissolution of human meaning. In order to prepare the inquiry of the present work, let us collect these features of humanitarian idolatry from Mahoney's text and, at the same time, gather his indications concerning the elements of a philosophical or religious alternative to this new and powerful form of idolatry.

Modern idolatry, Mahoney shows, is in one sense fanatically boundless and utopian[7] and, in another sense, fatally self-limiting (122). It is politically utopian (98, 100) because it is resolutely "anthropocentric" (69)—that is, because it denies access to any truth above the material. Christianity deprived of authentic transcendence (67), like plainly secular humanitarianism, reduces religion and morality to the provision of bread (5) and freedom (19, 79)—to material necessities and everexpanding, ever-equalizing social and individual rights (118). The idol of humanitarianism craves worldly power as the only hope for universal secular salvation, and it sees loyalty to particular moral, religious, and national traditions and communities only as irrational obstacles to its utopian project.

Traditional beliefs and loyalties impede progress toward humanitarian flourishing, according to this idol, because they locate the source of evil in human nature and not in the faulty construction of human institutions. The organization and mobilization of human power, unhindered by inherited prejudices, can transform the human condition because there is no permanent obstacle to such transformation residing in human nature itself. As we have seen, Tocqueville understood with remarkable prescience that the mobilization of humanitarian idealism against the obstacle of human nature itself necessarily tends toward the dissolution of concrete, livable human meaning in a pantheistic vortex of monistic obsession. The pantheistic vertigo—in effect, nihilism, or the collapse of meaning—is just the logical last stage of a process in which universalizing idealism consumes its own particular and materialistic content.

Post-Christian universal humanitarianism is unstable because it eschews any concrete experience of goodness or elevation. Nothing definite and actual can stand up fully to the pure formal criterion of universality since all truly human practices and institutions are built from or grafted upon materials affected by particular loyalties, beliefs, and prejudices. The ideal form of universality can never be fully reconciled with the givenness and particularity of actual humanity.

To state the problem at this extreme level of abstraction is to confront the radical difficulty presented by the idol of our age in its ultimately "pantheistic" implications. For how can universal truth (whether understood to be rational or revealed) accommodate human nature as inevitably inflected by particular loyalties and beliefs? Both secular reason and the Christian gospel propose an ethical horizon that transcends all divisions of nations and traditions; it is this shared commitment to universality that, for so many, blurs the difference between Christian love and humanitarian ideology. Love is love, in this Christian-humanitarian view, and love knows no barrier of race or nationality. If the surpassing Christian virtue is charity or love (1 Corinthians 13), then it seems that love must prevail over all particular creeds and loyalties. From this point of view, the humanitarian prospect is not the subversion of Christianity but its legitimate heir, its real fulfillment. The "falsification of the good" (Soloviev) would not be as powerful as it is if it were not able to "insinuate evil into the very heart of goodness" (46), if it were not a seductive counterfeit of the sublime standard of Christian charity.[8] As Mahoney suggests in his discussion of Auguste Comte's religion of humanity, secular society needs the institutional support of a secular religion; the ideal of a post-Christian society achieves its maximum coherence not in the form of a vague openness to the coexistence of a plurality of worldviews but precisely as the religion of secularism. Mahoney alerts us to the emerging ascendancy of such a post-Christian religion as a ruling vision, and this growing ascendancy can be verified almost every day in the latest political news.

SUBSTANCE AND UNIVERSALISM

The difficulty of anchoring the sublime and ethically revolutionary Christian idea of charity as surpassing all worldly ethical frameworks against the subversive appeal of secular universalism should not be underestimated. We can't blame the Beatles or contemporary Christian or post-Christian humanitarians too harshly for chanting that "all you need is love" if it seems to many that Paul the apostle said it long before Paul McCartney sang it.[9]

The central problem behind the confusing relationship between Christian charity and secular love can be articulated in terms of a tension between substance and universalism. Recently, I was conversing with an earnest and faithful young Christian scholar about the intersection between the church and the secular world, and I began to make the simple, if you will, "orthodox" case for the importance of defending a clear moral standard and understanding of the order of the family in a relativistic world. His heartfelt reply was, "Don't you want the church to be available to the widest possible group, even to all humanity? Does it not hinder the universal mission of the church to insist on barriers?" Another faithful young Christian scholar emphasized the importance of compassion toward those who struggle with traditional Christian teachings on sexual morality. I asked him: Would not sharing the principle of repentance be an important expression of love for a struggling sister or brother? No, he replied, if anyone needs repentance, it would be *only* the person who would presume to appeal to a principle held to be higher than the feelings of the person who is struggling.

Both of these thoughtful and faithful young Christians were effectively falling in with the "Love Wins" mentality, not out of any particular enthusiasm for sexual liberation or revolution in family structure, but according to the logic of universalism or inclusiveness that indeed seems to be a defining gesture of the gospel, and especially of Paul's letters, or of prominent parts of these letters. Conservative Christians are perpetually criticized for erecting "walls" when we should be "building bridges." But of course, there is a pretty simple logical problem with this movement of thought: universalism is by itself empty and meaningless; there must be some content, some substance, to be universalized, something to be shared. A bridge must be from somewhere to somewhere.

Every outreach presupposes an affirmation, every extension a center, every movement of compassion some understanding of the good and what it would mean to heal. The enthusiasm for inclusiveness, or the movement of compassion without regard to content, is not only religiously suicidal but logically incoherent.

THE GENEALOGY OF LOVE WINS (A SKETCH)

The costs of reading Christian charity as "love wins" may be obvious, but a diagnosis or genealogy of the disorder proves to be a challenging task. The philosophical and theological roots of a certain confusion between secularism and Christianity lie deep in the history of the West and entangled in the foundations of the modern age. To uncover these roots is a monumental task, and here I can offer only a few glimpses of the paradoxical relationship between Christianity and secularism that can be helpful in addressing the current confusion.

As I suggested earlier, the young scholars (universalist and compassionate) are not alone in their quandary since the tension between the universalizing form and the particular content of Christianity has been a challenge from the beginning. To spread the gospel beyond all ethnic and political borders while holding firm to some substance of what is to be shared is a problem coeval with the announcement of the good news, and one can, in fact, trace the history of Western thought as the unfolding of this problem.

We can bring this history into focus in a summary way by observing that there are two kinds of particularism, two sources of moral content or substance, that Christian universalism must aim to overcome. First, there is the particularism of the Jews, a chosen people defined by a rigorous, revealed law governing the details of daily existence. Second, there is the natural particularism of our political condition, authoritatively described by Aristotle: the natural virtues have a universal aspect, but they are always bound up with the common good of particular cities or political communities, or more particularly with the ruling ethos of these communities. Christian universalism thus necessarily confronts the particular claims of both revealed law and natural virtue, prior revelation and proud reason, Jerusalem and Athens.

In Paul's letters, both Jew and Greek are in question, but the confrontation with the Jewish law is the most obvious and immediate concern. The interpretation of the letters of Paul has always been central to the problem of sorting out the relationship between the gospel and the world. In many passages, Paul speaks boldly of the law that defined the covenant of Israel as being suspended or rendered inoperative, but he also speaks of the love announced by the gospel as "fulfilling" the law. So, the status of the law or of commandments in relation to the gospel's announcement of a love that includes the whole human race has been a tortured question in Christian theology from the beginning. The extreme, anti-Jewish view of the question was taught very early, in the second century, by a certain Marcion, who took Paul's writings to be foundational and used them to dismiss everything Jewish as completely foreign to Christianity and thus utterly reject the Old Testament, its commandments, and even its God. One could say that in this key respect, the "Love Wins" movement is a twenty-first-century revival of Marcionism.

St. Augustine (AD 354–430) was, of course, no Marcionite; he respected the canonical status of the Old Testament while interpreting it in a highly allegorical manner. The main concern of his universalizing effort, in any case, was not with the particular demands of the Jewish law but with the status of natural or pagan virtue in relation to the otherworldly faith of Christianity. The Augustinian view is summed up in the bishop's famous teaching that the virtues of the pagans are but splendid vices.[10] Although drawn to Platonism, he struggles to break with it decisively because he cannot accept Plato's belief in the natural capacity of a human being, the philosopher, to attain the good, a kind of natural salvation to be achieved by the perfection of one's own natural, intellectual powers.[11] Since, for Augustine, human beings cannot achieve the good by their own power, both Plato's claim to philosophical salvation (which Augustine does not lightly dismiss) and the more common human virtues praised by Aristotle as intrinsically good necessarily appear merely as socially and politically useful—as "splendid vices" of merely utilitarian value. In Augustine, we see clearly the tendency of Christianity to supernaturalize the goods of the soul, to refer them to another world, and thus to construe this world as the realm only of bodily needs and of vain pretensions. The natural virtues that humans everywhere tend to praise are thus debunked and, one can say, reduced to a "secular" perspective of mere instrumental value. In Augustine's thought, this tendency of supernaturalism to, in a way, depreciate the realm of nature and its virtues was contained by his residual Platonic regard for the contemplative ideal and by his practical good sense, but the Augustinian tradition has always contained the possibility of a relativizing that undermines what I have called virtue-religion—that is, an understanding of Christianity that provides support to the natural virtues coupled with an understanding of virtue that points toward a transcendent consummation.

Eventually, in book 10 of *City of God*, Augustine plaintively dismisses the elitism of the Platonist philosophers to whom he has shown so much favor in book 8, and thus he anticipates the mysterious power of the universalism that now envelops and pervades us. In book 10, the bishop of Hippo protests from the depths of his soul against the Platonic idea that philosophy is our only salvation and that only philosophers can be saved. Augustine's argument here is not exactly rational; it is certainly not simply logical. It is, rather, let us say, spiritual and existential: any adequate response to the human condition, he proclaims against the Platonists, cannot be a response that resigns itself to the final insignificance of our humanity, our common humanity. A true response to the human quest for meaning, a true idea of "salvation," must be true not just for philosophers but for all of humanity; therefore, it must save not only our rational part but our whole souls; it must redeem everything that is human in us. "And yet how could it [Platonism] be a genuine philosophy, if it did not offer this . . . *universal* way for the liberation of the soul."[12] A genuine philosophy must promise, as he writes further on, the satisfaction of all "honorable" desires.[13] The only salvation that addresses human existence is one that, in principle, saves every human being and thus saves everything human.

But what is "human"? What is "honorably" human? How can we define and affirm our humanity without affirming some good, ranking some possibilities above others, and qualifying some powers, faculties, or activities as most truly human? And how can this higher good of the soul not be informed by (tainted by?) what our particular community honors, what it looks up to, and our particular understanding of what is good and authoritative? Of course, it is attention to questions such as these of the meaning of the truly honorable or higher that had led Augustine's Platonic rivals to rank reason above spirit and desire, and

Greek republicanism above barbarian despotism, and so to violate human universality.

As soon as we try to supply our universal humanity with some content, some substance, we risk violating its universality. For us moderns, material progress—the original modern project of the mastery of nature for the relief of the human (bodily) condition—has long provided the default content of this universalism. But a default content cannot explain itself, defend itself, or stand up for itself. One does not have to believe in the inerrancy of the Bible to see that "man cannot live by bread alone." Our contemporary compulsive fascination with victimhood and self-hatred (even when these are made to pay quite handsomely) is now revealing the limits of a purely formal and implicitly materialistic universalism.

The risk inherent in Christian universalism is clear enough: if the gospel, in order to extend its reach, too enthusiastically negates both Jewish commandment and pagan virtue—whatever is esteemed as virtuous, lovely, of good report, and praiseworthy[14]—then it risks hollowing itself out, evacuating its own substance. And one can say that the modern, secular age, the age of this-worldly universalism, was founded on precisely such an evacuation.

LOVE WINS AND THE FOUNDATIONS OF MODERN SECULARISM

Modern secularism is founded on a kind of mutually eroding interaction between Christian faith and pagan reason: Christian humility debunks the "virtuous" pride of Greek reason, and Greek reason questions the supernatural claims of Christianity.[15] The resultant "rationalism" preserves the moral content of neither Jerusalem nor Athens, but only the open-ended promise of progress, of ongoing liberation from the limitations of the human condition.

The Protestant Reformation, a movement based on a reading of Paul and on a radicalization of Augustine, played an ironic role in the coming forth of this hollow modern universalism. By radically separating grace from nature in order to address the church's worldly exploitation of spiritual authority, the Reformers undermined the continuity between natural virtue and divine commandment and tended to deprive biblical commands of any rational support but a purely utilitarian understanding.[16] But a more explicit intention to deploy Christian motives (along with others, of course) to undo Christianity can be discerned in the philosophical founding of the modern age.

The modern political-philosophical project that took shape first in seventeenth-century Europe proposed that the Christian promise of salvation through the teachings and sacraments of the church had stifled human progress and that human beings needed to take responsibility for their own universal liberation from fear and want. But to do this would require a reorientation of morality in a decidedly this-worldly direction.

The mobilization of Christian motives for secular progress is already clear in the rhetoric of the philosopher regarded as the founder of the modern age, René Descartes (1596–1650). In his *Discourse on the Method*, Descartes crafts a story of his path of discovery and appeals to the public for support of his new scientific and humanitarian project. His aim, he says, is to demonstrate the advantages of his scientific approach so as to "induce all those who have the good of mankind at heart—that is to say, all who are really virtuous in fact, and not only by a false semblance or by opinion—" to support his project. He appeals explicitly to a secularized law of humanitarian love, arguing that we must not *sin* "against the law which obliges us to procure, as much as in us lies, the general good of all mankind." And we can avoid this sin against humanity only by cooperating in Descartes's project, by which, he promises, we humans can "render ourselves the masters and possessors of nature"[17]—that is, not beings limited by natural or divine law.

There is thus a direct line from the detachment of human love from the commands of the biblical law on the one hand and the natural virtues on the other to the technological project of mastery over nature, which implies the promise of a universal overcoming of the limitations of the human condition.

REASONING ABOUT LOVE

The subversion of Christian charity by the secular religion of love is speciously attractive as a moral ideal, one that is, of course, often very sincerely held. The appropriation of spiritual love and authentic virtue by the secular ethic of "Love Wins" is thus not just a mistake; it is, I feel bound to say, *the* mistake, the substitution of the one true thing by its alluring counterfeit. It is indeed *the* "falsification of the good."[18] The difficulty of extricating Christianity from its modern counterfeit is great because, as Pierre Manent has said, the moderns are too Christian, especially when they are not Christian.[19] It is, therefore, of critical importance to distinguish the counterfeit from authentic Christianity clearly and to spell out the opposing characteristics of the original as precisely as possible.

Given the often sincere and, for many, all-too-persuasive appropriation of Christian spirituality by the secular religion of love, just how is the authentic version to be distinguished? How is the first great commandment to resist complete absorption into the second, which is thereby adulterated and debased? How can the holy love of a neighbor be rigorously distinguished from the ideological project of the universal mastery of material need and inequality? How are we to understand God's kenosis or self-emptying, in the person of his son, in keeping with the Old Testament figure of the suffering servant, so as not to endorse or accede to the rule of the lowest common denominator or of the loudest claims of victimhood? In a word, how are we to discern the radical Christian virtue of humility in such a way that we do not renounce the classical virtue of magnanimity and thus sacrifice our souls along with our pagan pride? How can we bow before the mystery of a divine love that passeth understanding and still stand up with confidence for what is virtuous, lovely, of good report, or praiseworthy?

The significance of the "Love Wins" ideology can be clarified only by examining the secular idea of "love" in comparison with the Christian idea of charity. The key question, then, is this: Is the contemporary dogma "All you need is love" a legitimate descendent of the biblical teaching "Charity never fails"? The question for us is not same-sex marriage itself, as important as that question is, but the understanding of "love" in terms of which many Christians frame their support of this new "right" and all the "identity" rights that follow in its path. We need to understand what is at stake in this conception of "love" in order to be clear about what we are discussing, not only regarding the marriage question but wherever fundamental moral and religious principles are a matter of public concern.

I realize that just by asking what "love" means I am already taking a position that some find troubling or annoying. After all, how can love be the main thing, the one thing needful, the answer to all ultimate spiritual questions, if we must first achieve intellectual clarity regarding its meaning? To clarify, it is inevitable to divide, to separate light from darkness, and to invite "binaries," whereas love implies unity without reserve. By even raising the question of the meaning of love, I might seem to be ranking clarity above charity, light above love.

I want to acknowledge this conundrum at the outset; if it has any answer, I hope that what follows will help to bring it to light. But here, at the outset, it might be noted that where the question of reason (distinguishing, discriminating, dividing, clarifying) is concerned, the sides of the debate and the cultural struggle seem to have switched from what is generally assumed: it is the progressive liberals who tout love as an alternative to all reasoning concerning basic ethical, political, and religious principles, a moral trump card to silence all discussion, whereas it is "conservatives" (like me, indeed) who defend the essential role of informed, rational judgment in moral matters. Those who cannot agree that "love wins" is the answer to every moral dilemma or conflict must proceed with faith and hope that reasoning together—distinguishing and discerning—consulting what we can know of the human condition as a basis for understanding transcendent promises, ultimately contributes to our capacity to love rightly, that light and love somehow converge.

BEYOND EMPTY UNIVERSALISM

The emblematic dictum of Thomas Aquinas famously holds that "grace does not destroy nature but perfects it."[20] When Thomas taught this, the legitimacy, the givenness, of the natural desire of every being, including a human being, to persevere in existing, to affirm itself as the kind of being it is, was not in question. And since human beings are by nature familial, social, and political beings—and, for Christians, were created as such by God—the human inclination to form families and political communities and to defend our *particular* families and political communities (for there is no family or polity that is simply general or universal) was also a legitimate given. Today, however, nothing could be more questionable than the legitimate naturalness of our attachment to our particular families and nations or than the authority of these associations and so of their heads; all such mediating authorities are a flagrant scandal against the purity of the same and the other. Christians have for two millennia taken for granted the natural legitimacy and enduring reality of particular human bonds and focused their spiritual and intellectual energies on introducing a measure of relativity into these bonds from the standpoint of our universal humanity under a God whose love transcends all particular boundaries and borders. In modern times, Christians have, sometimes more and sometimes less willingly, become partners (by now, it is clear, junior partners) with modern rationalism or the modern ethic of scientism (including moral and political science) in dissolving the legitimacy of anything that particularizes and divides our humanity. To stand up for anything particular—therefore, to stand up for anything positive—is to stand against humanity.

We are thus all post-Augustinians now, believers and unbelievers alike, in the decisive sense of interpreting our humanity in terms of the universality of the city (the City of God) and of the soul. But our Christian universalism has been succeeded and swallowed up by our secular-humanist universalism. The universality of our Christianity has outlived the Christianity of our universalism. And this is in no way accidental. This may seem to be a concern only for Christians, but it is really a concern for anyone who can see that universalism without substance, without content, is a problem—that is, for anyone who can see that victimhood is not an adequate or viable or, finally, human idea of humanity.

To step back from the abyss of resentful victimhood as the meaning of our humanity, we must reconsider how an openness to what transcends particularity might be reconciled with the confidence or the courage to stand up for something—that is, necessarily, for something *particular*. We must consider how the beauty of the sacrifice of one's own good might be joined with the goodness of affirming some definite (and therefore never simply or immediately universal) good. We must rediscover, or perhaps, in a way, see clearly for the first time, how a Christian theology of the cross (denial of all-too-human goods) and a theology of glory (extension or expansion of what is best in humanity) must include each other.

The problem of reconciling our actual, concrete humanity with our universality is, then, a question intertwined with Christian theology, but it is not a question of interest only to professing Christians. All of us who are of the West, and therefore, virtually all who will read these words, are modern universalists and postmodern victims; we are now all either Christians or definitively post-Christians, marked, for better and for worse, by the Christian cult of the Victim who descended into humanity and put in question the natural, particularizing, meaning of humanity. Tom Holland[21] and Larry Siedentop[22] are right that we moderns are all Christians now in fundamental respects. In this they agree with Nietzsche and, as I will argue below, with Tocqueville. But Tocqueville as much as Nietzsche knew that this is by no means simply good news. The end of the Christian story will be the end of the human story if we cannot answer the compulsive turn to victimhood, the turn to suffering as the core of human identity par excellence, the act of repudiating all concrete goods, all acts of natural strength or virtue, as the last act of a self-effacing humanity, the residual spasm of human meaning. Is it possible to transcend our natural human particularism, to rise freely above the natural particularity of the good, without falling back on victimhood as the only surviving gesture of meaning? Is it possible for the universality of grace to perfect and therefore, first, to embrace and shelter the particularizing givenness, familial and political, of human nature? Is it possible for nature—including our familial and political nature—to be God's transcendently *free* creation and yet for us to affirm it rationally as intrinsically, eternally, *essentially* good?

This book is an essay in vindicating this possibility.

PART 1

Pierre Manent argues that we suffer from a "hypertrophy of theory" that obscures the essential goods of practical human existence. The overreach of theory can be traced to Machiavelli, but Machiavelli's revolt against the classical-Christian tradition was prepared and abetted by tendencies in Christian theology that come to a head in Luther and find their most radical expression in Heidegger's atheistic expression of fallenness.

Manent shows that Christian conscience can be interpreted either as the consummation of classical confidence in the inherent good of morality or, in the form of sheer consciousness of sin, as a tipping point tending to the subversion of morality.

The contemporary religion of humanity would consummate the victory of universalizing theory over the practical good, deploying the rhetoric of "charity" or "compassion" divorced from the substance of Christian faith. To resist this flattening, secular universalization will require an elevation of the virtue of practical wisdom or prudence.

Modern secular liberal and radical thinkers demonstrate and even celebrate the Christian derivation of modern universalist egalitarianism, the complicity between formal, immanent universality and the religious idea of absolute transcendence.

Leo Strauss understands that absolute transcendence is the deepest ground of a noxious synthesis between reason and revelation, and he promotes as an alternative the fulfillment of pagan honor in the idea of the self-sufficient goodness of the philosophic life. Strauss's discrete but penetrating diagnosis of the Christian complicity in modern rationalism, as well as the unsatisfactory alternative he proposes, challenges Christians to articulate more fully the status of practical nobility and moral agency in their otherworldly faith.

CHAPTER ONE

The Failures of Theory and Theology

Can reason preserve human purpose or provide the moral substance needed to resist its reduction to empty universality? Can reason discern and defend the goodness of what I have called "virtue-religion"—that is, the grounding of morality in a larger reality that both supports and transcends it? Can rigorous thinking support meaningful living? Friedrich Nietzsche posed this question in what may appear to be its most radical form when he violently opposed the requirements of "life" to those of "truth." But this radical opposition of life to truth can lead only (as it did in Nietzsche's case) to a desperate search for meaning ungrounded in any stable and eternal reality. This starting point leads to twin extremes: the will to power in the practical domain and the eternal return of the same in the theoretical, the fusion of pure activity and pure passivity. Nietzsche's failure has its nobility, and his scathing critique of the late modern, post-Christian faith in the "progress" of a purely materialist "happiness" ("a little pleasure by day and a little pleasure by night") is an achievement for the ages. But we, for our part, see too much good in actual human existence (as variously articulated in the Western tradition, philosophical and biblical) to be tempted by the grandiose rhetoric of the prophet of the Superman.

Rather than pushing the demands of "life" on the one hand and "truth" on the other to their opposite extremes and thus inviting an unnatural and monstrous fusion of pure power and pure acceptance of an inhuman reality "beyond good and evil," we will explore the possibility of a real harmony between practice and theory—between our practical natures (moral, political, and religious) and our openness to eternal truth, between our real freedom or moral agency on the one hand and being, or the fundamental character of reality, on the other. This exploration must begin with a truthful consideration of practice that is respectful of practice, one that takes seriously the natural moral-political point of view and seeks to attune rigorous reflection to what we propose is the necessary, permanent structure of practical existence. This attunement is of essential importance because the tendency of theory is to theorize practice in a way that dissolves it, which violates its nature from the outset. I here seek to explain practice without explaining it away, to "see" the good of action without seeing through it. This is admittedly a difficult task and involves a kind of balancing act: to theorize practice in a way that respects the substance of practice and that honors a certain opacity (albeit, I will argue, a luminous opacity) essential to our practical existence.

This practical approach to thinking about practice obviously owes much to Aristotle, whose account of the truth of our moral and political natures I will consult at some length. I will also borrow from Aristotle's Christian admirer, St. Thomas Aquinas, and recent authors who have developed Thomas's Christian-Aristotelian insights and propositions. More immediately, my approach owes much to the work of Pierre Manent, and in particular to his recent *Natural Law and Human Rights*. In this work, Manent repeatedly charges the "theoretical point of view" or "the hypertrophy of theory" with the obfuscation of the truth of practice.

PIERRE MANENT VERSUS THEORETICAL HYPERTROPHY

Pierre Manent's project of political philosophy already spans five decades and includes profound investigations of the broad arc of Western politics, such as *The City of Man* and *Metamorphoses of the City*, as well as brilliant readings of authors such as Tocqueville, Montaigne, and, more recently, Pascal. Manent's unrelenting pursuit of the truth of the condition of modern humanity combines Leo Strauss's devotion to political philosophy as an indispensable reflection on the human condition, Tocqueville's sober, even anxious understanding of modern democracy as a new age of humanity, and Raymond Aron's courageous and resolute attention to the political and social reality we see before us.

The term "theoretical hypertrophy" covers a broad range of philosophical and theological teachings in Manent's account. His most obvious target in *Natural Law and Human Rights* is modern reductionism, as represented by Hobbes and Machiavelli. Hobbes adopts a standpoint of mastery from which the human power to think asserts superiority over the human matter of thought. Hobbes promises scientific mastery over the human condition while reducing humanity to the sheer, unmitigated passion of fear. Tocqueville captured this characteristic modern stance of self-exaltation leveraging self-abasement in unforgettable terms: speaking of Hobbes's philosophical heirs, the self-styled "champions of modernity," he observes that "when they believe they have sufficiently established that they are nothing but brutes, they show themselves as proud as if they had demonstrated they were gods."[1] There have, of course, been materialist philosophers (Epicureans, most notably) about as long as there have been philosophers. The distinctive stock in trade of modern materialists is that they are keen to assure us that this reduction of humanity to blind material causes is good news. Thus, Vladimir Soloviev's delicious distillation of this hopeful reductionism: "We are descended from the apes. Therefore, we must love one another." In Hobbes's teaching, as Manent points out, the reduction of humanity is effected by the category of "fear." "Fear," Hobbes taught, "is the passion to be reckoned with." Political science, Hobbes promises, can make itself as certain and unequivocal as mathematics and can change the world on the basis of this reduction of all that is human to the single concern for material survival. But is the desire to survive, in fact, always and everywhere the dominant, overriding human desire? Of course, Hobbes knows that there are other hopes and fears in the human breast that, in fact, compete with this mathematicized concept of fear. But he asks us to count only on fear. Thus, as Manent notes, fear must be "moralized" in Hobbes. He *seems* to teach that the passion that is always really the strongest is fear, but in fact, he teaches that, in order to solve the human problem, we *ought to* take our bearings from this material passion, from fear of the body's violent death. This is the unacknowledged moral idealism upon which modern materialism has always been based.

In the first of his six chapters of *Natural Law and Human Rights*, Manent deftly exposes the bankruptcy of the contemporary "rights" discourse, which ultimately derives from Hobbes's radical reduction of humanity to an absolutely amoral "state of nature." Today's human rights ideology, he shows, is at once universalist and relativist; it promises both to liberate the person from his physical, sexual nature and to justify him on the basis of his natural or irresistible desires or "orientation." At bottom this ideology's only coherence is purely negative; it knows only what it is against: in the name of equality (the equality of a being defined only by the right to define and to redefine himself, or herself, or itself), "human rights" wages endless war against common sense, against what is best and richest in the spontaneous expression of our natures, against (as Manent wrote already in *Tocqueville and the Nature of Democracy*) "all that has human form." Manent bravely suggests, in fact, that the successful campaign for the recognition of homosexuality in the form of "marriage for all" must be understood as a fundamentally metaphysical demand, the demand that everyone renounce natural law, that no one recognize a norm or objective that is not the pure assertion of a human will.

In the second chapter, Manent begins to develop an alternative to the moral desert of subjective rights against the background of a sketch of the character and genesis of the modern project. The modern viewpoint is at once the perspective of the subject's unbounded power and that of a theoretical observer in absolute possession of his object. The triumph of willfulness is at the same time the ascendency of theory; our current practical impasse is the result of a "hypertrophy of theory." (In ch. 6, he will refer to "the tyranny of the explicit.") Hobbes's reduction of humanity to the bioindividual is of a piece with his imposition of a directly theoretical perspective on the human phenomenon. The "observer of human nature . . . is also the constructor of the new political order"; the practical phenomenon must be impoverished so that it can be "held in view," so that the "uncertainties of action" do not "overflow our vision."[2]

What is lost in the ingenious modern complicity between the hope of theoretical mastery and the reduction of humanity to fear, between idealism and material? What is crushed between these massive gears that drive modern "progress" is precisely the practical, human realm itself: the realm of choice and action as it naturally appears to the moral and political agent. (We will explore the enduring structure and content of this truly practical realm, with much help from Pierre Manent, in part 2.)

Manent is thus unstinting in his critique of the reductionist starting point of the modern theory of politics: the "irreparable, unpardonable error" of modern natural right, he argues, lies in the claim to alchemize law and morality out of nothing, or, in Manent's terms, to produce command starting from a condition without command, the famous modern "state of nature."[3] Insofar as it relies on this original mistake or this groundless pretension, modern liberalism, with the "struggle for rights" to which it gives rise, is haunted by nothingness. Stupefied by the liberal illusion of "autonomy," we render ourselves ever more subject to the abstract and impersonal machinery of the modern state. Hobbes's theory thus proves to be a self-fulfilling prophecy. The state of nature is not the truth of our nature or a true story of our political beginnings, but its lawlessness foretells the actual destiny of societies in the thrall of this theoretical liberalism. Hobbes's project truly foreshadows modern existence as the illusion of absolute freedom under the reality of absolute and inhuman sovereignty.

Did theory's monstrous overgrowth result from the influence of the new naturalistic physics over our understanding of the human world? Manent turns the tables on this conventional view of the history of ideas and proposes instead, as we shall see, that the rise of theory was irresistible because the character of practice had already been obscured by Europe's political and religious circumstances.

MACHIAVELLI'S VIOLATION OF THE "GAP" OF PRACTICE

Theoretical liberalism, or liberalism based on the premise of a lawless state of nature, commits liberal society to a ceaseless battle on behalf of an indeterminate and bottomless "equality" against human spontaneity and common sense.[4] But the health of liberalism depends on some determinate form of human life, some implicit law, that theoretical liberalism must perpetually undermine. Theoretical liberalism is a parasite whose only determinate principle of action is the ongoing destruction of its host. The state of nature is not society's true beginning, but it is truly the end toward which theoretical liberalism tends. "It is treating the effort of human thought lightly," Manent writes, "to imagine that we might effectively conceive and carry out a kind of 'de-creation-re-creation' of humanity without experiencing a moral upheaval" (53).

Manent agrees substantially with Leo Strauss that Hobbes's natural rights doctrine is based upon a theoretical "state of nature" derived from Machiavelli's "new modes and orders." Manent's understanding of natural law as *practical* is, in a fundamental sense, a response to Machiavelli's "realism," the master form, one might say, of the modern hypertrophy of theory.[5] And Machiavelli's "realism" is, in turn, a response, Manent avers, both understandable and disastrous, to the theological context in which premodern Christian natural law operated, a context that, as we will see, tended to draw natural law away from its practical conditions and toward a theological version of theoretical hypertrophy. To understand Manent's practical natural law, we must see how it responds both to Machiavelli and to Machiavelli's Christian provocation.

The problem Manent's Machiavelli sets out to solve is that of a great "gap" that defines the domain of human practice. The simplest description of this gap is in terms of the distance between what people say they ought to do and what they actually do, "between their limitless and essentially irresistible desires and the commandments of natural law that intimidate them without governing them" (31). However, as Manent explains, we cannot understand Machiavelli's response to the gap as an effort to reduce the space between ideal end and real performance; Machiavelli has no interest in helping us get a little closer to the end than we have so far been able to do. Machiavelli clearly does not accept the challenge of good action as it is in order to propose ways of meeting that challenge a little better than we ordinarily do. On the contrary, he proposes to transform the very meaning of action, to remove it from its natural context as ruled by an end it can never quite reach, and to set it free from all bounds. Machiavelli's new world will be defined not by our human subordination to certain intrinsically moral ends but by our amoral knowledge of the circumstances or obstacles, because these define only negatively the meaning of our actions. In this sense, Machiavelli does not promise to help us overcome or narrow the natural gap between human action and its end (either by improving our performance or, as proposed by Montaigne, for example, by lowering our goals) but rather to liberate us from all concern or respect for this gap.

The meaning of the natural gap thus becomes clear from the standpoint of Machiavelli's singularly radical response to it. To overcome the failure of our natural, practical humanity, to resolve the gap, it is necessary not to see it as a practical failure, a matter of immorality or of "sin," but rather to transpose this failure into a purely cognitive concern, or, as Manent writes, "what one might call a gnoseological failure. It is not so much that people do not succeed in doing what they should do; *the decisive point is rather that they do not achieve clarity on what they do*. They do not know what they do, and for this, Machiavelli does not forgive them" (28; emphasis added).

Machiavelli's radical innovation was not, then, to adjust in some way the relation between action and end so as to minimize the gap between them, but rather to instill in humanity "an excessive *desire for clarity*," to elaborate and promote "a nonpractical *view* of action" (34; emphasis added). What Machiavelli's "nonpractical view of action" must overcome or suppress are "the limits that spring from the fact that action is naturally produced by an agent and that it depends therefore on the virtuous or vicious dispositions of this agent" (32). As I will explain further in part 2, the intrinsic connection between action and virtue means that the "gap" of action can never be closed—must never be closed—not only because the successful attainment of the end of action is a problem that can never be "solved," since it depends on moral choice, but also because, as Aristotle already saw, the end of action is always bound up confusedly or mysteriously with the means of action.[6]

LUTHER'S GNOSEOLOGICAL CHRISTIANITY

Manent's confrontation with Luther in *Natural Law and Human Rights* is bracing in its force and clarity. Luther appears as a complicit mirror image of Machiavelli in that he considers human action from a purely theoretical standpoint divorced from the inherent character of moral agency—in Luther's case, from the standpoint of the problem of certainty of salvation. Commenting on Luther's *The Bondage of the Will* (a response to Erasmus's *On Free Will*), Manent shows that Luther deploys the principle of "faith alone" (*sola fide*) and so "escapes from the impasse of a life haunted by awareness of sin." While certainty of faith cannot be said to "belong to the theoretical order" in the usual sense, it certainly "tends to remove the believer from the practical order." For Luther, God, through his grace, "does not really transform or sanctify the sinner but shields the sinner from God's wrath by taking sin upon himself. One might say: where there had been an *acting* Christian or a Christian *agent*, now there is simply a *believer*" (37). Luther escapes the anxieties of action that are inherent in the perspective of the soul's guided improvement by embracing "certainty in [the believer's] will to be certain. The virtue of faith tends to become an art of believing, and the believer a virtuoso of faith" (39).

Manent thus presents Luther's doctrine of salvation by faith alone as a "gnoseological" approach that mirrors Hobbes's project of theoretical mastery or his "hypertrophy of theory," a hypertrophy that builds on Machiavelli's violation of the "gap" essential to natural human action. Setting aside for a moment Manent's discussion of Luther, I will expand briefly here on the Protestant Reformation as contributing to this violation or repudiation of the practical nature of humanity, albeit from a theological standpoint that appears opposite to Machiavelli's resolute attachment to this world.[7]

The persistent tendency of Luther's writings on politics is completely to collapse the traditional hierarchy between spiritual and secular functions. Thus, in "An Appeal to the Ruling Class of German Nationality" he states that the policeman and the cobbler are no less priests than those whose duty it happens to be "to expound the word of God and administer the sacraments."[8] This leveling is possible only because the dignity of such functions has been severed from any humanly accessible evaluation of lower and higher necessities and purposes, such as those that have framed the classical tradition of political reflection.

In what is perhaps Luther's most developed political writing, *Secular Authority: To What Extent It Should Be Obeyed*, Luther effects an ingenious and surprising breakthrough in Christian political theory, one that is rich in implications for modern thought. He accepts and, in fact, radicalizes the basic Christian dichotomy between the two kingdoms, the spiritual and the temporal. In the earlier tradition of Christian political thought, from Augustine forward, the drawing of this dichotomy had always implied a depreciation of the affairs of this world and thus redounded finally to the benefit of the spiritual power. The logic that had constrained political theorizing in the earlier Christian tradition, in fact, appears inescapable: if spiritual and secular concerns are considered distinct, and spiritual concerns are acknowledged to be of ultimate importance and therefore superior, then clearly these higher concerns must always in the end trump those that are merely political. If the secular realm has any dignity, then this dignity can only be derived from and considered subservient to the superior, spiritual realm. In a word, as long as humanity's ultimate purpose is understood as distinctly spiritual or otherworldly, as a Christian can hardly deny, then it seems inevitable that secular authority be subordinated in principle to spiritual or priestly authority.

Luther cuts through this Gordian knot of medieval Christian thought by radicalizing the basic Christian dichotomy and, in a way, liberating the secular from the spiritual. Salvation, or the spiritual kingdom, is radically inward, a matter of conscience, a secret, spiritual, hidden region dependent on no human power but entirely on the word of scripture. The kingdom of this world is wholly external; it deals with mortal life and with property. So complete is Luther's removal of the kingdom of God from the kingdom of the world that he proclaims the absolute uselessness of politics for true believers: The righteous do of themselves more than the law commands, attach no intrinsic importance to the things of this world, and have no need of compulsion. (Thomas Aquinas, by contrast, taught that political authority was essential to our humanity, even our uncorrupted humanity prior to the fall.) Luther is confident, on the other hand (despite, one might think, ample evidence that beliefs are considerably affected by material incentives), that the individual's conscience is immune from external force: "For faith is a free work, to which no one can be forced."[9]

Now, one would expect this radical separation to imply a radical depreciation of the political realm, as in the Augustinian framework. But Luther avoids this consequence by shifting the account of the purpose of politics entirely to the needs of the non-Christian neighbor.

Politics contributes in no way to the spiritual purposes of Christians, but only to the secular needs of their neighbors. Secular needs become authoritative for Christians *as someone else's needs*. By this remarkable displacement of the question of purpose, Luther bypasses the logic that seemed, in Christendom, to necessitate the subordination, direct or indirect, of political to spiritual authorities. Luther thus insulates the political realm from any higher purposes and thereby, he thinks, from the authority of priests. He refounds politics on material necessity yet does so in such a way that this secularization does not amount to a depreciation from a religious point of view. The key to Luther's ingenious rethinking is that the worldly or material necessity of politics is not left to rely on its own dignity but is considered as enjoined by the Christian duty of love. Luther accomplished what seemed impossible: securing at once the dignity of the political realm and its separation from any more authoritative spiritual ends. The linking of love to a material political necessity and the severing of any direct ties between this dutiful love and the authority of higher, specifically religious purposes is evident in Luther's uncompromising examples: "Should you see that there is a lack of hangmen, beadles, judges, lords, or princes, and find that you are qualified, you should offer your services." Or further, in the case of war, "it is a Christian act and an act of love confidently to kill, rob, and pillage the enemy, and to do everything that can injure him until one has conquered him according to the methods of war."[10]

Whatever the moral and spiritual resources of the Lutheran and, more broadly, Reformation traditions, Pierre Manent is right that in his core theological project, Martin Luther breaks decisively with the classical-Christian tradition of moral and political philosophy. We have seen that Luther accomplishes this rupture by a twofold strategy. First, he emancipates the spiritual and secular realms from each other by a radicalization of the Christian distinction between spiritual and inward things on the one hand and secular and external things on the other. Next, having severed secular, political matters from higher, spiritual purposes, he nonetheless secures the dignity and binding character of political authority by recourse to the Christian duty of love for the other. It is fair to call this duty of love operative in politics "secularized" because it concerns only external necessities, thus preserving the essential separation from concern for the good of the soul. My neighbor's material-political need is in no way intrinsically ordered with respect to a shared spiritual destiny; my duty to love my neighbor is commanded by God but in no intelligible way ordered by his love—that is, by charity as a supernatural *virtue*. Luther's Christian duty is commanded by God, but it aims at nothing divine except insofar as everything is God's creation. My Christian love has no other object, at least as far as politics and human action are concerned, other than the fallen needs of my non-Christian neighbor.

Beneath the now familiar dichotomy between the spiritual and the secular, or the internal and the external, this abstraction of duty from purpose is the lynchpin of Luther's remarkable attempt to do full justice at once to the claims of the soul and those of the body—spiritual transcendence and material necessity. The question Luther bequeaths to the future of political theory is whether the secular realm, now grounded in its own needs, can avoid encroaching on concerns of the spirit. Luther seems not to envision a situation in which a person's duty to the needs of humanity might appear to be in tension with, or might even claim to trump, the calling to some inward purity of faith.[11]

MANENT VERSUS BARTH'S *RÖMERBRIEF*

For Manent, the essence of Luther's "gnoseological" project is the attempt to concentrate religious meaning in a sheer consciousness of sin divorced from the potentialities and the perspective of moral action. In recent remarks on Karl Barth's treatise *Der Römerbrief* (*The Epistle to the Romans* [1922]), "Reflections of Practical Philosophy on 'Faith Alone,'"[12] Manent uncovers a still more radical version of the Protestant repudiation of the practical standpoint, an extreme form of the sublimation of a purely theoretical standpoint that tends at a deep level to abet the atheistic existentialism that has exercised a crippling fascination over the Western mind in the last century.

Introducing his lecture on Barth, Manent references the argument I have surveyed in my comments on *Natural Law and Human Rights*, above; according to this argument, "the Reformers, in order to utterly liquidate ecclesiastical mediation, tend to destroy the classical understanding of practical life."[13] By "classical," Manent intends both

Greek—especially Aristotelian—and Catholic understandings. Modestly disclaiming any expertise on the work of Karl Barth, he expresses no confidence in reaching a "clear and stable judgment" regarding Barth's teaching. Still, Manent cannot suppress the criticisms that arise from his "slow and difficult" reading of the *Römerbrief* of 1922.[14] These criticisms are as trenchant as they are far-reaching for our understanding of the bearing of Christianity on the natural, practical perspective.

Barth's teaching, Manent shows, is radically one of *Kritik*, a root-and-branch criticism of "the old life, the old man, in all its aspects." Abandoning the common, practical meanings of the "pair possible-impossible," Barth proposes an understanding of grace as "this impossible possibility . . . [that] excludes the possible possibility of sin" (214, paraphrasing Barth, 295–96). Going beyond Luther's formulation of the condition of the Christian as at once righteous and sinner, Barth argues, "I can only hold myself in conversion—*Umkehr*—(in the irreversible conversion!) *from* sin *to* grace" (214–15, quoting Barth, 285). Manent is puzzled by this idea of conversion as "a *movement* that does not seem to find completion or fulfillment in a stable disposition, a 'virtue' of the person" (215). The imperative of character development disappears completely for Barth in a kind of fusion of theory and practice. Manent quotes Barth: "Grace is the power of obedience. It is *theory* as such just as it is also praxis. . . . And it is *the* imperative, *the* call, *the* commandment, *the* demand that one cannot but obey, and which has the power of a plain fact" (Manent, 215, quoting Barth, 205). For Barth, Manent concludes, "theory dominates and envelops practice." This thoroughly theorized idea of grace must be understood, Barth writes, as "absolutely free of all possible confusion with the question of knowing what we can and must do or not do" (Manent, 216, quoting Barth, 215). For Barth, Manent continues, "what is decisive takes place on a level that is independent of and superior to the plane of practical life . . . the level of the *existentiell* (216); and "Barth has no place for an active understanding of obedience" (218). "A slave of grace or of sin, I do not obey in the proper sense, I simply find myself in one or the other condition" (218). Thus Barth grants "religion" in the usual sense little importance; he, in fact, writes that "the true act of conversion is in fact a *Denken*. . . . Repentance signifies a *conversion* of thought—*Um*-Denken" (Manent, 219; Barth, 460).

Barth's *Denken*, as Manent shows, has nothing to do with the classical idea of contemplation of eternity as an inward fulfillment of the soul; Barth's "thought" signifies neither action nor contemplation (223). True faith and true thought converge in the experience of crisis or the pure void of meaning, and thus "even faith, insofar as it wishes in any sense to be more than a void (*Holraum*), is in fact a form of unbelief (*Unglaube*)" (222, quoting Barth, 86). Barth understands thinking in an "existential (*existentiell*)" (222) way that resonates with Heidegger, and Barth believes that thinking "takes place within immanence and presents itself as an affirmation of immanence," or within "life exposed to time." Therefore, Barth's crisis-thinking, Manent writes, "takes place at a level of depth or of radicality that abandons the repentance of the agent to the vulgarity of a psychological experience stripped of any authentic spiritual relevance" (220).

FROM LUTHER TO HEIDEGGER

"One is tempted to say," Manent writes, that "in a certain measure, philosophy is the only thing that escapes Karl Barth's critique, however radical this critique may be" (223). But we have seen that what Manent considers Barth's excessively indulgent attitude toward philosophy has nothing to do with contemplation—that is, with any inward experience of some intelligible goodness. Barth's "philosophy" aligns with his radical Protestant faith in that it repudiates the practical point of view of action toward some good and, therefore, repudiates any philosophy oriented toward goodness or fulfillment. Significantly, the meeting point of Christian grace and philosophy for Barth is the experience—the "limit experience"—of suffering; this seems to be the only element of actual human experience that survives the radical critique of our natural humanity from the standpoint of faith.[15]

The tendency toward a convergence between a radical interpretation of salvation by faith alone and the deconstruction of practical meaning in atheistic existentialism is confirmed by the deep connection that Martin Heidegger, the father of existentialism and the author of the deepest and darkest existentialism, saw between his own thought and the work of Martin Luther himself. In Heidegger's response to

Luther, we see the most explicit and developed argument that radical conversion is, as Manent puts it, purely theoretical, in the sense that it involves not the instauration of a practical disposition that enables the convert progressively to overcome sin, but rather a kind of purely theoretical operation by which one comes to look at sin—that is, at human existence—in a certain way. For it has been shown from certain of Martin Heidegger's earliest writings that Martin Luther's idea of faith and sin played a decisive role in Heidegger's conversion from a staunch Catholic philosopher working within an Aristotelian-Scholastic framework to an atheist philosopher who embraced temporality or historicity as the insuperable horizon of human existence. To understand what Heidegger owed to Luther is to see the confluence between radicalized Christian transcendence and resolute secularism, or the absolute embrace of "temporality," in its starkest form.

John Van Buren has gathered several of Heidegger's early writings (or student notes from his lectures)[16] that include significant clues as to the bearing of the great philosopher's engagement with Christianity on his mature philosophy. In a 1919 letter to Father Krebs, a Roman Catholic mentor, the young philosopher announces without ire that his own "inner calling to philosophy . . . for the sake of the eternal vocation of the inner man" (70) requires that he sacrifice his attachment to the Catholic tradition: "Epistemological insights extending to a theory of historical knowledge have made the *system* of Catholicism problematic and unacceptable to me, but not Christianity and metaphysics—these, though, in a new sense" (69). This "new sense" of Heidegger's engagement with Christianity is perhaps most profoundly indicated in a set of texts edited by Van Buren entitled "The Problem of Sin in Luther." Here Heidegger notes that "the sense and essence of any theology are to be read off in light of *Justitia originalis*" (105)—that is, according to the original rightness of man as created by God. Luther's great breakthrough consists in his insight "precisely in opposition to Scholasticism," that sin or human corruption *"can never be grasped radically enough"* (106; emphasis added). In order to induce the spiritual despair that alone can truly bring humanity to God, Heidegger's Luther understands that "corruption is something to be amplified," that "hope comes not from works but from suffering," and that "on the part of man nothing precedes grace except rebellion." This implies a total rupture with any conceivable practical point of view ("All human action is presumptuous and sinful") and so with Aristotle ("The whole of Aristotle is to theology as darkness is to light"). A "theology of the cross" must therefore utterly displace any "theology of glory"—that is, all theology that holds that something in humanity is left unspoiled by the fall (107).

Against the background of Heidegger's appreciation of Luther, it is possible to see how Heidegger's entire project might be seen as a radicalization of Luther's rejection of the natural, practical standpoint, the standpoint inherent in human action. Whereas the Christian tradition held that, although the fall deprived man of the superadded gift of the three theological virtues, human nature retained sufficient integrity to allow man to understand himself as "natural being-placed before God"—that is, as standing before God, as by nature oriented toward divinity. Heidegger's Luther "rebels against this and . . . appeals to experience. . . . The being of man as such is itself sin. . . . Thus sin is not an affixing of moral attributes to man but rather his real core. In Luther, sin is a concept of existence." Luther's breakthrough, of decisive importance for Heidegger, is thus the claim that what Luther calls "sin" is, in fact, identical with human existence (108). "Fear, hatred, and flight from God" *are* what it means to be human; the imperative of flight is such that the human being "constantly wishes to distance himself further, he keeps on fleeing forever" (109). What the Scholastics disguise as an aspiration to good can only be a prideful and thus aggravated form of sin's flight. The human condition is one of sin, pride, rebellion, and flight, and there is nothing within human nature or human experience that can point beyond this condition.

Heidegger praises Luther's theology of the cross precisely for its denial of any orientation, any inkling, any vestige of good in human nature that might ground human action in any positive sense—that is, action for the good rather than as pure rebellion and flight. What, then, can be the meaning of Heidegger's claim that Luther's idea of the corruption of human nature can never be understood radically enough? Is Heidegger not suggesting that he proposes to understand this most fundamental Lutheran teaching more radically than Luther himself? This suggestion is bolstered by the last paragraph in this lecture manuscript: "Protestantism is only a *corrective* to Catholicism and cannot stand alone as normative, just as Luther is Luther only on the spiritual basis of Catholicism." Whereas Catholic degeneration is a decline into the disgrace of "worldliness," Protestants are equipped to praise "worldliness" as "godliness and frankness." To radicalize Lutheranism would be to sever it absolutely from its Catholic foil, to emancipate lucid and resolute worldliness, with its "mortal anxiety," from any sense of "a great spiritual trial"—which, after all, depends upon the foil of a conception of human goodness incompatible with the idea of sin as a pure description of human existence. Heideggerian "existentialism" is Luther taken at his word: human beings cannot hope for good because there is no "good" in them. If, then, the term "God" has any meaning, it cannot be anything positive or relevant to purposive human action. "God" is only what we hate and that from which we flee. Rebellion and flight are the human condition, and authentic human existence is nothing but the lucid and resolute embrace of this condition. If there is a "pure Lutheranism" (not to be confused, it must be emphasized, with the whole body of Luther's teaching, much less with the actual historical development of Lutheran Christianity), I conclude, a Lutheranism that takes at Luther's word the absolute rejection of any good inherent in practical human existence as we know it, then Heidegger has shown us what it would have to be like.

The Heideggerian radicalization of Lutheranism thus presents us with a stark and lucid reductio ad absurdum of Christian skepticism regarding the natural, practical human orientation toward some good.[17] The absolute denial of a natural orientation toward the good, whether in its Machiavellian or Lutheran-Barthian-Heideggerian forms, entails a wholesale repudiation of the practical standpoint of the insuperable "gap" of action.

CHAPTER TWO

Manent

Toward the Truth of Practice

In his critical examination of Karl Barth's *Römerbrief*,[1] Manent draws on Thomas Aquinas to suggest a more practical framing of the question of grace and obedience: "In the *Summa Theologiae*, Thomas Aquinas also emphasizes how the distance and the disproportion between God and man affects in an essential way the experience that a graced soul has of God: his presence and his absence cannot be known with certainty. Thomas borrows an audacious formula from Denys that seems to me very illuminating: to have grace is 'to be joined with one unknown'" (Manent, 219; *ST* I.12.13). Manent's practical understanding of grace and obedience depends upon the possibility that "we can learn to live with this God who is unknown." In affirming this possibility, we begin to see how far Manent is willing to go in defending the priority of practice to theory, in religion as well as in morality and politics: "To learn so to live: is this not in any case the only real knowledge that we can have—a knowledge that has nothing to do with 'mysticism,' and which gives us neither the desire nor the feeling of escaping our condition—that does not offend against God's transcendence? *Is not such a practical knowledge the most desirable and salutary of all, or rather the only desirable and only salutary knowledge?* These are questions one might pose" (219; emphasis added). The implications of Manent's profound suggestion that combines awareness of and respect for divine transcendence with a genuinely practical understanding of practice will be a central theme of part 2. But before leaving behind Manent's critique of modern theory as well as Protestant theology, let us gather a few more of his positive indications concerning the meaning of a practical philosophy, a philosophy attuned to the truth of practice, in the contexts we are now examining.

"Practical life," Manent explains in the course of his critique of Barth, "is always an adventure with its contingencies; that is also true of spiritual life in the strict sense of the term, since this life is also, fundamentally, a *practical* life" (217).[2] The practical "adventure" of moral and political agency, I conclude from Manent's indications, is, for the Christian, essential to his *spiritual* adventure of the life of faith—that is, to the human adventure understood as imbued with eternal meaning under a transcendent divinity. Manent leaves open for now just how this Christian understanding of the meaning of human existence relates to the understanding of human existence it proposed to replace. In the course of criticizing Barth's excessive trust in philosophy, or, more precisely, in a certain contemporary "existential" philosophy, Manent observes that "the Christian proposition necessarily involves, to be sure, a critique of Jewish law, but it also necessarily involves a critique of Greek philosophy, or of philosophy in general, this 'critique' being more or less destructive or conservative [*préservatrice*] according to the diversity of Christian confessions or schools of thought" (222). We are thus left to ponder just what, for Manent, Christianity should "destroy" or leave behind and what it should preserve in the Greek philosophical tradition. His answer, we shall find, is by no means simply "conservative" in relation to the Christian theological tradition.

Returning to *Natural Law and Human Rights*: What Manent clearly wishes to conserve is the moral and practical core of traditional Christianity, the framework of beliefs and institutions that supports a sense of "being engaged along a path of improvement, the fragile steps along which the conscience measures with prudence and justice." Practical life guided by the hope of eternal salvation is life "directed and judged by my *conscience*"—not a radically individualized conscience, and certainly not a pure Barthian awareness of suffering as a limit-thought or a post-Lutheran Heideggerian embrace of falling and flight as the meaning of human existence, but "a conscience that is more or less informed, more or less awakened, more or less scrupulous; and this direction and judgment normally require the help of sacraments and of the church as an institution."[3] True conscience is not absolute and purely individual, but a matter of "more or less" and decisively mediated by the institutional church.

Pierre Manent's preference for a Catholic as opposed to a Protestant understanding of the practice of faith—for Thomas Aquinas as opposed to Luther—is clear and, of course, hardly surprising. But to grasp the importance and originality of Manent's argument, one must not overlook his indications of the limitations of the medieval Christian understanding, even of a certain complicity of this understanding in the oblivion of the true character of practical existence, as Manent endeavors to restore this practical understanding in a way consistent with Christian essentials.

PIERRE MANENT ON THE MOST DELICATE QUESTION: CHRISTIANITY AND THE ECLIPSE OF PRACTICE

Manent's treatment of Christianity in *Natural Law and Human Rights* consists, for the most part, in two brief sections of the book. The first, found in chapter 2 in connection with the critiques of Machiavelli and Luther, is "The Human Condition and the Christian Condition"; the second, in chapter 3, is "The Christian Question." Manent's discussion of Christianity is careful and nuanced—even, one might say, discreet—as befits what he calls "the most delicate point of the situation," and, therefore, much is left to the reader in interpreting and comparing these two rich discussions. On close reading, it can be seen that the first section highlights the continuity between the natural condition (as articulated, notably, by Aristotle) and the Christian condition, while the second emphasizes a fundamental discontinuity.

The first section considers Christianity as the object of Machiavelli's critique. Of course, Manent's main point is a profound critique of Machiavelli, but it is striking how far he is willing to go in sympathetically understanding Machiavelli's objection to Christianity. Manent frames the Machiavellian problem, as we have seen, in terms of the "gap" inherent in human action between speech and deed, between what people say and what they do, between the end they imagine and the actual motives of action. Manent nowhere disputes the existence of such a "gap" or envisions any way of eliminating it. In fact, he blames Machiavelli for trying to collapse the natural gap of practice, and he will argue (as we will see in part 2) that respect for the true character of practice requires holding the gap open. But Manent does not contest Machiavelli's critique of Christianity's tendency to radicalize the gap between speech and deed in a way that leads to a kind of "pretentious *passivity*" (emphasis added), such as to justify "Machiavelli's piercing words [concerning Christian teaching], 'it is evil to speak evil of evil.'"[4]

The guiding thread of Manent's discussion of Christianity in this section is the question of whether Machiavelli's revolutionary theory was an attack only against Christianity or whether nature, as understood by the ancients, was also the target. It is in answering this question that Manent emphasizes the classical-Christian continuity: "If the Christian religion only expresses and thereby aggravates the natural condition of humanity, then it makes sense that in order to overcome *Christian* inaction or passivity, it would be necessary somehow to overcome the *human* condition" (35). The essential continuity, as well as the significant discontinuity, between man's practical nature and Christianity comes to view nowhere more clearly for Manent than in the question of conscience. By erasing or eradicating conscience, Machiavelli is negating a "human capacity brought to light only in a Christian context, that sums up and fulfills the leaving behind of the practical condition" (36). The dual object of Machiavelli's attack is further clarified in a footnote to this very passage: "Emerging in the context of Christianity, the notion of conscience supports and complements the Aristotelian analysis of practical life and of reflective choice so well that the two elements prove to be inseparable; once the notion of conscience is dismissed, modern practical philosophy (if these two adjectives can indeed be put together) will no longer be able to find its way in practical reasoning" (133n21). "Conscience" appears thus as the emblem of the continuity between nature and Christianity, the culmination of Aristotelian reflective choice and, therefore, of the true, practical condition of humanity.

This clear and even edifying portrayal of the "delicate" question of Christianity is perhaps not contradicted but is certainly unsettled by chapter 3's emphasis on the *discontinuity* between nature and grace. At least in the perspective that Manent adopts here, that of "social knowledge and political science, . . . the Christian religion presents a singularly resistant obstacle to Socratic political philosophy or to Aristotelian political science" (55). The "creature" enslaved to sin is hard to square with "the *political* condition experienced by the Greek city and analyzed by Greek political science" (55). The penitent seems to have little to do with the agent. The invisible and radically internal ("*in foro interno*") domain of the Christian soul is essentially incommunicable with respect to the visible realm in which the citizen acts, and there seems to be no way to translate between the "opinions of the citizen" and "the faith of the Christian" (55). The essential difficulty lies in the doctrine of "the invisible action of an invisible being *infinitely* different" from humanity (55; emphasis added). Machiavelli's antitheological ire (if not his resulting project) is at least understandable, then, in view of the fact that "under a Christian regime, the social *phenomenon* is at once overburdened and elusive," indeed unintelligible (56).

"As damaging as it was, *the disdain of the dogmatists of modern natural right for the social and political phenomenon can be said to have been inevitable* since it resulted from the overdetermination, or simply from the division or confusion, of the phenomenon itself" (57; emphasis added).

The reader is entitled to ask, then, just where Manent stands on the "delicate" question of Christianity from the standpoint of the natural perspective of action, the perspective of a certain "natural law" that he is preparing to defend. Does Christianity offer the fulfillment of the natural perspective of the human agent? Or does Christianity strain and burden this perspective to the point that its collapse into a perspective alien to moral action, either Machiavellian or Lutheran, is practically inevitable? Each of these interpretations has its truth, Manent suggests to us, but each also has its limits. To recover a true and natural perspective of action—to recover natural law within the perspective of an openness to a divinity that infinitely transcends our humanity—must then require honoring the moral truth of Christianity while knowing how to avoid its overreach and, therefore, its collapse, a collapse that brings with it the loss of the classical-Christian truth of moral agency.

CONSCIENCE AS THE SUMMIT AND PRECIPICE OF MORAL AGENCY

To explore this possibility of a defense of natural moral agency as compatible with openness to the supernatural will be the final purpose of part 2 of this work. For now, before concluding our review of texts in which Manent criticizes theoretical and theological hypertrophy, it will be useful to return briefly to the question of "conscience." Manent's treatment of conscience is particularly instructive in the way it shows Christianity to be, in one sense, the fulfillment of nature and, in another sense, to risk the undermining or liquidation of nature. On the one hand, conscience crystallizes the moment of individual responsibility, the deeply personal and individual character of moral agency. When motivated by conscience, the individual believer is lifted above and beyond contingent social conventions to ground reflective choice in a transcendent source of meaning and authority. In this sense, one can say that moral agency is never more truly moral or more truly active than when it is distilled in the idea of conscience. This is the sense in which Christian conscience is the supernatural fulfillment of the classical, natural understanding of reflective moral choice.

On the other hand, the individualizing and transcending claims of conscience risk destroying confidence in all concrete norms—which, after all, are always connected in some way with the natural goods of particular human individuals and communities—and collapsing into a pure consciousness of nothingness. In the face of "an invisible being infinitely different" from the agent and the reduction of temporal existence to enslavement to sin, we have seen "conscience" collapse into the sacrifice of the purportedly illusory goods of action to the idea of a "salvation by faith alone" (Luther), or, eventually, to a radically speculative idea of "conversion" now severed from moral action and understood as the pure *Kritik* of all mundane meaning (Barth).

Manent's practical preference is clearly what we might call a traditional, Catholic understanding of conscience, one that moderates its individualizing and radically transcendent power, its attempt to tie what is most interior and individual to what is furthest beyond our natural condition by offering the individual believer authoritative moral guidance and sacramental participation in ultimate goods. Of all the "many mediations [that] have been introduced between the political operation and the Christian operation, . . . the first of these [is] the Catholic Church itself" (56). Clearly, Manent has great respect for such attempted mediations. However, just as clearly, Manent understands the fragility of these mediations, given the intractable underlying problem of "seeing double"—that is, of the overburdened, unintelligible "social *phenomenon*" that has been the practical legacy of Christianity. Just how to hold together or at least coordinate the Christian truth of openness to infinity with the practical goods of the natural human condition is a question that we will explore in part 2.

Manent is thus content to be suggestive and not fully explicit on the "most delicate point" of the role of Christianity in what one might call the rise and fall of the humanizing gap of action. In portraying the relationship of classical philosophy to Christian theology, Manent is attentive both to a fundamental continuity (distilled in the Christian notion of "conscience") and a momentous rupture occasioned by the infinite expansion of the gap between human means and divine end. Christianity did not invent this gap, according to Manent, but it exaggerated it and thus brought it to light. Manent does not offer any obvious reconciliation of these two interpretive stances. Extrapolating somewhat from his argument, I would propose that Christianity absolutized the gap inherent in human action—a gap that Manent sees is inseparable from the meaning of human existence—by conceiving of the common good as perfectly realized only in a city of God understood to be so purely common (selfless) and so purely good (perfectly satisfying) that it was utterly beyond attainment by man's natural powers; thus it can be said that the problem Manent designates as theoretical "hypertrophy" appears already in premodern Christian theology, or in the Christian appropriation of the classical orientation of action by reference to a "best regime." On this view, Machiavelli and Luther were so affected by the intolerable tension of the infinite gap produced by this Christian-classical synthesis (at least in certain of its forms) that they proposed to close it definitively, either by replacing normative law with fear (Machiavelli) or by reducing the good, or salvation, to the subjective act of faith (Luther). In both cases, the gap inherent in action was suppressed, and human action was deprived of any elevated horizon. Thus, the Machiavellian fear that was mobilized to produce a fusion of "the appearance and the result" proved to be the effectual truth of radical Protestant faith and, more deeply, of an overly speculative or theoretical Christian appropriation of the classical tendency to close the gap essential to human meaning, the ambition to resolve the perpetual openness of action to something above and beyond it by an appeal to a determinate idea of the best regime and the best soul (that of the philosopher).

We can now see how Manent links the founding of modern rationalistic materialism by Hobbes and Locke, for example, with the theological revolution of the Reformation. Hobbes, Manent grants, was not wrong to complain that the European rivalry between church and state as ultimate powers caused Western people to "see double" and crippled their capacities for action. Machiavelli's and Luther's earlier and apparently opposite responses to this disabling double vision have proved to be mutually reinforcing; they have in common a repudiation of action itself in their attempts to seize some purely theoretical or "gnoseological" standpoint untainted by action's vagaries and uncertainties. The modern "realistic" or "scientific" option is ordinarily advanced (as originally by Machiavelli) as an alternative to the "idealistic" point of view of antiquity or Christianity (25). But "reality" was not discovered by the moderns; in fact, the reality of action was obfuscated: "If we look at human things from a 'realistic' or 'scientific' perspective, we do not so much see them 'as they are' but rather as they look when we dismiss or hide the acting human being's point of view. In effect, we cannot look at human things 'as they are,' since properly speaking, they *are* not; rather, they must be done or 'enacted.'"

In order to understand Manent's alternative to the modern "hypertrophy of theory" or "tyranny of the explicit" that results from this repudiation,[5] we must first appreciate how far he is willing to travel alongside Machiavelli (in the Florentine's effort to understand the roots of the medieval moral and political crisis) before decisively rejecting the strangely parallel strategies that Machiavelli and Luther conceive as a response to this crisis. There would have been no crisis of human action (Machiavellian or Protestant) if the point of view of action itself were not already fragile within premodern Christendom.

MANENT'S DEFENSE OF PRACTICE VERSUS CLASSICAL SYSTEMS OF TELEOLOGY

Before moving on from Manent's bracing critique of theoretical hypertrophy, both modern and Protestant, we should take note of the fact that, again somewhat discreetly, the French political philosopher departs as well from the teleological doctrines or gestures of classical political philosophy.

While an engagement with the ancients is not a focus of Manent's *Natural Law and Human Rights*, there are moments in his argument where he clearly distances himself from a broadly Platonic tendency to impose a certain philosophical template on practice in a way that covers over and distorts practical life. Thus, Manent explicitly dismisses as "a prisoner of the theoretical view that it shares with the philosophy of rights" any attempt to derive natural law from "a certain idea of nature . . . understood as the objective synthesis of all norms desirable for the good regulation of the human world" (101).

The classical gesture might be characterized broadly as follows: If we interpret the nobility or intrinsic goodness of virtue as indicative of a discrete and freestanding comprehensive highest good, then the complex of human motives and norms can be resolved into a unified and comprehensive system. All goods might then be interpreted as instrumental to a higher good, either of the city (the common good) or of the soul (philosophical communion with the principle of all being). These possible ways of anchoring the goods of practice in a determinate higher good might be said to characterize ancient or classical political rationalism. Thus, though the activity of deliberation activates and brings forth the cardinal virtues (as Manent emphasizes), for Aristotle, "the object of deliberation par excellence" is in principle a single rational standard, "the best form of government, the political regime." But to decide the question of the best form of government, one must define the best soul, and this task of definition leads to the proposition of philosophy itself, or the contemplation of eternal, self-sufficient truth, as the highest good and lodestar of human action.

Manent declines to follow the ancient Greeks, or such a conclusively "teleological" interpretation of the ancient Greeks, in reasoning from the practical virtues emergent from the requirements of political order to a single standard of the best regime and thus to the necessary standard of philosophy or contemplation as the best way of life. For Manent, the cardinal virtues, which are quite stable and universal in their manifestations in various regimes and cultures, are actualized not as independent ends-in-themselves to be grasped by theory but in practical, political deliberations relative to a particular regime and thus as means to further ends. These virtues may be said fully to come to light *as ends* only in the deliberation—the metadeliberation, one might say—of the statesman or his friendly shadow, the political philosopher. But whereas Plato and Aristotle invite reflection on a determinate comprehensive good, first of the city and then of the soul, Manent counsels deference to the practical structure of the good, the structure of the good as it operates in practice, and shows little interest in any final and explicit philosophical or theological determination of this practical good. In this respect, Manent may be said to take the side of Christian humility and even of modern skepticism against the inspiring but, in a way, overpromising speculations of the ancients.[6]

We have seen, moreover, that Manent's counsel of a certain philosophical humility is thus directed at Christian theology as much as it is at pre- or post-Christian philosophy. Any theory or theology that aspires to understand practice, to address moral-political agency, must situate itself within the realm of action; it must be attentive to and respectful of a certain necessary structure of action. Theology and philosophy must humble themselves in order to enter into what might be called the essential pride of human action, the confidence of action in an active human contribution to the good. This humbling of theory in order to release the inherent good of practice—which includes a necessary moment of pride—will be the theme of part 2.

CHAPTER THREE

From the Politics of Fear to the Religion of Humanity

The deep complicity between what appear to be extreme opposites—Machiavelli's and Hobbes's materialist realism on the one hand and the Reformers' (and Barth's) doctrines of the extreme transcendence or otherness of grace with respect to nature on the other—is grounded in their common repudiation of the evidence of practice, their utter rejection of the claim of the intrinsic goodness of virtue, or of the worthiness of moral improvement, which, Manent proposes, forms the necessary if implicit horizon of all real or passably sound human action.

The modern rationalist project of mastery over nature for the sake of material security and comfort has thus long been abetted, more or less knowingly, by a certain Christian renunciation of the claims of natural virtue. Secular humanism and what we might describe as a certain humble Christian pragmatism have effectively been partners for centuries, even when they were rivals. As Tocqueville wrote concerning the apparently providential march of democracy over seven centuries, "All men have aided it by their efforts: . . . those who fought for it and even those who declared themselves its enemies; all have been driven pell-mell on the same track, and all have worked in common, some despite themselves, others without knowing it, as blind instruments in the hands of God."[1] But now, in the twenty-first century, the effective alliance between rationalism and (explicitly or effectively) progressive Christianity has yielded to a new, awakened secular spirituality for which the rivalry between reason and revelation has been utterly forgotten. The human mind and the human heart devote themselves without division to the vision or feeling of an equal global humanity, such that neither reason nor faith can hear any call to a loftier soul or a better world.

The now ubiquitous and, therefore, somewhat tired term "woke" indicates that leftism has become a religion.[2] To those of us who reject this ersatz religion, it may seem to be a mental disorder, plain and simple. The woke contagion indeed expresses a spiritual disorder. But if wokeness is crazy, it is so in a profound way; its craziness goes deep and requires a philosophical and theological response. The woke denial of borders and limits points to an understanding of our shared humanity that would somehow transcend all particular, political, and cultural horizons. To refute the woke attack on limits and its remobilization of the militancy of "liberation" and to bring to light its madness will require a deep and brave reflection on the political and moral condition of humanity. Woke religion violates common sense, but common sense needs help defending against this violation. Contemporary madness thus challenges us to articulate the philosophy, and perhaps the faith, that must undergird common sense.

Pierre Manent has analyzed and challenged this final solution to the rivalry between reason and revelation in a remarkable collection of texts recently published in English translation under the title *The Religion of Humanity: The Illusion of Our Times*.[3] This volume well represents Manent's reflection, over four decades, on the problem of modern, "democratic" humanity in relation to what he calls "the Christian proposition."

CHRISTIANITY AND DEMOCRACY

The first text in this volume is a selection from a 1993 piece entitled "Christianity and Democracy." This includes a remarkably deft distillation of the unfolding of the "theologico-political" problem of the West, entitled "A Brief Political History of Religion." Here, it is immediately clear how little sympathy Manent has for any nostalgic evocation of a medieval ideal of Christendom: the attempt to instantiate the church as "the only true republic" inevitably failed, Manent acknowledges, "unleashing a permanent division and uncertainty" in the soul of the Christian citizen.[4] The national, confessional, and absolutist monarchy (exemplified by the reign of Louis XIV over France) then attempted to "reunite the two heads of the eagle" (language Rousseau borrowed from Hobbes), but the absolute Christian monarch was in a tenuous position from the outset since he needed both to appeal to a higher authority and to subordinate that authority to his own person (15). A similar tension or contradiction haunts modern democracy, as seen most clearly by Tocqueville, who wrote that in America, society was neither ruled by religion nor quite emancipated from religion, but rather that "society exercises [power] over itself by means of religion." "This equivocation," Manent observes, with a disarming boldness that is hard to gainsay, "contains the subsequent history of America." American history for Manent is marked by the exceptional privilege of a "sincerely religious people" imagining that "religion can be completely separated from politics" (17). The effectual tendency of this imaginary wall of separation is the complete sovereignty of politics over religion.

Manent's compressed account of the unfolding of democracy in France may be said, on close inspection, to arrive at the same destination and, finally, the same dead end by an opposite path. Having, not in this case by equivocation, but very deliberately, emancipated the secular republic from religious authority, the nation the French thus produced succeeds better than the church, empire, or the Christian king in "reuniting the two heads of the eagle" (18). In 1914, the secular French nation, somehow drawing upon the glory of its Catholic past, "inspired throughout Europe sacrifices that no king and no Church had ever obtained" (18). There was, for Manent,[5] something authentically Christian in the republican nationalism of the Third Republic.

But 1914 was to mark "the beginning of the end of the nation." And so we reach "the end of a cycle. . . . The Church has been completely domesticated by the nation; the nation, for its part, is exhausted" (18). It is this exhaustion of the nation that empties the arena of real action, which is always action for some concrete, practical human good— the good of a real and, therefore, particular community—leaving only the *illusion* of a humanitarian *ideal*, the illusion of "humanity" as a field of meaningful action. Meanwhile, Christianity—and Manent, himself a confessing Roman Catholic, is especially concerned with the action of the church—rather than preserving the alternative of a real community oriented toward an eternal salvation, now too often presents itself as "the bearer of [mere, ungrounded] ideals and values," in effect reducing itself to "humanitarian and egalitarian overbidding" (21). Christianity risks abetting the blind inertia of a "democratic humanity . . . that wills itself, without knowing itself." These are the core insights that frame the texts that Paul Seaton has gathered here: modern democracy, abandoning the concrete responsibilities of the nation-state, devolves into a religion of humanity; and modernized Christianity, forsaking the revealed requirements of salvation, collapses into the same ersatz religion. The ennobling rivalry between the assertion of the citizen and the humility of the Christian is dissolved in the empty, illusory notion of "humanity."

In concluding the 1993 essay that opens this collection, Manent finds a reason for hope in this exhaustion of the rivalry between modern, democratic humanity and Christianity: having, in the end, conformed to all of democracy's demands and abandoned all resistance to democracy's claim of political sovereignty, the church finds itself in possession of a fundamental "dialectical advantage": the sovereignty of humanity has been achieved, but the question "*Quid sit homo?* What is man?" (22) remains more than ever unanswered. That the church might step forward to propose a way of answering this question is the hope, no doubt by now increasingly forlorn, that inspires the profound and unique reflections gathered here.

THE ILLUSION OF "HUMANITY"

To analyze the humanitarian sensibility, Manent refers us to Tocqueville's idea of the *semblable*, a reductive human sameness, and to Rousseau's analysis of pity. We all now live according to the compelling evidence of the essential *sameness* of humanity—and we must note that Manent nowhere denies the immediate evidence of this sensibility. We are all touched and affected by a vivid sense of the simple humanity we share with other human beings as such. Manent does not present himself as an exception to this condition and this affect; indeed, he affirms, for example, that he has "only . . . admiration for the French doctors of

Doctors without Borders" (35). But he insists on pressing this question: Just what does this sameness mean? What is its *content*? The idea or feeling of humanity operates upon us in its *extension*, its universality, but what is its *intention*, its *practical* substance? This intention and substance, Manent argues, cannot be grasped or defined except in relation to *practice*—that is, to effective human action, to moral and political agency. The qualifier "political" here is critical because, as Manent has explained throughout his work, echoing Aristotle, all real, natural, practical action aims at a common *good*, a concrete good for a real community. "A profound, meaningful relationship between members of the human race can only result from a long time of living together, from common action, culture, and language." The particularity of community is thus implicit in the very nature of human agency. "We only really live where we act, and we do not really act except in the community of action that we form with our fellow citizens or our associates."[6] The "religion of humanity" is thus a pure *illusion* for the simple reason that the whole universe of human beings is not an actual arena of human action, which is always action for some concrete and particular good. "Justice has no meaning except where there is already a 'common thing.'"[7]

"Humanity" references no such effectively acknowledged and concrete good. Rousseau attempts to provide a substitute for such a real good in his feeling of pity or "compassion." But pity, Manent explains, however real an emotion, is, according to Rousseau's own perspicuous account, "very ambiguous."[8] "Pity . . . supposes that we perceive another suffering, but on condition that we are also aware that we ourselves escape from the suffering. We experience 'the pleasure of not suffering.'" The function of the feeling of pity in Rousseau's post-Christian humanism lies precisely in the fact that it "is not a disinterested sentiment"; it "does not demand any moral transformation or transcendence of the self." Therefore, it can never really aim higher than "the suffering *body*."[9] When "the notion of evil tends to merge with physical suffering," then human rights collapse into animal rights.[10]

The inadequacy and blindness of this understanding of humanity based on immanent pity, without reference to any shared understanding of distinctively human goods, Manent shows, was apparent in the "massive hypocrisy" of the NATO bombardments of Serbia in the war of Kosovo, where the "obsession with 'zero fatalities'" on the Western side shows that true sacrifice is hard to justify by a solely "humanitarian motive."[11] "The duty of [military] intervention is the new commandment of a new religion, the religion of Humanity"[12]—a religion that envisions no human bond but that of pity, a "weak and self-interested" sentiment.[13]

Manent deepens his analysis of the religion of humanity in part 3 of *The Religion of Humanity*. The author takes Victor Hugo's "poetic effusions" as early paradigms of this faith, and he identifies an early form of the new secular theology in the remarkably candid philosophy of Auguste Comte, for whom Nietzsche, "the great modern critic of altruism and humanitarianism," showed respect as that "great honest Frenchman."[14] It was Comte who made explicit the modern faith as a kind of doubling down on Christian love of neighbor. Modern altruism is thus revealed as an attempt to "out-Christian Christianity" (64). Nietzsche's contempt for this anti- or postreligious religiosity is hardly comprehensible to today's opinion leaders, who, in their sacrifice of reflection on the good to the abstraction of the "other," indeed in a way outdo Christianity in their total oblivion of the question of the soul's own good. Whereas Western humanity was once seized by the dual imperative of being a citizen and being a Christian, each a "task to accomplish" (68), we now think we have transcended both in our embrace of a universal, undifferentiated humanity. At the very moment we think we have separated religion from politics and attained a perfectly rational and secular society, we find instead that we have fused them, effectively worshiping humankind as the "Grand-Être" that determines our horizon. "It is at the moment when [humanity] embraces itself wholly"—without the mediation of nation or church—"that it ceases to understand itself" (67). We are sure, as was John Lennon, that if we just imagine "there's no heaven," then "the world will live as one."[15] There is nothing above us, and so we are left without purpose or vocation. This is the religion of humanity, beyond and beneath the claims of both the natural, political virtues and those that form us for another world. This is the "religion of the absence of God."[16]

CHARITY VERSUS COMPASSION

The crux of Manent's examination of the complicity between self-emptying Christianity and the ambition of or drift toward borderless global humanitarianism, and therefore the heart of this volume, is the author's effort to map the real distinction between Christian love and the emergent idea or feeling of "humanity." It is no exaggeration, I think, to say that the true meaning of humanity now depends on seeing the difference between the supernatural *virtue* of charity and the now omnipresent *feeling* of humanitarian pity. This is the subject of the texts gathered in part 4 of *The Religion of Humanity*: "Sifting the Wheat from the Chaff."

What is true Christian charity? "Charity is a common action, a common 'operation,' carried out visibly or invisibly by the Church and its Head."[17] This action aims at an otherworldly salvation, at eternal communion with God and the saints, and is by no means reducible to "the sentiment of human resemblance" or to an awareness of our vulnerability to physical suffering. "Charity is clearly a virtue, and even the culminating virtue, of the human being and the Christian."

Manent distinguishes Christian charity from secular compassion most boldly and incisively, in direct response to Pope Francis's blurring of the categories, in the three most recent texts presented in this volume: "Who Is 'the Good Samaritan'?" (2020), "Don't Confuse Christianity with 'the Religion of Humanity'" (2020), and "Migrations and Christianity: What Message?" (2021). We cannot enter here into the details of Manent's reading of the biblical parable, which aims to provide not an innovative interpretation but a restorative reading in the tradition of the Church Fathers. Manent observes that, in the parable, the Samaritan does not resemble today's "'Good Samaritan.' . . . There is an amplitude to his deeds, a liberty in his conduct, a competence in his care for all wounds, an authority to his word, and an ability to make promises worthy of belief, that are not those of a mere human being." The crux of the matter lies here: "The Church Fathers were right: the Samaritan is none other than Jesus himself." Manent continues, "The parable doesn't invite us to 'identify . . . with others without worrying where they were born or came from,' but to enter into a 'Christian discipleship' that has no other end than Christ. . . . The parable thus first teaches us that we have neither the charity, nor the strength, nor the reparative virtue, nor the patience, nor the hope, nor the faith, to be like the Samaritan."[18]

The good Samaritan does not teach humanitarian compassion; rather, it preaches Christ. In order to resist the collapse of charity into compassion, Manent must insist on the difference between what we humans may feel and what Christ alone can transform: "Charity is an *entirely different thing* from the sentiment of one's fellow human being, or from compassion.[19] It does not rest on a sentiment or the imagination. It is an active disposition of the will, a virtue. And what does it target? Inseparably God and one's neighbor, but first of all God. Why? . . . It is because we human beings are not very loving or lovable. The Christian claim is that it is only the mediation of Christ that can liberate us from the prison of the self."[20]

"Merely human compassion" is, at best, morally neutral in Manent's view; it may do more harm than good. Rather than presuming to do what Christ does, and identifying our fellow feeling with divine charity, we are called to put our faith in Christ. "The Samaritan is none other than Jesus Christ. There is no Christianity outside of Jesus Christ."[21] Humanitarian compassion, for its part, has no "interior principle" but is activated only negatively, by exterior occasions of suffering. The compassionate may be admirably active in their way, but "in the eyes of the Christian they are *spiritually passive*"; humanitarianism is "spiritually empty because it does not bring the Word and does not show the Way."[22] "The migrant" as a new "Christic" figure of borderless humanity "sums up humanity because he is the loss of the human, as Marx pretty much said about the proletariat."[23] One might conclude, then, that when we mere mortals, rather than looking to the virtue of Christ's charity, presume to imitate Christ's sacrifice or divine self-emptying (Philippians 2:7) by repudiating our moral and political humanity, then our action can have no meaning above the animal satisfaction and the animal pity in which Rousseau sought the ground of our humanity.

VIRTUE UNDER PROVIDENCE

Manent thus clearly divides the wheat of charity from the chaff of humanitarian compassion. To do so, he must emphatically distinguish the feeling of humanity from the divine act of charity. In insisting in this way on the radical transcendence of Christ and on our utter dependence on the action of his church in attaining our true end, the author might seem to adopt the language of fideism, which would certainly surprise those accustomed to the more Aristotelian framework of his oeuvre overall. But we can see even in these texts that Manent has in no way distanced himself from his insights into the continuity or friendship between the human and divine—that is, from a broadly Thomistic Christian sensibility, according to which grace does not destroy but perfects nature. In fact, part 5 of *The Religion of Humanity*, "Spiritual Mediation," centers on Christianity and, more specifically, the Roman Catholic Church as a moral and political mediator.

Charity is universal, but politics and true, virtuous action are always enclosed and particular. How can this supernatural openness be understood so as not to dissolve but to guide and uplift this natural closure? One thing is clear: the church must not confuse supernatural openness with the purely horizontal universality of humanitarian sameness. Referring to "the five great spiritual masses that determine the figure of the West"— that is, "Judaism, Islam, Evangelical Protestantism (mainly American), the Catholic Church, and, finally, the ideology of human rights"— Manent writes, "The Catholic Church is the least intolerant and the most open of the spiritual forces that concern us"; the church is thus positioned to be "the mediator *par excellence*."[24] (This was proposed, admittedly, a long time ago, in 2015.) The church's public role, its responsibility to a non-Christian humanity, is rooted in the connection between true action, or self-government, and Providence: active self-government depends on hope and on a confidence in the primacy of the good, and we have lost this along with our faith in providence. Human action at its best—that is, action according to the enduring cardinal virtues[25]—*naturally* opens upon a hope for and in something "bigger than us, too big for us." Action implies good implies hope implies providence. And we are called to active friendship with this Providence within the natural, moral-political realm in which we are placed, for "as citizens ... we address the Most High from the site of our action and for the common good of the city of which we are citizens." In this sense, Manent's embrace of the nation as a privileged arena of action has a theological ground: "If God, in creating man, left him in the hands of his own counsel, then the nation takes part in creation's goodness."[26] Rational, virtuous deliberation in the production of a political common good has divine significance.

Manent, we have seen, vigorously separates Christian charity from naturalistic compassion. But he does not radically separate the theological virtue of charity from nature simply: charity guides and perfects the natural virtues.[27] As a virtue and, therefore, inherently *active*, charity activates and extends our natural propensity to virtue. Daniel J. Mahoney makes this point concerning the interdependence of natural and supernatural virtue with particular boldness when he proposes, in the foreword to this collection, "that charity must be interpreted in the light of prudence" (vii). The pious will find this a surprising formulation, to say the least. It might seem more fitting and less jarring to Christian piety to say, rather, that we must see prudence in the light of charity. No doubt both formulations have their truth. But given our unnatural situation today, our addiction to the empty form of universality as a figure of humanity, we can see the urgent truth of Mahoney's elevation of the mediating virtue of prudence.[28]

CHAPTER FOUR

Christianity and the Progress of Liberalism

The deployment of Christian motives, or motives borrowed or extracted from Christianity, to drive the progress of rationalist materialism is an old story, a theme present from the beginning, often implicitly, sometimes more explicitly. Machiavelli lays mostly between the lines what his "new modes and orders" borrow from Christianity; Hobbes somewhat more candidly brandishes a certain Christian filiation of his project of absolute sovereignty; Descartes, for his part (and echoing Francis Bacon), turns the concept of sin against the Christian tradition in order to serve the cause of the mastery and possession of nature for the relief of the human condition. In one way or another, modernity has, from the beginning, been a post-Christian project and, therefore, one dependent on Christianity. Hegelianism is, of course, unthinkable without Christianity, and the story of Christian or Christianizing Marxism would fill—has filled—countless volumes. But perhaps only in the present awakening of radical egalitarian and identitarian animus against all substantive moral contents has the fusion of self-sacrificial purity of heart and boundless secular egalitarianism reached the point where any boundary or tension between spiritual purity and material demands seems to have been utterly effaced, and where a critical mass of people in the West cannot even conceive of a spirituality more concerned with an eternal soul than with the liberation of the self. The possibility, which Tocqueville glimpsed with horror, of a "pantheism" constituted by the convergence of absolute transcendence and absolute immanence now motivates masses within what I have called our "mirrored dome."

Still, certain moral and political philosophers, as well as contemporary scholars of the history of Western Christianity, find cause only for celebration in the confluence between the spirit of the Gospels and that of modern progress.

RAWLS'S "PURITY OF HEART"

The common tendency of what Manent has named "the hypertrophy of theory," in both its rationalist and theological forms, is the devaluing, the *Kritik*, even the repudiation of the practical point of view, and therefore of the "natural law" in its broadest and most elementary sense. The point of view of practice, the standpoint of the actual moral and political agent, *by nature*, respects the prior authority of norms and of goods[1] that are constitutive of the natural, practical standpoint. On the other hand, both the rationalist and the radical Christian forms of theoretical overreach undermine or directly attack the immediate practical experience of the intrinsic goodness of virtue and the intrinsic rightness of law in its givenness.

Manent's critique of theoretical critique may seem, well, rather theoretical and not of great practical relevance for moral and political actors today. But his claim is that our present practice is drenched with theory and thus at odds with practical realities in ways that must have momentous practical consequences. He argues, for example, that the modern theory of a "state of nature" has imposed upon us a dynamic of leveling universality, in which "freedom" is reduced to the equalized impulses of radically individuated biological beings, stripped of all normative characteristics including age, sex, and capacity. An abstract, theoretical equality thus wages ceaseless war against the spontaneous common sense of humanity. A recent result of the victory of theoretical equality over practical reality is the legalizing of same-sex marriage, which points to an essentially "metaphysical" ambition, a proposition that is "finally purely philosophical," the insistence that "the just or legitimate human order excludes all reference to a natural norm or purpose." Manent warns that the future consequences of this Promethean theoretical hypertrophy "will no doubt be commensurate with [its] audacity or imprudence."[2] Modern theory has defined the human person as "the being with rights," but "we say *nothing* concerning what *constitutes* or *gives form to* human life." The theory that replaces natural law with human rights progressively devours and obliterates human nature.[3]

In *Natural Law and Human Rights*, Manent does not explore the contemporary collusion of theological hypertrophy with the rationalist ideology of rights very explicitly. Switching our focus from French to American liberalism, we find that this collusion is presented with perfect clarity in the work of the most authoritative author of late progressive liberalism, John Rawls. The profoundly post-Protestant inspiration of Rawls's canonical and massively influential *A Theory of Justice* has long gone largely unnoticed or ignored,[4] but one cannot really understand the motive and the import of this theory without taking into account its essentially religious dimension. The whole, elaborate technical apparatus of Rawls's theory, from the "original position" with its famous "veil of ignorance" to the "two principles of justice" with all their ramifications in policy, depends utterly on Rawls's deep commitment to an obviously post-Protestant "purity of heart."

I will not undertake here to lay out the mechanics of Rawls's theory.[5] Suffice it to say that, claiming a Kantian legacy, he proposes to establish once and for all the absolute priority of the right (and thus of rights) over the good (and thus all substantive moral contents) (§68). The problem of the common good, as bound up with the question of human purpose, can be left definitively in the dustbin of history, and the parameters of rights can be defined in terms of the logic of a hypothetical situation (the "original position" behind a "veil of ignorance") in which calculations are made on the basis of "primary goods" essentially reducible to physical comfort and security, but, in a supposed improvement on Hobbes and Locke, now also including "the social bases of self-esteem." The result of hypothetical calculations in the hypothetical original position is a system of rights and policies that mirrors the moral and political views of late-twentieth-century American progressive liberalism.[6] Essentially, Rawls's understanding of justice is egalitarian in its fundamental inspiration but, at the same time, realistic in its recognition of inequality as a motor of economic well-being. Rawls is willing to use the engine of unequal initiative, competence, and material productivity to drive a system based upon a deeply egalitarian ethic. This is the basic meaning of his famous "difference principle," according to which inequalities are morally permissible only insofar as they serve the project of equality. More specifically, any unequal distribution of "primary goods" is to be allowed only when this inequality is tied to an increase in access to these goods by a class of persons deemed "least advantaged." The meaning of justice is thus defined decisively from the perspective of some materially and socially needy category of society. Rawls was eventually brought to acknowledge that how this category of the "least advantaged" is to be defined is a difficult technical problem for his theory. I am not aware that he ever recognized a much greater problem in placing such a premium on the status of victimhood itself. Had he lived a little longer, this problem might have become impossible for even him to ignore.

The details of Rawls's ingenious and elaborate justification for the liberalism that "we" are supposed already to embrace are not what interests me here. What interests me is the moment when, near the very end of his masterwork, the Harvard professor somehow opens his ears to the fundamental question of political philosophy, to the problem that has lain at the heart of political philosophy since Socrates and Plato: Just why should I be just? What is in it for me? What could possibly motivate me to put the good of the city before my own interests and even, in Rawls's thoroughly modern case, before any "private" conception I may have of a higher good of the soul or of heaven and hell?

Rawls finally confronts this question directly in the next-to-last section (§86) of *A Theory of Justice*, "The Good of the Sense of Justice." First, he affirms that human beings are naturally moral, but certainly not in the sense that they have by nature access to some understanding of a natural law, an understanding of what is right and good by nature or of what constitutes the human soul's true fulfillment. Rawls's strategy of the absolute priority of the right over the good excludes from the outset all such substantive answers to the question, "Why be just?" For Rawls, human beings are naturally moral in the sense that they naturally receive the stamp of whatever morality, whatever conception of justice, a society authorizes.[7] Our humanity as free, rational, and moral persons consists not of "hedonism" or the selfish pursuit of some good for ourselves but of honoring some "regulative principle" that governs all our actions. Nature, however, provides no such regulative principle; the human person attains no inherent good of human nature by ordering one's soul or character in a way that aligns with the good of society. Rawls will not and cannot appeal to some intrinsic good of virtue or to a natural law that would naturally align what the ancients called the good of the soul with the good of the city. In fact, any appeal to the good of the soul would place justice at the mercy of "hedonistic" incentives; from the point of view of justice based on the pure priority of the right over the good, an individual's pursuit of some philosophical or religious highest good has no more moral warrant than a life determined by the vulgar pursuit of bodily pleasures.

The only way to achieve true freedom, rationality, and humanity is to be prepared absolutely to sacrifice any concept of what is good, including emphatically any allegedly "higher" good, to a system of justice based on a pure conception of right, a sovereign conviction that there is no ground of morality beyond such a system of the reciprocity of rights as Rawls is here proposing. There is no right or natural or divinely ordained "order of the soul," but only a "unity of the self" defined by a purely social, purely horizontal reciprocity of rights, and thus by the conviction that "we participate in one another's nature. . . . The self is realized in the activity of many selves." The self is defined and ordered, not by any idea of the soul's natural perfection, and certainly not by a destiny of communion with God and with those other souls that God has sanctified, but purely and simply by the acceptance of the authority of "society" as the absolute horizon of human existence.

It is in the final section (§87) of *A Theory of Justice* that Rawls, having clearly left behind the neutral and often technical language in which he has defined the calculations that constitute his vision of justice, now speaks in devotional tones by which he clearly repurposes vestiges of his otherwise forsaken Protestant heritage to express the deepest inspiration of his liberal-progressive political project.[8] Explicitly renouncing any "perspective of eternity" or any dimension of transcendence, Rawls proposes that the standpoint of rational "autonomy" as identified with "justice," as he has defined it, is the one true perspective of human meaning, the ultimate convergence of rationality, morality, and freedom. "Purity of heart, if one could attain it"—our usually coldly analytical and seemingly pragmatic professor is ready to announce—"would be to see clearly and to act with grace and self-command from this point of view."

There is no mistaking, I think, the deeply Christian resonance of Rawls's lyrical conclusion to his scrupulously dispassionate and technical treatise on the meaning of justice. Nor, I think, can this evocation of purity of heart be dismissed as a gratuitous gesture without significance for the bearing of Rawls's theory as a whole. The repudiation of our natural pride in virtue, or our natural confidence in the intrinsic worth of action under law for the good, is the most basic premise of Rawls's project of the absolute autonomy of the right over the good, of the formal reciprocity of rights over all substantive contents of the good life. Rawls must entirely exclude considerations of moral desert from the conceptualization of justice;[9] the natural impulse to gauge justice in terms of (necessarily unequal) contributions to the common good is disqualified from the outset. Or perhaps it would be more accurate or more complete to say that the only "virtue" recognized by Rawls is the "purity of heart" that forswears all natural claims of virtue. The heart of Rawls's *Theory of Justice* is the sacrifice of natural and unequal virtue to a spiritualized project of material equality.

Rawls's *Theory of Justice* is thus an eminent case of what Manent has named theoretical hypertrophy and one that reveals the intimate collusion between the rational-materialist and radical- or post-Christian versions of the rejection of the standpoint of practical moral agency.

This rejection of our practical natures is inherently self-radicalizing because it is blind to its parasitical dependence on moral contents of one or another interpretation of natural justice. This vulnerability to radicalization is not hard to discern in the case of Rawls's attempt to give late liberalism a systematic final form. Rawls's theoretical and theological passion for some pure justice uncontaminated by the practical reality of human agency, by the blending of goods and rights, of ends and means, of transcendence and immanence, inherent in the natural standpoint of action, cannot long be contained by the technical and narrowly "practical" apparatus of Rawls's project. The hunger and thirst for a righteousness of equality and transparency—of equal transparency and transparent equality—will not long be contained within the momentarily "realistic" boundaries of Rawls's recipe for a welfare-state liberalism as the final solution to the question of justice. The "two principles of justice" would not long stand as an adequate fulfillment of the promise of "purity of heart." The demands on elite purity of heart by those claiming to be pure victims would soon enough explode the speciously prudent parameters of Rawls's final solution to the problem of justice.

SIEDENTOP: THE CHRISTIAN ORIGINS OF WESTERN LIBERALISM

Larry Siedentop's *Inventing the Individual: The Origins of Western Liberalism* provides an excellent historical complement to John Rawls's analytical presentation of a liberalism profoundly indebted to, even dependent upon, certain Christian motives. Siedentop's is a work of impressive scope and erudition, and at the same time of charming liberal simplicity; it argues that Christian belief is the wellspring of the moral ideal of a community of equal and free individuals that we associate with modern "secularism." And for Siedentop (unlike Leo Strauss, as we will see below), this religious genealogy of liberalism is clearly good news; he calls on Christians and secular liberals to embrace the Western heritage of equal freedom they share.

Siedentop argues that modern individualism sprang from the Christian revolution (especially St. Paul's revolution) against the hierarchical political, spiritual, and intellectual framework of pagan civilization. This pagan or classical framework, a certain conception of reason as ruling in the soul and in the city, was bound up with a hierarchical view of the cosmos. Siedentop sees that the ancient city, the ancient cosmos, and, therefore, the ancient understanding of reason were profoundly and inherently hierarchical. The analogy in Plato's *Republic* between a stratified soul and a stratified society is just the clearest example of the "aristocratic" moral and intellectual framework that pervasively structured the thinking and the sensibility of the ancient world.[10] According to Siedentop, St. Paul blasted this aristocratic framework, igniting a transformation with revolutionary social and intellectual consequences that are still unfolding in our times. The new view of reason prepares modern rationalism because it abandons the hierarchical claims of reason's rule and instead bases reason on an egalitarian and universalist faith. The effectual truth of Jesus Christ for Siedentop's Paul is the imperative of universal freedom and equality.

The moral revolution that Christianity would bring about was prepared, on the one hand, Siedentop argues, by the Jewish law and, on the other, by developments within Platonic philosophy. On the philosophical side, the "ancient sense of rationality" had been deeply conditioned by the experience of "public discussion and decision making in the polis" and thus by the belief "that reason could govern." The decline of the polis compromised the very meaning of classical reason. Philosophers began to look beyond "the model of a rational ascent up the great chain of being by a few—that ascent which tied thought and being so closely together"—and they "began to worry about the source of all being," considered as "the Absolute, a first cause that was beyond all comprehension." The emergence of this idea of the absolute "begins to reshape ethical thinking . . . for it led to moral rules being considered, not so much as rational conclusions from the nature of things, but as commands issuing from an agency that was 'beyond' reason" (53–54).

This philosophic reorientation away from the rule of reason in accordance with nature merged with the influence of Jewish monotheism, the belief in a God not beholden to the rule of reason, a God who "refused to be pinned down: 'I will be who I will be.'" With the waning of the polis's ethic of rational deliberation in an ordered community, "conforming to an external will was becoming the dominant social experience. And the voice of Judaism spoke to that experience as no other did. The message of the Jewish scriptures was radical. Virtue consisted in obedience to God's will."

The confession of human dependence on an absolute beyond reason would seem clearly to mark the end of reason's career: "All that could be said about the Absolute was negative: that it was not limited, not necessitated, not the subject of knowledge" (55). But the miracle of Christianity consists precisely in transforming this negation of humanity's alleged natural capacity for rational self-government into a liberation. Already within philosophy there had emerged the idea that the "act of submission" is "the precondition of knowledge" (55). But it is the apostle Paul's "vision of a mystical union with Christ" that "introduces a revised notion of rationality—what he sometimes describes as the 'foolishness of God'" (59). This new understanding of rationality "overturns the assumption on which ancient thinking had hitherto rested, the assumption of natural inequality. Instead, Paul wagers on human equality," a wager that "turns on transparency" between the self and others (59).

"In his conception of the Christ, Paul brings together basic features of Jewish and Greek thought to create something new" (60). Judaism's favoring of law and command over logos or reason (53), its preoccupation with "conformity to a higher or divine will," is miraculously combined with the maximal extension of reason's empire, with "the abstracting potential of later Hellenistic philosophy" (61). Greek reason had for centuries been extending its scope: "For the discourse of citizenship in the polis had initiated a distancing of persons from mere family and tribal identities, while later Hellenistic philosophy had introduced an even more wide-ranging, speculative 'universalist' idiom. That intellectual breadth had, in turn, been reinforced by the subjection of so much of the Mediterranean world to a single power, Rome" (61).

Siedentop's account of the rise of a universalizing, equalizing absolute reminds us of Manent's tracing of Western history in *Metamorphoses of the City* as that of the ascendency of the Roman and then Christian figure of the "one/all" over the classical tension between "the few" and "the many." In Manent's narrative, the aristocratic tension between the few and the many gives way, over the course of Western history, to the power of the one as guarantor of the all: "In the eyes of the One, all became the people, all were equal."[11] Manent traces a political and spiritual development that is structured by a double polarity—in fact, a polarity between two fundamental polarities: there is the classic, visible, and articulate polarity between the few and the many, and then there is the more radical, elusive, and disruptive union-and-separation between the one and the all. Whereas the few-many tension constitutes the natural life of the city, the one-all pair emerges in the boundless ambitions of Rome, finds theological expression in Christianity, and continues to haunt modern secular humanism.[12]

The cost of the rout, at the hands of the one-all, of the unjust partisan claims of the few has not been the simple victory of equality, the ascendancy, let us say, of the plain dignity of the common human being. Instead, equality and inequality, now uncoupled and unconditioned by each other, enjoy a joint and unlimited reign: modern society embodies extremes of equality and inequality, and we aspire at once to universal compassion and to unbridled competitiveness. "In brief, all are equal and everyone has his price."[13] Thus, for Manent, the extremes of glory (the perspective of universal empire) and of the reduction of meaning to individual consciousness tend to meet: the one and the all, radical transcendence and reductive equality, are two sides of the same spiritual coin.

Siedentop sees the same convergence between the absolute one and the formless egalitarian all that Manent sees, but Siedentop seems to regard their joint reign as altogether unproblematic; he embraces this dynamic with an enthusiasm that Manent cannot share. Manent is concerned about the evacuation of human and political content under the sway of the one, which is also all; Siedentop is very satisfied that the Christian synthesis of divine law and abstract, universal reason can ground a new morality, a new freedom and moral agency, radically individual and radically universal, that is "utterly different from the freedom enjoyed by the privileged class of citizens in the polis," a freedom that is bound up with a new understanding of "community as the free association of the wills of morally equal agents, what Paul describes through metaphor as the 'body of Christ'" (60).

The individual is liberated from family, tribe, and polis with the help of the idea of the one absolute divine will, but now this will is no longer understood in the Jewish way as "an external, coercive agency" (61). Rather, Paul's doctrine of Christ "overturns the assumption of natural inequality by creating an inner link between the divine will and human agency," a kind of fusion that justifies "the assumption of the moral equality of humans" (61). "The Christ provides a foundation in the nature of things for a pre-social or individual will. Individual agency acquires roots in divine agency. The Christ stands for the presence of God in the world, the ultimate support for individual identity" (64). This new universal standard overcomes the two great forms of mediation, the externality of the Jewish law on the one hand and the hierarchical presuppositions of Greek reason on the other. We see "the advent of the new freedom, freedom of conscience." Thus "the Greek mind and the Jewish will are joined." Rationality is now extracted radically from concrete social and political existence and therefore from "language as a social institution." "For Paul, the gift of love in the Christ offers a pre-linguistic solution, through a leap of faith—that is, a wager on the moral equality of humans" (65). Thus the believer's submission "to the mind and will of God as revealed in Christ" is at the same time the "beginning of a 'new creation,'" the revelation of human equality and autonomy. This liberation of the individual from law and reason and for his or her consecration to the moral equality of humanity is the object of Paul's "almost ferocious moral universalism" (64). Siedentop appears to see no practical tension between Pauline "Christian liberty" as, on the one hand, the liberation of the individual from all given social bonds and, on the other, the individual's submission to the Christ, a submission "in which charity overcomes all other motives." There is no problem in reconciling the liberal liberation of the individual with Christian submission to the demands of charity, as long as charity is interpreted liberally as implying "moral equality and reciprocity" (65). Thus, Siedentop believes that he has dispelled the illusion of an essential tension between Christian ideals and "Godless secularism" (360). The liberal idea of reciprocity based on moral equality is virtually identical to the New Testament injunction 'to love thy neighbor as thyself'; and the Christian doctrine of the incarnation cashes out as liberal commitment to "equal liberty": the "moral equality of humans implies that there is a sphere in which each should be free to make his or her own decisions, a sphere of conscience and free action" (361).

From Siedentop's point of view, then, the disposition of some Christians, Benedict XVI in particular, to combat some "Godless secularism" is utterly misguided since secularism, or the idea of universal, "subjective," and egalitarian human rights, is the very fulfillment of Christianity, "Europe's noblest achievement." Those Christians who "identify secularism as an enemy rather than a companion," and thus moralistically oppose abortion and homosexuality, "risk losing touch with the most profound moral insights of their faith." When we question the secular ethic of "equal liberty . . . charity is the loser" (360–62).

BADIOU: ST. PAUL'S UNIVERSALISM

The appropriation of St. Paul as the forerunner or even founder of one or another version of modern secular idealism is, of course, nothing new.[14] A recent and prominent such appropriation, very instructive in its unmitigated radicalism, is that of Alain Badiou's *Saint Paul: The Foundation of Universalism*. Badiou's version of Christian secularism does not culminate in Siedentop's rather complacent liberalism but rather in an extremely vague but unmistakable invocation of collective, indeed "communist" revolutionary action.

Like Siedentop, Badiou sees St. Paul's teaching as the overcoming of Jewish exceptionalism or particularism on the one hand and of Greek resignation to cosmic order on the other hand. But whereas Siedentop understands Christianity as preserving essential moments of these two alternatives (divine law and abstracting reason), Badiou breaks radically with both in the name of the "Event."

For Badiou, the event of the resurrection (which has nothing essential to do with some miracle of immortality) signifies absolute innovation beyond all claims of conceptual ordering; the submission of reason to the "folly of our preaching"[15] thus liberates human action from all "rational" limits.[16] The pure form of universality exhausts the meaning of this event of liberation. Philosophy is not transformed but is simply abolished, and the pure event of "the son" dispenses with all Trinitarian nonsense concerning the Father: "Jesus" is simply the name of this absolute and, therefore, purely formal and revolutionary "Event."[17] Human subjectivity is constituted by the Evental rupture; the Event evokes a process without end, a negation of law and reason without any stable content. The Event has no assignable content but only the form of revolutionary subjectivity and universality, radical individuality opening up upon radical collectivity. There is no truth to guide action; the only truth is the active response to the pure Event. Love is under the authority of the Event, and love converts thought into sheer power, "the real materiality of militant universalism."[18] Badiou's revolutionary "Event" is as formal and empty as possible in order to be as radical as possible. But in the end, the Event must "inscribe" itself in the world in some way, and I can assume that Badiou would not regard all inscriptions as equally faithful to St. Paul's universalistic revolution. Revolutionary "universalism" must imply some content, some stable features of the reality to be inscribed, or else any gesture of radical rupture with the given—say, throwing in one's lot with a violent Völkisch movement or waiting upon gods poetically—might be considered as authentically "Evental" as another. We know the tenor of Badiou's "Event" from his undefended allusions to communism, and we can discern the content of his "rebirth" in the phrase "the real materiality of militant universalism." As a good communist, Badiou projects mankind's universal material redemption—the overcoming by and for humanity of the realm of material necessity—as the horizon and implicit telos of his passion for the radical destruction of all given horizons.

In its content, Badiou's interpretation of the ethical meaning of Christianity is not that far from Siedentop's reduction of charity to "reciprocity." However, in contrast to Siedentop's very comfortable progressive liberalism, which is content to progress within a revolutionary ethical frame inherited from the distant past, Badiou's intransigent radicalism must perpetually reenact the exemption of grace from nature and defer the content of reciprocity to a new world beyond the natural economy of liberalism. To state this comparison in terms of the figure of transcendence of the absolute one or universal all, whereas Badiou longs (at least rhetorically) for a final eradication of all inequality in the consummation of the marriage of the one and the all, Siedentop is content that the absolute has done its revolutionary work at the Christian or Pauline origins of Western civilization; for us today, he thinks, the prosaic work of universal equality, freedom, and reciprocity can proceed in the now familiar world that the absolute produced long ago by blasting the aristocratic paradigm of reason, which presupposed an eternal tension between the few and the many.

KOJÈVE'S POST-CHRISTIAN UNIVERSALISM

Leo Strauss considers Alexandre Kojève's philosophy as exemplary of the interpretation of secular rationalism as the real fulfillment of Christian universalism.[19] Following Hegel, Kojève understands modern secular rationalism as a transformation and fulfillment of Christian universalism and subjectivity. His Hegelian version displays a firmer grasp than Siedentop's of the philosophical stakes of such an interpretation and, in a way, combines Siedentop's prosaic liberal and democratic sympathies with Badiou's revolutionary resolution.

Kojève agrees with Siedentop in cashing out the meaning of universalism in the rather prosaic democratic morality of reciprocity. For

Kojève, the great political, military, and religious actors who drove the march of history understood themselves as serving some god or some understanding of truth and right, but the only real and abiding motive in the historical process proves to be the desire to be recognized in one's humanity by other human beings. The medium or currency of this recognition can be nothing other than the effective satisfaction of the simple material needs and interests of our common, bodily humanity. The Christian leveling of aristocratic pride released the energy of human labor for the service of common human needs; thus, the effectual truth of a God who transcends social differences is an ethic of formal universality, and this can have no concrete meaning except a universal society of equal recognition. Kojève's advantage in sobriety over Badiou's enthusiasm for the revolutionary "Event" lies in his acceptance of the prosaic and democratic and therefore humble or low substance of the revolutionary telos: there is no meaning of life except the satisfaction of the most ordinary desires of the most ordinary human beings. Kojève's advantage in realism over Siedentop lies in his awareness that the fulfillment of the idea of a universal society of equal freedom and reciprocity will leave Christianity far behind and require a coercive apparatus—the universal and homogenous state. Thus, Kojève acknowledges, the final and absolute ascendancy of the plainest democratic satisfaction is the only real truth of the ecstatic religion of grace: a collective life supported by total technological mastery, the absolute victory of a final, rational tyranny, a prosaic life in which all poetic projections have been banished along with the cruelty of history—this, Kojève sees, is the final and irrefragable meaning of the transcendent Christian Event that first laid the axe to the root of all aristocratic pretensions.

For Kojève, one might say, history has a rational meaning, but this meaning is finally meaningless—this is the shadow of nothingness that Heidegger casts over Kojève's Hegelian story of rational completion. And here we see the culmination and exhaustion of the dynamic polarity between the one and the all that, as Pierre Manent has proposed, has driven Western and therefore world history. The complicity between absolute transcendence and formal universality has progressively dissolved the human tension between the few and the many; neither the ambitions of nobility nor the simple duty of common decency seem able to resist the allied force of the notions of absolute freedom and universal necessity.

Resistance to this pincer movement of the one and the all against the natural and limited space of human existence was, I propose, the central purpose of Leo Strauss's philosophical career. The great debates he engaged in or staged, notably the questions of ancients versus moderns and of Athens versus Jerusalem, can be adequately grasped only as responses to this dehumanizing dynamic of Western history.

CHAPTER FIVE

Strauss's Response to the Victory of Universalism

On Tyranny

The quarrel between the ancients and the moderns concerns eventually, and perhaps even from the beginning, the status of "individuality."
—Strauss, *Natural Right and History*

This is the next-to-last sentence from Leo Strauss's *Natural Right and History*. In the last sentence, Strauss takes the side of virtue and "sound antiquity" against individuality. He does not advertise the connection he clearly sees between modern individualism and the Christian break with sound antiquity concerning the eternal status of the individual human being. The preceding discussion of three celebratory versions (Larry Siedentop, Alain Badiou, Alexandre Kojève) of the derivation of modern secular individualism or rationalism from Christianity will serve to frame Leo Strauss's discreetly anti-Christian defense of "sound antiquity."

Despite impressions that Leo Strauss willingly conveys, he agrees fundamentally with Siedentop's diagnosis of the Christian roots of modern liberal democracy. The important difference, of course, is that Siedentop celebrates this development, whereas Strauss deplores it. In his "Restatement" to Kojève concerning *On Tyranny*, Strauss does not really contest the Hegelian thesis (whether in Kojève's or Voegelin's version) of the Christian root of modernity. In fact, he explicitly leaves open the question of "how far the epoch-making change that was effected by Machiavelli is due to the indirect influence of the biblical tradition," but insists only that first "that change" must be "fully understood in itself."[1] In other words, once the Machiavellian effectual truth of modern rationalism is understood, then Christians and others inclined to give the modern revolution a Christian baptism, to cover this very this-worldly project with a veil of vaguely Christian humanitarian "spirituality," can judge for themselves whether they want to be responsible for this interpretation. Let us not sugarcoat modernity, Strauss is saying, by evoking its "spiritual roots" before we ask in all sobriety: What *is* the modern project? Thus, although Strauss emphatically prioritizes the question of the character of modernity over that of its "indirect" biblical origins, he quite clearly does not either refute or even dismiss the proposition that such religious influences were a significant factor in the rise of modern rationalism.

Strauss is thus less immediately interested in the historical question of "influences" than in the essential character of modernity, and nowhere does Strauss make clearer than in this text his fundamental assessment of the modern project, understood in its full implications—that is, as Kojève understands and embraces it. He makes clear, that is, that he abominates this project and considers it antithetical to any adequate understanding of genuine nobility or of plain human decency. The identification of philosophy and tyranny in Kojève's Hegelian-Marxist project, the liquidation of philosophic transcendence in total devotion to the cause of an utterly unphilosophic humanity, the extreme separation and fusion of the high and the low, the one and the all, represents for Strauss the collapse of all human meaning, the end of humanity. Kojève is, of course, resigned, with more than a touch of irony, to this inhuman or posthuman culmination of secular humanism. But Strauss bends every effort to resist this culmination, even allowing himself (no doubt with a touch of his own irony) a militant call to resistance: "Warriors and workers of all countries, unite, while there is still time, to prevent the coming of 'the realm of freedom.' Defend with might and main, if it needs to be defended, 'the realm of necessity'" (210).

Freedom as an all-too-human project has necessarily degenerated, Strauss sees, into a rational and technological tyranny; the compulsion to make humanity completely at home in this world, a world of human beings' own making, has left them utterly homeless. To turn to the "realm of necessity" would be to recover an appreciation of the permanent contours and, therefore, the permanent limits of the human condition. But how can "necessity" provide a home for human existence, for meaningful action and reflection? Strauss is perfectly aware of the irony in this militant call to action on behalf of a supposed realm beyond the reach of all human action. The irony lies precisely in the fact that the "realm of necessity" does indeed need to be defended. The idea of an eternal realm of pure, impersonal necessity untouched by human concerns is the projection of a very human claim to rule, the mostly implicit horizon of an essentially aristocratic assertion of human meaning.

Strauss here tips his hand more than once to reveal the human and political springs of the philosophic idea of a "realm of necessity," but he also provides plenty of encouragement to the pride of philosophers who would not wish to be reminded of their dependence on common moral and political sources of meaning. He appeals to the pride of philosophers even as he defines philosophy as beyond human pride. Strauss tips his aristocratic hand, at least for those who are paying close attention, when he more than once resorts shamelessly to argument by high-minded assumption or by peremptory definition: we must *assume* that philosophers do not desire to rule (they do not care what other people—at least common people—think); and a "philosopher" who is concerned with recognition is, by definition, not a philosopher. Moreover, Strauss explicitly concedes to Kojève that his (Strauss's) pure, transhistorical idea of philosophy depends upon the thesis of eternal, immutable being—but then he explicitly acknowledges (in a critical concluding paragraph that was withheld from the original English edition) that this thesis is altogether questionable (213).

Strauss most extravagantly indulges the pride of the self-styled philosopher when he proclaims that "the philosopher's dominating passion is the desire for truth, i.e., for knowledge of the eternal order, or the eternal cause or causes of the whole. As he looks up in search for the eternal order, all human things and all human concerns reveal themselves to him in all clarity as paltry and ephemeral, and no one can find solid happiness in what he knows to be paltry and ephemeral" (198).

Any would-be "philosopher" who has not already detected the tone of hyperbole in this celebration of philosophy will likely not pause to reflect on the implication of the sentence that immediately follows: "He has then the same experience regarding all human things, nay, regarding man himself, which the man of high ambition has regarding the low and narrow goals, or the cheap happiness, of the general run of men" (198). That is, the philosopher is to the political man, "the man of high ambition," as the political man is to the common man. The philosopher's ambition is to be beyond ambition. Strauss's philosopher defends his autonomy or self-sufficiency without recognizing the irony implicit in the need to defend it by the very human and personal assertion of an eternal, impersonal necessity.

For Strauss, the possibility of satisfaction in serene contemplation grounds wisdom's moderation. But it would be at least as true to say that the virtue of practical wisdom, the noble reserve represented by Jane Austen (as opposed to Dostoyevsky) (198), the aspiration to resignation concerning common human hopes, is the very *human* ground of the idea of the contemplation of an inhuman eternity.

Strauss's most decisive concession to Kojève is his acknowledgment that "subjective certainty" is impossible and that all knowledge is embedded in a social-political context. He does not disagree with Kojève's view that the "classics were fully aware of the essential weakness of the mind of the individual"—but affirms the superiority of an aristocratic over a democratic-universalist social and political frame (195). The Straussian philosopher takes his bearings from the admiration of the few; his orientation is determined originally and fundamentally by a concern for *honor*, whereas the modern philosopher is conditioned by an original motive of "love" for human beings, or concern for the "love" of other human beings, irrespective of their humanly esteemed qualities (156–58). This critical examination of "love" makes it clear that Kojève's universal recognition is indeed for Strauss a descendant—a perversion, to be sure, but still in a very significant sense a descendant—of the Christian idea of universal charity.

Strauss recognizes that friendship (as opposed to charity or universal love) is fundamental to the classical idea of philosophy and that such friendship always arises from and depends upon some prephilosophic understanding of the meaning of the noble. Thus, the risk of or tendency toward "sectarianism," Strauss avers, is inherent in philosophy. This tendency, of course, should be resisted, but with the understanding that the only alternatives to the "noble" conception of philosophy, the linking of philosophy with an aristocratic understanding of "things beautiful," are (1) the reduction of philosophy to its impact on the many and thus on history—that is, to ideology and propaganda—or (2) the dilution of philosophy to a superficial and unserious academic exercise, a "Republic of Letters" detached from vital human concerns (196).

There is, of course, another move that Strauss makes, which almost all readers take to be his most adequate and, therefore, final move—namely, his proposal that philosophy be understood as Socratic "knowledge of ignorance," or knowledge of the permanent questions or fundamental problems (196). Certainly, there is truth and, indeed, beauty or nobility in this characterization of the philosophic life. I am convinced, however, that this "zetetic" teaching finally has a certain exoteric bearing for Strauss; it is addressed precisely to the pride of philosophers who aspire to transcend pride. The "fundamental alternatives" share a common core that now has a moral and political bearing because now, at the end of history, this core is threatened with extinction precisely by a perverse but powerful synthesis of the radicalized alternatives, aristocratic and democratic, Greek and biblical, the absolute and the universal, the one and the all. To retreat from the modern synthesis is necessarily, for Strauss, to distrust the Christian impulse toward synthesis and to wish to restore the original tension between the few and the many. But such a restoration is inseparable from a moderate partisanship on behalf of the few; it is bound up with that "noble reserve" that characterizes the person of classical prudence and that implies an aristocratic metaphysics and cosmology associated with resignation to the limitations of human action and therefore with serene detachment from human concerns. Thus, Strauss's proposal of the zetetic option is here embedded in an account that seems to culminate in the metaphysical idea of an "eternal order" but that finally acknowledges, for the attentive reader, that the taste for such an order is rooted in a practical hierarchy, or, as Strauss writes, in "the immediate pleasure which we observe when we observe signs of human nobility" (202). The fundamental alternatives are certainly real, but they are also presented as a pair to the modern or postmodern classical philosopher (the Straussian philosopher), as noble possibilities anchoring his aristocratic pride, as an eternal horizon worth defending "with might and main" against the "realm of freedom."

I do not mean to say that Strauss reduces philosophy to narrowly "political" motives. My view is that Strauss recognizes that the truth of "philosophy," classically understood, is, in a very deep sense, a partisan truth, or a truth inherently tinged with a certain pride and a certain partisanship on behalf of excellence, on behalf of "the noble." The intrinsic satisfactions of understanding come to light only by being positioned "above" common necessities. In the absence of this vertical orientation, the activity of reason cannot avoid being drawn into the horizontal field of universalization and technology.

GRACE AND NATURE IN THE SPINOZA PREFACE

The fundamentally moral-political bearing of Leo Strauss's defense of classical philosophy indeed lies deeper than his formal openness to the perennial questions of the Western tradition. For Strauss, the recovery of the primordial *unity* of Athens and Jerusalem, a unity that he often leaves all but unspoken, now depends upon respecting their *difference*, even their incommensurability.

Strauss's English preface to his *Spinoza's Critique of Religion* is an extremely dense and sinuous text, a rare venture of Strauss's into autobiography, and therefore, a potential holy grail for seekers of the deepest intention underlying Strauss's sometimes gnomic utterances. What has not been appreciated is that his critique of the "new thinking" leads him to provide glimpses of a deep unity or convergence between Jerusalem and Athens.

Strauss argues in this preface that the crisis of Judaism is embedded in the crisis of liberal rationalism; Judaism has hitched its wagon to a train that is heading for a major wreck—in fact, a conflagration. The honorable pretensions of Judaism to rationalism have led it to throw in its lot with modern rationalism, which turns out to be fundamentally irrational because it has tried to provide its own ground and thus has flouted the limits of human nature. Modern rationalism is thus fundamentally constructivist, and it has seduced Jews into thinking of God as a product of the human mind. But a New (antirationalist) Thinking (e.g., Franz Rosenzweig) has opened up the possibility of moving beyond metaphysical rationalism in order to ground Judaism in an "immediate experience" of God, man, and the world. This Jewish embrace of the New Thinking is very ill-advised, however, Strauss argues, because, first, the Jewish version is hard to distinguish from the Christian version, but, more fundamentally, because this thinking in its Jewish form has not yet hit bottom; it has not plumbed the consequences of the forsaking of reason. It is Heidegger, instead, who reveals the dark depths of the rejection of the philosophical tradition, the fall into an abyss of death and nothingness.

How can we respond to Heidegger's critique of rationalism and his abyssal thinking? It is at this point that Strauss directs us, as he did in *Natural Right and History*, to a ground common to the Bible and to classical philosophy. And this statement brings us to the heart of Strauss's project of a "return" to classical political philosophy and, indeed, in a deeper way, to the alternative Athens/Jerusalem. Against the antirationalism of the New Thinking, Strauss affirms that the biblical experience is not contrary to nature; indeed, he writes, strikingly adopting the most recognizable Thomistic motto: "Grace perfects nature, it does not destroy nature."[2] The Bible and the classics agree, he says, on the natural authority of nobility and justice: every noble person is concerned with finding transcendent support for justice. "The biblical God forms light and creates darkness." A truly "empirical" reading of human experience would reveal not the radical otherness of some absolute, but rather the ground common to Aristotle and to Judaism expressed in the traditional Jewish belief in "the Torah as prior to world" (13). Our openness to grace must not tempt us to forget the authoritative character of law: Against the Jewish version of the New Thinking that reinterprets the law as "liberation, granting transformation" (that is, along the lines of Heideggerian "possibility"), Strauss insists on the primordial meaning of law as prohibition, which recognizes the power of evil and thus the "necessity of coercion" (14). Further on, he refers to "the law of reason or the natural law as the right mean between hard-heartedness and soft-heartedness" (33).[3]

Spinoza, on the contrary, anticipates Nietzsche and Heidegger, Strauss argues, in that his God is beyond good and evil; this God's absolute transcendence implies an absolute freedom to be what he will be. Thus, Spinoza "lifts Machiavellianism to theological heights" (18): just as Siedentop (and in their own ways Badiou and Kojève) would wish, the absolute transcendence of the one clears the space of this world of all given norms and hierarchy and makes way for a universal religion of humanity. This religion of humanity appears first in its realist or Machiavellian-Spinozist version, in which the necessity of the cruel substitution of human coercion for divine authority is embraced, and then in Hermann Cohen's idealist or Kantian version, which radically differentiates morality from nature and thus obfuscates the necessity of coercion by dreaming of infinite progress.

Strauss here thus implicitly traces the self-destruction of modern reason through what he has elsewhere named "the three waves of modernity": Machiavellian-Spinozist, Kantian (which includes Cohen), and Nietzschean-Heideggerian (which includes the Jewish New Thinking, especially Rosenzweig). This much is familiar to students of Strauss. But the additional element that is clearly, if delicately, present here is the fundamental complicity of Christianity in this collapse of reason. The "New Thinking" that is centered on the notion of the experience of a "call" from an "absolute" radically removed from all human meaning is described as "a secularized version of the biblical faith as interpreted by Christian theology" (12). Rosenzweig, who tried to redeem the New Thinking for Judaism, is blamed for displacing the law in favor of a "sociological" notion of the Jewish nation in a way that emulates the doctrine of Christ. Christianity seeks to replace the *law* with a more "spiritual" *teaching* that turns away from the reality of law as prohibition, from a sober awareness of the power of evil and the necessity of coercion, and redefines the law as "liberation, granting, transformation"—that is, as openness to some vague possibilities beyond the world as we know it. Thus, Strauss associates "the law of reason or the natural law" (22) with the right mean between hard-heartedness and soft-heartedness, the moderate acceptance of the necessity of coercion. The Christian attempt to place both reason and biblical faith under the notion of some "absolute" (11), and thus to transcend the authority of a law understood to be inscribed more or less clearly in an eternal order (the first wave of modernity), tends ultimately to liberate the individual from the natural limits of the human condition and to subject him to the authority of history (second wave) and finally to the abyss of nothingness (third wave). The promise of a transcendent home for the individual spirit alienates human beings from the primordial experience of the law and finally leaves them radically homeless.

This reading of the Spinoza preface, of course, goes against the grain of many interpretations of Strauss by uncovering Strauss's awareness that, at the deepest level, the idea of absolute transcendence is the ground of a noxious synthesis between reason and revelation. In other, more accessible texts, Strauss proposes the "brute fact of revelation" as an obstacle to the completion or the sealing of this synthesis. My suggestion is that it is Strauss's *esoteric* teaching that biblical law and classical reason spring from a common root in the orientation toward an eternity that limits and defines humanity; he sees this natural, finite horizon as opposed to the Christian and modern destruction of a finite moral order in favor of the "spiritual" teaching of a "transcendent" or fully open possibility, whether Christian or "rationalist." Strauss's *exoteric* teaching presents biblical law as pure command and thus as reason's other, a check on the modern instrumental rationalization of law. Thus, the familiar Straussian opposition between a life based on revelation and the life of autonomous reason, a choice that he sometimes presents as fundamentally arbitrary, is a staged showdown, a stopgap measure that attempts to use modernity against itself, one facet of modern willfulness against another.

A further consequence of my interpretation is a reversal of priority between Strauss's two famous polarities: ancient/modern and Jerusalem/Athens. Contrary to a common reading, the moderns-versus-ancients distinction, or, more precisely, the "progress or return" alternative, proves to be the more fundamental—once we see why Christianity belongs for Strauss clearly on the "modern" side. Classical nobility and Jewish law, while by no means equivalent or even compatible in their full ramifications, are both "ancient" in the decisive sense that they represent two rival versions of "return" to a finite horizon; the absolutizing of the Jerusalem/Athens distinction, which Strauss blames on a Christian radicalization of Platonic transcendence, in fact lies at the root of modernity. The rejection of concrete form and limits (whether these limits are articulated as divine law or as natural virtue) is the common root of Christian transcendence and of modern immanence.

The primordial unity, the common root, of Jerusalem and Athens consists of a tension between broadly aristocratic and democratic motives or sensibilities that is inherent in the moral phenomenon. As we read in *Natural Right and History*, the prephilosophic origins of natural right are also, or are at least bound up with, "the most elementary premises" of the Bible. The Bible and the classics agree on the primacy, the givenness, of the two natural poles of morality, namely nobility and justice, but the articulation of nobility and justice requires favoring one over the other of these primordial norms. Classical political philosophy favors nobility; it wants to believe that justice can be subsumed without remainder under nobility. Jewish piety distrusts prideful claims to nobility and tends to subordinate nobility to justice and the duty of obedience to the divine law, to which we are all equally subject. Strauss is respectful of both of these developments because each, in its own way, honors the natural or primordial human phenomenon. On the other hand, the Christian project of producing a universal synthesis of nobility and justice, of overcoming the tension between the self-assertion of virtue and openness to the needs of the other, undertakes too much. It makes a promise it cannot keep, at least "in this world," and thus prepares humanity for the modern project, which associates the pretension of transcendence, the adoption of a standpoint outside nature, with devotion to the needs of our most common humanity. First in Christianity and then in modernity, for Strauss, the tension between the few and the many is overcome by the conflation of the one and the all.

THE FRAGILITY OF THE STRAUSSIAN PROJECT

It is now clear why, in the Spinoza preface, Strauss employs Thomistic language (natural law as the right mean; "grace perfects nature") while blaming Christianity for the modern collapse of reason. Is Thomism part of the problem or part of the solution? The answer is elusive because it is "both": though Strauss might prefer Aristotelian Christianity to, say, Pascal or Kierkegaard, he is convinced that the Christian promise of the individual's salvation beyond the polis and beyond the law necessarily contains the germ of modern irrational rationalism.

There is, of course, a truth in the figure of universality as a mark of transcendence, as Strauss clearly recognizes. This is another aspect of the biblical side of the natural or primordial condition of humanity that precedes and grounds the very idea of "nature." It is also reflected in the egalitarian, apolitical understanding of natural right that Strauss acknowledges as among its primordial meanings. But Strauss's project requires his favoring of the political and aristocratic tradition of natural right over its social and universalist aspects. Noble contemplation, the aristocratic configuration of philosophy, provides, he thinks, a very necessary shelter for the natural and ordinary power of "sacred restraints," the rudimentary distinction between good and bad that "we learn as children." Without the shelter of this horizon of eternity and its inherent recognition of the limits of human action, tyranny can claim the excuse of the highest ideals for the lowest deeds; humans can be tempted to do obviously bad things in the name of universal, transformative ends.

The great Catholic novelist Flannery O'Connor, in her introduction to *A Memoir of Mary Ann*, saw this danger as clearly as anyone: "In the absence of this faith now, we govern by tenderness. It is a tenderness which, long since cut off from the person of Christ, is wrapped in theory. When tenderness is detached from the source of tenderness, its logical outcome is terror. It ends in forced labor camps and in the fumes of the gas chamber." The universalization of Jewish righteousness in Christianity and then modernity, the transformation of simple justice or decency, ultimately yields the project of universal recognition as understood by Hegel and Kojève. For Strauss, the only alternatives to this universalization are (1) a return to orthodoxy, to the Jewish law, or (2) a return in some form to classical, political (that is, aristocratic) natural right. This is not the place to develop the practical implications of such a postmodern "return" to the classics, except perhaps to signal the two key elements of the practical side of Strauss's project: (1) liberal education, the promotion of a corps of academic gentlemen led and defended by the spirited warriors of serene contemplation or what Peter Lawler once called "transerotic solitude," and (2) liberal democratic constitutionalism as the best possible approximation of a classical mixed regime. These two elements translate essentially into what are called the "East Coast" and "West Coast" Straussian projects.

I will not attempt here to assess the current prospects for these academic and political visions. It is important to emphasize, though, that Strauss is very aware of the one-sidedness of his grounding of morality and politics. He is aware that his aristocratic strategy gives short shrift to another dimension of morality and, indeed, of the meaning of human existence. This is the dimension he refers to, as it were, in passing when he asserts quite flatly that humanity is unthinkable without reference to "sacred restraints." We are subject to mysteriously grounded limits, divine commands that cannot be accounted for from the perspective of the nobility of aristocratic self-sufficiency. These commands issuing from a divinity beyond the reach of natural, political reason suggest to the mind the universality of humanity and tend to elevate common human hopes for the redemption of what is dearest to us as simple human beings. This is to say that the idea of sacred restraints suggests a divine, universal lawgiver who humbles the proud and commands love for our fellow human beings regardless of claims to excellence.

Strauss, however, judges it best to preserve philosophy from the hazardous task of the articulation of personal love or of the hope of universal salvation associated with love; instead, he prefers to keep sacred law separate from the nobility of philosophy, to keep Jerusalem (i.e., Judaism) separate from Athens: proud reason on the one hand and divine law on the other—and never the twain must meet. But the decisive point that has not been appreciated in interpretations of Strauss is that his insistence on the separation between Athens and Jerusalem is intended as a means of preserving the sense of eternal order and natural limits that they share. It is precisely this sense of a limiting order that Strauss believes is undermined by Christian spirituality, which craves a synthesis of Greek philosophical transcendence with the mysterious God who gave the law to the Jews. The modern, progressive synthesis of reason's pride with the claims of universal justice was directed against but also prepared by the Christian project of integrating Athens and Jerusalem.

Strauss's praise of the nobility of philosophy as contemplation of the permanent questions is a fragile strategy tailored to a post-Christian age. It requires the downplaying of the demands of simple justice, or their relegation to the biblical law as observed by a particular people, because these demands soften up the soul and make it vulnerable to Christian and modern universalism. The strategy is fragile because the cementing of the alliance between the aristocrat and the philosopher requires the suppression of the gentleman-philosopher's very natural and also biblical doubts about his own righteousness, the suppression of the humbling claims of conscience, the dismissal of the claims of "purity of heart" as meaningless apart from the allegedly gratuitous assumption of a God who searches hearts, the subsumption of justice under virtue, and the promotion of a kind of mutual admiration society between gentlemen and philosophers.

A THOMISTIC ALTERNATIVE?

But what of Catholic and, in particular, Thomistic Christianity? Does not Thomas Aquinas's Christian appropriation of Aristotle, or Aristotelian interpretation of Christianity,[4] provide an alternative to the inevitably leveling tendency of Christian universalism, the alliance between the one and the all against the claims of the few and the proud, just as suggested by the Thomistic motto, "grace perfects nature"? Much like Siedentop, Strauss sees Thomas as an exception, a detour, an outlier in relation to the necessary and dominant path that leads from Christianity to modernity. But the difference is that Siedentop disapproves of the Thomistic pause in the progress of Christian universalism-individualism, whereas Strauss conditionally approves of Thomas's efforts, which he regards as well-meaning but inevitably flawed.

From Strauss's point of view, the Thomistic synthesis of Christianity with an Aristotelian philosophic elevation must finally fail; it is inherently vulnerable to the more consistent modern synthesis of extreme elevation and extreme generalization. The problem with the modern synthesis is not that it is incoherent. Rather, it is an all-too-coherent conflation of the one and the all, the attainment of a transmundane absolute purified of all content by the open process of universalization itself. This modern fusion of the one and the all can, in fact, be understood as the perfect synthesis of the two ways of life Strauss posits as representing the essence, respectively, of Athens and Jerusalem. Free understanding, understood classically as the aristocratic ascent from opinion, necessarily retains an aristocratic cast. But absolutely free understanding (detached from its aristocratic vertical orientation) would have no end, no content but the production from itself of the universal. Obedient love, on the other hand, as understood traditionally, would necessarily involve understanding of the kind of being one is called to love, and, thus, of the good proper to such a being. But such a good must be of at least one of the two following kinds: (1) the good of the soul or virtue, which necessarily draws upon a hierarchical frame of reference, or (2) plain bodily needs, to be served as directed and within limits set by the commandments of the law.

Noble contemplation, the aristocratic configuration of philosophy, had provided, most notably in the form of Thomistic philosophy, a very necessary shelter for the natural and ordinary power of "sacred restraints,"[5] the rudimentary distinction between good and bad that "we all learn as children."[6] However, if purified of all reference to Greek virtue as well as Jewish law, obedient love as Christian charity becomes reducible in practice to Kojève's "recognition" (or Siedentop's "reciprocity"—the Golden Rule) and thus open to the instrumentalities of rational tyranny called for by universal technological reason. As Badiou's appropriation of St. Paul exemplifies, devotion to the cause of revolutionary universality is the effectual truth of Christian love purified of virtue's pride and of particularist law.

Thomas would, of course, be shocked and appalled by this reduction of charity to its secular humanist effectual truth, as any serious Christian ought to be. But Strauss would say that when natural, aristocratic reason is subordinated to faith, then natural virtue and its classical extension and purported ultimate ground, the virtue of contemplation, become ministerial to charity, which is then left without any definite "higher" content. The notion of a good above bodily necessities depends for its content upon some minimal political and social hierarchy transposed in the very notion of "elevation." But the pretension to pure charity, Strauss thinks, humbles the pride implicit in all such hierarchical virtue and thus fatally opens the horizon and undermines the implicit teleology of natural right. The effectual truth of the evacuation of any worldly finalities (in the name of the absolute transcendence of the one) in favor of an end projected by faith but understood to be beyond all human comprehension is the eventual filling of that horizon with the all, the plain and universal needs of humanity and the self-defined and sovereign "dignity" of every individual.

Strauss's discreet but powerful critique of Christianity is proving its pertinence every day as the residues of Christian "love" are exploited in a movement of universalization with no content but liberation from law and virtue. But he knows his alternative to be fragile because it posits as an end of all aristocratic striving the ultimate reality of a "realm of necessity" utterly indifferent to our humanity. Part 2 of this volume may be read as a response to Leo Strauss's discreet but profound critique of Christianity and effort, drawing on Thomistic sources, to articulate Christian other-worldly faith as a friend of practical elevation and moral agency.

LEO STRAUSS FOR BELIEVERS

Strauss does not publicize the affinities or parallels between the Christian and modern syntheses because he values a practical alliance with Christian natural law and because he prefers to hold the founders of modernity rationally accountable for their momentous and ill-advised project. Only if we consider the rise of modern universalistic hopes as a rational project can we hold reason responsible and thus hold open the possibility of a more responsible view of reason. It is thus on eminently practical grounds that Strauss resists portraying modernity as the "secularization" of Christianity (as in Voegelin's "immanentization of the eschaton," for example).

Whatever one thinks of Leo Strauss's disposition on the question of biblical religion (and he certainly seems not to have been a believer in any familiar sense), he remains an indispensable thinker for believers because of his unrivaled deconstruction of the faith of modernity. The modern rationalist critique of religion is itself based, he shows, on an unexamined faith in the mastery of nature as the end of knowledge. This critique is invaluable to all who would resist the blind colossus of modern rationalism, whatever we think of the alternative Strauss proposed—that is, the alleged self-sufficient goodness of philosophic inquiry itself within a horizon ultimately defined by a radically impersonal "realm of necessity." In any case, Strauss's proposed solutions appear, on close examination, to be quite nuanced and deliberately political. Strauss offers the most perspicacious of all critiques of modern rationalism because he never loses sight of the question of the good of thinking and, therefore, of the problem of the relation between the goods of theory and practical goods. The moderns deny the lynchpin of classical thought, the intrinsic good of philosophizing, and thus make knowing instrumental to power. Power, in turn, can be interpreted only according to the most "natural"—that is, universal—human needs and appetites, at least until Nietzsche's attempt to liberate the will to power from this democratic conception of nature.

Even—or especially—serious Christians can appreciate the force of Strauss's very discreet argument that Christianity is vulnerable to cooptation by "social justice," since its Jewish humility undermines aristocratic pretensions, while its Hellenism undermines the particularity of Jewish commandments. To be sure, some Christians will appeal to Holy Scripture as a check on progressive interpretations of "spirituality," others mostly to "conscience," and others mostly to the mediating authority of the church. But the very pertinent question with which Strauss confronts us Christians is this: Can any of these alternatives to the progressive synthesis of divine otherness and human "progress" stand without relying on content derived from Jerusalem and from Athens in their original, pre-Christian forms—that is, from sacred commands and from the pride of human nature?

This is Leo Strauss's implicit advice to Christians: the only possible brakes on the secular appropriation of Christian humility and universalism are Jewish law and pagan honor. A very sober and pious Christian "Straussian" would hold on to the promise of a salvation beyond worldly limits while acknowledging the inescapability in this world of both pagan pride and coercive law. "Il faut avoir l'esprit dur et le coeur doux" (We must have a tough mind and a tender heart).[7] How to welcome the grace of a soft and open heart without sacrificing the natural virtue of a clear and firm mind—how to be lucidly in the world (a practical world that I believe Strauss has understood on its own terms as clearly as any human being has done) yet finally not of the world—this is a problem without a definite, conceptual solution, and we must believe that wrestling with this problem, both in theory and in practice, is not only a mortal necessity but somehow an apprenticeship in our eternal freedom.

This is the task to be undertaken in part 2.

PART 2

The contemporary idea of the equal dignity of every unique human individual derives historically from Christian teaching but now must be regarded as an irreversible datum of human experience. It is the deepest ground of our essentially democratic sensibilities. Tocqueville understood the insuperable authority of this democratic experience of the essential sameness of humanity but also knew that the practical "moral analogy" on which meaningful human existence depends requires some "aristocratic" complement to this democratic orientation. His practical integration of the moral truths of democracy and aristocracy is most concisely expressed in his praise of "liberty under the sole governance of God and the laws." Daniel Mahoney's response to secularized Christianity as "the idol of our age" indicates the elements needed today for a recovery of such an ennobling understanding of liberty: natural moral order, divine authority, the intrinsic good of virtuous action, and the embrace of political mediation.

Manent helps us further to articulate an alternative to leveling and vacuous universalism. He proposes to renew our understanding of natural law by emphasizing its grounding in the inherent structure of the practical good, the natural "grammar of action." Manent's understanding supports our confidence in the practical human goods that depend upon us while opening our souls to divine aid and to possibilities beyond our mortal powers. Such a perspective on the real but incomplete good of human action provides the most complete support for the "mixed law," Christian and rationalist, of modern liberalism.

Further investigation of Manent's understanding of the natural good of practice proposes that a "gap" or indeterminacy is essential to this good. The luminous opacity of this gap holds open the space for the practical synthesis of will and reason that is essential to the performance of "the noble" and, thus, to the very grammar of action. Manent's "gap" of action can be seen, moreover, as consistent with the circularity between the noble and the just that reappears in each level of Aristotle's ascending account of human ends. At the same time, Manent's vindication of the natural pride of human virtue declines to defer to the classical claim of philosophical self-sufficiency and thus remains humbly open to understanding the goods of virtuous action ultimately as a free gift of the Creator. Practical philosophy can thus be understood as a kind of "first theology," a touchstone of human meaning that Christianity necessarily transcends but that it must never finally leave behind.

CHAPTER SIX

Liberty within a Christian (or Post-Christian) Horizon

We have seen in part 1 that both theoretical and theological hypertrophy (to use Pierre Manent's term) threaten to occlude the practical perspective from which the natural law comes into view. Modern theory—that is, rationalist materialism—is blind to or unreflective upon its own idealism or spirituality, its commitment to some universal humanity, and therefore tends to make human beings beasts as it promises to make them gods. Postmodern liberationism radicalizes the modern idealistic negation of natural law, the natural goodness of the cardinal virtues, investing all meaning in the emancipation of the individual, which portends the collapse of the self into the "pantheistic" nihilism evoked by Tocqueville. Christian theology, when in the thrall of an extreme transcendence, offers no alternative to this ultimately nihilistic dynamic but, at its limit, presents a mirror image of its modern theoretical accomplice, concentrating all hope upon a radically transcendent grace that, in the end, must evacuate as prideful all substantive content, leaving only humanity's universal desire for material security and comfort, with no spiritual content but the formal and empty concept of "equal recognition" to fill the void.

What stable moral and metaphysical content can we identify with confidence that will resist this drift of freedom and universalism into the vortex of nihilism? How can we articulate some solid middle ground between the complicit extremes of idealism and materialism, the vaulting ambition of cosmic gods allied with the debased realism of needy beasts? Our challenge is to limn a region of some satisfactory stability between a formless transcendence on the one hand and either a flat and soulless or a demonically leveling, deconstructing immanence on the other.

The dilemma we face is neither an imponderable historical accident nor a product either of obvious error or of recent manifestation. The roots of the present disorder can certainly be traced with more than a little plausibility to contestable philosophical and theological projects; Leo Strauss's discovery of a full project of modern secularism in Machiavelli's "new modes and orders" and Eric Voegelin's tracing of modern ideological extremism to the Christian heresy called Gnosticism are eminent examples. But the temptations of modern ideology would not be what they are if the natural order of the soul and of the city were not exquisitely fragile and subject to disruption by the inherent pressure of humanity's spiritual freedom.

My evocation of "spiritual freedom" may seem to suggest flights of philosophical or theological speculation. But here, I wish to stay as close to common experience as possible without by any means claiming that the experience I relate could be abstracted from its moral and religious context. For this reason, I turn for a moment from my intellectual interlocutors and beg the reader's indulgence as I speak in a more personal voice. I offer first a brief, true story and then a fictional one from popular culture in order to show how the openness of the human spirit to transcendent possibilities is also a vulnerability to longings and to notions very difficult to reconcile with a stable moral and political order.

TWO STORIES

The first story concerns a woman—let's call her Alice—whom I came to know, a sister in my church congregation, who was entering middle age as I made her acquaintance. I was serving as her lay minister, and so I felt a special duty to offer her what loving care I could as she faced considerable practical challenges in life. Fulfilling my duty to love did not come easily in her case. Loving Alice did not come naturally to me. Her manners were abrupt, and her voice was shrill. My mention of these details, of course, says more of my limitations as a Christian than of Alice as a person. As it happened, I believe I held my personal responses in check and did my best to serve Alice along with others in the congregation. But I knew that in this case (and certainly not only in this case), I fell far short of the commandment to love my neighbor as God loves me.

Eventually, what I learned from fellow congregants helped to soften my heart. I learned something of Alice's personal story and how her bright prospects as an attractive and talented youth had been shattered beyond recognition by forces beyond her control. But the complete opening of my heart to Alice as a person came from a moment of grace that I shall never forget. We had decided in our congregation to experiment with the introduction of a new practice in our Sunday services. Once a month, we would add an extra hymn to the hour of worship; members would take turns introducing a favorite of theirs. Alice's turn came to introduce her special hymn, "Come Ye Children of the Lord." The hymn is simple musically and lyrically, a plain expression of hope in a quite literal Christian conception of a glorious end time when sin will cease, the earth will be cleansed from all iniquity, and we will dwell in love, beauty, and peace in the presence of our Savior.[1] All this was quite familiar to me, and as we as a congregation joined in singing the simple and lovely song, perhaps I was not giving it my full attention. But then the moment was transfigured for me as we sang these words: "All arrayed in spotless white, / We will dwell 'mid truth and light." At this moment, I seemed to see Alice as a glorified being, arrayed in white, her youthful beauty and grace restored, transfigured by divine love, and all the promises her parents and friends had once seen in her fulfilled a thousandfold. Of course, the vision or glimpse soon passed, but I never again looked upon Alice without some of its light surrounding her. For me, the idea that Alice was a unique personal being of eternal worth had become, for a moment, a concrete perception.

As I noted in the last chapter, Leo Strauss remarks somewhat cryptically, in the next-to-last sentence of what is perhaps his most foundational work, *Natural Right and History*, that "the quarrel between the ancients and the moderns concerns eventually, and perhaps even from the beginning, the status of 'individuality.'"[2] The question of individuality *eventually* comes to the surface because it has always been there. It has been there since the writings that became the Hebrew Bible taught that human beings were created in the image of God, and so much more since the news was proclaimed that God had taken on humanity in his own person in order to conquer sin and death and redeem the hope of glorified individual personality. "There are no ordinary people," C. S. Lewis observed. And, "It is a serious thing to live in a society of possible gods and goddesses."[3]

Strauss preferred "the spirit of 'sound antiquity,'" with its "concern with virtue," to the notion of the ineffable preciousness of every individual that is, in his view, somewhat irresponsibly, fostered by Christianity. A thoughtful Christian today cannot deny that Strauss had his reasons. In light of the ravages of modern individualism and of the liberationist and identitarian delusions it prepares, it would be foolish to dismiss Strauss's concern or his classical and pagan judgments. There is nothing automatic in the coupling of Christian individualism or personalism with the sense of elevation and noble resignation inherent in classical virtue.

If I may be allowed another lapse from my usual resort to philosophical and theological discourse, I propose to illustrate both the truth of Christian individualism and the weight of Strauss's classical reservations with an example from the popular culture of my youth. A scene from a well-known musical play and movie, *The Music Man* (1962), may help to illustrate the fundamental problem that concerns us. Most readers will recall that the main protagonist, the con man who styles himself "Professor Harold Hill," has sold musical instruments to most of the children in an Iowa small town, backed by the promise of musical instruction. But, alas, the sham professor knows not a note of music. To save his skin from the mounting anger of the townspeople, he has no recourse but to rely upon the "think system" he has imparted to his young charges, a system by which each child's positive thinking about producing music is supposed to enable the children to produce music. Following one last, desperate reminder of this system, the "professor" picks up his baton and commences to lead his poor little band in what emerges as a barely recognizable desecration of Beethoven's Minuet in G.

It would appear that the jig is up for the phony music professor, that his deception is exposed, and that his fate is finally sealed. But just as the evidence of the disastrous nonperformance seems clear to all with ears to hear, a mother's voice emerges from the audience: "That's my Barney! That tuba's my Barney." Soon, other parents succumb to the same vision or illusion, and the motley and incompetent ensemble is transfigured into the magnificent marching band led by the famed "76 Trombones" that graces the finale of the movie.

What has this to do with the question of the "status of individuality" that Strauss considers the hinge of the quarrel between ancients and moderns, in effect the quarrel between virtue and individuality? Simply this: from the Christian point of view, Barney's mother is, at some level, profoundly right. Of course, Barney is not an excellent tuba player, if he is a tuba player at all. But, of course, that is not the point; the point is that Barney's mother perceives him to be wonderful, even glorious. And if the gospel is true, then it is true that, without musical talent, or for that matter any distinguishing virtues, Barney bears the image of God: Barney's soul was redeemed at an infinite price; Barney is a unique individual whose personal story matters from an eternal standpoint. This sense of the incalculable dignity of every individual person, a worth that transcends all worldly economies, was first articulated on the basis of biblical teachings, but it is felt or experienced by many a nonbeliever and exercises an unquestioned authority over our post-Christian civilization. This openness to transcendent individuality is the wellspring of the ethic of the other that we have seen at work in contemporary victimhood-identity politics.

By now, it should be clear that this unquestioned authority of the idea of the dignity of every individual is far from simply good news. When this idea was contained within a more or less comprehensive, shared religious understanding of our temporal pilgrimage, the affirmation of the individual was given ritual structure and moral meaning by authoritative sacraments and commandments and by membership in a visible community of shared vocation. Even then, as Pierre Manent has rightly insisted, the coordination of this religious vocation, of this membership in a heavenly city that somehow transcends the hierarchies of this world, with the practical imperatives of a particular human city posed an insoluble problem for the human agent. Now, as the conviction of an infinite and mysterious individual dignity has been flung entirely out of the orbit of any substantial and authoritative sacramental and moral community, the practical implications of that dignity can only be negative and destructive: all individuals are equally exempt from the normative structure of any particular authoritative community (and all authoritative communities are particular), which may be considered to have no more importance for enlightened individuals than the norms of tuba proficiency had for Barney's mother. We post-Christians dare not affirm any particular world of moral and political authority; we know only that the individual is not of this world, the world of practical accountability, the world defined, limited, and oriented by what is given in the moral and political nature of humanity. Whatever alternate world we might imagine for our infinitely free individuals is not a world in which true freedom is formed by virtues commensurate with our real natures or attuned to any determinate vocation.

This post-Christian understanding, which contests any definite moral-political world without replacing it with another world, cannot sustain our humanity. To put it simply, Barney is a lousy trombone player, and he had better face this deficiency for the sake of his own soul and for the sake of his city. Societies need competence, and they need excellence to produce the physical and symbolic goods that sustain them; individual human beings, moreover, need concrete, more or less determinate standards by which to judge their own and their fellows' contributions and deficiencies, and no amount of abstract talk about infinite personal worth will supply such needs or such goods. Strauss's "spirit of sound antiquity" is informed by his awareness of the need for virtues that will always be tainted by natural necessities of production and reproduction as interpreted through the hierarchy of a particular society, virtues that will never adequately reflect a pure sense of the equal dignity of every human person. Similarly, Tocqueville recognizes the compelling sense of justice that informs the democratic idea of equality, but he also knows that without some residue of or substitute for aristocratic honor, in all its imponderable particularity or "bias," the glorious, spiritual ideal of equality can only sink to the lowest common denominator of insipid materialism, and beneath that to pantheism and nihilism.

Christian love cannot dispense with classical virtue. Barney's mother—and perhaps, indeed especially, his father—owe it to their son, after expressing proper love to him and encouragement in his musical efforts, to acquaint him with harder truths about his talents and their limitations and about the discipline that would be needed to play the tuba or to practice other arts of civilization. Similarly, my duty to Alice, however informed and enabled by the grace of seeing her in the light of eternity, was, after finding ways to show her that I loved her just as she was, to help her become a better person, a more competent person according to the ways and circumstances of our society, and a more virtuous person according to the enduring forms of the virtues as inflected by the character of our particular communities.

TOCQUEVILLE ON DEMOCRACY AS A CHRISTIAN PROBLEM

Everyone knows that religion is a major part of Tocqueville's understanding of a cure for the ills and the temptations of modern democracy. It is not well understood, however, that Tocqueville sees Christianity (or, more generally, biblical monotheism) as a major factor in the rise of democracy and in its coming ascendancy. In a word: for Tocqueville, before revealed religion was the solution, it was the problem. When Tocqueville avers in the course of his introduction to *Democracy in America* that the prospect of democracy's total conquest of the Christian world fills him with a "religious horror" (*terreur religieuse*), we need to take his word choice seriously.

This is not at all to deny that Tocqueville writes, if not necessarily as a believing confessional Christian, then certainly as a friend of Christianity who greatly respects the moral and political legacy of the Western religious tradition. While in no way claiming that Tocqueville was omniscient regarding democracy and its future or that he adequately addressed all questions surrounding the new form of society and of human existence, I am still inclined to embrace Harvey Mansfield and Delba Winthrop's judgment that *Democracy in America* is the best book ever written about democracy as well as the best ever written about America.[4] Tocqueville's two-volume work (1835, 1840) remains peerless as a perspective on modern democracy that at once affirms not only the power but the essential justice of the emerging type of society while being fully alert to its pathological potential for society and for the soul. The profoundly religious bearing of modern democracy lies at the heart of both

Tocqueville's embrace of the benefits of democracy and his dread of its dark side. What do Enlightenment rationalism and Christianity have in common that situates them both as essential drivers of the democratic movement or impulse? What they share is a hostility to mediation—a hostility, therefore, to what Tocqueville names "aristocracy."

The deeply Christian source of democracy, for good and for ill, is clear from the first pages of *Democracy in America*. In Tocqueville's sweeping and eloquent introduction, the irresistible rise of democracy in "Christendom" is presented as authorized by Providence and growing from a seed planted by Christianity. The eligibility of all men for the priesthood regardless of rank of birth is the plainest evidence of this seed of democracy, a seed that is nourished even by forces and events that seem to oppose or contradict the idea of equality. The deepest source of this irresistible dynamic of democracy is traceable to the religious idea or sensibility according to which all the intellectual attributes and capacities that might seem best to illustrate the manifest inequality of human beings are interpreted as "gifts that Heaven distributed haphazardly" (5). As random or humanly mysterious "gifts" of "Heaven," these extremely unequal human attributes redound to the profit of democracy, even when they are possessed by democracy's adversaries, because, precisely as fundamentally unmerited gifts, they point up "the natural greatness of man" (5). Here, in this linkage between talents as unmerited gifts and the natural greatness of humanity as an undifferentiated mass, we see already the paradoxical collusion between a providential view of history and its apparent opposite, the Enlightenment idea of human progress by human means. In their common opposition to the natural, aristocratic tendency to understand the most important human characteristics and assets as possessions of kin and of class, Providence and Enlightenment collude in the irresistible march of equality.

The power of equality is no historical accident. The aristocratic claim to a secure possession of natural superiority is inherently fragile; it is vulnerable as much to the fascination of a mysterious Providence transcending human agency as to the claims of a rationalized universalizing Enlightenment. Tocqueville is fully aware of aristocracy's fundamental fragility in the face of this leveling, eviscerating collusion of the extremes of faith and reason. Of course, he nurtures no hope for, nor would he indeed wish for, a return to the aristocratic world of Europe's *ancien régime*. Indeed, a central purpose of *Democracy in America*, and particularly of its rhetoric of irresistible Providence, is to dissuade his aristocratic fellows in France from the futility of any direct or wholesale opposition to the massive flow of the river of history toward a democratic future. The river cannot be dammed up or turned around, but it may yet be diverted in a direction that might leave room for true liberty, decency, and even a certain greatness. The religious, indeed metaphysical terror of democracy must not be evaded but faced and engaged.

THE DEMOCRATIC-CHRISTIAN THREAT TO MORAL ANALOGY

The shape of the terror that Tocqueville confronts is already clear in this compressed and brilliant introduction. The author's clearest statement of what is necessary for a cogent response to the irresistible march of "democracy" is his deep and intriguing paragraphs warning of the "abolition" of what he names "moral analogy." Nowhere in Tocqueville's whole oeuvre, I would suggest, is the fundamental problem at the heart of modern rationalist and individualist democracy presented more profoundly. It follows, then, that nowhere is what is essential in responding to the problem more clearly apparent, at least to the alert reader.[5]

The notion of "moral analogy" arises in the course of Tocqueville's evocation of the violence and confusion of the French Revolution as illustrative of the dark possibilities inherent within the rolling revolution of modern democracy more generally. He describes the extremism of the French Revolution as symptomatic of a rupture of "the natural bond that unites opinions to tastes and actions to beliefs." He then characterizes this rupture as destroying the "sympathy" that has "in all times" obtained "between the sentiments and ideas of men." It is because of this rupture that "all the laws of moral analogy have been abolished" (10–11). Gathering and aligning these formulations, we see that the democratic revolution tends to sever and oppose opinions, beliefs, and ideas on the one hand from tastes, actions, and sentiments on the other. A concise and abstract formulation of the problem is this: the rupture of theory and practice—or, more precisely, the destruction or perversion of the natural bond or necessary feedback loops between theory and practice. When our conceptual universe falls out of alignment with or loses attunement to what we know "in our bones" as practical agents in the world, then we lose touch with our humanity.

It must immediately be added, however, that this disastrous rupture is at the same time a calamitous fusion: in imagining ourselves to be theoretical gods, we become practical (ideological and revolutionary) beasts. Our idealistic abstractions do not remove us from the world of action but commit us to perpetual violence against our natural moral-political condition. The oblivion of agency accompanies the rise of activism. Tocqueville later captures this perverse rupture and fusion of theory and practice in an unforgettable apothegm that captures the essence of the modern ideological obsession: "When they [modern materialists] believe that they have sufficiently established that they are only brutes, they show themselves as proud as if they had demonstrated they were gods" (519). This is a pellucid characterization of the internal contradiction that lies at the heart of the modern democratic or rationalistic project, the frame of mind that has proven to have bottomless seductive power over peoples increasingly severed from a traditional social order supportive of "moral analogy." This patent contradiction, the calling card of the self-styled "champions of modern civilization" (11), proves, alas, to operate as a powerful implicit motive for ever more radical action, for addictive commitment to revolutionary transformation. The rupture between theory and practice produces a flight from reality, an ever-renewed attempt to produce a new "ideal" reality, but this "ideal" has repudiated in advance any touchstone in actual human reality, the reality of a condition in between gods and beasts.

Tocqueville's account of the "deplorable" (10) spiritual and intellectual condition that is the abolition of "moral analogy" (11), the divorce (in terms I have extrapolated from his highly suggestive characterization) between theory and practice, clearly points to the one thing needful for thinkers who are moved by Tocqueville's appeal to other friends of true human greatness—that is, for those who resonate with his call for a new kind of liberalism based on the conviction that human freedom cannot stand up for itself and thus cannot endure without reference to some figure(s) of greatness or elevation. This one thing needful, the opposite of the abolition of moral analogy, would obviously be the conservation, defense, and now, in our day, no doubt, the reconstruction of the conditions of moral analogy.

In the simplest and most abstract terms, moral analogy is the coordination between theory and practice, ideas and feelings, concepts and intuitions. This coordination is healthy and, in that sense, natural—that is, in accord with human nature and the human condition, but not immediately available in any "natural law" understood as an explicit and universal philosophical or theological system. The simplest (and therefore necessarily quite abstract) statement of the wholesome coordination of theory and practice I am evoking here might be this: First, practice must look up to, defer to, or be aware of the superiority of something above it, something eternal and beyond the scope of human action. It is important to add as well that this "something above," though by no means susceptible of being exhaustively captured or constructed by theory, must be available in some practically meaningful way to discursive thought—to philosophy or to theology, to theological philosophy or philosophical theology. Practice must find some realizable guide and compass in theory. Second, at the same time, theory must never betray its practical touchstone. The good that is the end of action is not some ineffably transcendent "ideal"; nor is it an ever-elusive, ultimately incoherent, and therefore self-undermining idea of "progress." Nor can the end of action be located within a system in which practical goods are somehow transparently ministerial to some absolute transcendence that admits no continuity or analogy with the natural goods of human agency—for example, the cardinal virtues. As Aristotle and Pierre Manent remind us, the end we seek is always in an important sense in some way already present within the practical means by which we seek it—that is, in the practical, habitual dispositions, the virtues that, for the most part implicitly, shape our understanding of a good life and of a good society. In an important sense, *theory must rule practice, while at the same time practice must rule theory.* This is the circularity of theory and practice that must always come to light for the thinker who honors what he knows as a practical human being, as for the practical agent who cannot shun the pleasure or shirk the responsibility of thinking what is eternal.

"Moral analogy" is thus Tocqueville's way of evoking the harmony or coordination that characterizes any passably healthy soul and city, that between thinking or deliberate reflection on ultimate purpose and the good inherent in practical action in the human world. The abolition of moral analogy is the neglect or repudiation of this harmony, the refusal of the feedback loops that tie transcending ideas to the intuitions of commonsense morality and tie commonsense morality to conceptions of eternity. This neglect or repudiation lies at the foundation of the project of those Tocqueville calls out with some sarcasm as "the champions of modern civilization," those who abandon the natural condition of moral analogy in pursuit of a project that would try to do great things with human beings without making human beings great, to progress toward a better society without attending to the conditions of raising good human beings, and ultimately to make themselves gods on the basis of a bestial understanding of human nature.

DEMOCRACY, CHRISTIANITY, AND GENERAL IDEAS

Tocqueville's vigorous and profound opposition to the champions of modernity is thus of a piece with his understanding of "moral analogy" as fundamental to the health of the soul and of the city. It remains to show the specifically religious dimension of Tocqueville's "religious terror" in the face of the providential march of equality. This dimension is often overlooked, owing to the author's very clear embrace of Christianity, and especially of Christian morality, as a ground of resistance against the powerful undertow of the democratic tide. All readers of *Democracy in America* know that Tocqueville argues that human beings can be trusted with freedom only if they understand it to be limited by a divinely sanctioned code of morality. The most fundamental check on the democratic drift toward majority tyranny is the belief that the popular will is ultimately answerable to a moral God. Moreover, the desires and longings unleashed by the passing of aristocratic hierarchical restraints are moderated by the deferral of ultimate hopes to a life beyond mortality. We forget none of these benefits of religion for democracy as we now turn to a consideration of the deepest source of Tocqueville's "religious terror"—that is, to a consideration of the fundamental way in which Christianity risks abetting the democratic dissolution of traditional or aristocratic social order and thus undermining moral analogy.

It is only in volume 2 of *Democracy in America* that Tocqueville explores this deepest source of the terror he experiences in the face of democracy. In part 1, he traces what can fairly be called an ontology of democracy—of the way of understanding reality or being that accompanies democracy, as well as of the self-understanding of the democratic soul or subject that is bound up with this orientation to what is. (In parts 2 and 3, we might say Tocqueville develops the social-psychological and, finally, in part 4, the specifically political ramifications of this ontology.)

The key to Tocqueville's ontology of democracy is the intimate connection between the democratic spirit and the affinity or passion for "general ideas." The progress of democracy as a social condition is inseparable from an orientation to the world that is defined by an increasing aversion to what is concretely given and that is, therefore, increasingly determined by the seductive power of broader and broader abstractions. Tocqueville refers to a "taste" for general ideas, but the word is perhaps inadequate to the phenomenon he is describing or, rather, to the ontology he is evoking. Generalizing or abstracting is the democratic subject's fundamental orientation toward what is, and generality or abstraction is the fundamental way in which reality manifests itself to the democratic or democratizing subject.

Tocqueville's most fundamental discussion of this problem is in 2.1.3, "Why the Americans Show More Aptitude and Taste for General Ideas Than Their English Fathers." This aptitude and taste are presented in contrast to an idea of the perfection of divine knowledge: "God . . . has no need of general ideas" (411); God has no need to filter and, therefore, distort reality, either through the general ideas upon which democratic people fall back or through the aristocrat's partial and imperfect hierarchy of particulars. God needs no constructed general category of humanity but sees each and every human being at once in what she shares with others and in her individual differences. But for human beings, all knowing is distorted through aristocratic particularity or—or rather, and—through democratic generality. As societies progress in knowledge, they master more general concepts and so tend to rely more and more on them. The democratic social condition reinforces this tendency of civilization to generalization until it becomes "a frenetic passion that one must satisfy at every turn" (412). (The English people, by contrast, though "very enlightened," remain "very aristocratic" and thus relatively allergic to general ideas (414). The French, on the other hand, as Tocqueville will explain in the next chapter, 2.1.4, are even more unhinged from concrete reality in their passion for general ideas than the

Americans. This is largely owing to a lack of actual political experience on the part of the French.)

Tocqueville seems to display a quite equable, nonpartisan disposition toward democratic generality on the one hand and aristocratic particularity on the other. Both fall far short of divine perfection of knowledge, but both, in a way, represent facets of God's perspective. Our author certainly understands the contributions of democratic generalization to the progress of civilization. Like Hegel, he posits that the best minds of classical antiquity were blinded, by the concrete aristocratic conditions of their own societies, to the manifest injustice of slavery and so were at pains to prove that slavery was somehow authorized by nature. It is here that Tocqueville most clearly pronounces the fundamental linkage between Christianity and the modern movement of generalizing equality: "It was necessary that Jesus Christ come to earth to make it understood that all members of the human species are naturally alike and equal" (413). No sentence in *Democracy in America*, I propose, is more essential than this one for Tocqueville's understanding of the democratic problem and thus for his project of saving democratic (and Christian, or post-Christian) souls. Beneath the democratic revolution lies the Christian revolution.

Introduced by Tocqueville here in 2.1.3 in connection with the manifestly unjust practice of slavery, the Christian subversion of the aristocratic orientation to society and to reality appears in a clearly favorable light. But no sooner has the author implicitly evoked the holiness of Jesus Christ and the injustice of slavery than he describes the condition of human beings in centuries of equality as "independent of one another, isolated and weak" (413), and therefore not so much the condition of those who are free and equal agents but that of those vulnerable to a sense of the irresistible march of humanity in history. The point of view or disposition of equality is bound up with the passion for general ideas and the oblivion of the practical standpoint of deliberate action. (He here describes democratic individuals as "so practical, so complicated, so agitated, so active that little time remains to them for thinking" [414].) There are, to be sure, general ideas "that are products of a slow, detailed, conscientious work of intelligence" (414), and these appear to include the ideas of "the similarity of men and of the equal right to liberty that each one of them bears by birth" (413). Tocqueville clearly faults the aristocratic mind for its resistance to such true ideas: "Aristocratic nations do not make enough use of general ideas and often show them an inconsiderate scorn" (415). But Tocqueville's concern here in 2.1.3, and indeed throughout the whole of this volume 2, is clearly the fact "that democratic peoples are always ready to abuse these sorts of ideas and indiscreetly to become inflamed over them" (415).

This ontology of leveling or homogenizing abstraction is inherently negative or deconstructive; the mind determined by abstractions always knows much more clearly—more concretely—what it is negating (traditional or aristocratic social and moral forms) than what it is affirming (an abstract general idea). Democratic ontology is thus fundamentally at odds with what Tocqueville has called "moral analogy"—that is, with the tempering of the abstract idea by the concrete experience, as well as the informing of the concrete experience by the idea that aims to transcend particular experience. This is not to say that the democratic subversion of moral analogy can be answered simply by an unqualified embrace of the traditional or aristocratic pole of the human condition. Human beings are rational animals, in between gods and beasts, and can never find a final home in any particular social matrix of meaning. But Tocqueville clearly sees that in the modern, democratic age, the most fundamental threat to humanity clearly comes from the dissolving power of democratic abstractions and not from excessive attachment to particular habits, customs, or hierarchies.

Tocqueville continues throughout part 1 of volume 2 to diagnose various manifestations of the passion for abstraction and of democratic citizen's resultant impatience with mediation—that is, with figures or representations of meaning that are on a human scale and thus sustained by residues of aristocratic meaning. This theme is most fully and explicitly developed in chapter 17, in which Tocqueville explains, echoing Pascal, how the democratic poetic imagination produces the diremption of the human soul into a pair of abyssal infinities: a groundless, infinitesimal self on the one hand and a vast idea of an infinite God on the other. (This divinity is, during a certain phase of the history of democracy, associated with a vast and empty notion of a collective human destiny.) Tocqueville's account of "two abysses" (462), a clear evocation of Pascal,[6] immediately implicates Christianity in the democratic dynamic of "general ideas" Tocqueville is challenging. Tocqueville shows little interest in the possibility of unmediated divine revelation; he considers the political and poetic possibilities of humanity as these emerge in natural human experience, and thus considers "religions only from a purely human point of view" (419). The difficulty of dispensing with the human point of view of religion is apparent in the fact that Christianity itself has appeared historically in two essentially different forms, aristocratic and democratic. A Christian might well ask: Does Christ's mediation provide a substitute or alternative for the natural mediation of the poetic/political? The fact that Christianity itself, according to Tocqueville, seems to subdivide into traditional ("aristocratic") and modern ("democratic") forms seems to belie the possibility of a total exemption of revealed religion from natural mediation. To put the question in terms of Trinitarian theology: Can the meaning of God's manifesting himself as "fully human" in the Son be grasped or received without some implicit natural interpretation of the human? Or can God's kenosis, or self-emptying, escape the negativity of the modern subject/self without drawing upon the political poetry or poetic politics of nature?[7]

As Pierre Manent has helped us to see, the secular humanitarian ideology of "human rights" obviously provides no path toward a religion of virtue or an idea of virtue open to divinity. But Tocqueville has also suggested to us that Christianity itself is vulnerable to a generalizing, leveling view of humanity and thus to a Pascalian fascination with dual infinities, abysses that can provide no foothold for virtue or moral analogy. Revealed in an aristocratic age, the gospel had to aim its rhetorical weapons at the excesses of natural human pride to counsel humility. In democratic times, Tocqueville understands, Christians must find a way to give due support to the pride that is inseparable from the nature of human agency or moral analogy and thus to restore confidence in the natural, mediated goods of practical virtues and bordered political communities.

To understand grace as the perfection of nature, we must first see nature for what it is.

LIBERTY UNDER GOD AND THE LAWS

Tocqueville never presumes to supply a complete theoretical account of the standard by which he proposes to evaluate and guide modern statesmen or "legislators of democracies" (518, 622). He alerts us to the existence of a "mother thought" that runs throughout the two volumes of *Democracy in America* and leaves us to suppose that his most animated interjections, such as the kind of call to arms with which he concludes his diagnosis of American "pantheism" (2.1.7), reveal something of the heart of his thought: All those who are still in love with "the genuine greatness of man" (426), he pleads, must join together to fight against the pantheistic self-subversion of democracy. The closest thing we have in Tocqueville's writings to an articulation of the mostly implicit standard by which Tocqueville judges and acts may be the passage in *The Old Regime and the Revolution* (bk. 3, ch. 3) where his impatience with those who are "made for slavery" because they have no sense of the intrinsic goodness of freedom ("its own peculiar charm, independent of its benefits") produces this poetic evocation: freedom, he writes, "is the pleasure of being able to speak, act, and breathe, under the government of God and the laws alone."[8] Let us pause to consider the meaning and resonance of this declaration.

"Freedom" implies something elusive, undefinable, even "spiritual" in the sense that it transcends the common categories of human discourse.

What we learn about freedom from this passage is, first, that freedom is an intrinsic good, or that it at least somehow points to a good that is good in itself, "independent of its [external] benefits." Thus, freedom is "noble" or elevated; it is contrasted with the ignoble or slavish disposition of people who are "made for slavery" because they are insensitive to goods that transcend mere material utility. Thus, one can also say that freedom is spirited and spiritual; it is associated with human pride and self-assertion, and at the same time, it aspires toward an undefined elevation, toward something beyond the all-too-human.

Freedom involves pleasure but is not for the sake of pleasure, but rather for its own sake. Freedom is expressed in "speaking, acting, breathing" without constraint—that is, without merely human constraint. "Acting" is central to freedom. The free person acts in the world; he or she in some way contributes to or changes the world. The person who acts freely intends to act meaningfully in and upon the world, to "make a difference," as we say.

But this free action is bound up with "speaking"—with reasoning and deliberation, and thus with a sober assessment of what is given by

God or by nature, a clear view of the permanent features of reality that provide the largest context of action. Free action is action upon nature and yet somehow according to nature. For meaningful freedom to be possible, it must be the case that the world is made or constituted in such a way as to allow for or invite human action; the meaning of all things must be friendly to human meaning. Speaking and acting, reason and freedom must belong together or spring from a common root in the way things are—that is, "under God and the laws."

Finally, freedom is also the freedom to "breathe." This breathing points to the simplest, most common, or "democratic" aspect of freedom's meaning. Not everyone rises to the full possibility of rational action or of active or practical rationality, but everyone breathes, and everyone can appreciate the freedom of breathing, the inspiration inherent in the simple gift of life itself. And even the simple and universal gift of life must be defended against those who would act even against the freedom to breathe—that is, against our very survival. The most elementary and universal understanding of freedom is bound up with every person's and every political community's right to secure and defend their own life and own breath.

Freedom is thus spiritual, and therefore somewhat elusive and not subject to a complete theoretical definition. But freedom is not altogether limitless, boundless, or undefined: freedom expresses itself within a meaningful horizon in which there is commerce between the most elevated and the most common. Freedom, let us say, is both voluntarist and lawful; freedom is ordered by virtue, and virtue is free. In Tocqueville's terms, freedom experiences itself as "under the government of God and the laws alone."

Of all Tocqueville's elliptical formulations, this is the one in which the most meaning and the most tangled problems are distilled in the fewest words. Freedom is without merely human or arbitrary constraint, but freedom is limited and defined by its relation to some higher authority. This higher authority is expressed by the twofold government of "God" on the one hand and of "the laws" on the other. But this formula of Tocqueville's is at least as much a question as an answer; indeed, one might say that the central question, the problem that drives the whole history of political philosophy, is bundled up in this dual reference.

What does the author mean by "laws"? Since Tocqueville is referring to the laws as a legitimate authority, clearly he does not mean just any law or anything that human beings might call laws; he means true laws, laws that are morally binding, and therefore natural laws or laws that derive their authority in some way from natural laws, from what is right or just by nature.

But what, then, is the relation between God and the laws? Are the laws just and good just because God commands them? Or does God command them because they are inherently, in and of themselves, just and good? Readers of Plato's *Euthyphro* will recognize here a problem almost as old as philosophy. I do not propose to resolve the problem; instead, I propose that we embrace the problem as the sign of our closest approach to the source and structure of human meaning, the ultimate or most general parameter of the good life. The freedom of a personal, Creator God and the intelligible, unchangeable truth of impersonal law—these two aspects of meaningful existence, these two faces of a purposive cosmos or creation, must both be honored in any articulation of a life that is right and good. Tocqueville's "freedom under God and the laws" is as fine an encapsulation of the highest possibilities of human existence as could be wished for.

This duality within the highest possibilities of meaningful existence corresponds broadly to the two great sources of the Western tradition, Jerusalem and Athens. I undertake here to understand the bearing of each of these sources on the question of the free human good, then to appreciate the tradition of Western Christianity as the effort to hold these sources together, and then to assess the consequences of the modern collapse of the biblical-Greek alliance, a collapse that is inseparable from a certain attempted fusion of Greek rationalism with biblical free transcendence.

The Jewish Bible confronts us with a personal and mysterious Creator God, whose ways are not our ways but in whom we recognize the sovereign instance of free activity: "I am that I am"—God's self-naming before Moses—has been understood (by Augustine, for example) to refer to "Being" in the sense of a pure, immutable Platonic or Platonistic essence; but the Hebrew, I am told, indicates something more like "I shall be as I shall be"—that is, that the meaning of divinity cannot be contained or restricted by any laws conceived by the human mind.

Greek philosophy, for its part, invites us to take our bearings by a lawful or rational order, to situate ourselves within a cosmos governed by impersonal and immutable truths.[9]

I propose (contrary to what Leo Strauss seems to teach) that neither of these alternatives, when reduced to its pure form, is either livable or thinkable. Freedom and reason, creative action and immutable, impersonal truth are both absurd when purified of the other. Freedom is unthinkable without truth—a truth available in some way to natural human experience and reason—and truth without freedom. The divine must be understood in a way that supports both the lawful quality and the freedom or independence of human action; Providence, the ultimate guarantor of a truth whose face is not turned away from humanity, must be a friend of freedom.

Freedom and reason, creative action and immutable truth, depend upon each other as two sides of the same coin of human meaning.

MAHONEY'S ALTERNATIVE

We are now prepared to return to Daniel J. Mahoney's *The Idol of Our Age* with this problem in mind: Just how are we to identify the moral content necessary to resist the self-evacuation of Christian or post-Christian universalism? Mahoney's examination of authors from Auguste Comte to Pierre Manent includes many elements of a response to this question and thus can help us trace a path to a fully articulated alternative. Let us review those key elements.

For Mahoney, to resist humanitarian idolatry it is clearly essential to recover confidence in a moral truth above human construction, "a natural moral order" or an "objective hierarchy." The Christian concept of "conscience" is understood as the "portal" to this moral order or hierarchy. This order is grounded in both the will and the intellect[10] of a loving (22) and merciful (3) God. Orestes Brownson was clear and emphatic on this basic point: the rights of man are dependent on the rights of God.[11]

Before consulting other key markers laid out by Mahoney on the path to an alternative to relativistic and ultimately "pantheist" love, it will be helpful to acknowledge difficulties or reasonable objections that might be leveled against such appeals to an "objective moral order" (69, 124) and to divine authority. These difficulties are mainly two; we can call them "epistemic" and "substantive." The epistemic objection: How can we know of this objective moral order? And if we can know it, then why do we need divine authority? Or, if moral order is a matter of revealed divine command beyond the grasp of reason, then does it make sense to speak of an "objective" or knowable moral "order"?

The substantive objection: If we grant the possibility of some objective and/or divinely authorized moral order, then would it be consistent with human freedom and dignity, with human "autonomy," to be simply subjected to its "heteronomous" authority, to bow before and conform to a law whose source is altogether outside us, a law in which we, as rational and personal beings, have no part? In a word, even if we could know such a law, why should we, how can we, as thinking and self-aware, self-possessing or "subjective" beings, embrace such an "objective moral order," an order that seems to stand over against us as a kind of brute fact?

Important responses to these objections are already adumbrated in Mahoney's examination of proponents of the religion of humanity and of the witnesses against secular idolatry. I will collect these responses here in order to develop and further ground them throughout this book in a fuller account of the natural preconditions of Christian (or, for that matter, post-Christian, humanitarian) love, of love's dependence on virtue, or more precisely, on virtuous agency. And we will see that the answers to what I have called the epistemic and substantive objections to objective/divine moral law are ultimately one: while the moral law must indeed be understood as "objective" in the sense of grounded somehow above us, it must not be understood as simply outside us, as absolutely "other" with respect to our rational and spiritually self-aware humanity. Kant's dichotomy between "autonomous" and "heteronomous," which now effectively governs almost all our discourse on fundamental questions surrounding agency and morality, is wholly inadequate for grasping the relation of the human subject—or, more properly, as we shall see, the human agent—to an authoritative moral order. Properly understood, the appeal to a higher law is not alien to, but in fact, deeply continuous with, the full, responsible exercise of human agency.

With this outline of the problem in mind, we are prepared to understand the significance of the further indications we can gather from Mahoney's text. These are the indications the present work will explore and develop into the essential elements, at least, of a robust philosophical and theological alternative to the contemporary idolatry of "love."

Objective moral order and divine authority are not the only prominent features of the alternative limned by Mahoney and the witnesses against humanitarian idolatry he cites. The other principal indications we can group under two headings: virtuous action and political mediation.

To resist the "immanentist humanitarian ethos" is to relearn "how to look up to everything in the order of things that was truly substantial and truly noble" (69, a propos of Kolnai). Awareness of a higher "order of things" is inseparable from the authority of what is "truly noble" in human things. Respect for "the cardinal and theological virtues" is integral to respect for the "meaningful transcendent reference points" (1) of an "objective moral order."

To recover our bearings and resist the humanitarian subversion of Christian love, we must appreciate magnanimity as well as humility, the justified pride of "a Lincoln, a Churchill, or a De Gaulle" and not only the humility of "a self-giving Mother Theresa"; we must look up to the lofty hero as well as the sublime saint.

These references to great statesmen bring us to the fourth essential indication to be gathered from Mahoney's outline: the mediation of the political. Beginning with the title of his first chapter, Mahoney closely links resistance to the humanitarian subversion of Christianity with "authentic political life." The elevation of the noble seems necessarily to involve a "corporate" (67) dimension, the self-affirmation of a collective body of persons (and not of the church alone). A Christianity resistant to subversion must be "tough-minded" (87); it must "encourage citizens and believers alike to take seriously the full range of one's political and civic responsibilities" (88). "The Church needs to learn the language of humane national loyalty" (104), and thus to recover a freedom and individuality "rooted in the [political] common good" (41).

While bemoaning the secular "self-limitation of reason" (123)—the suppression of attention to what is higher or transcendent—Mahoney thus proposes the acceptance of another kind of limitation—that is, the limitation of the abstraction "humanity" by the reality of nations and peoples as realms of meaningful action. The acceptance of borders and democracy as "territorial" seems to him and his witnesses (Brownson, Manent) to be essential to our access to what is higher.

We are now prepared to see how the four elements of Mahoney's response to the humanitarian idol—natural moral order, divine authority, virtuous action, and political mediation—respond to the two main difficulties noted above—that is, the epistemic and the substantive. This response will, in turn, begin to reveal the interrelation among these elements to bring them to light as parts of a larger whole. To trace the contours of this whole and thereby to provide an alternative to the reigning reductive humanitarianism is the present book's central aim.

To link the authority of God and of an objective moral order with virtue in action and the political common good is to begin to see that what is "transcendent" and, in a way, "objective" is not divorced from the practical experience or performance of meaning in the actual human world. Mahoney's alternative to secular fanaticisms and democratic indifference, as well as to religious fundamentalism (123), proposes to bring together and to hold together will and intellect (125), politics, and the truth discerned by conscience (127). This perspective reconciles the word of God and moral law with the spiritual needs of humanity (71)[12] precisely because human spirituality is understood to embrace human liberty or the nobility of responsible choice and action. Divine providence is understood as holding open the space of human prudence; "attention to grace" is thus understood as friendly to the ambition "to govern oneself by the guidance of one's own reason" (104).[13] The openness of divine law to human action supports the dignity of political life in general and specifically that of the nation-state, the fundamental arena of action in the modern world, "the home of self-government and free and dignified political life" (103).

Mahoney's alternative to secular-humanitarian religion thus implies an understanding of Christianity that "affirms the truth of pagan nature, the Jewish Covenant, and political reason and political civilization." Such a synthesis appears grounded, moreover, in a Christianity that embraces "Hellenistic influences" (18), including those of Greek philosophy and Roman law. The "moral point of view" supported by this synthesis would transcend "both nationalism and cosmopolitanism" while managing 'to preserve what is positive in them'" (44).[14] Finally, the deepest ground of such a synthetic understanding of Christianity comes to light in the teaching expounded by Pope Benedict concerning Logos as the "creative reason at the heart of the universe."

If "faith in God and Reason" (122) is to provide the ground of moral and political understanding and action resistant to a leveling, vacuous humanitarianism, then it must be that both God and Reason can be understood as friends of human action understood in the fullest sense, action that takes responsibility not only for prescribing general rules but for shaping the world of meaning in which we live. If "choice is never merely arbitrary, bereft of rational moral guidance," then it must also be the case that the ultimate guiding principles of morality and the ultimate religious truths are such as to hold open the possibility of meaningful human choice, choice that partakes in some way in the "creative" character of eternal Logos. The truth that guides active human choice, the truth to which "conscience" or "the listening heart" opens a portal, is in a deep sense a truth of action, an eternal ground of the intrinsic good of human agency.[15]

These are the indications I have gathered from the fecund suggestions available in Daniel Mahoney's timely and eloquent challenge to a vacuous secular humanitarianism, the idol of our age. True human virtue and sound Christianity alike require respect for an authority above human will and interest in a good higher than material needs or formless freedom. At the same time, this authority and this good must be attuned to and in some way extend the dignity or nobility of human agency and of its fullest natural expression in prudent political action.

This book's purpose is to further articulate, defend, and expand upon these indications and thus to trace the contours of an understanding of virtue-religion substantial enough to resist the humanitarian and, ultimately, pantheist subversion. It is Christianity that has saddled us—or gifted us—with the problem of the practical management of a society of potential gods, and we cannot address the problem without returning to its Christian matrix.

CHAPTER SEVEN

Pierre Manent's Christian Aristotelianism

Only freedom ... creates the light that makes it possible to see and to judge human vices and virtues.
—Tocqueville, *The Old Regime and the Revolution*

Pierre Manent's Christian Aristotelianism is profoundly consonant with Alexis de Tocqueville's firm but measured and even anxious defense of modern and democratic liberty in *Democracy in America*. Indeed, Manent's political, philosophical, and discreetly theological project can be understood as an elaboration of Tocqueville's animated praise of "liberty under God and the laws."

We have seen that Manent, like many critics of modernity, including Catholics and Straussians (and Manent is indeed a Catholic who acknowledges a great debt to Strauss), locates the fatal weakness of modern rationalism in its reduction of humanity to a materialistic individualism. In Strauss's terms, the project of modern rationalism was to "lower the standards in order to make probable, if not certain, the realization of the right or desirable social order or in order to conquer the chance; one must effect a shift of emphasis from moral character to institutions"— that is, a shift to institutional design based upon a reduction of human motives to material self-interest.[1] The alternative to this materialistic "rationalism"—this modern reduction of reason to the service of material needs and desires, to security and comfort—has long seemed obvious (in its general character, that is, if not in its particular determinations) to conservative critics of modernity, whether philosophical (e.g., Straussians) or religious (e.g., conservative Catholics): the recovery by philosophy or theology of a premodern understanding of a higher purpose, an end of human striving clearly distinct from and higher than the merely material—the intrinsic satisfaction of the life of philosophic investigation, for example, or the consummation of happiness in a divine beatific vision. It may seem obvious that the answer to the reductionist metaphysics of modern rationalism must be a better, "higher" metaphysics, a theory or theology of the good, that can enable us to rise above the endless Hobbesian pursuit of desire after desire or the belief in some phantom of "progress" toward some secular salvation.

Pierre Manent does not answer modern rationalism in the way we tend to expect. Certainly, he intends to make available to us certain authoritative goods undermined by reductionist materialism and extreme individualism. But to open up the possibility of substantive goodness, he does not propose to provide us with a new or restored theory or theology of the good or some unified, authoritative vision of the whole that might serve as an antidote against the acids of modernity. Instead, he directs our attention again and again to the inherent character of human action itself, to the very "grammar of action."[2] It is precisely the "hypertrophy of theory" that blinds us to this inherent grammar,[3] and we shall see that, although Manent levels his critique mainly against reductionist modern theory, he does not exempt visions of the good, philosophical or theological. This is the audacious modesty of Pierre Manent's practical natural law: he renews a root-and-branch critique of the theoretical foundations of modern, rationalistic liberalism and then, one might say, disappoints our hope for a theoretical alternative. If, however, we suspend our disappointment in order to grasp the full ambitions of Manent's project, its unique audacity comes into focus: he invites us to recover our practical bearings by setting aside not only modern theory, based as it is upon denial of the good, but even premodern (classical and Christian) forms of the hypertrophy of theory, at least long enough to pay the most careful attention to the essential character of practice itself—that is, to the precise way in which the notion of goodness is always already at work in action itself, prior to any theoretical articulation.

Just what Manent sees (if "sees" is the right word) when he turns his attention to the essential, inherent character of practice itself, of the structure of action as experienced or performed from the inside, as it were, the inescapable logic of human agency, we will now consider. But let us first acknowledge a difficulty that must be taken up more fully following this exploration of agency from within. Harvey Mansfield put his finger on this difficulty in a discussion of a thinker who, in important respects, may be considered a precursor of Manent: Edmund Burke. Burke's critique of the abstract rationalism that set the stage for the French Revolution is, in important respects, akin to Manent's critique of the "hypertrophy" of modern, reductionist theory. Mansfield's question for Burke is a good question for us to keep in mind with respect to Manent's project: "Our question in assessing [Burke's political philosophy] is: can theory serve solely as a watchdog against theory and never be needed as a guide?"[4] Our answer, as it were on behalf of Manent (and perhaps Burke), will be that, although the functions of watchdog and guide cannot be severed entirely, a good philosophical and theological watchdog over natural law, properly understood as the intrinsic meaning of human agency, must be scrupulously modest in order to avoid usurping the unsurpassable good inherent in action itself, and at the same time must be uniquely audacious in holding open space in eternity for this good.

Manent's philosophical deference to the practical point of view can be understood as an exercise of Christian humility. Christian humility may serve human agency by constraining the pride of reason from a destructive attempt to solve the political problem—either, as in classical political philosophy, by determining a highest good above moral agency and political deliberation or, as in the modern project of rational mastery, by dismissing the problem of the good in order to liberate human action from its inherent moral structure. On the other hand, an extreme theological interpretation of humility (the radical subjection of the soul's works to an externalized grace in Luther and Barth, as we have seen) may subvert human agency and thus contribute to the inhuman dynamic of the expansion of rights untethered from human goods.

Manent's Christian Aristotelianism follows Aristotle very closely on the implicit structure of human action, the subtle economy between means and ends that emerges in a patient phenomenology of the goods of practice. But Manent departs from Aristotle by setting aside any attempt to determine philosophically the best city or the best soul, thus allowing for the appreciation of the modern nation-state, a political form "of Christian mark," as a framework of human action and deliberation deeply oriented to a hope beyond human power, a hope inclusive of ordinary human beings (not just the great of soul or the ultrarare "philosopher"). Manent's Aristotelian humility, or humbled Aristotelianism, counters the pride of reason, modern-theoretical as well as teleological or theological, in order to liberate the ordinary pride that is inseparable from human action.

In order to advance his proposition for this Christian Aristotelianism—I have already suggested—Manent must deflect three opposing interpretations of the political implications of Christianity: we can call them (1) modern-humanitarian, (2) Protestant-existentialist, and (3) traditional Catholic natural law, at least when understood as an exhaustive and explicit synthesis of all human purposes.

The most visibly powerful of these interpretations today is obviously the first, the humanitarian appropriation of Christian charity. The religion of humanity, Manent argues, would never "have attained its empire over our souls if it did not appear as the extension and the consequence, perhaps the effectual truth, of Christianity, of the religion of the neighbor."[5] But Mahoney, following Manent, points out that this reduction of charity, the greatest theological virtue, to compassion and fellow-feeling, ignores the fact that genuine love of one's neighbor is possible only because one discerns in him or her "the image of God."[6]

I have summarized Manent's authentically Christian response to the post-Christian religion of humanitarianism in part 1. The more challenging task of rescuing the natural "grammar" of human action from more serious theological forms of "hypertrophy" remains.

MANENT'S POLITICAL THOMISM

In his very original articulation of the problem of natural law in *Natural Law and Human Rights*, Manent employs considerable delicacy in deflecting the most respectable alternative to his Christian Aristotelianism, which is the traditional understanding of natural law itself. As we have seen above (pt. 1, ch. 2), without expressing any direct criticism of St. Thomas or his followers, Manent puts the question of natural law on what appears to be a completely different footing from the scholastic tradition, at least in its more didactic or "manualist" versions. He speaks broadly of the temptation of responding to the moral vacuity of modern human rights by reference to an objectifying communitarianism or natural law understood as the objective synthesis of all desirable norms, the resolute counterassertion of an "objective [moral and metaphysical] order."[7] He also acknowledges, in his most recent sketch of the genesis of modern rationalism, the role played by the double vision created by the incommensurable claims of the political city and the City of God. The overreaching of a certain Christian idealism, the attempt to posit a theological and, therefore, theoretical end of practice wholly beyond practice, seems to have led inevitably to the reaction that produced the modern reduction to a world without inherent ends. In comparison with the theological and philosophical systems of natural law, Manent's natural law, which starts with the universal motives of the pleasant, the useful, and the upright or honest (*honnête*),[8] is both more modest and more firmly grounded in the natural structure of human action. Manent is not blind to what we might call the transcendent orientation of the *honnête* and its orientation toward the noble, what is higher and more beautiful, but he observes that, as a motive or essential movement of the human soul, the noble is stronger than any idea, any cultural, philosophical, *or theological* representation. Rejecting the claims of theory and of theology, the "tyranny of the explicit,"[9] he judges it wise not to try to capture the élan of the noble in any determinate idea but rather to keep it both tethered to the common goods of practice and open to a hope as much beyond human conception as it is beyond human power. He thus not only rejects any systematic and comprehensive development of the objective rules of natural law but implies further that theology and philosophy would do best to refrain from articulating ideas of perfection, which he considers finally unknowable and incoherent. (Rather than aiming to define some ultimate "perfection," he thus prefers to speak of "satisfactory fulfillment."[10]) It is natural and Christian to hope for a divine good beyond the goods of practical action, but Manent sees reason, in our present circumstances of theoretical hypertrophy, as investing too much in speculations on goods beyond those we actually experience in some way in the practice of moral agency and political deliberation.[11]

In a beautiful and lucid Lenten lecture titled "Reason and Faith," Manent shows how a humane understanding of reason opens itself to faith and how both reason and faith are bound up with politics or with our attachment to and dependence upon human communities:

> The believer, like his rationalist or agnostic fellow-citizen, is always "outside himself," always already taken up in human bonds that, like the non-believer, he is striving to strengthen, to make more just and sweeter. Each as much as the other must give a reasonable account of these bonds. . . . But this extension of the self, this enlargement of the self, this participation of the self in something larger than itself, which is implied in every human bond, from the slightest to the grandest—can reason ground this, can it first even understand it? It can if it engages itself with all its strength in the search for being, for the being such that no greater being can be conceived. But then, at this extreme limit of its strength, it is necessary to accept, or not to accept, suspending its effort, but not its movement, and to let the greatest being come towards it; and then rational man must consent, or not, to let the truth come towards him.[12]

This text evokes the continuity between our natural human interest in securing and enhancing the "sweetness" of social bonds and our interest in our hope for a higher and more complete good. At some point, our quest for such a good exceeds the limits of reason, and so we must choose whether or not to let the divine truth come toward us. I interpret Manent as suggesting that we exercise a reasonable faith, or "let the truth come towards" us, when we surrender the ambition of theoretical or theological mastery and allow God's grace to supervene upon our natural practice of moral and political agency. This is the practical appropriation of the fundamental insight of Thomas Aquinas that Manent continues to honor: grace does not destroy but perfects nature.

The modern tyranny of theory, in the end a result of the medieval ascendancy of theology, requires Manent to insist that the nature to be perfected is inescapably a practical, moral, and political nature. The divine truth can come toward us only as we assume practical responsibility for the common goods of the real communities of which we are a part. Neither (1) modern rational mastery for the sake of humanity nor (2) the humble Protestant or postmodern abnegation of responsibility for human goods nor (3) classical or medieval speculation on a highest good altogether beyond practice can relieve us of our responsibility as rational, moral, and political beings for the only goods available to us by nature, and thus the only goods of which we can coherently speak—that is, the goods inherent in our moral and political agency and inseparable from the very practice of that agency.

Manent's originality in relation to traditional Catholic natural law may thus be understood in the light of his diagnosis of our modern ills and confusion as a result of "theoretical hypertrophy." In response to the modern tyranny of theory (which is itself, at bottom, an excusable if not necessary response to the medieval ascendancy of theology), Manent insists that the nature that grace promises to perfect is inescapably a practical—a moral, and political—nature. The divine truth can come toward us only as we assume practical responsibility for the common goods of the real communities of which we are a part and honor those stable, natural cardinal virtues that are bound up with any wholesome idea of the common good.

Any theory or theology that aspires to understand practice, to address moral-political agency, must have some grounding or footing within the realm of human experience, which is ineluctably a realm of action, of agency in view of some substantial, actionable understanding of what is good. Theology, no less than philosophy, must be respectfully attentive to a certain necessary "grammar of action." Theology and philosophy must humble themselves in order to enter into what might be called the essential pride of human action, the active human contribution to the good. As we shall explore further, although in *Natural Law and Human Rights* Manent only sparingly quotes the Angelic Doctor,[13] his project might well be understood as a performative and postmodern appropriation of Thomas Aquinas's teaching that the natural law consists of human participation in eternal law; indeed, the natural law consists of human participation in the active and productive realization of eternal law.

DEATH IS NOT THE END

The audacious modesty of Manent's retrieval of natural law, his great reserve or circumspection in discussing the divine or transcendent, can be seen in his discussion of the problem of death ("The Obstacle of Death," ch. 5 of *Natural Law and Human Rights*). In this confrontation with what is often taken by philosophers and theologians to be the ultimate existential question, we find an instructive example of how he situates what is divine or transcendent in relation to practical philosophy, or the "natural grammar of action."

In this section, it is clear that not even the ever-looming fact of mortality, ground zero for the deconstruction of common, "inauthentic" human being-in-the-world in both atheistic and transcendent discourses of absolute otherness, can distract or discourage Manent from his faithful attachment to the practical ground of human meaning:

> If the agent, the acting human being, despite his fear, his great fear of death, does not, unlike the free individual, spend every effort to avoid or avert death, this is precisely because he is an agent, an acting human being, and as such obeys his nature and the logic of action. . . . As an agent he is in search of the right action, which has its rules and priorities, and which thus may include and even command acting in a way that implies mortal risk. It is not that he looks at death without blinking; it is that in acting he looks first at the rule of action, and death or the fear of death cannot be the main thing on his mind.[14]

On the contrary, Manent continues, within the secular-individualist perspective of human rights "the death of the body does not open up a new domain, an unprecedented experience; it introduces no essential or urgent interrogation into the substance or the intimate texture of life. It is simply the greatest material obstacle with the potential of interrupting the material and necessary movement of life." Within this secular perspective, death can be approached only as another problem for which a technical solution must be found.

Manent describes the alternative to this secular perspective as the possibility of "surveying the horizon of life, . . . calling up thoughts worthy of its formidable magnitude, rather than inviting the imagination to evoke *the splendors or the misfortunes* that may await us beyond the tomb."[15] While Manent is certainly well disposed to such reflections on the eternal horizon of life and on the splendors and misfortunes of immortality, he does not allow such reflections to distract him from his "essential or urgent interrogation into the substance or the intimate texture of life." It is very striking that his response here to the problem of death does not turn to such meditations on eternity. His concern, on the contrary, is to secure our understanding of the immanent meaning of human existence—or let us say, rather, of its natural transcendence—and, in particular, to secure our understanding of the practical meaning of human agency:

> A free agent does not relate to death in this [modern] way. [Fear of death] is not the standpoint from which he views his life: though he wishes to avoid death, he does not take it as his main task to avoid death; this is not the way he sees things. . . . One might say: the individual who sees in life a series of obstacles to avert ends up seeing in life only the threat of death, whereas the agent, finding in life a plurality of motives and rules of actions that it is important to combine rightly, sees before himself a very rich field of practice, which death, however much it may be feared, cannot come to occupy all by itself, nor even in general to dominate.[16]

The primary foil of Manent's argument here is clearly the secular-individualist standpoint of the mastery of nature, which suppresses the question of mortality by the promise or simply the distractions of the technological project. But it is striking—and characteristic of Manent's approach, I would venture—that he does not answer the secular project of mastery directly with an otherworldly promise of transcendent hope (to which he obviously holds himself open). Instead, he defends the legitimacy and the goodness of the practical standpoint of action itself, in this world; he would have us relate to the promise of eternity, it seems, from this standpoint of the reasonable combining of knowable, practical goods.

For Manent, neither our mortal fears nor even our otherworldly hopes should distract us from the now urgent task of appreciating the immanent, practical goodness of human action: to preserve the human good, the link between humanity and divinity, against the dehumanizing abstractions of modern theory or of unreasonably otherworldly theology, the one thing needful is attention to the intrinsic goodness of human agency itself, to that commanding and obeying with a view to the good which, already for Thomas Aquinas, is best understood as human participation in divine providence.

THE INDETERMINACY AND PROMISE OF THE GOOD

Manent's *Natural Law and Human Rights* shows how the very idea of human nature has been obscured and all but forgotten under the sway of the modern idea of the "autonomous individual." He presents a renewed understanding of natural law as an alternative to the dehumanizing liberal-democratic regime of "human rights" and provides the essential conceptual tools for recovering an understanding of the nature of the practical human good and thus for holding the practical and spiritual worlds together. While open to the truth of Christianity and profoundly consonant with Aristotle's practical philosophy, Manent's approach is an altogether original recovery, at once modest and audacious, of the meaning of humanity as moral agency.

Manent's minimalist restoration of a philosophy of practice and a practical philosophy implies a profound and wholesale transformation of the way we conceive the relation between acting and thinking, practice and theory—or rather a reversal of the parallel transformations effected by Machiavelli and Luther at the beginning of the modern period. Manent's great reversal, his great recovery or rehabilitation from within the perspective of practice of the natural good of human action, of moral and political agency, proposes a radical rethinking that bears on theology as well as on secular theory.

An indispensable window on Manent's understanding of the priority of the practical is chapter 5 of *The City of Man*, where he produces Aristotle as an alternative to Kant and Nietzsche. The highest expression of the moral and deliberative means as the noble end of action, Manent here suggests, is the statesman's active composition of the common good from the various parties' propositions of incommensurable goods. The explicit debate that constitutes the city, Manent explains, concerns the meaning of justice and, thus, the character of the regime. The plurality of claims of justice arising from different characteristic parts of the city typically comes down to the contest between the few and the many, oligarchs and democrats. These two parties advance, respectively, the claims of property and of free birth, but beneath these, the political philosopher discerns the city's raison d'être—that is, the aim "to make the citizens good and just . . . and by that very fact happy."[17] Aristotle, in his *Nicomachean Ethics*, develops a rich understanding of virtue and its happiness, culminating in the divine activity of pure contemplation, but even there, I have argued elsewhere, the philosophical end remains implicated in the practical-political means.[18] Manent here notably leaves aside the contemplative culmination of virtue in the *Ethics* and instead traces the problem of authoritative ends to its political culmination in Aristotle's *Politics*. The problem is that the "true city," the city of the virtuous, must take into account the real city, with its challenging plurality of legitimate claims (birth, liberty, wealth, virtue, military valor). The commensuration of all such legitimate claims is "insoluble theoretically."[19] Still, "every political regime, as a particular regime, imposes a [practical] solution to [this theoretically] insoluble problem" (166).

Manent's Aristotelian view is that the judgment or decision that resolves this problem is seen neither as derivable from some theoretical principle (as an exponent of universal human rights or certain advocates of natural law would hold) nor as an arbitrary act of the will (as Nietzsche concludes from the failure of a theoretical law or right of nature). "Indetermination is not an abyss, but the complexity that holds out the promise of the good" (166). The genius of Manent's entire project may be glimpsed, I suggest, in this "promise of the good" that lies within political deliberation. And I believe it is not accidental that Manent does not here limit his claim to "the promise of the practical or political good." His suggestion is, rather, that the human good itself is, not exactly limited to, but inescapably bound up with the mind's and soul's engagement with the plurality of substantive claims that emerge in our natural, political existence: "In advancing his claim, each [claimant to the meaning of justice] proposes a certain equivalence between his own good and the goods of others, a certain relative measure of the goods that constitute the city, which is generally not unfavorable to it. Faced with having to acknowledge that this equivalence is less certain than it seemed to him at first, he moderates his claim and lowers the relative measure of his own good. The result is the practical commensuration of the theoretically incommensurable goods" (167). This practical commensuration of political claims is, of course, a compromise, but it is not merely a compromise, not simply a bowing to necessity:

> Thanks to this moderation, the sum of the goods in which my party, my family, or I myself will share will be increased. The statesman's work of compromise is not a mere necessity but a particularly noble and delicate task. [The statesman] must give each good its due, in conformity with the intrinsic dignity of this good as he judges it. In making this judgment, he applies a principle of personal and private appreciation, for example, of a philosophical or religious sort. But he must do it in such a way as to assure the integration of all the goods in the unity of the same city. Here he acts in his specifically political role of a statesman whose task is to preserve and promote the common good. (168)

Both the nobility and the delicacy of the statesman's task are on fine display in this discussion, but the reader may still judge this task to be lower than the ultimate concerns of philosophy and religion. I think, though, that Manent's presentation puts this ranking in question, at least. Note that he qualifies philosophical and religious principles as matters of "personal and private appreciation." Compare this qualification to his praise of the end of statesmanship—that is, the common good:

> The common good is not, then, a good that can be isolated from the different goods and elements that constitute the city. Nor is it a sort of common denominator, unlike the good of self-preservation which for the modern philosophers will be the foundation of human rights. It is both *the supreme good* and the good which binds the different goods together that can have no direct rapport with

one another because they are incommensurable. It is the good without which the other goods could not coexist, that is, could not be present at all in the human world. (168; emphasis added)

Manent does not say that the "common good," the good that results from the statesman's mediation, is the "supreme *political* good"—although it would not be unreasonable to infer that qualifier from its context. I propose instead that we honor the omission of the qualifier "*political*" and consider the possible implications of Manent's presentation of the common good produced by the statesman's free commensuration of rival goods as "the supreme good." Just as the intrinsic good of virtue arises from a deliberation in which virtue appears explicitly or directly only as a means, so the dignity of the highest good crowns the noble and delicate task of operating the practical compromise that, in effect, suggests or points to an actual commensuration of the rival claims that are at work within the city because they are at work in the human condition. The highest human good, the good actualized in the statesman's responsibility for the political community, appears thus to consist in reflective or rational responsibility for the practical viability and cohesion or consistency of the irreducible plurality of human goods. The good comes to light not as a theoretical (philosophical or theological) hierarchy of explicit ends but as the implicit understanding that graces the practical operation of a good that is common and, therefore, higher.

PROVIDENCE, ACTION, AND THE NATION-STATE

To translate Aristotle's insight into our moral and political natures, and to address the concerns of a faltering liberal-democratic nation, one must take account of the insights and problems presented by Christianity and of the development of liberalism as at once a rival to Christianity at a theoretical level and a partner with it in the development of the Christian nations of the West. For Manent, a recognition of the inescapably Christian (even when post-Christian) dimension of modern statesmanship is bound up with his espousal of the case of the modern nation-state.

Manent has made the case for the vital importance of the national political form in a number of works, most notably *Democracy without Nations?* (2006). But it is in his more recent *Beyond Radical Secularism* (2015)[20] that he more fully explains his attachment to the nation and especially the inescapably Christian meaning of this political form. It should not surprise us that it is in this very topical and urgently practical book that we find a deepening of his reflection on man's political nature in connection with the central proposition of Christianity.

Beyond Radical Secularism ranges from the most practical and immediate problems the French confront today (its French title is *Situation de la France*) to the largest questions of politics and religion; it shows, in fact, how the great questions of the Western tradition are at stake in the urgent challenges confronting France, Europe, and the West today. Problem Number One is the growing presence of Islam in France. It is in the context of the challenge of Islam that Manent provides a bracing characterization of the spiritual and philosophical task demanded by the present political situation. To grasp this task requires an understanding of the nation-state as originating in a political community of Christian confession that arose as a response to the debilitating division and confusion of political and religious authority that characterized the Christian Middle Ages.

Europeans, Manent explains,

> progressively abandoned the idea of a Christian empire for the form of the nation-state in the ardent pursuit of new and ever-more-intimate alliances between the government of men and divine benevolence. It was necessary for human beings endowed with free will and conscience to gather in political communities at once smaller in extent and more open to divine initiative. It was necessary to govern oneself by the guidance of one's own reason and with attention to grace. It was necessary to find place for the collaboration of human prudence and divine Providence. In this collaboration, the theology of *Saint Thomas Aquinas was able to provide the principles, but not to show the way to put them concretely into practice.*[21]

St. Thomas provided the principles for the collaboration of human prudence and divine providence, and now, as secular liberalism displays its decadence and exhaustion in the face of the Islamic challenge, Manent proposes at least to show what it would mean to put these Thomistic principles into practice. The fundamental proposition of *Beyond Radical Secularism* consists thus in pointing the way toward a completion of the task of Thomism, not only a political correction or supplement but, I would suggest, a consummation of the Thomist project of human-divine partnership through an articulation of its deeply political implications.[22] For Manent, "the collaboration of human prudence and divine Providence" has political implications not articulated by Thomas himself. Manent, in a way, proposes to update the Thomist project for our times and in a way to highlight its deeply practical character through another return to Aristotle's ethical and political anthropology in the framework of Christian hope. The truth of Thomism—that is, of the divine-human collaboration at the heart of the Christian proposition—is at once a deeply political truth and a truth in which political reasoning acknowledges its limitation before a divine source of hope.

The decisive moment in Manent's proposition of a new, political Thomism, which appears in the thirteenth section of the book, must be quoted at length:

> We have lost faith in the idea of self-government that animated European nations since they began to take form in the high Middle Ages. Simultaneously—and here I ask permission to call attention to this coincidence—we have lost faith in Providence, in the benevolence and protection of the Most High; or, if these expressions appear really too obsolete, we have lost faith in the primacy of the Good. . . . The two operations of freedom are inseparable, as are action and hope. Every action, and especially civic or political action, is carried out in view of some good, especially in view of the common good. Doing what depends on us as best we can, [we can] decline to appropriate this good that is greater than us, and, softening our pride a little, suspend internally our action in order to confide the common good to the Agent who is greater than any action and than any human good. As vacillating and prone to fail as we are, it makes sense to put our common goods, so mysteriously substantial and durable, under the protection and the direction of Providence: . . . We address the Most High from the site of

our action and for the common good of the city of which we are citizens.[23]

Action necessarily envisages some good, and the common good, the political good, necessarily appears to us as elevated above merely private or personal goods. But this higher, common good both depends on us and exceeds us, transcends our power as actors.

Whereas, in his lecture read at Notre Dame Cathedral, Manent concludes with a passive gesture of faith ("to let the truth come towards him"), in the present work, he foregrounds our active participation in the covenant ("alliance") God has offered us. "We will not be able to re-open the domain of action if we do not dissipate the prestige of this false providence [progressive history], if we do not recover a reflection on the political order as the framework and the product of choice for the common good, if we do not rediscover the desire and hope of the Covenant" (72).

In extending action into faith, Manent, like Thomas, of course, goes beyond Aristotle, whose articulation of the good depended finally on the possibility of a purely human representation of the good, if only in the rare life devoted to pure contemplation. Human action is, therefore, inseparable from faith in a greater Agent; the most complete human action must understand itself as dependent upon and in cooperation with a higher Providence. The pride of action must not evacuate itself but humble itself in accepting the divine invitation to partnership in Providence.

The Truth of the Christian covenant or partnership between God and man exceeds Aristotle's truth, the truth of human action as possessing its own ends in the limited sphere of the polis (or its projection in the self-enclosed, impersonal eternity of a self-thinking thought). The good envisioned in human action includes and transcends the end inherent in the great means of the cardinal virtues. This good transcends even the statesman's mediation, which glimpses a higher good in the very act of adjudicating the reasonable claims of the worthy parts of the city. Faith as an act of partnership with a universal personal God achieves an eminent expression in the great politics of the providential nation-state, a task that compels the Christian statesman to attend to the partial truths asserted by the major claimants in today's contest for the soul of civilization.

For Manent, the imitation of Christ's mediation thus has an essential political dimension; it includes mediating among human goods. And in a civilization bearing the indelible mark of Christianity (the human-divine partnership represented in the providential nation-state), this mediation addresses not only the natural claims of the pagan city but the very universal claims of Christianity itself. The Catholic statesman produces and glimpses the highest good by attending prudently and faithfully to and thus moderating the claims of the great spiritual masses of humanity, including those of Christianity itself as a social body. The highest good is a political as well as a transcendent and spiritual good; the Thomistic synthesis of faith and reason is fulfilled at least in part in the Christian statesman's production of the common good of a civilization bearing the mark of Christianity as it weighs the truths embodied in the great spiritual masses that make a claim on the government of the modern world.

Pierre Manent's refusal to abandon or to fly beyond the meaning inherent in action itself provides him the key to "recovering law's intelligence"[24]—that is, to rediscovering the natural and practical meaning inherent in an existence under law. A true and natural understanding of law would allow us to appreciate the goodness of human action as this goodness points beyond practical virtue to a divine goodness that, like the goodness of action itself, must always exceed the grasp of theoretical or theological reasoning. The good is not a rational construction; reason honors and evokes a good that transcends reason as it labors to articulate the shape and implications of the good with reference to the practical situation at hand. In practice, the claims of goodness always point beyond practice to what is highest and ultimate. At the same time, the language with which we praise what is highest and ultimate always falls short of a complete articulation or manifestation. The good exceeds language and reason, but the straining of language and reason toward the good is not alien to or accidental to the meaning of the good. The excessive or overflowing meaning of the practical on the one hand and of the divine on the other color each other. It is confidence in this goodness that forms the untheorized horizon of action that carries Manent as an agent as well as a thinker beyond the delicate historical question of the philosophical and theological genesis of the modern hypertrophy of theory to embrace the possibility of an unprecedented recovery of natural law.

This recovery, while grateful and deferential to Thomas Aquinas's Christian and premodern natural law, does not despise the intimations of the good that resonate in the practice of modern liberty. Our situation as practical, rational beings is no longer defined, as was Thomas's, by the contest between philosophy and theology, but instead by the good that is at work in both, but that both, in their mutual rivalry in our Western history, have tended to obscure. As he explains in the appendix to *Natural Law and Human Rights*, "The problem is no longer to define the border and to order relations among two institutions, one political and the other religious, both equally ambitious and proud, but to measure the content in terms of the common good of this mixed law that has defined the Christian custom of Europe over the centuries and that is rediscovering an unexpected ordering power."[25] The rivalry between philosophy and theology that determined Thomas's framing of the question of natural law has long been superseded by a "mixed law" not susceptible of any final theoretical articulation. The common ground between reason and revelation has been demonstrated in practice by liberal nations "of Christian mark." In the development of the modern liberalism of Europe's Christian nations, natural law has been demonstrated in practice, while obscured by the liberal theory that descends from Machiavelli via Hobbes and Locke. Manent's proposition of natural law is modest or minimalist theoretically, but practically and spiritually it is momentous. He invites us to recognize the spiritual good that beckons beyond the visible arena of practical liberalism. He invites the discerning reader, that is, to register the humanity of a liberal natural law "of Christian mark" (that is, indelibly stamped by the spiritual and practical experience of Christian nations). The good of what he names this "mixed law" exceeds both liberal theory and any systematic and, finally, "otherworldly" theology.

Manent's primacy of the practical, his "recovery of law's intelligence," thus involves a respectful but firm adieu to the long Western rivalry between the two versions of theoretical hypertrophy, to the framing of the conflict in terms of what Leo Strauss has famously labeled the "political-theological problem." Stepping away from this rivalry, the author invites us to open our minds and hearts to the goods, at once practical and divine, useful and noble, that have long summoned us both to act and to pray. To choose the right means for the right reason, and in doing so to know oneself as participating in, even as contributing to, the very unfolding of the order of creation—this is the humble simplicity and the glorious promise of the perspective Manent proposes to us.

We have seen that this perspective involves not quite a theoretical synthesis but a certain coordination of a biblical understanding of God with an Aristotelian understanding of human action. Up to this point, I have been concerned with defending the practical realm of human agency against tendencies of theory (philosophical or theological) to undermine the integrity of practice. The two poles of my analysis, then, have been the claims of theory and the irreducible reality and responsibility of moral and political agency. It is time, though, to recognize and to begin to account for a dimension of human meaning that cannot be aligned simply with either my theoretical or my practical pole. This is the dimension—obviously central to the West's Christian inheritance—of interpersonal *love*. As illustrated plainly, if perhaps rather crudely, by the unstudied prejudice of Barney's mother (in *The Music Man*) in favor of her son, the phenomenon of love for a person as a distinct and irreplaceable individual is an undeniable dimension of human meaning, an important factor in any reasonably capacious understanding of the good life and of what is ultimate or divine. This dimension was not invented by, but was brought to light with irreversible power by, biblical revelation. My attempt to arbitrate the claims of theory and practice, and thus to map the principal factors of the good, must hold open a space for this third corner of the triangle of human meaning, or the third pillar supporting the structure of meaning—that is, love.

CHAPTER EIGHT

The Grammar of Action and Its Eternal Resonance

The main target of Manent's critique of theoretical hypertrophy (as we saw in chapter 1) is clearly the modern doctrine of natural rights, which has necessarily evolved into the doctrine of human rights. Indeed, the problem is precisely that the idea or project of natural rights, as understood in the modern tradition of political philosophy and most eminently and symptomatically by Thomas Hobbes, slides irresistibly into the assertion of ever-expanding human rights. The original appeal to a standard of nature dissolves into sheer human assertion. As Manent shows, this dissolution is inherent in the modern project because the "nature" to which Hobbes and his followers appeal, nature as the radically individuated biological being, ultimately reduces to the individual's boundless assertion of "rights." Despite Hobbes's effort to define desire by the one desire he anoints as "rational"—that is, the fear of violent death—in the end, the normative authority of the state of nature as an absolute void of authority prevails. The governing law of modern liberalism is lawlessness; modern liberalism is flight from law—a perpetual, obsessive, ever-self-radicalizing flight from law as the essential structure of human action.

Manent's critique of the modern rationalist and secular theory of "natural rights" as grounded in a radically reductionist and individualist state of nature is consonant, in many ways, with diagnoses attractive to "conservatives" or "traditionalists." As a critique, it shares much, for example, with Leo Strauss's deconstruction of modern rationalism, as well as with traditionalist Catholic antimodernism. But in responding to the modern deformation of reason, Manent does not appeal either to the Straussian idea of an autonomous philosophic life content somehow with the serene contemplation of "the permanent questions" or to the massive theological apparatus of the school of Thomism. Certainly, he shares with these critics of modern rationalism the intention to make available to us again the authority of certain goods, or the goods of a certain authority, that have been undermined by reductionist materialism and abstract, ungrounded individualism. However, to open up the possibility of substantive goodness, he does not propose to provide us with a new or restored theory or theology of the good or some unified, authoritative vision of the whole that might serve as an antidote against the acids of modernity. Instead, in *Natural Law and Human Rights*, he directs our attention again and again to the inherent character of human action itself, to the "grammar of action."[1] It is precisely the "hypertrophy of theory" that blinds us to this inherent grammar, and we shall see that, although Manent levels his critique mainly against reductionist modern theory, he does not exempt premodern propositions of the good, philosophical or theological. This is the audacious modesty of Manent's practical natural law: he renews a root-and-branch critique of the theoretical foundations of modern, rationalistic liberalism and then, in a way, disappoints our hope for a fixed theoretical alternative. But if we suspend our disappointment in order to grasp the full ambitions of Manent's project, its unique audacity comes into focus: he invites us to recover our practical bearings by setting aside not only modern theory, based as it is upon denial of the good, but even premodern (classical and Christian) forms of the overreach or "hypertrophy" of theory, at least long enough to pay the most careful attention to the essential character of practice itself—that is, to the precise way in which the notion of goodness is always already at work in action itself, prior to any theoretical articulation.

THE GAP BETWEEN REASON AND COMMAND

It is in chapters 4 and 5 of *Natural Law and Human Rights* that Manent most closely investigates the natural grammar of action as obscured and all but suppressed by the collusion between the "ideal" of individual autonomy, which, in fact, reduces the human person to the brute assertion of a *conatus*,[2] and the abstract, end-less state that hides its governing power behind the function of guarantor of the asserted "rights" of this blind and mute *conatus*. Here, Manent's brilliantly original account of natural action hovers delicately between poles that one might name voluntarism and rational teleology. On the one hand, action is necessarily, inherently, "archic": action commands, it initiates, it rules. Action is active—one might almost say, creative; it is in no way reducible to the straightforward or automatic application of a rule or preexisting template. Action involves an irreducible element of personal initiative, a singular ruling response to a singular practical opportunity. "Thus there are only commands and the act of commanding, *in this world or in the other*, because action and the human agent are naturally and necessarily under the rule of action" (emphasis added).

Manent amplifies this argument concerning the necessarily archic character of action in a section of chapter 6 entitled "The Primacy of Command." "[An] action is either commanding or commanded" because "human life, whether public, social or private is always essentially in tension," the tension "contained in the fact of having to act, in the fact of the agendum," in "the urgency of what is to be done and the desire to do well" (113). Action is commanding because it requires a break "with passivity, with the inertia of immanent life," because it envisages "a future that must be opened up" (114). Action and its good can neither be simply deduced from an authoritative good nor predicted as the mechanical result of some *conatus*.

On the other hand, action is never arbitrary or purely "creative"; action always asserts a reason for its rule: "Action and the human agent are naturally and necessarily under the rule of action. The practical world is never given over essentially to the arbitrary commands of gods or of men, because along with action come the reasons for action, and because the human agent cannot engage in action without entering to some degree into its reasons" (emphasis added). Thus, on the one hand, to act is always, in some form and to some degree, to "command," to initiate and thus to produce practical meaning and order; yet, on the other, action is not an ex nihilo creation; to act is to propose and assert a general rule of action as right and good in a certain concrete situation.

Thus, Manent's understanding of action is, we can say, neither voluntarist nor rationalist, because it is, if you will, in a way both voluntarist and rationalist: commanding is at once initiating and productive; yet, at the same time, commanding action appeals to or participates in the rational authority of the good. The human good of commanding action consists in human initiation and production—not in just any human creation or assertion, but in the proposition of a human good. The good of commanding and the commanding of the good are inseparable features inherent in true action—that is, good action for the good.

This practical synthesis of will and reason is essential to the grammar of action.

Human action and practical reason naturally ally commanding (archic ruling/initiating) with reasoning: virtuous action accomplishes reason in a rational and commanding act, an act at once of reason and of will. In this context, we can see more clearly what is at stake in the natural "gap" of action that Machiavelli rejected or violated in founding modern, transformative political activism. The "gap" inherent in human action is not simply a gap between good intentions and inevitable moral failure, but rather, more profoundly, a kind of irresolvable circle: acting as ruling-initiating involves an appeal to or a claim upon some recognized or recognizable good, and yet there is no separate, freestanding good, no simple substance of the good apart from the ruling-initiating act that asserts its claim upon the good. *The good is, in a way, both above the act and in it.* "The practical good . . . has no existence outside of the action that aims at it and produces it" (115). Action is *essentially* a kind of gap—or, rather, action essentially performs a kind of gap, it inherently involves a dynamic tension—in which what it affirms or asserts is at once itself and inseparably something beyond itself, some authoritative "good" above itself. The good is, in a way, in the action itself and in a way above and beyond it. We know no goodness that does not partake in the quality of the gap.

LAW, NATURAL AND HUMAN

This same gap or circle of meaning or dynamic tension appears in Manent's discussion, in chapter 6, of the relation between natural law and human law. He notes, and in fact acknowledges the pertinence of, the common and, as it were, the official objection that is addressed to the very notion of natural law: nature cannot make laws; only human beings, only human reason and will, are capable of producing law, since law has meaning only in relation to a human being who produces and obeys it.

Manent by no means dismisses this objection; it is, in fact, true that natural law has no meaning except as it guides the active human production of human law. Natural law becomes fully real only in practice—that is, in actual human commands. At the same time, however, our modern experience unhappily demonstrates that human law depends utterly on natural law: human law has been "emptied of its meaning" by being severed from natural law. Thus, *"natural law and human and political law, far from being incompatible notions, are on the contrary in solidarity and mutually implicated"* (112). This solidarity-in-difference between natural law and human law is another manifestation of the "gap" (or circle, or tension) essential to the practical world. Natural law must be understood to be "above" human law, but law has no determinate practical meaning until instantiated in actual practice.

This is the inherent gap and living tension between action and the good of action, between will and reason, between natural and human law that both Machiavelli and Luther—and Hobbes, and the whole regime of naturalistic rights that follows—wish to resolve or collapse, and it is Manent's whole purpose to sustain and defend it. This is an essential element of the grammar of action that must not be explained away by theoretical or theological hypertrophy. As I will suggest further on, this grammar of action has implications far beyond the narrowly practical realm (moral and political); the fecundity of the gap must extend to our understanding of the temporal and the eternal.

THE USEFUL, THE PLEASANT, AND THE NOBLE ("HONNÊTE")

Examining more closely the argument of Manent's sixth and final chapter, "Natural Law and Human Motives," we see more clearly just what in the realm of action can be seen and described, as it were, from the outside (what is passably determinate and therefore universal) and what must be left to action itself, including the action of the practical theorist or scientist (and what is therefore necessarily indeterminate and characterized by a gap or circle or tension resistant to a spectator's grasp). The gap/circle/tension inherent in human action and, therefore, in the human good (surely a necessary touchstone in any meaningful speech about the good, even the summum bonum) appears again in this final chapter in the form of the relationship between the fact of natural motives and the norm of natural law. This account of the mutual dependency of natural motives and natural law is the last step in Manent's survey of the "grammar of action," and thus of his counsel that we not attempt to close or resolve the gap natural to action but rather that we respect it and hold it open.

According to Manent, action is necessarily opaque to us as theorists or spectators precisely because it depends upon us. The problem is not only that the "passage to act" always retains something mysterious but also that we are dealing here with an aspect of the human soul that is especially opaque. It would not be wise to seek more clarity than belongs to the practical domain (104). The noble cannot be transparent to the gaze of theory, or the practical understanding of practice is lost; the noble cannot be the object because nobility is performed in the activity of practical science itself; practical science knows the noble as the practical experience of noble action itself. Reason as practical science must leave place for commanding, for the pride and nobility of commanding, and thus for "the 'play' proper to practical life" (111)—and so, in the very practice of practical science, the motive of understanding must accompany but not preempt the practical motive of the scientist himself; the rational operation of the science of practice must itself rise to the responsibility of action. Practical reason is bound up with practical responsibility.[3] Natural law, the basis of practical science, "leaves the agent as well as the evaluator great latitude for exploring paths of improvement" (110).

Action's opacity is not an insuperable obstacle to understanding; it is, rather, a luminous opacity—once we learn to look at it in the right way, with the right focus, from the right distance. It is the stability of this familiar mystery of action as reasoned commanding or commanding reason, natural law as realized only in human law, that makes practical science possible—that is, a science that is respectfully attentive to practical reality and does not attempt too much, does not attempt to usurp the place of practice. A theory of practice must honor the luminous opacity of practice and not destroy it in an attempt to achieve transparency.[4]

Given Manent's critique of theoretical hypertrophy and his resolute respect for the meaning inherent in practice, the reader will be prepared to appreciate the audacious modesty of his outline of a positive account of natural law in his final chapter. Manent dismisses so swiftly and deftly as "defensive and reactive" the approach to natural law based on an "organic" or "communitarian" vision of a "certain idea of nature" as the objective synthesis of all desirable norms (while acknowledging the "very legitimate need" this approach addresses) that one might fail to notice how much traditional theorizing has been set aside. In its place, the author posits natural law as deliberate, commanding action in view of the three basic kinds of motives available to human beings, motives that recall Aristotle's three kinds of friendship: the pleasant, the useful, and the "honnête." The honnête names our natural human interest in what is decent, upright, and honorable; it involves our attraction to the just and the noble, our recognition of the obligation to do what is right by others, as well as the aspiration to distinguish ourselves for excellence of character. When Socrates in *The Apology* eventually (29b) sets aside his pretense of total skepticism by claiming "I do know . . . ," what he is affirming is precisely, I suggest, the foundation of natural law in this primordial commitment to decency and honor.

A practical science is possible because these motives are universal; Manent strikingly refers to them as "objective components of human nature" (101): human motives reveal an "objective and sharable character" (103), and thus "the bases of practical life are much more stable and constant than we are inclined to admit, carried away as we are by the theoretical point of view of the social sciences, and more generally by the point of view of the observer or spectator" (106).

Of course, natural law cannot be reduced to what is objective, stable, and constant from a theoretical point of view, or there would be no "gap" or no "play" open to commanding action, no freedom, and no residual mystery of practice. It is the last type of motive, the desire to be upright and honorable, even to attain nobility, that is clearly the most interesting and, in a sense, the most variable, elusive, and problematic of Aristotle's and Manent's three motives.

It is this third motive that provides a bridge between motive and law, between description and evaluation in Manent's account. It is indeed apparent on close examination that the noble or honorable appears in two different levels of Manent's scheme. Most obviously, the "honnête" is one of the three universal and natural motives that must be addressed or taken into account in all responsible action—that is, all true action. But there is also what one might call the second-order nobility of the action itself of taking responsibility for the three natural motives, the nobility that qualifies reasonable pursuit of the common good as the right balancing of the three natural motives. The motive of the honorable/noble is at once one of the descriptive, determinate "givens" of the natural human condition and at the same time the very motive of the agent in the fullest sense, the political agent, in his effort to secure the common good. The noble appears both as the upright—an immediate, universal human standard of normal humanity—and as the distinctive crowning achievement of the human agent par excellence.

And since the true science of practice is always necessarily a practical science, the author of an account of such a science is necessarily himself a moral and political agent—if not a statesman, then at least a potential or would-be friend or adviser to a statesman or potential statesman. Thus, we understand Manent's arrestingly personal response to the alleged "naturalistic fallacy" of confusing "is" with "ought," the supposed barrier to a normative natural law grounded in a descriptive account of universal human motives. "But in reality there is neither a leap nor a chasm nor an abyss between 'is' and 'ought,' but only a gentle slope, along which we can walk with modest confidence. *This, I say without vanity, is what I am now doing.*" (107; emphasis added). The author can follow the gentle slope from "is" to "ought," from an objective description of universal human motives or "reasons of . . . actions" to a practical effort "to discern the best way to judge and guide such actions" (107), first, because he shares an interest in what is morally right and noble with the human beings he is both describing and addressing, and, second, because the idea of what is just and noble itself cannot be finally or exhaustively determined theoretically, since it must include a "gap" open to determination by the agent and the author. The indeterminacy of the noble, its openness to the commanding reason of the agent (and to the author as agent), defines the gently sloping bridge from "is" to "ought."

THE NOBLE: STABILITY AND OPENNESS

Manent recognizes but is not alarmed by the variability in human conceptions of "the noble." Despite and across this variability among civilizations and cultures, he thinks, human beings can reason together about good action. As I read (and perhaps extend) Manent's argument, the stability and universality of the noble are grounded in a dynamic triangular structure of the city, the soul, and the divine.

The City

The noble is instrumental to the just; it is bound up with and thus tethered to the imperative of justice, of doing right by others and serving the common good; the noble and the just may be seen as the two essential dimensions of the "honnête," or the basic moral goodness of human beings or rightness of human conduct. And the content of justice is inseparable from the useful (to which the pleasant surely cannot be irrelevant): no person is just—and therefore, no person is noble—who does not act with some reasonable regard for the plain utility or reasonable interests of his neighbor or fellow citizen.

The Soul

The noble is, by nature, held to be intrinsically good. This is necessarily inherent in the nature of the noble because nobility must produce and reproduce itself; nobility must "stand up for itself" in order to be productive of nobility. In this sense, the useful requires and is fulfilled in the intrinsically noble and thus is associated with the highest pleasures.[5] Noble action must preserve the conditions of noble action. Virtue is the principle as well as the end of virtuous action. Virtue must be understood to be noble or intrinsically good, good for its own sake, above and beyond its connection with utility.

The noble expresses the "gap" inherent in action in that it is at once instrumental to and higher than common utility. The noble is grounded by the useful, and the useful is ennobled by the noble. The useful (the intelligibly instrumental) points beyond itself to some higher order of meaning, which yet cannot be articulated without reference to the useful.

Tocqueville brilliantly and concisely exhibits the gap of action or the circularity between the useful and the noble in his little allegory of the angel and the beast:

> There is more of a bond than one would think between perfecting the soul and improving the goods of the body; man can leave these two things distinct and view each of them alternately; *but he cannot separate them entirely without finally losing sight of both.*[6]

> In men, the angel teaches the brute the art of satisfying itself. It is because man is capable of elevating himself above the goods of the body and of scorning even life—of which beasts do not have any idea—that he knows how to multiply these same goods to a degree that they cannot conceive of.[7]

In his discussion of the "bond" between the noble and the useful in this chapter, Tocqueville is most concerned with supporting the intrinsic goodness of the noble as essential even to the useful. But his understanding of the gap and circularity between the two is by no means blind to the need, in circumstances other than those of modern democracy, to affirm the other side of the gap: Were he addressing an aristocratic society that "held [men's] souls almost numb in the *contemplation* of another world," Tocqueville writes, in the immediately preceding chapter, "I would wish it possible for me to stimulate the sentiment of needs among such a people; I would think of discovering the most rapid and easiest means of satisfying the new desires I had made to arise, and, turning the greatest efforts of the human mind toward physical studies, I would try to excite it with the search for well-being."[8] The vital circularity between the noble and the just/useful goes both ways.

The greatest variability in the noble stems from a third finality of the noble, which, in a way, traces a second and higher instrumentality, as we will see below.

The Divine

The instrumentality of the noble to justice or the common good, the natural perception that the common good is higher than the individual good, holds the noble open to a higher good beyond the self-satisfaction of the soul as well as the necessities of the city. The noble thus serves—that is, it is experienced as in part instrumental to—some divine perfection beyond itself. Above and beyond its usefulness and its intrinsic goodness, the noble must point beyond itself to some glorious plenitude, some completeness of being that cannot be a direct end of human action. We have seen that, as in Aristotle, the structures of human action are inherently circular and immanent in at least two ways. But what we might now call the immanent circularity of the noble/just and the useful would collapse if the noble were not held open to the possibility of transcendence, the promise of some glorious perfection, plenitude, or infinity beyond the circle. As Tocqueville's imagery of the "angel" suggests, the circle of the noble and the useful must be open to the spiritual or transcendent. Moreover, as I will propose further on, the transcendent or divine must form a circle—the circle already traced by the Thomistic "analogy of being"—with the naturally noble. Manent, following Aquinas, goes beyond Aristotle in tracing the natural passage from the noble to the supernatural; this passage is opened up by a readiness to do justice to the transcendence implicit in plain, universal moral agency and by a humbling of the classical, aristocratic pretension to achieve a philosophic transcendence that escapes the gaps and circles of the practical (moral and political) good.

THE CITY, THE SOUL, AND THE DIVINE
IN ARISTOTLE'S PRACTICAL PHILOSOPHY

Aristotle's inquiry into virtue's goodness in the *Nicomachean Ethics* already reveals a kind of gap (nonidentity) and circle (mutual dependence) between the city and the soul, between the claim of justice and the claim of the beauty and intrinsic goodness of nobility: the just (doing one's duties as regards others, "doing the right thing," serving the common good, held to higher than individual good) refers itself to the noble; the noble (what elevates the individual agent, what is intrinsically desirable and satisfying, what fulfills or perfects the agent), for its part, refers itself to the just. Aristotle's decision to preserve and sustain this virtuous circle rather than resolving it into some linear rational economy clearly subordinating means to ends reveals itself in the somewhat surprising argument he makes that virtue is concerned not with ultimate ends (the objects of wishing) but only with *means*. Aristotle's ethics defines the practical human good as virtue, and yet a gap is left open between, on the one hand, virtue as a means that is within one's power and thus a matter of choice and, on the other, the ultimate good for which one might wish. Thus, Aristotle directs our attention not toward the indeterminate question of the final good of the city or of the soul but rather to the means, the ways of acting that, in fact, are reasonably thought to be within normal human competence. Our actions seem to presuppose some end or ends that surpass our powers, but there is an end that falls within the domain of our responsibility and, thus, of our power—that is, moral virtue. This virtue concerns the means that we choose in view of ends over which we are not finally masters.

Aristotle thus focuses on moral means rather than ultimate ends in order to bring to light means *as* ends, in order to reveal the truth inherent in moral virtue—that is, that there is goodness in the way in which things are done, independently of any theoretically posited final good, a good that aims at what respected, public-spirited people hold to be good (as Aristotle loves to repeat, the good of doing things in the right way, at the right time, toward the right persons). Our actions presuppose final purposes beyond our power, but there is a good in itself that is within our reach, and that is moral virtue, the virtue that concerns the means we choose in view of ends beyond our choice.

And what might be this end beyond our power of choice? Some ultimate good of the soul beckons beyond the horizon of practical virtue. Aristotle will, of course, eventually (book 10 of the *Nicomachean Ethics*) propose to identify this ultimate end with purely theoretical activity. However, although Aristotle seems to attempt to specify this highest good as a human possibility whose actualization our experience can directly verify, it proves impossible to characterize it without acknowledging its elusive transcendence—that is, without reference to what the best citizens of the city honor on the one hand and what is divinely beyond us on the other.

Let us descend from this peak of Aristotle's account of the most honorable and divine possibility to consider virtue at the most elementary level. The tension inherent in virtue is never clearer in Aristotle's account than in his discussion of the first virtue, courage. Is courage, he asks, pleasant for the courageous agent? It must be considered to be pleasant since virtue is noble, and it is good to be noble—any normal person would surely prefer to possess a noble soul, a soul that is in a good condition, rather than the contrary. Still, it must be admitted that this virtue, which is displayed especially in the armed defense of the city, can lead to consequences that are hardly pleasant. There is no need for Aristotle to describe the suffering of a brave fighter; he mentions with ironic delicacy that the pleasure intrinsic to this virtue may be "obscured by the attendant circumstances." It is somewhat deflating to consider the vulnerability of the goodness of proud courage to the stronger sword or perhaps the random arrow of the enemy.

The case of the virtue of courage shows a truth that applies to the whole ethical life: it is true that the virtues are, in a sense, intrinsically good and noble and thus inherently pleasant since they serve to complete or perfect human nature. For nature to be fully what it is is inherently a good and pleasant condition. But it is also obvious, not least in the case of the virtue of courage, that virtue is constituted as it is with a view to the obvious material necessities of the city. I must brave the enemy's sword and arrow for a good that must be held to be higher, the common good, the good—or simply the survival—of the city. Moral virtue exists in eternal tension between the poles of the noble and the just, between the good of the soul and the good or the needs of others.

What does Aristotle make of this tension that lies at the heart of virtue and of human action? It may appear that throughout the remainder of the *Nicomachean Ethics*, he undertakes to resolve this tension by ascending from the plane of morality first to that of practical wisdom, and then to friendship, and finally to the pure pleasures of theoretical wisdom and the contemplation of immutable truths. I would maintain, however, that at every step in this ascent toward the pure good of the soul, the noble remains implicated in the just, the good of the soul never escaping the horizon of the city. Practical wisdom, which is supposed to guide moral virtue, is found also to be guided by it; and friendship, which Aristotle presents as a means to the good of the agent himself, nevertheless is shown on closer inspection to be irreducible to this teleology of the higher egoism of a self that aims at possession of the good: even the philosopher never escapes the need for another person with whom to engage in the activity of philosophy. Aristotle famously or notoriously teaches that the friend is another self, but the underside of Aristotle's argument shows that the self is also another friend—that otherness or transcendence of the self is inherent in the good of friendship. Finally, the quest for a self-possessed plenitude that culminates in the purity of theoretical wisdom (ostensibly an asocial wisdom) fails to escape the economy of the city: the best pleasures are the most noble—that is, those most apt to govern or to command the lower parts of the city. The circularity between the noble and the just reappears at each level of Aristotle's ascent in his account of human ends.[9]

How might Aristotle's subtle appreciation of the circularity or irreducible gap that defines the meaning of the good and the just be reframed within a Christian understanding? Christian humility may serve human agency by constraining the pride of reason from a destructive attempt to solve the political problem—either, as in classical political philosophy, by determining a highest good above moral agency and political deliberation or, as in the modern project of rational mastery, by dismissing the problem of the good in order to liberate human action from its inherent moral structure. On the other hand, as I have already suggested, an extreme theological interpretation of humility, one that subjects the practical good to theological hypertrophy, may subvert human agency and thus contribute to the inhuman dynamic of the expansion of rights.

PRACTICAL PHILOSOPHY AS FIRST PHILOSOPHY AND THEOLOGY

Manent's Christian and metaphysically minimalist recovery of an Aristotelian understanding of natural law shows what it would mean to overcome our modern, post-Christian addiction to the illusion of boundless progress and boundless mastery—an illusion that appears in its full form in totalitarian regimes but that also pervades liberal democratic societies. To overcome this addiction would be to repent of our addiction to the horizontal infinity of progress and humanity and to situate the infinite, the divine, on a vertical vector that is "above" us, in the direction we know, practically, as "the noble." Such a repentance would not, of course, deny the characteristic Christian virtue of humility, but it would require holding open a space of meaning in which the justifiable pride of moral and political agency can be received humbly—that is, received as a free gift from our Creator. The supreme complete entity does not destroy our human nature as practical agents but mysteriously and beautifully redeems and completes our practical natures.[10] The goodness of God's rational creation, so understood, participates actively in, and in its way manifests and thus extends, the Goodness of the Creator.

While open to the truth of Christianity and profoundly consonant with Aristotle's practical philosophy, Manent's approach points toward an altogether original recovery, at once modest and audacious, of an understanding of moral agency as central to the meaning of our humanity from the perspective of eternity.

PART 3

Nostalgia for paradise is man's desire not to be man.
—Milan Kundera, *The Unbearable Lightness of Being*

All meaning necessarily circulates between the same and the other, the familiar and the mysterious, the practical and the transcendent. Greek and biblical transcendence privilege different practical touchstones of meaning, political self-sufficiency for the Greeks and familial love for the Bible. The Christian tradition undertook to synthesize these two orientations toward what is highest, rational order and love, in what Benedict XVI named the "personal logos." Here I propose that the integration of reason and love depends upon another touchstone of meaning, that of moral agency.

There is truth in the modern claims of subjectivity, or the insistence on the personal self as a locus of ultimate meaning. But these claims must not be severed from the prideful propositions about the order of the whole that are implicit in human action: the self is also a soul. Care for "the other" thus implies responsibility for an understanding of the good and, therefore, of the whole.

What understanding of the whole can support moral agency? The Thomistic theme of an "analogy of being" between the human and the divine seems to promise such support, but a one-sided emphasis on the transcendent pole of this analogy tends to reduce the meaning of action to a "service" vulnerable to naturalistic interpretation. But other contemporary readings of Thomas Aquinas accord a higher place in eternity to the essential grammar of action, while honoring the freedom of creation and grace.

Our Christian response to the "woke" exhaustion of liberalism matters only if Christianity bears something essential of what Pascal named "the truth about man." It does, but neither Pascal's exquisite understanding of the misery of man without God nor Joshua Mitchell's uniquely discerning Protestant response to contemporary secularized victimhood adequately appreciates the goodness and responsibility of active virtue.

CHAPTER NINE

The Same and the Other

Western Configurations of Transcendence

The premise of my attempt here to extend Manent's efforts to affirm the primacy of the practical may be stated as follows: every understanding of the "highest good" or of "heaven"—that is, every conception of transcendence—involves some mingling of what we can call "the same"—what we affirm as intelligible and in principle present to our articulate experience—and "the other"—that which surpasses, while somehow addressing, our understanding and our experience. This is as true of perspectives on human meaning that claim to owe nothing to religious revelation as it is of explicitly religious views. Every passably thick and consistent understanding of the meaning of human existence somehow situates that existence and that meaning within a larger whole. And every such understanding must in some way hold open the circulation of meaning between the same and the other, between what we in some sense grasp and possess and that which leaves its trace on us in transcending our experience.

What is ultimate—our answer to the question of the meaning of divinity, the question "Quid sit Deus?"—must be other than ordinary experience, or it would not be transcendent and would not offer the hope of some condition free of the burdens, the conflicts, the confusions, the tensions, or the simple boredom of our mundane existence. "What no eye has seen, nor ear heard, nor the human heart conceived," the scripture promises, "God has prepared for those who love him"

(1 Corinthians 2:9 NRSV). At the same time, the goods of heaven, or of any conceivable representation of transcendence, cannot be simply and wholly other than our actual experience, or the promise of such goods would have no meaning or attraction for us. What our eyes have not seen, nor our ears heard, we must somehow be able to imagine, or, if not adequately to imagine, at least to project as a fulfillment and extension of known goods: "And of which of you that is a father shall his son ask a loaf, and he give him a stone? or a fish, and he for a fish give him a serpent? Is there anyone among you who, if your child asked for a fish, would give a snake instead of a fish? Or if the child asked for an egg, would give a scorpion?" (Luke 11:11–12 NRSV). If there were no continuity between actual experiences and possible goods, then the promise of transcendence would have no meaning for us. The promise of a heaven absolutely *other* than any enjoyments we have experienced in this life would have no meaning *for us*; in fact, it could not be a promise addressed to beings such as us, but only to a wholly other sort of being in whom we could have no conceivable stake.

For the promise of heaven (or of any figure of the "highest good," or of the meaning of a divine and supremely fulfilling existence) to matter to us, this heaven must at once be other than or beyond our mortal experience and at the same time somehow continuous with this experience. More precisely, the promise of heaven must highlight and build upon features of our actual experience that seem to rise above our ordinary and defective mortality and articulate these features (however imperfectly) into some conception of a higher state of existence and, therefore, of another, better world.

It is uncontroversial, I think, to say that Christian theology was decisively conditioned in its origins and throughout its history by its inheriting and adapting of key elements of Greco-Roman philosophy. In fact, we can see that essential features of what was to be the traditional Christian view of God emerge already in the elementary political theology that Plato proposes in book 3 of *The Republic* as an alternative to the Athenians' traditional and morally unreliable (to say the least) gods and heroes. To provide a good model for the education of the guardians of the best city (who eventually will be shown to be philosopher-kings), God must be depicted as the cause of good things but not of bad. He must be perfectly good and therefore in need of nothing and unchangeable—for why would a perfect and perfectly self-sufficient being ever change? Such changeless perfection and self-sufficiency, we learn further on, implies immateriality: Divinity must be conceived as wholly exempt from the mutability, the corruptibility of the material realm.

Any conception of transcendence, of some higher state of existence, I have proposed, must be grafted upon some actual experience. What are the experiential sources of the Platonic (or, more generally, the Platonic-Aristotelian) conception of divinity as self-sufficient and changeless immateriality? We must note at the outset that the original context for this conception is plainly political: the attributes of divinity are set forth plainly with a view to their political function—an indispensable function, to be sure, in the fashioning of a civilized existence. Those who are to rule over the passions of others must first rule their own passions in view of a good above material desires.

ST. AUGUSTINE AND THE PROBLEM OF TRANSCENDENCE, GREEK AND BIBLICAL

We begin to see already, then, that the Greek idea of transcendence, without which the tradition of Christian theology would be unthinkable, was rooted in the moral-political condition of humanity and, more particularly, in certain experiences and concerns of the Greek polis. Let us briefly consider in this connection Thomas Pangle's *Political Philosophy and the God of Abraham*,[1] a very penetrating interrogation of the political roots of Greek philosophical transcendence. Just as, for Pangle, biblical piety is rooted in the patriarchal family, so, he argues, philosophy springs from the city's "radical subordination of many or most individual goods that are ordinarily associated with happiness," a purification of "preoccupation with corporeal, familial, and mundane needs." The call beyond family, Pangle further argues, introduces the prospect of "passionate" male friendship, which itself "is ultimately transcended, in and by an ascent toward the divine spiritual self-sufficiency that is the dimly beheld highest aspiration of the life of the city."[2] The very idea of divine self-sufficiency in the Platonic antecedents of Christian theology appears then to be an extension of the city's virtue and of virtuous friendship, and thus an inherently politically conditioned interpretation of transcendence or of human possibility. This is to say that the goods of family, those "corporeal, familial, and mundane needs," are sacrificed, first in the name of the city and its idea of manly nobility, and then, in the next higher level of refinement, in view of the goods of male (and possibly homosexual) friendship, and then, in a final stage of ascent, in the name of the philosopher's "divine" self-sufficiency. The city's aspiration toward self-sufficiency is said to be realized only in the purely intellectual satisfactions of the philosopher, whose mind at its best participates in the self-sufficiency of a purely intellectual and impassive God (Aristotle's "self-thinking thought"). As Pangle's teacher, Allan Bloom, has written, "The subjection of the family to the ends of both the city and the intellect is a primary task of classical political philosophy."[3]

The Bible parts company with Plato's *Republic*, even proceeding in the completely opposite direction, to resolve the tension between the family and city, as scholars such as Allan Bloom have observed. From the biblical point of view, moral norms are rooted in the requirements of the family, and love of family is finally subsumed in love of God. The Bible teaches an "intense but severely limited eroticism" limited by the requirements of familial order, whereas the Greeks teach us to question the family for the sake of eros, "which in turn metamorphoses into the passion for free self-discovery." (Bloom apparently takes the Greek idea of divine intellectual self-sufficiency to be a figure of "free self-discovery.") Thus, while the Greeks demote the family and use the city as a stepping stone to an intellectual divinity, the Bible ignores the city and takes the family as a stepping stone to divinity, interpreting God (at least in the Old Testament) as a devoted but also commanding father.

For Thomas Pangle, biblical transcendence is finally incoherent, it seems, because one cannot make human sense of the motive for obedience to the commands of the biblical God. Pangle examines this problem through a very searching reading of the story of the Akedah, Abraham's binding of Isaac. For Pangle, either Abraham knew that God would somehow avert or reverse Abraham's sacrifice (as the writer to the Hebrews suggests in Hebrews 11), and so it was not really a sacrifice, or Abraham was ready to sacrifice all his hopes to a God whose command, therefore, becomes wholly unintelligible. It seems biblical obedience must either be purely calculating and thus not at all ennobling, or else it is simply mad and humanly meaningless.

It seems difficult to fault the logic of Pangle's analysis, but Leon Kass's reading of the Akedah reveals another possibility, though one not easily reduced to simple logic or calculation:

> God does *not finally* require that men choose between the love of your own and godliness. Though it took a horrible episode to demonstrate this fact, harmonization is possible between a reverence for God (who loves righteousness) and the love of one's family or nation, rightly understood. God, the awesome and transcendent power, wants not the transcendence of life but rather its sanctification—in all the mundane activities and relations of everyday life. Thus, God displays Himself to be exactly the sort of god whom one could not only fear-and-revere, but even come to love—"with all thy heart, with all thy soul, and with all thy might."[4]

Pangle's logic, or, more precisely, his rationalist teleology, cannot account for the intrinsically relational character of biblical transcendence. In a word, he cannot account for love as a good that enriches the lover only when he releases his rational hold on it, his claim of secure possession. He cannot account for the possibility that biblical sacrifice does not leave behind "the mundane activities and relations of everyday life" but redeems and sanctifies them.

The dynamism of mainstream Christian theology may be said to derive from the infinite task of holding together these Greek and biblical understandings of transcendence. Nowhere are the magnificent travails of this project more visible than in the writings of the greatest of Christian Platonists, Augustine of Hippo. There are no more poignant moments in *The City of God* than those where Augustine must confront the Christian limits of his Platonism as concerns the questions of time, the body, and interpersonal love.

Augustine cannot ignore Paul's warnings against "useless" and "misleading" philosophy (see Colossians 2:8), but he straightforwardly exempts the Platonists from such warnings. "These philosophers have been raised above the rest by a glorious reputation they so thoroughly deserve; and they recognized that no material object can be God . . .

that nothing changeable can be the supreme God . . . that in every mutable being the form which determines its being can only come from him who truly *is* because he exists immutably. For him . . . life is [not] something other than intelligence."[5] In fact, he goes so far as to suggest that the mysterious name for himself God gives to Moses, "I am HE WHO IS," is the source of the Platonic notion of a pure intelligible Being.[6] But further on, he must confront the Platonists' contempt for the body, on which basis they proudly dismiss central Christian doctrines of incarnation and resurrection.

The superiority of Christianity over Platonism, Augustine argues, lies in its *universality*: "This is the religion which contains the universal way for the liberation of the soul since no soul can be freed by any other way. . . . How could [Platonism] be a genuine philosophy if it did not offer this way? For what is a universal way for the liberation of the soul if it is not a way by which all souls are liberated, and therefore the only way for any soul?"[7]

Any true way to the liberation of the human soul, Augustine is convinced, must be a universal way; that is, it must, at least in principle, be available to human beings as such and not only to a few philosophers. Clearly, the force of this argument is not a matter of logic, for there can be no logical objection to the proposition that only certain superior human beings can be raised above the limitations of the human condition. The force of the argument lies rather in a sense that there is something of eternal significance in human existence itself, and not only in the perfection of the rational faculty but something in our humanity as such that must have some eternal significance and destiny. Human beings have a spiritual dignity that does not depend on their being philosophers and is not limited to rationality per se. There is something in all human beings—that is, in each and every particular individual human being, and not only in the activity of philosophical reflection—that transcends the limitations of the human condition. Thus, the deep meaning of Augustine's "universality" is not confined to the imperative of including in principle all human beings; such a formal universality must be understood as derivative from a qualitative or substantive universality, a sense of the dignity of the human person as a whole: Christian salvation, Augustine thus writes, "purifies the whole man, not just the intellectual part. . . . The Savior took upon himself the man *in his entirety*."[8]

To affirm the dignity of particular individuals in their whole selves is to embrace the eternal significance of the body and of temporality. The Platonist identification of perfection with immutability implies that nothing important can really change. Time must be considered as cyclical, and any embodied soul that goes up must eventually come down. There can be no radical temporal rupture in the order of reality.

Augustine thus confronts the necessity of a sharp break with the most basic premises of Platonist intellectualism, although he is never able fully to question the Platonic origins of his own conception of God as immutable and impassive self-sufficiency. Christianity insists, Augustine points out, that there can be something radically new under the sun, that "Christ died once for all for our sins . . . [and] we shall be with the Lord forever." The incarnation breaks through the eternal cycle of reality and produces a linear history of the soul, leading to an everlasting salvation *of the individual person*. Augustine recognizes the logical force of the Platonist insistence on the immutability of the structure of reality, but he does not believe human beings can live by such a "truth." Platonists measure God by the standard of human reason, he argues, but "our faith ought to laugh at these theories [of] 'walking in circles.'"[9] The cyclic theory implies that "our misery should never have an end. . . . If it were true, it would be more prudent to suppress the truth, nay, wiser to be in ignorance—I am trying to find words to express what I feel."[10] That is, philosophy as a way of life cannot stand by itself; the attitude of resigning one's personal hopes to the idea of an impersonal necessity, of contemplating the idea of an eternity utterly indifferent to our integral humanity, and thus of regarding the meaning of life as a learning to die (and never to live again), is not, Augustine thinks, viable in practice.

This critique of the cyclical view of time clearly strikes at the heart of Platonism. And it implies a rejection of the Platonist understanding of the body as essentially base and inherently corruptible. Against this view, Augustine argues that the body is not a prison or a punishment, but a gift or a blessing.[11] Whereas for the Platonists, the ideas of body and corruption are inseparable, Augustine maintains that the problem is not the body itself but "corruptible body." Turning the tables on the Platonists, he argues that they are "carnal" in their rejection of the body; that is, what separates us from God is not our corporeality but the very pride of reason in its disdain for the body. In these passages on time, the body, and the salvation of the whole person, Augustine reaches his most intense awareness of his distance from the core assumptions of Platonism. He is too intellectually invested in Platonism, however, to complete the rupture; he continues, for the most part, to think in essentially Platonic categories. Most notably, Augustine continues to conceive God in terms of Platonic categories of immateriality, immutability, and impassiveness.

To summarize my discussion so far of transcendence in its Hellenic and biblical forms, eros evokes an elusive but meaningful longing for some fulfillment, some completion in a better world, or some rest in the soul's true home. In (Thomas Pangle's) Platonism, this eros is best understood as directed toward a fulfillment in the philosopher's comprehensive self-knowledge, which is at the same time a knowledge of the (problem of the) whole or of the home of the self, at least insofar as the self is a soul and has a home; such knowledge requires a radical abandonment of ordinary human hopes pertaining to love and family. In Leon Kass's reading of the Jewish Bible, on the contrary, the longing for divine righteousness is reconciled through sacrifice with the ordinary goods of family and posterity. The founders of Christian theology, including, notably, Augustine, made the momentous choice (already arguably indicated by the author of the Gospel of John's identification of the Christ with the logos) of grafting the personal understanding of divinity and thus of salvation onto a Greek philosophic conception of eros as directed toward a purely intellectual good. Inevitably, then, historic Christianity has found itself tasked with the challenge of holding together this Greek understanding of the good as rational impersonal necessity with the biblical elevation of love (typified especially by familial affections and bonds) to eminent status in the conception of the righteous and good life.[12]

LOVE, THE PERSONAL LOGOS, AND MORAL AGENCY

A more Protestant strategy for the management of eros can be found in the influential work of Denis de Rougemont, *Love in the Western World*. De Rougemont offers an uncompromising critique of eros from the standpoint of Christian brotherly love or "agape."

In his analysis of "The Tristan Myth," de Rougemont depicts eros as an abstract, lawless, and finally nihilistic passion. Tristan and Isolde, on close inspection, do not, in fact, love each other or any real person, but are driven by blind passion that finally considers itself more real than the world, beyond the world, and thus beyond good and evil. The lover is finally a mere moment in a vaulting and abstract passion that makes of all that is real (including the lover) an obstacle or obstruction to be overcome in a boundless quest that can end only in the decision for death over life; love is the "active passion of darkness."[13] Eros can find no stable footing and no satisfying fulfillment in the actual world, and so its essence is fundamentally negative and destructive.

Christian agape must thus rescue pagan eros, and marital love, properly understood, is thus to be understood as the most exemplary expression of agape. Real, constructive love, love in action or "active love," is neither a passion nor a calculation but a choice—the choice of fidelity or keeping faith, the choice to share one's life with another. It is through such fidelity that we become persons, that we freely enter into the particular, finite world into which the Creator has placed us.

De Rougemont's alternative to eros is beautifully set forth, but its loveliness ought not to conceal from us the sacrifice that it requires. The author observes that there is something "absurd" and inhuman in the fidelity that grounds marriage as an expression of Christian agape. We become persons through a free act of belief that cannot be explained in terms of any higher good (such as contemplation) but must be embraced as an expression of obedience: to be in love is not a choice but a duty. The Christian's fidelity to marital bonds is of a piece with his or her acceptance, as a created being, of the limitations of our finite existence. "It is on the earth that we must love"; we accept this sacrifice of eros "in *obedience* to the Eternal."[14]

De Rougemont observed that "the pledge exchanged in marriage is the very type of a serious act because it is a pledge given once and for all. The irrevocable alone is serious."[15] The question is, How are we to regard the deepest engagements of our mortal existence not only as serious but somehow as *good*, as bound up with our eternal happiness?

The sanctification through sacrifice of the "mundane activities and relations of everyday life" that Leon Kass understood to be the central promise of biblical piety reminds me of a response the great

French intellectual historian Rémi Brague gave to a student's question at Brigham Young University concerning the eternal significance of the family. Brague ventured on this occasion that, since our memories of this earthly existence will be with us in eternity, there is a sense in which the precious goods of family endure forever. This, in turn, recalls a passage in Marilynne Robinson's exquisite epistolary novel *Gilead*. The fictional writer, Reverend Ames, is addressing his very young son in letters the son will be able to understand only some years after his father's death:

> I feel sometimes as if I were a child who opens its eyes on the world once and sees amazing things it will never know any names for and then has to close its eyes again. I know this is all mere apparition compared to what awaits us [in heaven], but it is only lovelier for that. There is human beauty in it. And I can't believe that, when we have all been changed and put on incorruptibility, we will forget our fantastic condition of mortality and impermanence, the great bright dream of procreating and perishing that meant the whole world to us. In eternity this world will be Troy, I believe, and all that has passed here will be the epic of the universe, the ballad they sing in the streets. Because I don't imagine any reality putting this one in the shade entirely, and I think piety forbids me to try.[16]

Further on, Ames's best friend and fellow minister Boughton offers this reflection on the meaning of "heaven": "Mainly I just think about the splendors of the world and multiply by two. I'd multiply by ten or twelve if I had the energy. But two is much more than sufficient for my purposes."[17]

The fictional John Ames's proposition of a fundamental continuity between earth and heaven, the temporal and the transcendent, recalls a remarkable moment in Homer's *Odyssey*. Odysseus might have lingered forever in the embrace of the divine Calypso, but he felt that he and the mortal Penelope belonged to one another: "Goddess," replied Ulysses, "do not be angry with me about this. I am quite aware that my wife Penelope is nothing like so tall or so beautiful as yourself. She is only a woman, whereas you are an immortal. Nevertheless, I want to get home, and can think of nothing else."[18] Personal love is defined by a fundamentally noninstrumental, nonteleological, and therefore infinitely mysterious attachment to an imponderably unique individual person. But personal love, considered as an active virtue, requires or projects a teleological context; to act implies some understanding of what is good, for the lover and for the beloved. Radically personal love and the generality and intelligibility inherent in purposive action must somehow be held together.

This is not the place to attempt a historical review of the problem of the personal and the intelligible in Christian theology,[19] but we can learn much in this connection from a brief consideration of the teaching of the late former pope Benedict XVI (formerly Joseph Ratzinger) on the meaning of the Logos in Christianity.

The prologue to the Gospel of John, Ratzinger reminded us, already in his early *Introduction to Christianity* (1968), put "the concept of Logos . . . at the very center of our Christian faith in God." "Logos" means "word" or "reason," he explained: "The God who is Logos guarantees the intelligibility of the world, the intelligibility of our existence, reason's accord with God, and God's accord with reason." Paradoxically, though, he adds that since God's understanding "infinitely surpasses ours," his reason "may . . . often appear to be darkness." Still, "reason can speak about God, it must speak about God, or else it cuts itself short."[20] For Benedict, then, God is somehow both continuous with reason or logos as human beings know and experience these ideas, yet also, in some sense, infinitely beyond our understanding. It is possible and meaningful for us mortals to speak about God because, in some way, God is speech/reason, and at the same time, "there is relationship within God himself."[21] We can speak of God reasonably and relate to God personally, we may conclude, because God is both logos and a person. In my late friend Peter Lawler's pithy formulation, God is "personal logos."

Returning decades later, as Benedict XVI, to the idea of "logos" in what is known as his "Regensburg Address" of 2006, the pope contrasted (controversially, in the event) Muhammad's idea of God as "absolutely transcendent" and therefore beyond all "our categories, even that of rationality," with the Christian integration of faith and reason. He proposed a "profound harmony between what is Greek in the best sense of the word and the biblical understanding of faith in God." The essence of this understanding comes down to this: "God acts with logos." Thus, the "Hellenization" of Christianity was neither an accident nor a violation of Christianity's essence; the intermingling of "Biblical faith and Greek inquiry" stems rather from an "intrinsic necessity."[22]

Benedict traces challenges to this fruitful intermingling from the "impenetrable voluntarism" that arose within late medieval Christian theology to three phases of a movement for "dehellenization" that began with the Reformation of the sixteenth century. Most notable for us is the second stage of dehellenization, best represented by the thought of Adolf von Harnack. The central idea of this stage was to recover "the man Jesus and . . . his simple message" from beneath "the accretions of theology." This dehellenized Jesus proved to be "the father of a humanitarian moral message" that was understood to be in "harmony with modern reason." For Benedict, therefore, the gospel, when unnaturally severed from its Greek complement, risks devolving into the all-too-familiar, if finally incoherent, partnership of dogmatic scientism and humanitarian moralism.[23]

My approach in this book is obviously broadly in sympathy with Benedict XVI's impressive effort to hold together Jerusalem and Athens under the master idea of a personal logos. The difficulty, however, is precisely the tension or the mystery inherent in this theological formulation. It would be a mistake to imagine that the sheer verbal conjunction "personal" + "logos" somehow renders clear the condition of the human being in relation to the whole of which he is somehow just a part yet, in another sense, drawn to the possibility of communion with the whole. "Personal logos" must be respected as an aporia that reminds us of the partly clear and partly mysterious character of our existence, a distillation of the most "fundamental and permanent problems" (Strauss).[24] But this is not to gainsay Benedict's proposition that this fundamental problem is also, in a way, the most fundamental answer, or the best touchstone of an answer to the human condition. There is perhaps no better epitome of the elusive yet substantive meaning of all things than this proposition of an ultimate, immutable reality that is somehow open to and responsive to the deepest longings of the particular beings we are. We can see, then, how the fundamental *problem* distilled in the "personal logos" can, in a way, serve us as a fundamental *answer*, or let us say, as a touchstone of fundamental *practical* guidance.

The term "practical" is by no means secondary in this formulation. As suggested by Manent's critique above of the "hypertrophy of theory" or the "tyranny of the explicit,"[25] an ultimate, architectonic concept such as "personal logos" is always at risk of being overtheorized at the hands of ecclesiastical theologians or ambitious intellectuals and thus becoming sterile and instrumental to the authority of one or another system of thought. One might characterize the danger or the temptation in the following simple way. On the one hand, the personal might be subordinated to the logos, with the result that Christianity is reduced to the status of a junior partner to an intellectualist Platonism or Neoplatonism, with its ruling idea of a rational-impersonal-necessity. Here, the Christian idea of "contemplation" risks becoming overhellenized in a *theoretical* sense and tilting decisively toward the primacy of sheer intelligibility. On the other hand, the modern "rationalist" philosopher or intellectual tends to embrace the standpoint of the human person, all desires and passions included, and reduce logos to a mathematical construct, projecting an understanding of ultimate reality as a pure object of human mastery for all-too-human ends. I conclude that the complementarity between Athens and Jerusalem must not be pressed to yield a final and comprehensive theoretical system but rather must be sustained and, as it were, "kept in play" by vigilant attunement to its practical implications.

Such attunement to practical implications could not be more evident than in Benedict XVI's rich and nuanced discussion of the problem of love in his first encyclical, *Deus Caritas Est*. Here, Benedict shows how the combining of "personal" and "logos" entails or is bound up with a kind of synthesis of agape and eros. *Eros* (a word that appears only twice in the Bible, both usages in the Greek Old Testament) designates a love that is both "worldly" and "ascending."[26] It may be called "worldly" because it is "self-seeking" and because it tends to "a sinking in the intoxication of happiness." Eros, we may say, seeks the fulfillment or wholeness of the self or the completeness of the soul. Eros seeks the consummation of "the same." But "seeking" here is the operative term: since the self-identity of the same is ever out of reach, eros is ecstatic, ever seeking its happy fulfillment. What we might then call an ecstatic selfishness accounts for the promiscuously intoxicating quality of pagan eros (399). But it is the seeking or searching quality of eros, I conclude from Benedict's analysis, that makes possible the synthesis he envisions with the *sacrificial* and other-regarding quality of agape. "True eros tends to rise 'in ecstasy' toward the divine, to lead us beyond ourselves; yet for this very reason, it calls for a path of ascent, renunciation, purification, and healing" (398). This "ascent" then meets the path of a kind of "descent": "Love now becomes a concern and care for the other. No longer is it self-seeking, a sinking into the intoxication of happiness; instead it seeks the good of the beloved: it becomes renunciation and it is ready, even willing, for sacrifice" (399).

The purification of eros, which requires a renunciation of the selfish, intoxicating ecstasy of pagan eroticism, is not at all a renunciation of the body or of the embodied particularity of human persons: "By contrast with an indeterminate, 'searching' love, this word [agape] expresses the experience of a love which involves a real discovery of the other, moving beyond [eros's] selfish character" (399). The "elevation" is also love's "definitive" quality—its embrace of the individuality or "particularity" of our humanity; eros redeemed by agape elevates individuality to eternity: true, divine love is "definite . . . both in the sense of exclusivity (this particular person alone) and in the sense of being 'forever'" (399). This is why "love between man and woman, where body and soul are inseparably joined," provides a privileged "glimpse" of the "promise of happiness," of that "beatitude for which our *whole being* yearns" (398; emphasis added). This love is in no way "cut off from the complex fabric of human life" or "detached from the vital relations fundamental to human existence" in some "world apart" (400). And this love, which, rightly understood, is both eros and agape, this definitive yet ongoing "real discovery of the other," is one "where body and soul are inseparably joined" (396). "Man is truly himself," Benedict writes further, "when his body and soul are intimately united; the challenge of eros can be said to be truly overcome when this unification is achieved" (398).

The unification of man and woman signifies the unification of body and soul and the transcending of the dichotomy between eros and agape. True love, or charity, is both ascending and descending (400), of both soul and body, and is at once a sacrifice or renunciation and a fulfillment or beatitude—a fulfillment that is not self-enclosed or "inward-looking" (399) but, as expressed in the evangelist's logos, ever open to, in communion with, another.[27] True love honors both the character of the same and that of the other in the human orientation toward the good. Thus, Benedict clearly refuses the "antithesis" (400) between eros and agape that forms the basis of de Rougemont's reflections. "When the two dimensions are cut off from one another, the result is a caricature or at least an impoverished form of love" (401). "Man cannot live by oblative, descending love alone. He cannot always give; he must also receive. Anyone who wishes to give love must also receive love *as a gift*" (emphasis added). And this antithesis is not rejected only in its application to human beings: "God loves, and his love may certainly be called eros, yet it is also totally agape" (402).

Thus, "receiving as a gift," the more "ascending" or fulfilling dimension of love, may be designated by the venerable term "contemplation" (as in the Pastoral Rule of Gregory the Great). But, then, it must immediately be noted that the object of contemplation is not an object, a Being reducible to self-identity and self-sufficiency, however elevated. The idea of God as Love, Benedict writes, may be said to be "a strictly metaphysical image of God: God is the absolute and ultimate source of all being." But the very meaning of "contemplation" is correlative to an understanding of the Being to be "contemplated." And that meaning here, in Pope Benedict's first encyclical, is surely far removed from the classical or Neoplatonic aspiration to a final intellectual possession of a ground of rational, impersonal necessity. The "strictly metaphysical *image* of God" as "the Logos, primordial reason," must be held together with our understanding of God as "at the same time a lover with all the passion of a true love. Eros is thus supremely ennobled, yet at the same time it is so purified as to become one with agape" (403; emphasis added).

ETERNAL GOOD AND INFINITE SACRIFICE

The Catholic teaching represented here by Pope Benedict XVI's reflections on the personal logos attempts a reconciliation or even a synthesis of the dimensions of love represented by pagan eros and Christian agape, contemplative fulfillment and open or relational personality. The Protestant teaching tends rather to require the suppression of eros in favor of the duty of the embrace of the finite conditions of our created existence, including the imperative of love motivated by nothing but love. To be sure, the (Protestant) Christian's embrace of the actual, particular world of faithful marital personhood through the renunciation of the infinite longings of eros seems to have its inherent attractions, but to resist the appeal of eros it must finally be defended, in the Protestant perspective, not as an alternative fulfillment of natural human longings, not through any intelligible, representable connection with an understanding of the whole, but as an act of obedience and of faith, a kind of this-worldly asceticism in which the inchoate sense of higher purpose that emerges from natural human existence is sacrificed on the altar of radical transcendence.

How might the conflict between eros and agape, between the greatest hope for eternity and the greatest sacrifice to infinity, be reconceived as a productive tension? Such a reconceiving would not wish to replace the broadly Catholic vision, in which eros is sublimated into a residually but still fundamentally intellectualist, contemplative conception of human fulfillment, with the broadly Protestant sensibility that favors a sacrificial agape and the consequent humble or mute acceptance of the duties of finitude. Instead, the productive tension—or, if you will, coprimordiality of eros and agape—suggests a cosmology and soteriology that would project creative and procreative desires upon an eternity understood as open possibility as well as consummating fulfillment; it would conceive transcendence in terms both of the other and of the same. Such an eternity would be understood at once as free and as ordered by immutable laws enacted through divinely guaranteed covenants; it would imagine or configure the highest good or heaven as in some deep way grounded in and continuous with the concrete though imperfect experiences of familial and communitarian love expressed in shared *projects* of eternal significance.

Eternity without love is an impersonal abstraction, an unlivable, self-enclosed divinity, Aristotle's God as self-thinking thought, the ultimate reality conceived as utterly indifferent to the hopes and fears of the actual human person. Personal love, on the other hand, is attuned to the mysterious individuality of the person; it is radically individuating—and therefore, being translated into a pure concept or project, it is, in its own way, radically abstract and universalist. Love of "the other," an agape severed from any bond with an intelligible eternal good of the soul, is not a stable idea, not a concept that can guide action or inform a concrete understanding of a good life. De Rougemont's love as pure Protestant duty to commandment must be parasitic on a residual "Catholic" hope for the soul's fulfillment in eternity. Without some trace of some such hope for the soul's good, the ethical imperative of "love," the "infinite" claims (Levinas) of the other, can tend only toward one of two possible reductions: the mysterious, radically unmotivated sacrifice of the good either (1) yields the radically individualized finitude of Heidegger's *Dasein*, human existence reduced to an arbitrary "thrown project," which can be taken up only as a fateful task assigned by a particular "history," or (2) yields a formally universal humanitarian project of "love" emptied of higher purpose in which all that is left of the human person is finally only as the vanishing point of a radically liberated individual freedom or "authenticity." (Jean-Paul Sartre's existentialist Marxism, radically individualist and radically collectivist and historicist, is thus not an anomaly.)

I propose that only purposive action, or moral agency "under God and the laws" (Tocqueville),[28] can provide the essential, life-giving mediation between generalizing rationality and individuating personality. Only the mediation of active virtue can prevent each of these extremes from collapsing into and fusing with the other. Practical moral agency situates the engagement of the person as a rational being with a lawful reality at the heart of individual personhood; it therefore binds love to liberty under law. Love for persons *as agents* is neither passive nor world-transformative but both lawful and world-constituting. Moreover, ultimate truth, in this view, is not understood to be impersonal but, rather, to open upon an arena of active personal participation.

Action is a personal claim on enduring truth. The integration of intellect and personhood is not a philosophical or theological construction but is already at work in the microstructure of agency, what Manent calls the grammar of action itself—that is, in a practical instrumentality that is inseparably joined to a self-affirming and stable nobility, which in turn holds itself open to something other than itself, to something and someone beyond, something and someone divine.

Finally, we must add to these already expansive claims the following: the mediation of moral agency can never be wholly exempted from the particular context of action under a common authority—that is, from the political and sometimes ecclesiastical context in which choice operates. The lawful context in which the grammar of action is always already embedded is inevitably conditioned by or interwoven with practically authoritative norms of a given community or of interwoven communities. Moral agency aspires to affirm its meaning within a horizon of transcendent eternity, but this aspiration is always grounded in and ineluctably colored by the concrete institutional setting in which the aspiration of transcendence arises. "The laws of moral analogy," as referenced by Tocqueville,[29] hold together time and eternity, practical action and infinite longings, and neither can sustain its meaning without this mediating bond with its other pole. Hope in the goodness of eternity depends upon a bond with practical moral agency, with purposive action on a human scale in a visible community. Agency is necessarily moral-political agency. And love of persons must not be severed from love of the natural beings we call humans—that is, the beings who are bidden to be responsible agents in contexts always defined by mediated moral law as well as natural necessities.

Moral agency in a concrete community is the essential complement to the idea of love as the gift of the self to the other.

MORAL AGENCY AND FIRST PHILOSOPHY OR THEOLOGY

Truth must be not only in some way available to human beings but also in some way meaningful to us as human beings. If philosophy is the most rigorous and unrestrained pursuit of truth, then it cannot ignore the imperative to articulate a place for the truth-seeker within the whole of the truth that is sought. This is, of course, the imperative that Socrates was heeding when, as praised by Cicero, he brought philosophy down from the heavens to consider politics and ethics. One must also acknowledge the premise of Heidegger's powerful investigations in *Being and Time*—that is, that an understanding of Being, or fundamental reality, must give a central place to the being, "Dasein," for whom Being is a question of fundamental concern. (Alas, Heidegger resolutely severs Dasein from practical human nature.) A philosophy—and I will venture to add, a theology—that has not considered the human source, origin, and character, the ground of possibility, of our interest in the heavens or the whole has missed its calling, not only morally or religiously but rationally and philosophically.

This statement of an inescapably human ground of any possible meaningful speech about the heavens or about the whole is the furthest thing possible from the affirmation of some purely immanent, "rationalist," "naturalistic," or "materialist" humanism: I say *inescapably* human; I do *not* say simply or exclusively human or all-too-human. If the human is not always already in some way—a way that is fundamental and ineradicable—oriented toward what is divine, what is eternally good, true, and beautiful, however vulnerable we know this orientation to be to distortion, corruption, effacement, subversion, and perversion, then we quite simply have nothing to talk about beyond the technical management of our material needs (as if those can be defined and limited on their own terms), and we are not the rational animals in between gods and beasts whom Aristotle described or whom he invited us to be. It is because we are speaking beings who cannot, without utterly failing the human vocation, escape the imperative to order our lives with a view to some higher purpose, however dimly discerned, that we must be open to the possibility of and the calling to some manner of participation in a divine and eternal meaning that lies at the very heart of being *and of our human being*.

Any philosophy or theology worthy of the name and true to its calling must then, I propose, be attentive to its own conditions of possibility—that is, to the problem and the promise of the human spirit's openness to the eternal whole. Reflection on the humanity of philosophy, or the place of human being with respect to being or to the whole, is bound up at once with what is most urgent and what is highest for the calling of thinking in its fullness: such reflection is philosophy's first duty in its essential pursuit of rigor and probity; and this reflection is also inseparable from philosophy's ultimate and highest calling in sparking and sustaining human openness to the divine. First philosophy cannot spare itself the labor of self-reflection, and, thus, of reflection on the human sources and conditions of philosophy.

The theme of "first philosophy" finds its classic source in a text of Aristotle's that has come to be known as the *Metaphysics*. Here I can honor this origin only by briefly noting the fecundity of its aporias.[30] Aristotle invites us to envisage a science that would be primary both in relation to an ontological order and in the order of human knowledge—at once the noblest knowledge in itself and the most effective for human beings—a science that would crown the best life for human beings and that would at the same time provide a foundation for the unity of all the sciences, a common summit of choice and necessity, practice and theory. But an ambiguity unsettles this conception of first philosophy from the beginning: Would such a science be found in theology, the science of the highest beings, divine beings described by Aristotle as "separate," or rather, would it be found in what we have learned to call metaphysics—that is, the science of being as being, of being in general, and thus of all beings? To remove this difficulty would require overcoming the distinction between theology and metaphysics, and this Aristotle never claimed to have accomplished.

The result of this difficulty is an apparently irremediable gap between what is first in itself and what is first for us, for human beings. This is the gap that Nietzsche allows to open to an infinite chasm in his absolute antagonism between "truth" and "life." Here we stand upon the Platonic premise that Nietzsche rejected—that is, that the tension between truth and life must not be considered absolute, that the imperative of truth cannot be truly conceived or authentically heeded without solicitude for the meaning of life, and that the meaning of life—and in the first instance of that form of life from which we must begin, human life—is a life inescapably oriented toward or concerned with (or haunted by, or fleeing from) truth.

"Theology" might be derisively defined as the human pretension to speak of things beyond human capacity. But if we define philosophy as the love of a wisdom we never fully possess, the eros that longs to articulate just what it is we do not know, then the line between the pretensions of theology and the modesty of a Socratic philosophy becomes very fine indeed.

Aristotle's rhetoric in the last book of the *Nicomachean Ethics* may be taken as exemplary on this point: if the contemplation of divine truth indeed surpasses our humanity as such, it is nevertheless the case that "the divine in us" allows us to conceive the possibility of rising to a participation in the divine. This temptation to overreach our humanity is, it seems, inherent in our humanity. Simply to coincide with our own being, to fail to stretch and strain toward some good, some truth, some beauty that exceeds us, is to sink beneath our humanity. The two meanings of "first philosophy" cannot be held in absolute separation. The love of truth cannot be divorced from the truth of love, of our erotic interest in the truth as the possibility of our own fulfillment.

The main point of the present book is to propose a further consideration, or a third focal point of truth, beyond the love of truth and the truth of love. This third part of a triangulation on truth is the standpoint of human action or moral agency, of the active production of good in a practical world shared with other human beings. The truth and love that orient our attempts to honor our humanity cannot be divorced from what we know of the necessity and of the good of actual human souls in actual human communities. In this way, we might understand Aristotle's proposal, in book 1 of the *Nicomachean Ethics*, of what appears to be another conception of first philosophy, neither theological nor metaphysical but practical. It is no accident that he calls this "architectonic" science neither "philosophy" nor "ethics" but "politics."

CHAPTER TEN

The Claims of Subjectivity and the Limits of Politics

If man were completely ignorant of himself, he would not be at all poetic; for one cannot depict that of which one has no idea. If he saw himself clearly, his imagination would remain idle and would have nothing to add to the picture. But man is uncovered enough to perceive something of himself and veiled enough so that the rest sinks into impenetrable darkness, into which he plunges constantly and always in vain, in order to succeed in grasping himself.
—Tocqueville, *Democracy in America*

All who remain enamored of the genuine greatness of man should unite and do combat against [pantheism].
—Tocqueville, *Democracy in America*

MICHAEL DAVIS ON GREEK TRUTH AND MINENESS

Michael Davis's meditation on Aristotle's *De anima* in his *The Soul of the Greeks* is a subtle and penetrating effort to hold together subject and object by reflecting on the puzzle of an impersonal truth claimed by a personal being, the tension between truth and mineness. His reflections are a worthy complement to Leo Strauss's effort to excavate a natural understanding of humanity from beneath the sediments of Christianity and modernity.

Davis is very attentive to what might be called the necessarily performative or even existential dimension of philosophy—that is, of the soul's attempts at or movements toward self-understanding. The soul exhibits and enacts itself in the act of trying to understand itself. The soul is an act, but not simply and purely an act (if indeed the notion of a pure "act" has any meaning), because it has a form and limits, a structure, and, if you will, a "nature." The soul cannot be known as we think a simple object can be known, but it has a kind of form and limits that come somewhat into view, however elusively, in the soul's attempts at self-reflection. The soul's natural desire to know is necessarily a desire to embrace or grasp and thus, in a way, to be all things, and yet in this very desire, the soul is irreducibly other than the whole it seeks to know. But then the whole must somehow include the knowing and desiring soul, and so the soul's exceptional way of being cannot be simply other than the being of the whole.[1]

Davis proposes his unfolding of classical Greek insights concerning the soul as an alternative to Christian and post-Christian ideas. The Greek way is proposed as "a more natural way" or "a more natural beginning" that can help us break through the obstacle to clarity that the Christian tradition represents. Drawing upon a rich and provocative metaphor that Leo Strauss adapted from Plato, Davis suggests that Christianity has dug us into "a cave beneath a cave," from which the Greeks, and perhaps only the Greeks, provide the necessary tools for digging ourselves out—for acceding to the natural cave from which, then, presumably, an ascent toward the sun becomes at least possible (2).

Davis recognizes, though, that what Christianity wrought was not unrelated to the soul's actual nature—and how could it be, after all, and still appeal so powerfully to so many people over so many centuries? Our natural awareness of ourselves as other than causally determined things, as "splendidly, if mysteriously, free" and therefore as "morally responsible agents," lies at the bottom of the idea of the soul as "immaterial, atemporal, and free" and as having some destination beyond this "vale of tears" that emerges in Plato's *Phaedo*, for example, before it is developed in Christian theology. It appears, therefore, that the Christian idea of the soul, centuries' sedimentation of which Davis proposes to excavate, may be one-sided, an elaboration of a partial truth, but it cannot be without connection to nature. We must note, though, that we are now digging down toward what we hope are natural sources of ideas and notions, but the question whether we have access to any pure point of nature from which we can start to "ascend" without beginning to accrue our own layers of sediment is not clear.

The soul is naturally alienated from the world but also somehow at home in the world. This connectedness between the soul and the world is to be understood, Davis proposes, "in the end as philosophy." Davis's idea of philosophy does not seem to exclude the poets, and he seems to find as much understanding of the nature of the soul in poets as in philosophers, if, indeed, there is finally any difference; perhaps we are to understand that "philosophy" privileges the soul's connectedness to the world and that poetry privileges the soul's *existence* as problematically other. But can philosophy articulate this connectedness without drawing upon politically authorized ways in which "we differentiate among kinds of souls"—in which we rank souls as better or worse, higher or lower? Is not the idea of philosophy itself bound up with a necessarily partisan conception of "actualized potentiality"? "There is thus," Davis writes, "a political aspect to soul"—and is there not, I would then ask, a political aspect also to philosophy, and not only to its beginnings (4–5)? Davis indeed writes, following his teacher, the great classicist Seth Benardete, that "political philosophy is the eccentric core of philosophy." But is philosophy's very center not then implicated in this partisan core?

One way to understand Christianity's critique of philosophy would be to see the critique as an attempt to overcome this necessary partisanship of philosophy by positing, as Davis has suggested, some purely transcendent and atemporal soul with an otherworldly origin and destiny. To be more precise, one might say that Christianity attempts to overcome the essential partisanship of classical philosophy by radicalizing it, by pressing the insight that Davis shares with Christians (and with Heidegger, or the early Heidegger) that existence must lie somehow at the heart of being, that the whole would not be whole without its manifestation in human existence (or Dasein). Essential to the whole, on this view, is the existence not only of worldly beings but especially of un- or other-worldly beings such as we are: "But how is it possible for a being with a particular disposition or bent to be so self-effacing as to be 'somehow all beings'?" (22). Must not the good proper to my nature interfere with the truth of my awareness? Put differently, how is it possible for awareness to be "mine" and still "true"? Extending Davis's investigation, I would suggest that, for truth and mineness to be reconciled, it would have to be the case that my very mineness, my existence as a person, would have a correlate at the origins or peak of the whole. God would have to be a person, in other words, or, let us say, more cautiously, there would have to be something personal about the divine. There would have to be a *personal logos*. Deeper than Christian theological atemporality, therefore, is the Christian embrace of temporality and personality as lying at the heart of the meaning of the whole.

Of course, this Christian move is irreparably problematic as well, from a philosophical point of view, because the only "persons" we know are people, and we cannot really know what we are talking about when we say that the Creator and Sustainer of the whole is a "person." In any case, the dilemma inherent in the human soul—the tension between the need (as much intellectual as affective) for impersonal, eternally present, and cognizable meaning on the one hand and the need for temporal, personal meaning on the other hand—this tension is fated simply to be repeated in the gigantomachia of Christian theology: Is God the eternal necessity of reason, or the ineffable mystery of will?

Classical philosophy is *political* philosophy because, while conveying an awareness of the inherent tension of the soul that Davis so expertly dissects, it tends finally to ground the goodness of its own activity in a hierarchy of knowable goods necessarily "rooted in a particular tradition" (5) and therefore ultimately positing an intelligible eternal (impersonal) necessity. I by no means assume that this positing is dogmatic; in fact, I think it is, for philosophers, always knowingly political as well as poetically playful; the point, though, is that some such gesture is essential to the coherent articulation of classical philosophy, and to its coming into speech through a worldly self-affirmation. For example, when Aristotle says that "the friend is another self," he is no doubt aware, as Davis suggests, that it would be just as true to say that the self is another friend (74). But it remains the case that the coherence of Aristotle's discourse depends on privileging the self, the virtuous self, the soul of the philosopher, the self-sufficiency of the same as opposed to the relationality of other, as grounded finally in the philosopher's serene contemplation of an impersonal divinity.

Christian theology is both more and less partisan than classical, political philosophy: it posits another world, another universal city, where my individual existence and self-responsibility, and that of every human being, has eternal meaning in the design of a personal God whose love for me and mine is never dissolved into some impersonal necessity.

Christianity is fundamentally erotic, Davis sees, because its desire "includes within it a desire for the continuation of the being that is desiring—the soul as a self" (224). It is fundamentally relational, like "the beautiful itself"—although, to be sure, its theologians attempt to sever the ecstatic from what appears to be the logical implication of incompleteness and imperfection. Christianity wants to hold together the beauty of sacrifice with the good of fulfillment, to hold together the call of otherness and the satisfaction of self-possession. And who can blame it?

I would ask Mr. Davis, however: Does not classical political philosophy necessarily perform this same erotic tension between the same and the other, but from the other, thumotic direction? It affirms itself as the peak of the attempt of human beings "to gain control over their lives" (226). But it evokes erotically the beauty of sacrifice in its very affirmation of the good of fulfillment; it enacts incompleteness and personality as it affirms impersonal completeness, rational impersonal necessity. Thumos and eros cannot finally be separated, Davis suggests; what one aims at cannot be fully articulated any more than the other, and each, in a way, falls back on the other.

Davis seems to me not so much to have shown the superiority of the Greeks to the Christians (as he would wish) as to have brilliantly traced the fundamental aporia in which we must stand regarding the fundamental question of Athens/Jerusalem. Christianity, as much as political philosophy, begins in an insuperable (at least as far as we can know by nature) human experience; and political philosophy, as much as Christianity, cannot help putting a partisan stamp on our most fundamental experiences.

THE DIVINE APORIA

Davis concludes by exploring the possibility that Socrates provides a viable example of drawing life from the fundamental experience without being drawn along by it and therefore away from what is primary and originary: "For Socrates, love of himself means love of whoever draws him out of himself. He is, therefore, at once genuinely smitten and, at the same time, never altogether loyal. . . . The trick is apparently to allow yourself to be drawn out of yourself but not hold on to the image that draws you and threatens to trap you in a new version of yourself" (228). One might say that Davis's statement of the approach of classical philosophy attempts to ground human meaning, to "gain control" over one's life, not in a grasp of the self or in an actualization the self's inherent potential of a pure self-grasping, but rather in fidelity to a kind of primordial and evanescent moment in which the self necessarily produces some "image" of the whole. That is indeed some trick—and I mean this as a compliment: Davis seems to me to have identified very precisely what would be required to establish the supremacy of the classical viewpoint. In this his ambitions may surpass those of Leo Strauss, who coyly acknowledged philosophy's insuperably political springs as well as the answerability of the biblical humbling of human pride. But it is unclear whether it is possible to capture and be faithful to this "drawing out" without being effectively drawn to one or another figure of transcendence. And so I remain, I confess, more attracted to the possibility of being drawn out a little further still, toward the good or toward God, toward the logos of the personal, toward the ground of either an impersonal whole or a personal destiny or calling, subject then to the necessity of considering the road not taken. But then, is it not plausible that what draws me out is the personal logos?

Western thought would, in general, prove more fascinated by the notion of a first philosophy or theology than respectful of the aporia inherent in the personal interest in an impersonal truth, which Aristotle's ethical invocation of the divine seems to honor. In the case of theology, the revelation of a personal God who created and who loves the world—if the stories *and the witnesses* are to be believed—seems to remove any permanent obstacle to the hope of bringing together divinity and humanity, truth and mineness. However, as Nietzsche understood, such a revelation risks being interpreted in all-too-human terms, identifying salvation with relief from physical suffering and material need. Modern philosophic rationalism embraced without reserve such an interpretation of salvation, as we see in Descartes's effort to define divinity as available without remainder to human purposes, or rather to the project of mastering human necessities.

The love of truth untethered from practical goods and from the rank order in which such goods are naturally proposed, however inchoately, resolves to an "awareness of the fundamental problems" that cannot answer for the goodness of those problems.[2] The pride of philosophy then risks collapsing into the philosophic vanity that Augustine rightly deplores. The vacuum of purpose may then be filled by a project of material mastery: the thinker who would try to conceive the good of thinking apart from any natural goodness thereby adopts the standpoint of a pure subject transcending the world and thus in a position to maximize leverage upon the world, now reconceived as the pure object of his or her mastery.

The good indicated in the very "grammar of action" (Manent), or in what I have referred to as the microstructure of moral agency itself, provides the only touchstone by which we may honor both the love of truth and the truth of love. Moral agency is our best clue to understanding personal logos, our privileged point of access both to what is high and to what is universal. Only by returning to this touchstone can we resist succumbing to the reduction of divinity, or what is highest, to the service of universal humanity conceived as a lowest common denominator of necessity and desire. The following reflections on the idea of subjectivity in Tocqueville, Leo Strauss, and Emmanuel Levinas illustrate my claim that any viable understanding of eternal truth in relation to personal existence must accept the mediation of our moral-political condition.

MINENESS AS MODERN SUBJECTIVITY

The modern discussion of "mineness"—of the soul's relation to itself—centers on the concept of the "subject" or of "subjectivity." The term "subject," however, contains a deep and very revealing ambiguity. On the one hand, "subject" can suggest the desire for or claim to self-possession and self-transparency; on the other hand, it can refer to the determinism of the pair subject-object, the self's constitution as a subject over against an object, and vice versa. This epistemological pair subject/object can be seen to mirror the political configuration subject/state; the "punctual self" (the term is Charles Taylor's)[3] is not a soul and has no enduring content, and is thus "subject" to an "objective" power beyond its capacity to ground or to explain, except as a correlate of its own empty subjectivity. These apparently opposite connotations of "subject" and "subjectivity" are thus complicit: the claim to transparent subjective self-possession tends powerfully to accompany or to call forth a surrender of human agency to some nonrational power, whether naturalistic or divine.

I will argue, through engagements with Tocqueville, Strauss, and Emmanuel Levinas, that the only alternative to the abyss opened up by these complicit extremes is the soul's acceptance of the mediation of a politics and of a poetry respectful of the mutual dependence between the order of the soul and the order of the whole. We can never fully possess ourselves—that is, grasp our subjectivity immediately and transparently. In attempting such transparent self-possession, we must suppress our partial but substantial awareness of the greater whole within which we live and have our being since any such understanding is necessarily mediated by some more proximate political and poetic orientation, some impure and particular, and therefore partisan commitments. The suppression of this political and poetic mediation cannot emancipate us from the authority of the (partisan) whole but only *subject* us to an inhuman orientation in which the meaning of being collapses into pure power. Whether we name this power "matter," "history," "God," or even "the other," its effectual truth, at the limit, can only be nihilism.

We have seen that Davis, in *The Soul of the Greeks*, recognizes the political moment that lies at the heart of classical philosophy. Unlike Leo Strauss, however, Davis seems not to acknowledge the necessarily partisan character of this rejection of the Christian and modern quest for the emancipation of subjectivity from all worldly authority. Strauss, I will argue, responds to the threat of nihilism by discreetly abandoning the Christian and modern search for "subjective certainty" and the horizon of universality and equality that accompanies this quest, implicitly counseling resignation to the rule of classical and aristocratic figures of transcendence. Next, I intend to show that Emmanuel Levinas's assertion of a ground of ethics prior to all worldly mediations fails to uncover a nonpolitical ground of the ethical subject and, in fact, renders his ethics of the other vulnerable to a progressive and universalist ideology. Only Tocqueville, I hold, appreciates the appeal of both aristocratic pride and democratic-universalist subjectivity, and so he provides a worthy example of honoring both "elevation" and "justice."

It is hard to disagree with Pascal's famous observation that we know too little to be dogmatists and too much to be skeptics, but it is even harder to know what to do with this insight, or to know where it leaves us. I suggest that it leaves us at the threshold of three human possibilities: we are poetic, we are philosophical, and we are political beings.

We are poetic beings because we are productive of meaning: our very existence secretes meaning; we cannot exist without acting, we cannot act without imagining—that is, without conceiving purposes. And we cannot conceive purposes without conceiving (however dimly and implicitly) some understanding of the whole, of the way things are, and of our place in the whole among the things that are.

Philosophy is the natural (albeit rare) extension of this natural interest in conceiving the whole, which cannot be severed from our interest in understanding our place in the whole (and the whole's place in us)—from man's interest, as Tocqueville says, "in grasping himself."[4]

We are political beings because our natural interest in understanding the whole and our place in it can never be naturally consummated. This failure to fully grasp ourselves or the elusive whole in which we find ourselves leaves us dependent upon the conventional wholes—the practical orders—that precede us and in which we live, breathe, and have our being. Politics is the natural (albeit not effectively universal) extension of our awareness that the conventional whole whose authority precedes us can be conceived as an arena of human reflection and choice.

And what of religion? We are beings open to—or vulnerable to—the claims of revealed religion because neither poetry nor philosophy nor politics can fully respond to our interest in understanding the whole and our place in it, in grasping what is, and in grasping ourselves.

TOCQUEVILLE ON THE DYNAMICS OF SUBJECTIVITY

In the chapter "On Some Sources of Poetry in Democratic Nations," Tocqueville begins by defining poetry broadly as "the search for and depiction of the ideal" (458). Poetry is the imagining of what is as a meaningful context for human existence, as a whole that can be a home for purposive action and reflective self-understanding. Traditional or "aristocratic" societies, for Tocqueville, are those in which inherited ways and hierarchies provide a ready matrix for the generation of "the ideal"; human beings may not fare well overall in such societies, but they find themselves within an inherited home, morally and spiritually, and the more poetic among them can project images from this conventional home, images that extend and elaborate the meaning of lived hierarchies, and that therefore will have meaning for others who live within them. Aristocratic poetry springs from what is concrete and particular, and thus reinforces the meaning of purposive action within a largely inherited world of meaning (459).

Equality, Tocqueville argues, tends to "dry up" these traditional sources of "poetry"—that is, of human meaning. Poetry requires the leisure to conceive of possibilities that extrapolate from received hierarchies and thus to populate the world with "supernatural beings," but modern democracy undermines these social and poetic hierarchies and leaves people preoccupied with improving their material existence. Democracy thus tends to confine the imagination "to the visible and real world" (460).

This confinement to the actual would seem equivalent to the end of imagination and poetry, but Tocqueville shows that this is not the case. In the first movement of post-Aristocratic poetry, the democratic imagination devotes its gifts to the praise of inanimate nature, the depiction, for example, of rivers and mountains. But this descriptive poetry, this attempt to project meaning upon indifferent things, proves to be "only a passing phase": "I am convinced that in the long term, democracy turns the imagination away from all that is external to man to fix it only on man." The "visible and real world" to which modern democracy confines the imagination is not some simply inert, given world without human meaning, but in fact, a pure field for the projection of human meaning: "Democracy turns the imagination away from all that is external to man to fix it only on man. . . . Democratic peoples . . . only become really animated at the sight of themselves" (460). But this "themselves" that animates the democratic imagination is no concrete and actual body, formed and distinguished by meanings largely inherited from the past. No, this collective democratic subject is defined only by its negation of such past meanings and even of "nature," which can now be understood only as the obstacle against which human beings as a collective democratic movement define themselves: Democratic human beings do not even see an awesome primeval forest except as it falls beneath their collective axe (461).

The twentieth century witnessed the paroxysms of modern humanity's animated attempt to grasp itself through the active projection of meaning upon a whole evacuated of inherited and concrete hierarchies. The last feeble spasms of this attempt to grasp our humanity as the collective subject of a progressive history are still being felt, especially in America, as the salt of "hope and change" loses what little savor it may have had. Tocqueville had already seen that universal historical man was a momentary illusion that only seemed to interrupt the collapse of the pure self (the self purified of all inherited and conventional meanings) into pure infinity: "Man comes from nothing, traverses time, and is going to disappear forever into the bosom of God. One sees him for only a moment wandering, lost, between the limits of the two abysses" (462).

Tocqueville shows the fusion of the two abysses in his brief and powerful portrayal of "pantheism," discussed above in my introduction. The passion of modern democracy to grasp itself or ground itself purely or without mediation, to reduce meaning to one pure ground, culminates in the total eclipse of meaning: the self is swallowed up into an undifferentiated God or all, and human action, particular or individual action, becomes strictly inconceivable as continual flux and changeless eternity, time and being, are revealed in their perfect complicity.

The only alternative to this pure complicity of being and time is the mutually dependent differentiation of the soul and the whole. The soul and the whole are both differentiated and held together by some concrete and conventional substance of poetic imagination, some hierarchical field of meaning fit to orient human action. Human action requires such a field that is substantial or determinate enough to give it traction in the given or "real" but open or indeterminate enough to leave scope to the imagination; politics and poetry together define this intermediate realm of mutual dependence between the soul and the whole. The soul's attempt to grasp itself without the mediation of an understanding of the whole and the attempt to grasp the whole without the mediation of an understanding of the active human soul both issue into the abyss. The self and infinity (or God as severed from a concrete human whole) are really the same abyss that is opened up by the severing of the soul from any partly intelligible whole.

The emancipation of the modern "self" from the acting "soul" and its world, its whole, issues necessarily into the modern "subject": active (acting or political) humanity depends upon a given (yet poetic—that is, partly indeterminate and open) whole, and the project of liberating humanity from such mediation, the promise of a pure self-grasping or self-grounding, can only *subject* humanity to the abyss of an ever-more-abstract and elusive infinity: first that of material nature and its supposedly inherent negative purpose, then that of history as supposedly rational, and then, finally and most consistently, the infinity of "pantheism" or of being as nothing but time (Heidegger). To split the natural atomic bond between the soul and the whole unleashes the explosion of history in its three waves,[5] culminating in politics and poetry's collapse into the fusion of the abyssal self and the abyssal God.

The attentive reader will have noticed that I seem to have left revealed religion out of this discussion of the collapse of the soul into the subject self, the self subjected to history and finally absorbed into being. It might seem that this omission is justified by the idea of revelation itself: whatever depends wholly upon revelation from a source beyond humanity is hardly amenable to rational discussion and must be left to God and those to whom God reveals what he wills to reveal. On the other hand, though, if what God reveals is meaningful to human beings, it seems it must somehow enter into or engage the problem of man's poetic and political nature as I have tried to describe it. If divine revelation is relevant to the human soul, the acting and imagining human soul, then it would seem it cannot be exempt from the economy or the dynamic of soul and whole that I have described. What cannot inform human action or appeal to human imagination would seem irrelevant to humanity—unless revelation simply creates another humanity wholly other than the one I have limned, in which case, again, there would be nothing for us humans to talk about.

Tocqueville seems to show no disrespect to the possibility of unmediated divine revelation, but this possibility does not stop him from considering the political and poetic possibilities of humanity as they reveal themselves to a human being, or thus from viewing "religions only from a purely human point of view" (419). In fact, it can be shown that Tocqueville considers Christianity to be fully vulnerable to, and, in fact, at least complicit in, the erosion of the soul/whole and the preparation of the subject of infinity. The Pascalian resonance of Tocqueville's evocation of the "two infinities" immediately implicates Christianity in the dynamic he is challenging, even if we neglect the implications of a rare mention of the Son himself: "It was necessary that Jesus Christ come to earth to make it understood that all members of the human species are naturally alike and equal" (413).

I cannot here fully develop the question of Christianity's standing, according to Tocqueville, in relation to the diremption of the soul into the two infinities of self and "God."[6] But the question perhaps reduces to this: Does Christ's mediation provide a substitute or an alternative for the natural mediation of the poetic/political? The fact that Christianity itself, according to Tocqueville, tends to subdivide into traditional ("aristocratic") and modern ("democratic") forms seems to belie the possibility of a total exemption of revealed religion from natural mediation. To put the question in terms of Trinitarian theology: Can the meaning of God's being "fully human" be grasped or received without some implicit natural interpretation of the human? Or can God's kenosis or self-emptying escape the negativity of the modern subject/self without drawing upon the natural understanding, upon political poetry, or poetic politics?

EMMANUEL LEVINAS: THE VULNERABILITY OF PURE ETHICAL SUBJECTIVITY TO THE PROJECT OF PROGRESSIVE HISTORY

Emmanuel Levinas's work is an effort to answer this question in the affirmative: ethics can be reduced to the evacuation of the self in favor of the other. As a Jewish philosopher, he draws not on a Christian theology of kenosis or divine self-emptying but on a parallel Jewish theme of ethical law as the absolute obsession of the self by the other—in fact, the very constitution of the self or subject in the ethical bond to the other. Levinas's radical ethic of the other proposes a radical break with the Western rationalist tradition. However, in its absolute rejection of classical solicitude for virtue's pride, his project, in fact, tends to fall into alignment with modern secularism. Levinas seeks to ground human meaning in a primordial truth, in a first, unconditioned movement of *ethical* transcendence, but, unlike Davis's classical Greek approach, he would achieve this precisely by eschewing altogether the West's attempt to "gain control over life" through reasoning. At the same time, he claims to locate an absolute beginning and thus not resort, like Strauss, to any politically conditioned intersubjectivity.

In *Éthique comme philosophie première* (Ethics as first philosophy; based on a lecture delivered in 1982), Levinas argues that the absolute ground of subjectivity can be discerned in the subjection to "the other" that precedes any cognitive self-awareness. Consciousness precedes reason, and conscience grounds consciousness.[7] Since, according to Levinas, all knowledge amounts to a totalizing grasp, every *Auffassen* a *Fassen*, there can be no question for him of providing a new foundation for knowledge or of founding a new knowledge. It is rather a question of going back "behind knowledge and its grasp of being," back to where there "arises . . . a more urgent *wisdom*." And to arrive at this, it is necessary, Levinas argues, to take up Husserl's phenomenology in order to overturn (*renverser*) it: "Although he succeeded in clarifying the idea of an original, non-theoretical intentionality of the affective and active life of consciousness, Husserl maintained representation as its basis" (78).

Levinas thus undertakes to complete the freeing of this nontheoretical intentionality from its links with representative knowledge, to discern a "consciousness of consciousness" that would precisely not be a self-consciousness, but "indirect and implicit, without initiative going back to a self, without envisioning . . . [that is,] a 'non-intentional' consciousness" (80). Such a nonreflective consciousness would be nonreflexive but not prereflexive, since it would not be understood as oriented toward an essential fulfillment in the "good conscience" of reflexivity, in self-identity (82–83), but would know itself rather as the "bad conscience" of "the stranger on the earth." Such a consciousness would arise (*pace* Heidegger) not as the question of being but as the question of the justification of my own being in the face of the other.

Ethics is thus first philosophy, according to Levinas, inasmuch as the primary question is not "to be or not to be" but rather the question of bad conscience, "the question of my right to be, which is already my responsibility for the death of the other, interrupting the non-circumspective spontaneity of my naive perseverance [in being] . . . not: why being rather than nothing, but how being justifies itself" (107–9).

Let us set aside for a moment this summary of Levinas's argument in order to attend to a question that the text does not treat but that seems necessarily to arise: Can this "primary," transontological "ethical" questioning or interpellation be the key to a "first philosophy" in anything like the traditional sense? Can it serve human beings or certain human beings as a principle, a foundation for life, or for thought? Can one articulate on its basis an "ethics" in anything like the usual sense, as some kind of response to the questions of the basis of knowledge and the purpose of life? Does it allow one to judge among the possible responses, to distinguish between a body of knowledge (or way of knowing) or a life that is somehow in harmony with this foundation or origin of the humanity of the human and other propositions of knowledge that are not in such harmony? In other words, can such a primordial ethics either illuminate or guide human choice?

This problem recalls a parallel difficulty in the thought of Husserl: If truth is grounded in the absolute consciousness of the ego, then how can one distinguish a true or truthful consciousness from a false? In much the same way, Levinas risks obscuring the character of choice or ethical discrimination by making an "ethical" moment prior to the distinction between conscience and consciousness the inaccessible basis of both. This is to suggest that Levinas risks proving too much—that he may ground the ethical so deeply as to lose it in the humanly inaccessible recesses of human being and thus may lose touch with the very phenomenon of choice in his effort to ground it in a kind of nonnatural necessity.

Let us keep this problem in mind as we return to Levinas's text: "The dimension of humanity behind the persevering in being," according to Levinas, would be "like the suspension—the *epochē*—of the eternal and irreversible return of the identical to itself and of the intangibility of its logical and ontological privilege; a suspension of its ideal priority, a priority that negates all otherness by murder or by englobing and totalizing thought; a suspension of war and politics which pass themselves off for the relationship between the Same and the Other" (104–5).

As Jacques Rolland has suggested (following Derrida), the thought of Levinas may thus be considered as "an epochē of phenomenology itself, in addition to or rather than a phenomenological epochē."[8] But just as—by Levinas's own account—Husserl's epochē leaves intact the interior meaning of the suspended lived experience, even while severing every link between this meaning and a supposed external world, would not Levinas's ethical suspension have a strictly analogous tendency? Has he succeeded only in laying bare an "immemorial freedom more ancient than being," a freedom beyond or prior to the phenomenological freedom of absolute consciousness, but a freedom incapable of translating its otherness from being into a meaningful differentiation of the interior of the world thus suspended?

Following, in this matter, Heidegger, Levinas found Husserlian freedom still too "natural"; to have done once and for all with the ascendency of nature it was thought necessary to liberate nature from the hold of theory itself, including in particular from the primacy of knowing, the last remains of "the natural attitude." The only true liberation of humanity, in Levinas's view, thus has nothing to do with "choice" but resides rather in an "obsession" of or by the other.

It is certain in any case that Levinas is consistently, resolutely hostile to the notion of a world configured by one or another supposedly natural ethical differentiation. And yet it is no less certain that he intends his ethics, an ethics prior even to consciousness, to be translated in some way into an ethics in the more usual sense, into a source of criteria for choice and action in the world. At least at the time of the writing of *Humanism of the Other* (1972—thus only two years before the appearance of his second and final major statement, *Otherwise than Being*), Levinas did not hesitate to speak of a clearly *moral* and notably universalizing extension of his research into a primordial "ethical" moment, a subjectivity prior to reflection and even to consciousness: "Platonism is overcome by the very means furnished by the universal thought issuing from Plato.... To glimpse the meaning of a situation prior to culture, to envision language as stemming from the revelation of the Other,—which is at the same time the birth of the moral ... this is to return in a new way to Platonism. It is also to make possible the judging of civilizations on the basis of ethics.... Moral norms are not implicated in history and in culture" (60–61). But how, we must ask, can the intention to establish an ethical criterion be reconciled with hostility to the idea of the qualitative interior differentiation of a world?

Let us return to *Ethics as First Philosophy*, where this hostility reveals itself in an insistence that Aristotle's world collapsed into the world reduced by Cartesian doubt or in the Husserlian epochē. In section 1 of this lecture, we find that, for Levinas, Aristotle's "happy solitude" of philosophic self-sufficiency differs in no significant way in its implications for the meaning of the world from what Levinas calls thinking as the "work" of thinking, or the identification of thinking with egoistic freedom, the appropriation of being by knowing—in a word, technological thought. Thus, Levinas proceeds as if the ancient theme of philosophic solitude did not evoke in its ascending motif the notion of an order of the whole surpassing all human power. The same resolute refusal on Levinas's part of any articulation of an ethically meaningful world excludes the possibility of an ethical meaning articulated in relation to some conception of the political whole, of human community: rigorously ethical responsibility, he writes, "consists in not presupposing community"; ethical liberty requires "a fraternity in extreme separation" (98). Levinas's rejection of classical philosophical self-sufficiency along with modern technological mastery severs ethical transcendence from any orientation toward a meaningful whole.

But what, then, can be the meaning, the content, the effectual truth in the world of this fraternity without community and without relation to the constitution of the world? It seems that for Levinas, it is not so much the world in itself as the world understood as an effort toward some meaningful and intelligible unity that poses a problem for the ethics of the other. Only the world understood as a rival to a radically "altered" humanity, a world tending to resist the postphenomenological reduction, would have something to fear from this reduction. Consider this text from *Otherwise than Being*: "Entities *are*, and their manifestation in the Said [the non-ethical, the impersonal] is their true essence.... To enter into being and truth is to enter into the Said; to be is inseparable from its meaning. It is spoken; it is in the logos. But then there is the reduction of the Said to the Saying, beyond Logos ... the reduction of meaning to the one-for-the-other."[9] Levinas is not troubled by the non-sense of the being of entities; indeed, he regards it as a condition of the purity of his primordial ethics. To be as being is meaningless, and it poses no problem as long as it does not claim significance. Significance or meaning inheres only in the postphenomenological reduction itself; it is finally this very "ethical" reduction that brings to fruition "the effort of the philosopher, and his position against nature."[10] Thus, the reduction of consciousness to a primordial moment of ethical subjection undermines the philosophical aspiration to a self-grasping self-sufficiency, but at a deeper level, in radicalizing philosophy's suspension of "the natural attitude," it fulfills philosophy's implicit promise of pure subjectivity.

Human meaning will thus be properly fulfilled in those rare minds who are able to conceive this ethico-phenomenological reduction—not to grasp, certainly, but to glimpse and to honor this sublime prereflective subjectivity. But how is this ethical subjectivity to be lived or honored by the nonphilosopher? The answer that follows from Levinas's ethical reduction is that human beings, in general, are to comport themselves toward worldly entities now reduced to being only what they are—that is, entities that in no way point beyond themselves to some larger whole that might incite reason's totalizing ambitions. Already in *De l'existence à l'existant* (From existence to the existant), Levinas relied on "Husserl's phenomenological reduction" to affirm that "it is not from within the world that we are able to speak the world." Worldly motives must be understood as radically self-contained; they indicate no possibility of transcendence. "Desire knows perfectly what it desires. . . . We breathe in order to breathe, eat and drink to eat and drink, find shelter in order to find shelter, and study to satisfy our curiosity." In short, "the world is profane and secular [*laïc*]."[11] There is no meaning of the world that it would be up to a philosopher or some other figure of human elevation to fulfill. Levinasian elevation resides precisely in a renunciation of all claimed meaning beyond the "profane and secular" character of the world. There is thus no need to be a philosopher or even a postphilosopher in order to embrace the radical transcendence effected by the epochē of the phenomenological epochē. The Jewish proverb so dear to Levinas is enough: "The material needs of the other are my spiritual needs." There is no choice *above* necessity.

It is clear, however, that Levinas does not insist on a traditional interpretation of this proverb. In this same text (*De l'existence à l'existant*), he follows a critique of Heideggerian "authenticity" with praises of "the great strength of Marxist philosophy based upon economic man. . . . Locating itself in the sincerity of intention, in the goodwill of hunger and thirst, the idea of struggle and of sacrifice that it proposes . . . is only the extension of these intentions."[12] Decades later, in 1981, we find Levinas again confessing his admiration for at least a certain aspect of Marxism: "In Marx's critique, we find an ethical consciousness that undoes the ontological identification of truth with intelligibility and an ideal questioning that requires that theory be converted into the concrete praxis of concern for the other."[13] There is of course no question, for Levinas, of endorsing an entire Marxist system. Still, in this appreciation of the "ethical" character of Marxism we can observe that the orientation toward the other is not limited to an exclusively private domain or simply abstracted from concrete moral and political concerns. The meaning that supervenes upon the radical reduction of the world directs the regard of human beings (including the great number who do not grasp this postphenomenological reduction intellectually) not only or especially toward the daily or banal needs of the neighbor but toward the *future*. Thus, in a text praising the memory of Popular Front leader Léon Blum, Levinas sets aside the question of "the philosophy by which [he] justifies this strange strength for working, without working for the present," in order simply to praise Blum's belief "in an unrevealed future." "To act for distant things in the moment when Hitlerism triumphed . . . was undoubtedly the height of nobility."[14]

Without questioning the substance of this praise, is it not still necessary to ask if it is possible so easily to put aside the question of the "philosophy" or content of the noble hope that elicits action "for distant things"? Can an ethical concern with human necessities avoid the question of the character or meaningful context of these necessities, of the often implicit articulation of the world that orders an orientation toward the future? In a word, can an expression of progressive idealism be judged apart from a consideration of its conception of the common good? To see the problem with the formalist futurism implicit in Levinas's praise of Blum it suffices to observe, without of course suggesting any simple equivalence, that not only those who worked against Hitlerism could and did claim to work "for distant things."

Levinas's case thus seems to demonstrate the inescapability of the question of the meaning of the whole. Levinas's reduction of subjectivity to an ethical moment of subjection to or obsession by "the other," a moment ostensibly prior to theoretical awareness and even to consciousness, cannot evade some reference to the meaning of the world in which human beings find themselves. After rejecting classical self-sufficiency as complicit in modern rationalistic mastery, and thus rejecting nature as cosmos of hierarchical differentiation along with nature as a field of technological transformation, Levinas, in fact, falls back into the technological and progressive or historicist attitude. A subject that negates all wholes, cosmic as well as communal, albeit in the "ethical" name of "the other," is not exempt from the natural orientation toward some larger meaning relevant to human action, a meaning understood as encompassing both my own subjectivity and that of "the other," and thus reducible to neither.

Thus the case of Levinas, despite the author's intention, provides powerful vindication of Tocqueville's insight into the complicity between the reduction of concrete hierarchies and the embrace of a vast and indefinite collective project. Levinas's maximally antinatural subject is saved from falling into the infinite abyss of time as being only by his smuggling into it the "ethical" substance of the authority of history.

LEO STRAUSS'S IMPURE PHILOSOPHICAL PRIDE

I by no means intend to dismiss Levinas's critique of the "good conscience" of the philosophic tradition. For, as Strauss himself recognizes (see above, ch. 5), such a critique strikes at the vulnerable heart of the classical idea of philosophy. The classical understanding stands or falls with the claim of the self-sufficient happiness of the philosophic life, the life of putatively untrammeled questioning. And despite soaring rhetoric to the contrary, Strauss evinces a distinct awareness of the fragility of this claim. Notably, in his exchange with Alexandre Kojève on Strauss's *On Tyranny* (a reading of Xenophon's *Hiero*), he does not really contest Kojève's refusal closely to examine the "philosopher's" motives: "It is practically impossible to say whether the primary motive of the philosopher is the desire for admiration or the desire for the pleasures deriving from understanding. The very distinction has no practical meaning unless we gratuitously assume that there is an omniscient God who demands from men a pure heart."[15] We cannot assume, according to Strauss, that there is a God who could verify the philosopher's purity of heart, and so the question of such purity is, in a way, strictly meaningless. There is no transcendence that is pure of all mediation, no pursuit of truth that is not guided and configured at some level in some way by aristocratic honor.

The question of the purity of the philosopher's heart is not, then, one that touches only the personal worthiness of the philosopher; it concerns the possibility of philosophy itself as a self-sufficient form of human existence and thus the lodestar of moral-political reasoning. The nobility of philosophy serves in Strauss's argument as the anchor of virtue and excellence more generally. Thus, a moral-political concern lies at the esoteric heart of Strauss's recovery of "political philosophy," and the thinker's orientation to the political is much more than an exoteric front or a propaedeutic ladder that is finally kicked away. Any transpolitical grounding of the soul would require recourse either to "a God who sees clearly into men's hearts and judges them according to their intentions (which may, of course, be unconscious)" (161) or to the authority of Kojève's "Society" as the new divinity who passes judgment at the end of history. Thus, the three available alternatives in conceiving and guiding human existence come into view: (1) classical-political, (2) biblical, and (3) modern. Strauss clearly recommends the first and more subtly suggests the derivation of the third from the second. The idea of a final and objective solution to the human and political problem arises from the perceived failure of the Christian recourse to a truth beyond humanity yet available to humanity by a miraculous revelation. Strauss rejects both Christian and secular versions of transpolitical solutions. And yet, as we have seen, he hesitates in his dismissal of the biblical critique of aristocratic pride.

I argued above (ch. 5) that Strauss is very aware of the one-sidedness of his aristocratic strategy for saving the integrity of philosophy as the ultimate touchstone of our humanity. He knows that the philosophic guardianship of transcendence that he proposes depends on a judicious flattering of those who claim philosophic self-sufficiency and self-containment; he knows that this stewardship cannot be justified on purely rational grounds in an apolitical sense, but that it is informed by the most deliberate of moral and political judgments.

Strauss surely knew that this strategy was quixotic, since as soon as he says we must be open both to the pride of Athens and to the humility of Jerusalem, to the excellence of philosophers and to the righteous obedience of the pious, he has made it impossible not to wonder how these dispositions can be integrated, or at least held together in the same soul. But Strauss suppresses any such integration because he abominates the modern synthesis, which harnesses philosophic ambition to the project of universal salvation. In other words, he sees, with Tocqueville, that the idea and sentiment of equality—or, for that matter, the ethic of the self's subjection to "the other" (Levinas)—is vulnerable to the limitless passion for technological mastery.

Tocqueville, for his part, fully understood the drift of equality toward the project of technological mastery and the suppression of all concrete and finite forms of human virtue, but he also judged that it was impossible definitively to subordinate the ethical claims of our common humanity to the prideful assertion of human excellence. No one has surpassed Tocqueville's exquisite awareness of the need to manage the tension between the fundamental ethical and political demands he names, respectively, "elevation" and "justice"—that is, between the insuperable political truth of prideful rule and the irrepressible revelation of humble subjectivity and its correlate, universal humanity. Tocqueville did not, however, have the leisure to undertake, or did not choose to prioritize, the philosophical or theological task of articulating his noble and sublime equilibrium of elevation and justice as a touchstone for understanding reality and divinity. He devoted his quite short and encumbered life to upholding "liberty under God and the laws," but was not able to propose a comprehensive vision that might hold together and sustain the bonds between freedom and law and divinity. In what follows, I will venture an outline of such a philosophical and theological complement to Tocqueville's defense of human greatness as liberty under law.

CHAPTER ELEVEN

Analogy, Virtue, and Politics

What understanding of the whole and of the divine would accord with (while, of course, transcending) the "grammar of action" that has emerged from my reflection of Manent's understanding of natural law? Or, to put the same question in other terms, what vision of God, the soul, and true community would reasonably extend and support Tocqueville's exquisite equilibrium between the "aristocratic" and "democratic" dimensions of human being? Or, in yet another formulation, what answer to the perennial question of political theology, the question on which theory and practice ultimately must converge—that is, "Quid sit Deus?"—would honor and account for Strauss's bracing pagan response to the Christian and democratic subversion of philosophic nobility while remaining open to the biblical truth of subjectivity and universality, to the mysterious, infinite value of the human person under a personal God?

Even to announce such questions reminds me of moments in the classroom when, responding to similarly capacious questions from students, I like to fall back on the excuse, "If I could answer that one, you couldn't afford me!" It goes without saying here, I trust, that I will not venture to propose anything like a final, complete, and systematic answer to the question I have been unable to resist raising. Still, the significance and full meaning of the questions I have raised can hardly be vindicated without at least striving to suggest in what way we might respond to them. Since my suggestion will, in large part, take the form of building upon certain teachings of Thomas Aquinas, I will avail myself here of this Thomistic excuse for my immoderate ambitions: a little knowledge of the highest things is more valuable than perfect knowledge of ordinary things.[1]

I have proposed above that to prevent a flattening and hollowing-out of Christian love that makes its merger with secular humanitarianism all but inevitable and invites the furious resentment of identity politics, we must understand the essential truth of "the old virtue-religion." While remaining open to and humble before the holiness that must always surpass our understanding, we must have the confidence to articulate "the feedback loops between what is virtuous and what is holy." The divine ground of morality, I have said, must be in a sense "objective" and grounded in a reality beyond the full reach of our will and our reason, yet this divine ground must not be understood as "wholly other" with respect to our concrete and reasoned experience of high and low, as well as right and wrong.

I am persuaded by Mahoney's and Manent's arguments that Providence must be understood as holding open the space of human prudence. And I have shared Mahoney's suggestion that such an understanding must finally invoke divinity as logos, or the "creative reason at the heart of the universe." This Creative Reason (aka Benedict XVI's "personal logos"), though, must be coordinated with the broadly Aristotelian understanding of human action advanced by Manent, one that is neither voluntarist nor rationalist because it is in a way both; action is *archic* or commanding even as it appeals to the rational authority of the good. To preserve what Tocqueville so evocatively named "the laws of moral analogy," the unprogrammed fecundity of action must be held together with a respect for "God and the laws." Our view of the whole and of divinity must open space for the essential "gap" of action that can be articulated theoretically only as a kind of irresolvable circularity: the good must be both in action and above it. It is this circularity or luminous opacity of real, practical action that must be respected and not sacrificed to the inherent tendency of theory and theology to hypertrophy. At the same time, the nobility of practice, of moral agency, must not assert itself as some absolute and transparent ground of meaning but must be held open to some glorious plenitude that transcends it. Moral analogy must know itself as pointing to some holiness that ever exceeds it; moral analogy must take responsibility for itself, not as a final and absolute ground of meaning, but as always pointing beyond itself to a divinity that it reflects but does not possess. Moral analogy participates in an "analogy of being" that holds together the human and the divine without collapsing them into an inert monism.

THE ANALOGY OF BEING (*ANALOGIA ENTIS*) IN ROMAN CATHOLIC THEOLOGY

Tocqueville's concept of "moral analogy," as we have seen, points up the critical importance of holding together the practical and the theoretical or ideological meaning of moral terms. It is a disaster, for example, as Tocqueville so well understood, for "enlightened" (or now "woke") political righteousness or a wish to be "on the right side of history" to be divorced from ordinary moral responsibility "under God and the laws." The "analogy of being," on the other hand, is a rather specialized theological term that has arisen in the centuries-long elaboration of and debates surrounding the theology of Thomas Aquinas. It refers to the problem of "divine names" that has its classical source in the writings of an early sixth-century Neoplatonist theologian commonly referred to as "Pseudo-Dionysius." The question of divine names is that of the status of terms we use in attributing qualities to God, such as "good," "wise," and "just": since these are terms that we use to describe human beings, what meaning can they possibly have as predicated of a radically transcendent divinity? How can words used to describe created beings have any meaning with reference to the Creator?

The theological debate concerning an *analogia entis* has figured significantly in Roman Catholic theology, at least since its discussion by influential Scholastics such as Francisco Suárez and Thomas Cajetan in the fifteenth and sixteenth centuries. It is not clear whether—or, if so, in what way—Tocqueville was referencing this theological tradition when he warned of "the abolition of moral analogy" in the author's introduction to *Democracy in America* (1835). Indeed, it may seem that Tocqueville's moral and political concerns are quite removed from the technical discussions of the meaning of theological terms that we find in the Scholastic tradition. I will argue, however, that Tocqueville's "moral analogy" and the Thomistic "analogy of being" are ideas that ought to be thought together—indeed, ideas that need each other. "Moral analogy" (the essential bond between ideas and practical existence) and "analogy of being" (the linkage between divinity and humanity) are best seen as two approaches to the same fundamental moral, political, philosophical, and theological problem. Sound morality and politics need the support of some understanding of the whole, or what Tocqueville alludes to as "a very general idea that men have conceived of God, of his relations with the human race, of the nature of their souls, and of their duties toward those like them";[2] and philosophical theology must connect God-talk with the practical, moral-political existence of human beings. Human agency inevitably references some understanding of what is best and highest, some answer to the perennial philosophical and theological question, "Quid sit Deus?" And words about God—even a Creator-God said to be radically distinct from his creation—must have meaning for human beings—that is, meaning for personal beings who are embodied agents in the practical world.

The prehistory of the theological theme of analogia entis might be traced to the very beginnings of Western philosophy in the question of the "one" and "the many," as this question emerged already before the Socratic turn in thinkers such as Heraclitus and Parmenides.[3] Is reality one, and are plurality and change mere illusions (Parmenides)? Or is the ever-changing manyness of becoming the only reality (Heraclitus)? If these are the only options (and we leave aside here the question whether the thought of these great pre-Socratics can be reduced to these opposites), then there can be no analogy of being. It is in the works of Plato and Aristotle that the first clear attempt is made to navigate between these extremes. Plato's *Republic*, for example, speaks of the temporal world as (in John R. Betz's terms) "something between being and non-being, and likewise as something between the forms and the formless."

"It is in Aristotle . . . that we first see analogy employed in a more technical sense in connection with ontological questions."[4] Aristotle saw analogy as a kind of mean between univocity (a word's meaning is always the same) and equivocity (one usage of the word in question is absolutely different from another). He introduced a distinction between a *pros hen* ("to one") analogy, which Cajetan would later label as analogy "of attribution," and a second kind, the analogy of proportion. The first kind of analogy refers to cases where various usages are associated together owing to a common point of reference. Thus, we may refer to a healthy human being, to healthy medicine, and to healthy urine, but the latter two references clearly depend upon the first. It is the analogy of proportion that came to play a pivotal role in Western Christian theological debates. Its original, Aristotelian, meaning was rooted in Greek arithmetic and involves the comparison of two different proportions. This kind of analogy, Betz observes, "clearly comports with metaphor and, as such, could be said to indicate a greater dissimilarity between the things compared."[5]

The problem of analogy has for centuries been a major theme of Thomist theological debate. It was not, however, a prominent or explicit topic in the Angelic Doctor's own writings. Rather, the principle of analogy can be seen as a "central governing principle" of Aquinas's teaching, one that is not so much "thematized" as "*used* constantly, and indeed quite explicitly," to address the most fundamental of questions, that of the relationship between the Creator and his creation. In this sense, the analogia entis, or the "affirmation of an *analogia proportionalitatis* between the being of God and the being of creatures," is one of the "central, governing principles" of Aquinas's thought.[6] The question of being, divine and created, issues directly, moreover, into that of "the relationship between reason and faith, nature and grace," and thus "philosophy and theology."[7]

ERICH PRZYWARA'S PHILOSOPHY OF *ANALOGIA ENTIS*

The problem of the analogy of being can thus be said to be as old as the Western philosophical tradition itself, with the qualification that this problem was decisively sharpened and made, as it were, urgent in light of the Christian teaching of a radical difference between Creator and creation, between grace and nature. Most eminent and influential among those who have articulated this problem in the last century is Erich Przywara,[8] the Jesuit theologian of German-Polish extraction and author, among other important works, of *Analogia Entis: Metaphysics; Original Structure and Universal Rhythm*. The debate between Przywara and the great Protestant theologian Karl Barth goes to the heart of the Catholic/Protestant divide and can well be considered, in Betz's terms, "a debate about everything." I, for my part, am certainly convinced that the proposition of an analogy between humanity and divinity that expresses at once a fundamental difference and a vital continuity between the two terms is one that resonates profoundly with the aim of this book—that is, to preserve the practical good of humanity against the humanitarian subversion of Christian love.

Przywara's main thesis may be stated thus: either the things that constitute our plural and temporal reality are identified with what is immutable and infinite (pantheism), or there is an analogy of being according to which "mutable and finite things are grounded in their ultimate essence in something immutable and infinite, which is essentially distinct from them."[9] In terms that are at once biblical and the basis of any natural theology, the alternative to a pantheistic collapse of reality into a lifeless Parmenidean one is the idea that "ever since the creation of the world, his invisible nature has been clearly perceived in the things that have been made" (Romans 1:20).[10] The creature is the image of the Creator, and thus an analogy of the Creator. God is incomprehensibly beyond all things, yet "tangibly present" in all things. This is the inherently paradoxical basic structure of Przywara's analogy of being: God is "in-and-beyond"[11] all things. The paradox extends to the very relationship between reason and revelation, between, on the one hand, a purely natural and rational theology and, on the other, theology understood as dependent upon revelation and grace: the idea of an analogy of being arises, as it were, necessarily from rigorous thinking about the relationship between Oneness and manyness, between the whole and its parts, the eternal and the temporal; and yet this natural, rational insight into the character of reality bears within itself the invitation to an openness to what necessarily transcends nature and reason. The principle of analogy—of holding together immanence and transcendence, nature and grace—thus applies reflexively to itself: the analogia entis is at once natural and supernatural.[12]

The thought-form of analogy as a fundamental structure may come to view, moreover, either from the more subjective or the more objective side of our apprehension; it may emerge either as a primordial form of the orientation of the human part to the divine whole or as the deep structure of the whole as it manifests itself "through a glass darkly" to rational and spiritual beings as they participate in the whole. The analogy of being affirms the radical difference between the divine and the human, and yet, as unveiled to mortals, whether simply by miracle or as emergent from their reflective thinking, it establishes some linkage, an elusive yet vital continuity. The revelation of such an analogy establishes, not quite a *bridge* between human beings and the divine ground of being— not a stable, calculable middle ground or ever-available passageway— but a kind of intellectual and spiritual structure that, when we try to grasp it as permanent and cosmic, translates itself into mere categories of human language and consciousness. But then, as we seek to map it in an immanent phenomenology of human consciousness, it lures us into uncertain speculations on the meaning of all things. The modes of opening to and responding to the whole that we call respectively "reason" and "revelation" are very distinct and even opposed options for the ordering of human life (as Strauss, most notably, insisted), and yet these alternatives prove hard in practice to keep apart.[13] If nature's ground is both in and above it, then the rivalry between reason and revelation is not a problem to be solved, whether by the victory of one or the other rival or by some final intelligible synthesis, but a manifestation of the *way* things are.

The core meaning, then, of the analogia entis, which, according to Erich Przywara, the acknowledged master of this problem, in fact lies at the heart of Thomas Aquinas's thought and indeed of Christianity itself, is the idea that the divine is at once in and beyond the natural world of human experience. The meaning of existence can be sustained, the musical[14] tension between immanence and transcendence developed and unfolded, only by an analogical sensibility that "holds open,"[15] rather than attempting to resolve, the polarity between Creator and creature. Przywara's wariness of any final, propositional resolution of the analogical tension seems to signal a definite counsel of modesty to the enterprise of systematic theology: a theology of analogy must remain as much a kind of poetry or music as a self-contained propositional system. Such a musical theology would necessarily evoke actual human experiences of one kind or another as natural pointers to supernatural reality. This analogical theology, moreover, would have to be ever vigilant against the pretensions of theory or theology to favor one pole or the other, the natural or the supernatural, and thus to risk the collapse of the musical tension.

Betz cites Przywara's observations on the "wide variety of concrete religious experience" that would provide the substance of our "natural knowledge of God":

> At one moment one might ascend from the perfections of finite things to the infinite source of all perfection; at another moment one might catch a glimpse of the majesty of immutable shining through the flitting back and forth of mutable things; at another moment one's experience of other persons may give one a lively sense of the personality of God as the fulfillment of everything we intimate in personal greatness; or, at yet another moment, we may happen to perceive in the restless activity of creation the "active repose and reposing activity" of the Creator.[16]

In these examples it may be possible to discern references to natural experiences of, respectively, ethical, aesthetic, erotic, or agapic (that is, grounded in the experience of love for a unique individual), and properly philosophical-theological transcendence. The question naturally arises whether one of these experiences would not tend to serve as the dominant tone in the music of the analogia entis. In Przywara's favored musical analogy of being's analogy we perhaps already see a certain tendency to the dominance of the aesthetic. Here I make the case for the prominence (which is not to say the exclusive dominance) of the ethical.

A certain aesthetic sensibility, a disinterested beholding of the beauty of the dynamic polarities of analogy, may seem to be the ideal disposition of the soul on the basis of which to advocate for the maintenance of an equilibrium between the "in" and the "above," between the poles of immanence and transcendence. But there are inevitably theological and even ecclesiological stakes involved in the articulation of the analogical polarities, and it is clear that these interests have tended to pull the discussion distinctly toward the transcendent pole. This emphasis on transcendence is, of course, unsurprising in what is, after all, theological discourse, or part of an essentially theological conversation. But it is noteworthy that the special solicitude for the transcendent pole appears in Przywara and in twentieth-century Roman Catholic theology more generally as a pointed and somewhat defensive response to a critique of Catholic analogism (if I may coin a term) by the great Protestant—radically Protestant—theologian Karl Barth.[17] Przywara and his advocates, such as our guide, Betz, are at great pains to disprove Barth's claim that the theology of analogia entis is at least vulnerable to an impious natural theology, to the tendency, that is, to claim far too much for the natural understanding and thus too much continuity between God and human beings. In response, our Catholic theologians, it is fair to say, are determined not to be outdone by any Protestant in their proclamation of divine transcendence. The defensive posture of our analogists here is indeed unmistakable. Thus Betz: "For Przywara the stress of the theological analogy falls not on the side of proximity, similarity, and immanence but rather on the side of distance, dissimilarity, and transcendence." Here, in Betz's masterful chapter, as in so many friendly accounts of the analogia entis, the reference to the Fourth Lateran Council's formulation (1215) is de rigueur: "No similarity can be observed between Creator and creature, however great, that would not require one to observe a greater dissimilarity between them."[18] In the end, all talk of "continuity" or "bridge-building" between the human and the divine must be forsworn. God's likeness to the creature is beyond all likeness. Analogy is after all "only analogy," and the "ever greater" God must finally be situated "beyond all analogy."[19]

PRIDE, HUMILITY, AND SERVICE

An outside observer of this Thomistic dance of speculation and retraction might be forgiven for wondering what all the fuss has been about: the music of analogy seems abruptly to stop, as the in-and-above/beyond must finally be categorized as unequivocally *beyond*. To be sure, what may seem to be a rather self-defeating theological gesture might be understood and excused in terms of Aristotle's advice regarding the virtue of the mean: in practice, we should be sure to stay furthest from the extreme that most tempts us. Since we fallen and prideful beings are obviously tempted to claim too much for ourselves, one might think that we can hardly go wrong by insisting on the absoluteness of divine transcendence. But such a rhetorical and practical stance betrays ignorance of the dialectic of transcendence and immanence—a dynamic as often infernal as edifying—that I have traced earlier in this volume.[20] The pride of the modern ideologue, of the intellectual or "influencer" who craves participation in some version of the modern transformative project, is not continuous with the prideful claim of Aristotle's magnanimous man to possess virtues worthy of the greatest honors, or with the classical philosophical pride that understands itself as an extension, a further perfection, of practical magnanimity.[21] The pagan philosopher, Manent has observed, claimed to be superior to other human beings; the modern social scientist presumes superiority over (or absolute otherness with respect to, I might say) our very humanity.[22] The pride of moderns considered as persons is no doubt very much a version of the same human vice that is coeval with our fallen humanity, but the specific pride of modernity is not the ordinary vice of the person who claims more for himself or herself than is warranted, and it is certainly not the virtuous magnanimity, the confidence in standing up for virtue according to a shared standard, praised (with discreet qualification) by Aristotle. Modern pretensions to transcendence of the common condition of humanity are not based on a positive analogy or continuity between human and divine natures, but on the assumption of a standpoint of absolute otherness—on a kind of secularized negative theology! The fulcrum upon which modern humanity proposes to deploy the lever that will master nature and transform the world must be absolutely other than the world; the human subject must be totally emancipated in principle from the tutelage of the natural object. The boundless and incoherent presumption of modernity is that which somehow claims (at least implicitly) the standpoint of God while pretending to prove that human beings are nothing but animals. Tocqueville, again: "When they believe they have sufficiently established that they are only brutes, they show themselves as proud as if they had demonstrated they were gods."[23] Tocqueville's practical conclusion, based on this observation of the abasing pride of the moderns, is the same as mine: this modern, democratic age is no time to teach humility: what we need now is pride.[24]

But of course Tocqueville's outburst in favor of pride cannot be the final word for us. However much we may sympathize with his rhetorical gesture in the face of the modern and democratic subversion of humility, it remains the case that humility is a Christian virtue and, moreover, that the Christian critique of the pride of philosophers (as in Augustine's *City of God*) is a telling critique. We must therefore return to the Thomist theme of an "analogy" between humanity and divinity in the hope of discerning a way of composing the truth of pride with that of humility.

Let us return, then, to Przywara.[25] While leaving no question but that the negative moment of analogy must finally be dominant, the author of *Analogia Entis* is also at pains somehow to preserve a positive link between Creator and creation. Let us see if there is indeed a space for the natural pride of human action within an understanding of analogy that considers itself, in the last instance, a "negative" or "apophatic" theology—that is, one that concludes with a confession of God's absolute difference from man and thus his utter incomprehensibility.

The fundamental context that determines the discourse of analogia entis is that of the absolute difference between Creator and creation. God is being itself, the very act of existence, in whom there is no gap between essence and existence. Created beings exist not of themselves but only through the act of creation. The terms of the analogia entis are fundamentally determined by the dogma of the creation ex nihilo. We must pause, then, briefly to consider the bearing of this doctrine on our concern with moral analogy, mediation, and the concrete substance of virtue. The idea of God's creation of the world from nothing has, at best, a debatable scriptural basis, but this doctrine proved essential to the early doctrinal development of Christianity within the conceptual universe of Greek philosophy. For Neoplatonism, the body of speculation from which Christianity had to wrest its distinctive teaching about God and the world, there is no "creation," just as there is no fall and no redemption, but rather an eternal *emanation* of lower orders of reality from an impersonal first principle. In the eminent and massively influential case of Plotinus (204/205–270 CE), for example, from the eternal self-identity of the one, there emanates the logos, and from the logos, the cosmos. The ultimate reality is a *rational impersonal necessity*, and all that is emanates eternally from this first principle. Reality is, therefore, essentially timeless, and temporality is a mark of a defect of reality.[26] Within this classical, pagan philosophical framework, there can be nothing truly new under the sun, no catastrophe of a fall resulting from the choice of evil over good, and no good news of redemption.

Things seem to change, but in reality, everything must stay the same, as determined by the same rational impersonal necessity.

Christian theology was confronted with the task of adapting the terms of this Neoplatonic framework to the biblical idea of a God who creates and cares for his creation. The biblical God had to be emancipated from the rational impersonal necessity of Neoplatonism. The decisive expression of this emancipation is the idea of God's radical freedom and of the radical gratuity of creation. The world is in no way a necessary emanation from God; God was under no rational necessity to create the world; he created the world in absolute freedom. To create absolutely freely is to create from nothingness. The doctrine of a creation ex nihilo is a strict correlate of God's absolute freedom defined in opposition to the Neoplatonic rational impersonal necessity. From within this perspective of resistance to Greek rational self-sufficiency, the Christian analogy of being must, therefore, insist upon absolute divine freedom, a freedom that absolutely transcends rational necessity and, therefore, is, in the end, absolutely incomprehensible. This is why the last word in the Roman Catholic doctrine of analogia entis must be a gesture of negative theology as prescribed by the Fourth Lateran Council: every positive affirmation of a likeness between God and man must issue into a confession of God's absolute and incomprehensible transcendence. *To wrest a personal God from the Greek categories of rational impersonal necessity, freedom embraces nothingness.*

The assertion of freedom from rational impersonal necessity, however, comes with its own risk: that of a radical, inhuman, and ultimately unlivable arbitrariness. One can say that late-medieval nominalism succumbed to this risk, the risk of understanding divine freedom as pure, arbitrary will, and thus leaving human freedom with no standard but will. The Thomistic theology of analogia entis, of which Przywara's work is exemplary, aims to avoid this risk by somehow preserving the positive moment of likeness, some meaningful continuity of the human and the divine, within the confession of God's absolute otherness.

Przywara's solution is to find a kind of positivity in the radical negation of any natural or ontic continuity between humanity and divinity. It is the very absolute transcendence of the divine that opens the natural to what is beyond it and frees it for "activity" within its own, natural realm. The supernatural end, the "vision of God as eternal life," is at once utterly beyond nature and yet inherent in nature, not as a natural potentiality, but as the *potential oboedientialis* (or "negative potentiality") already discerned by Thomas Aquinas. This potentiality is best named not "positive" but "active," since it is "active . . . wholly and utterly on the basis of the 'negative' of negative potentiality"—that is, a potentiality consistent with God's radical transcendence of the natural.[27] Here, I am clearly venturing with the great German philosophical theologian into the realm of theological mystery, and it would be wrong to ask for any kind of univocal or programmatic clarity. Still, I think it is always pertinent to ask, Just how does this mystery of the positivity of pure negativity "play out"—*positively*, as it were—in actual human existence in the world in which humans exist? And Przywara's text does not leave us without instruction as to this question: the practical meaning of the right understanding of negative theology, a theology faithful to the absolute difference between Creator and creation, is "unlimited 'service to God.'" Our very "powerlessness" is summoned to "service." Thus "our utterly passive potentiality . . . is a summons to action."[28]

This positive activity based upon a purely negative potentiality Przywara esteems as "the crown that Thomas Aquinas places atop our entire discussion of potentiality." This crown is, in fact, the "doctrine of secondary causes," or Thomas's teaching that God's power of creation is so great that he can share even the divine "power of operation." Here, Przywara quotes the Angelic Doctor: "Out of the eminence of its goodness, the first cause gives to other things not only their existence but the power also to be causes themselves." At the "maximum of its giving," the "divine Is" shares even "its property of being 'cause of all good,'" imparting even the very ability to give. The very immediacy of man's dependence on God, of human being on the Being that simply Is (that is, whose essence is His existence), "leads to the creature's greatest possible independence—even to the property of being 'self-caused.'"[29]

Przywara's vision of independent and expansive human action enabled by divine transcendence itself is such, I dare say, as to inspire men and women of faith and goodwill to the cultivation and application of their best faculties. The author is very careful, at the same time, to differentiate his Christian vision from a Pelagian or Aristotelian pride: active service reflects a fundamental awareness of "the distance of the servant from the Lord." Despite the praise of action, then, and not withstanding Thomas's own efforts (or so it seems to me) to appropriate as far as possible rather than reject "the Philosopher's" account of the nature of choice and action, Przywara regards this Thomistic vision as "the decisive *reversal* of Aristotelianism."[30] Aristotle, he explains, understood action in the framework of a final end conceived as a "concentrated possibility," a pure actuality that presides over "an eternal cycle of change." Przywara thus understands Aristotle's practical philosophy not on its own terms but as decisively conditioned by what Heidegger named a "metaphysics of presence," and he seems to agree with Heidegger that Aristotle's action is destined to decay, along with its metaphysics, into Heidegger's own "productive Nothing."[31] However, the Christian alternative of a "summons to action" as service to a radically transcendent God in no way disposes of the question—as natural, I dare say, as it is eternal—of the good of action. The term "unlimited" in Przywara's praise of Christian service as emancipated from natural finalities evokes a saintly commitment, but it does nothing to answer the question of the purposes of action. Presumably, "service" is to be informed by "love," which in turn would bifurcate into love of God and love of neighbor, as enjoined by the two great commandments stated by Jesus in the Christian Gospels. But this of course simply returns us to the question of the content of that love and of that service, which has informed the present inquiry from our first pages.

To a Christian heart, the question "What is service?" may well seem impertinent, even blasphemous. We think we know the meaning of service immediately from the example of the Savior himself in the Gospels. What can philosophic questioning possibly add to the sublime teaching that whoever has fed the hungry and clothed the naked has served the Lord himself? But Manent has already alerted us to the danger of interpreting Christian love of neighbor in exclusively materialist and humanitarian terms.[32] The modern project of the mobilization of collective rationalized power for the purpose of material security and comfort has, in a way, upstaged the Christian spirit of service and left it entangled in alien motives and ideas. Christ's teaching was addressed to human beings, first Jew and then Gentile, for whom certain basic elements of the constitution of human nature and the limits of the human condition were not in question. As Leo Strauss has observed, Jerusalem and Athens agreed from the outset on the centrality of morality to humanity. The only question was how to articulate what stands above morality; what understanding of eternity (a loving Father? a serene rational impersonal necessity?) can support and vindicate or redeem the moral order that is essential to our humanity as individuals and as communities? This, of course, is the question I find myself here in the midst of attempting to map. But now, today, as our natural awareness of the authority of moral law is increasingly obscured by the overlay of the modern secular-progressive morality of equal comfort and ease, both physical and psychological, it seems we can no longer assume that the idea of "service" is to be understood as service to human beings understood as beings for whom morality and law are not merely temporary necessities on the path of technological and democratic progress, but constitutive of their being. Jesus's audience knew what all passably civilized peoples have always known about the human condition and the human good as first of all a moral and spiritual good. Humanity is unthinkable apart from questions of what is *intrinsically* good and bad, right and wrong. Such an understanding cannot be assumed of the materialist or postmaterialist audience who today hear the call of "service."[33]

THE EPISTEMOLOGICAL REDUCTION OF NATURAL MEANS TO DIVINE ENDS

When Przywara praises activity as "service" at the conclusion of his argument for an analogy of being as the ultimate framework for understanding Christian teaching, he, as a true Christian, surely assumes a genuinely humane view of the subjects of the "service" he praises. But he assumes more than can safely be assumed in an era when the very question of the nature of the beings to be served, of the substance of the human good, can hardly gain a hearing. In his eagerness to distance himself from Aristotle and the pride of self-sufficiency, he risks forgetting or neglecting Thomas Aquinas's own doctrine of human action as informed by natural law and structured according to a hierarchy of natural finalities (self-preservation, reproduction, rational sociality, and knowledge of God). In here passing over the question of the *substance* of the human good, he misses an opportunity that might have been provided by his brief discussion of Aristotle and the problem of the "transcendentals"—that is, the true, the good, and the beautiful.[34]

Rather than sustaining these three faces of the transcendent in his metaphysics of analogy, Przywara makes a decisive choice in favor of the "true," approached from a decisively "noetic" or epistemological perspective. Having asked "whether one may simply rest content with this *de facto* play of the transcendentals within one's method, or whether one must rather consciously and critically include the transcendentals *in one's method* at the outset," Przywara observes that to phrase the question is already to have answered it in favor of "the true."[35] And he understands this truth, following Husserl, as the culmination of the "noetic" in Western philosophy—that is, in terms of the priority of "consciousness."[36] Thus Przywara, in his theory of analogy, will decisively subordinate the practical (the actuality of virtue) and foreground a *theoretical regard* upon the fundamental "rhythm" or oscillation between immanent humanity and absolutely transcendent divinity.[37]

From the standpoint of Manent's Christian-Aristotelian understanding of natural law, Przywara may then provide another example of the "hypertrophy" of theory or theology. By adopting a fundamentally "noetic" or *epistemological* approach grounded in the supposed Cartesian consistency of something called "consciousness," he misses an opportunity to take practical human existence, moral-political existence, as a necessary touchstone for the articulation of the "in-and-above" quality of the human condition. If the "in-and-above" dynamic is always already at work in what Manent names the "grammar of action," the most elementary structure of actual, practical human existence, then one might say that nothing is more immanent than what passes for "absolute transcendence," the "ever-greater" quality so emphatically touted by the Fourth Lateran Council.

If God is nearer to us than we are to ourselves (Augustine),[38] might this not be best interpreted in terms of a positive resonance between divine transcendence and the aspiration of action itself to what is "ever greater," to a nobility that is at once pridefully claimed by the agent and the inspiration for a beautiful sacrifice of the agent to an ever-elusive beyond? A truly good and truly beautiful understanding of the analogy between humanity and divinity, I propose, would have to honor both the grounded pride and the sacrificial humility of action. Consider in this connection Przywara's intriguing remarks in chapter 6, "The Grounding of Analogy," concerning the relation between the natural and the supernatural. Following Aquinas, Przywara argues that "the truly supernatural, the vision of God as Eternal life," corresponds in human nature to a "being prepared by God"—that is, a *potential oboedientalis* or capacity to receive grace, a "most intense negative potentiality" that becomes positive when the supernatural "incorporates itself entirely into the relational edifice of the natural." Within this supernatural absorption, as it were, of the natural, "the supernatural 'concerns the end itself, . . . while the natural is 'underway' to the end." In this "relational structure," the "correct mode" is supernatural, while the "correct content," grounded in "the relational structure of ends and means," is natural. Thus, "the vision of God as Eternal life becomes the 'ultimate perfection' of the natural," in which the natural desire for happiness at last finds rest.[39]

Note that, somehow, in Przywara's evocative formulation, based on Aquinas's *De veritate*, the ultimate *end* is located in the supernatural, while the right *content* or substance is in the natural. The "right content" thus seems to correspond to the natural "relational structure of ends and means." But just what is this natural relational structure? If Manent and Aristotle are right, then the ends-means structure is no simple linear instrumentality of means to ends. The end of virtuous action is (to use Przywara's term) "in-and-above" virtue itself; it is always in a sense in the good of the virtuous *means* itself (doing the right thing in the right way for the right reason with respect to the right people . . .), and yet in another sense again beyond the end inherent in virtuous action in the end at which the action aims (a "higher good" prefigured by the common good of the community and, for Aristotle, finally associated with the pure actuality of the intellect).[40]

The question for us is whether the supernatural incorporation of the natural must not also be, in a way, "the natural incorporation of the supernatural"—or, if that formulation is too hazardous, then let us say, more circumspectly: the inevitable interpretation or evocation of the supernatural in terms that reflect the natural, practical existence of humanity. Can the elevation of the supernatural be in any way comprehended or expressed, or simply meaningfully evoked, if not as an echo of the play inherent within the natural goodness of action for the good? Przywara's supernatural incorporation of the natural "relational structure of ends and means" risks reducing natural action to a purely economic and linear relation. The "right content" would thus tend to collapse into a naturalistic instrumentality, and the "correct mode" of the supernatural would reign from some infinite distance over a naturalistic economy of functions.[41] And any "unlimited service to God" would tend inevitably to be interpreted within this naturalistic frame.

Przywara is intent on honoring the basic Thomistic insight that grace perfects nature. I mean to ask here whether grace can perfect nature without perfecting the *perfection* of nature, without extending or echoing the imperfect or open-ended perfection of nature. If we do not understand "nature" as "in-and-above," as always already pointing positively beyond itself to grace, as oriented both toward self-sufficient actualization and toward the open possibility of ecstatic sacrifice, then we will end up interpreting grace or the effects of grace according to a naturalistic nature. And unless we take our bearings consistently from the practical in-and-above, we can only end up interpreting "love" and "service" within the horizon of naturalism and then, eventually, from within the pantheistic vortex that naturally succeeds naturalism.[42]

VIRTUE'S SPLENDOR

In two important books on Aquinas, Thomas S. Hibbs has proposed an interpretation of Aquinas's theology that is profoundly consonant on many points with my understanding of practical virtue—that is, virtue understood according to what Manent has described as the natural "grammar of action." Hibbs shows how an understanding of transcendence that positions divinity far beyond the reach of prideful classical reason at the same time opens up space for the eternal significance of practical human existence.

Hibbs reads Aristotle, who seems to rank theory higher than practice, as in fact holding that the supremacy of the question of wisdom means that "practice, in at least one important sense, is more fundamental than theory. If theoretical contemplation is to be considered the highest human activity, it will be so only in light of a conception of excellence internal to the notion of practice."[43] For Hibbs, Christian theology in a way both humbles and elevates the classical understanding of wisdom. Citing Aquinas, Hibbs proposes that "wisdom is not so much an achievement as a receptivity, not so much a property of the philosopher as a participation in that which exceeds all human fathoming."

The distinction between classical "achievement" and Christian "participation" merits careful examination. Participation is here understood to be more "receptive" and less self-sufficiently active than, say, pagan wisdom. But participation cannot be sheer receptivity in the sense of passivity; the participant in "that which exceeds all human fathoming" in some sense has a part in what transcends him. Following Iris Murdoch's thesis—which is that "rival accounts of ethics and inquiry will be predicated on divergent concepts of human agency as 'continuous with some sort of larger structure of reality'"[44]—Hibbs proposes that the soul's "participation" in what exceeds it is that of a special "part of the whole, . . . that part of the world in which, and through which, the whole is made manifest." But then of course everything will depend upon just how one conceives the specialness of the human as part of the whole. And one's conception of what is most special or highest in our humanity cannot help but color one's understanding of, or the character of one's orientation toward, the divine. What one might call such "feedback loops" between humanity and divinity are inevitable, in no way reductive, but indeed beautiful and good, and so, we must believe, not irrelevant to our discernment of what is true. Hibbs understands Aquinas as integrating or at least coordinating a broadly Platonic and Augustinian understanding of "participation"—in which the divine pole of meaning may be said to be dominant (since humans are only parts of a whole that far exceeds them)—with a more Aristotelian emphasis on the integrity of nature and thus of human nature. The human, natural pole is understood, moreover, following Thomas's Aristotelianism, as grounded in the moral-political condition of humanity. Aquinas defines natural law, after all, as human *participation* in eternal law. And eternal law is of course undistinguishable from God's very being and goodness.

Hibbs pointedly distinguishes this participation-cum–natural law interpretation of the relation between the human and the divine from what he calls the "perfect being theism" characteristic of Aristotle's medieval Arab interpreters and still attractive to some contemporary interpreters of Aquinas.[45] Perfect being theism envisions God's wisdom as the peak of a hierarchy of goodness defined by the philosopher's own ideal of theoretical contemplation. It is from this standpoint that the great Arab Aristotelians denied that God's providence extended to lowly, particular things. But Thomas criticizes this way of construing divinity as a kind of idolatry and "always vulnerable to the vice of self-love." This "anthropomorphic view of God" was thus ridiculed by Ortega y Gassett as that of a "philosopher admiring himself in the mirror."[46] Aquinas's alternative in one sense removes God further from humanity and in another draws him closer. God as pure "subsistent being" (aka the "pure act of being" as announced in Exodus: "I am that I am") is in one sense much more mysterious than the Aristotelian philosophical idol of pure, self-sufficient theoretical activity and yet in another sense, as Augustine famously said, nearer to each of us than we are to ourselves. God is the immediate cause of the being, and is the ground of the goodness, of every being in every moment of its being.

Hibbs's mobilization of the tool of "negative theology" (talking about what God is *not*) in order to reject the pridefulness of philosophic idolatry, of the conception of God as continuous with the human practice of theory, does not, however, by itself dispose of the question of the linkage or analogy between divinity and humanity. There must be some positive content in the human language by which we reference God, whether in doctrinal description or in devotional praise, or else our doctrines and our praise are strictly meaningless. By disqualifying philosophic contemplation as the touchstone of positive analogy between humanity and divinity, Hibbs has cleared the way for the elevation of other human practices as most suggestive of what transcends humanity. If we grant that God is nearer to us than we are to ourselves, then we are still left to ask: What is it deep within us that is divine? What experience or practice or feeling can best serve us as a touchstone for an understanding of and orientation toward divinity?

Hibbs's answer is essentially to interpret divine goodness as deeply consonant with the highest human *practical* virtue—that is, prudence. To be sure, a more conventional interpretation of the Angelic Doctor's thought conceives divinity according to the superiority of theory to practice; thus, divine activity is understood according to a purely contemplative or intellectualist understanding of what is highest. As Hibbs writes of Aquinas's teaching in the second part of the great *Summa Theologica*: "There is one end unifying the whole of human life and that end is contemplative union with God." And he acknowledges that "the characterization of the end of contemplation seems radically to subordinate action to contemplation and thus to invite forgetfulness of the life of prudence and the moral virtues." But he goes on to argue that "the Christian account of the end as union with God is not nearly as 'intellectualist' as has usually been thought."[47] Hibbs then strives, with considerable success, I think, to reconcile such statements with a more "practical" understanding of the divine. Or, to be more precise, Hibbs shows that Thomas's Providence can be understood in continuity with the supreme practical virtue of *prudence*—albeit a version of prudence that is in a way synthesized with *techne* or "divine artistry." Hibbs credits Aquinas with "a very rich rethinking of *techne* as allied to a type of practical wisdom or prudential discretion." So "corrected," he writes, such an understanding of "divine artistry provides a fertile model for rethinking art and its relationship to prudence and truthfulness."[48] This inflection of Providence-prudence toward the beautiful work of a divine artist cannot fail, of course, to reflect back on the Christian's understanding of human virtue, giving it a "creative" and narrative dimension, an appreciation of the individual's production of meaning in an open horizon on the path of return to God, a dimension that is absent in Aristotle's practical philosophy. The prudence of Christianity, like its Providence, is more attentive to and solicitous of individuals and their history than its classical antecedent.[49]

The simple yet far-reaching insight we can derive from Hibbs's interpretation of Aquinas's theology is that the very meaning, tonality, and practical implications of the idea of "contemplation"—that is, of a conception of transcendence as intellectual fulfillment—must depend on a prior understanding of the being to be contemplated. The idea of a personal God must radically destabilize, to say the least, the classical Greek idea of the contemplation of eternal being as rational impersonal necessity. But the idea of the highest object of contemplation as *personal* does not resolve the perennial question, "Quid sit deus?," but only opens it within a certain perspective. It always remains to ask: What *is* a *person*? Just what is it that is closer to us than we are to ourselves? Either these words highlight and thus "privilege" certain features of human experience or practice, or else they are strictly meaningless.[50]

Hibbs, we have seen, shows that Aquinas's understanding of divinity is informed by an analogy between Providence and natural prudence that inflects prudence toward an openness to creative "artistry" attentive to the eternal significance of individuals and that appeals to an aesthetic sensibility not prominent in Aristotle. Still, Hibbs sees that this aesthetic openness and a certain individualism must not forget their grounding in the political nature of humanity; reason and virtue are by nature oriented toward the common good of the political community: "The passions are formed," Hibbs writes, "with respect to pleasure and pain by social practices of praise and blame; we gain an understanding of what is good and best for us by imitating the exemplars of human action embodied in the practices of our community."[51] These exemplars of virtuous action represent a natural bridge from narrow self-interest to a higher good whose original form is the common good of a particular community: "The legislator's art does not eradicate natural motives and attachments, but moves the individual from the private and narrow bounds of self-interest to a gradual appreciation of the common good." At the heart of the natural inclination toward the good that is presupposed in the supernatural perfection of the good is the formation of the soul according to a community's customs: "The laws of the community are intimately connected with and must operate in conjunction with the inveterate customs of a society."[52] The human person as revealed by Christianity remains in a fundamental sense a political being, or, if you will, a political-traditional being, a person formed by particular laws and customs oriented to the good as presented in the common good.

NATURAL LAW AS POLITICAL

Jean-Rémi Lanavère's recent work on natural law in Aquinas's thought is indispensable for a reflection on the status of politics and ethics within a Christian or post-Christian understanding of humanity. In other words, Lanavère's Aquinas provides invaluable aid in reconciling the universality and the transcendence of the ultimate human good with the natural mediation of the political community and of the natural virtues as attuned to the common good.

Lanavère's thesis is that the Thomistic doctrine of natural law is essentially political—that is, that "natural law, without political law, has as it were no meaning from the point of view of practical reason, for it is insufficient to guide action."[53] "'Political justice' is the key to understanding justice."[54] Whereas the tendency of political Augustinianism is to "absorb natural right in supernatural justice, the law of the State into that of the Church," Aquinas exhibits just the opposite tendency; that is, he "seeks to discern natural law in its naturalness."[55] The integrity of natural law within Thomas's supernatural framework derives from the liberty of the "New Law"—that is, the law of the gospel or of the New Testament, which removes politics from the determination of the "Old Law." Politics is in a certain way removed from theology, distanced from the direct authority of theology, precisely for theological reasons. The lack of determinacy in the new law creates space for another "sufficiency," that precisely of natural law.[56] Thomas's natural law "is not depoliticized due to its anchoring in the metaphysical-theological, but, to the contrary, rendered political for this very reason."[57]

For Lanavère, therefore, the linkage between humanity and divinity is in an important sense mediated by the political condition of humanity: "Divine providence can be thought on the model of the human virtue of prudence, while, conversely, since man is in the image of God, human prudence can be authentic only insofar as it takes divine providence for its model." Thus, Lanavère proposes, "the concept of providence" may be considered the "primary analogy" (*analogie de départ*) that links human experience with our understanding of divinity.[58]

The rational creature participates in eternal law—that is, in divine providence—not only as a recipient but also as an active, provident agent. This active participation *is* the natural law.[59] "God is not content to rule over men by his law, but he makes them lawgivers" (178).[60] This "lawgiving" activity, moreover, is by no means limited to the promulgation of general rules or principles, but is essentially involved in addressing particulars: "The perspective that rules the Thomistic vision of the law as a whole remains very much that of the particularization required by practical rationality" (194). This elevation of the practical and the particular implies a notable elevation of the idea of *human* law: "It is human law that makes it possible to overcome the gap that exists between the universal and the particular. What distinguishes political laws is not a falling off in comparison with the universality of the natural law, but a necessary extension, or even an indispensable fulfillment" (199–200). Natural law itself is by no means received passively by the human agent; rather, natural law is *constituted* (202) by human reason, and then *fulfilled*—not distorted, or compromised—in its particular application. This understanding of concrete human law as fulfillment is bound up with Thomas's well-known departure from the Arab Aristotelian doctrine that divine knowledge is limited to universals: for Thomas "it is of the highest importance that eternal law includes knowledge of singulars" (207), down to "the slightest detail" (211). This must be the case, since divine knowledge must be conceived as practical, not theoretical (207).

The surprising and marvelous conclusion that can be drawn from Lanavère's careful examination of law in Aquinas is thus that, in an important sense, actual human law, law in the most practical and concrete and political sense,[61] is tied more intimately to eternal law, to the divine mind itself, than is human reason in its work of constituting the general principles of the "natural law":"The raison d'être of the *lex humana* should thus not be conceived as the final completion in the order of practical knowledge of what God has supposedly left incomplete, but as the final completion of what is incomplete in the natural law in its participation in eternal law. In other words, it is because natural law is incomplete that human law must complete it, and not because of any incompleteness of the eternal law in which human law is the participation" (214). The "indigence" or "insufficient participation" of natural law in eternal law opens up the possibility of "the function of the particularization of natural law by human laws" as "the expression of the dignity of being a cause which is that of the human being in the execution of divine providence" (221).

Human beings are God's intermediaries in the actual execution of human government (217, citing *ST* I.103 ad 6 resp.). This divine sharing of Providence with human prudence is not the sign of a defect in Providence, but, on the contrary, an indication of its generosity and abundance (218) in inviting the *participation* of human reason—the deeply *political* participation of human reason—in eternal reason (219).

WHAT ABOUT GRACE? AND LOVE?

My presentation of Thomas's understanding of human agency as fundamentally political—that is, oriented toward the concrete, natural, common good of a community as politically determined—may seem to have taken us far afield from distinctive Christian teachings concerning supernatural grace and the supernatural virtues of faith, hope, and charity. Don[62] Lanavère of course recognizes that, "since man's ultimate end is a supernatural beatitude, natural law, together with human law, does not suffice to direct human life." The new law—that is, Christ's good news—is a "reality of grace." The vital paradox that has interested me is that it is precisely this new law of grace that "leaves politics to human decision." Natural human agency in the fullest sense—that is, moral freedom as inclusive of political responsibility, of the "archic" prudence (Manent) that cooperates with God's providence in determining and commanding what natural law has left indeterminate—is not effaced by grace but rather liberated and heightened. This exercise of such an expansive agency, *the responsibility of reason under God*, is not merely, as for Augustine, an unfortunate effect of the fall that aims no higher than a compromise of human wills in view of material necessities. Indeed, Lanavère observes, "just as the ultimate end of man is supernatural, so also is the end of human society."[63]

Of course, my purpose here is not to provide, not even to sketch, a complete Christian teaching, whether according to the Angelic Doctor or anyone else. My purpose, rather, has been to recover an understanding of the natural, political beings to whom Christian revelation is addressed and whose nature must not be canceled by the revelation of grace and of a supernatural purpose. I have proposed that what Manent calls "the grammar of action" is central to such a natural understanding of human nature and that this natural grammar must be given its due in any articulation of the analogy of being that makes it possible for us mortals to speak of God. The moral and political health of citizens or subjects of late-liberal democracies is at risk as modern societies and states flirt precariously with totalitarian temptations. These temptations can be countered only by discerning just what is at stake for us today in the Thomist proposition that grace does not destroy but perfects nature. Extreme notions of "grace" and of "love" that prescind radically from human nature, sublimely "spiritual" as such expressions may seem, cannot address what Tocqueville so evocatively named "the abolition of moral analogy"; without a recovery of the natural goodness of virtuous action it is impossible to prevent the descent of liberal humanitarianism, or the perspective of universal human rights, into the pantheistic vortex of victimhood identity politics. That said, the revelation of grace and charity in Jesus Christ cannot leave us just as we were, ethically and politically. In some sense Christian revelation changes everything. But just how is this "changes everything" to be understood in relation to the *nature* that must not be destroyed, but rather perfected?

In order to begin to explore the relationship between, on the one hand, the revealed offer of grace and the supernatural virtue of charity and, on the other, the good by nature—a good that must be understood as grounded in the political nature of humanity and thus in the natural excellence of the virtues—let us return for a moment to Przywara's account of the relation between the supernatural and the natural. The mystery of human agency is that it consists on one hand in "an essential ordination . . . towards the 'positive' of a rounding-out to perfection . . . and is therefore in itself 'good.'" Yet, on the other hand, it is precisely this orientation of the created nature toward the good that "lays the ground for the possibility of evil. . . . In virtue of its essence [created being] is capable of falling away from essence." Natural possibility as orientation to perfection or completion is thus suspended from the radical, supernatural possibility of either receiving or rejecting this gift of the very possibility of goodness, which is also the gift of "sharing [the divine] property of being 'the cause of all good.'"[64] The gift of this active, practical goodness is thus inseparable from the mighty responsibility of consenting to its sheer givenness, and thus joined as well to the dreadful "possibility of saying No to God." The natural orientation of the creature toward good and away from bad, the free possibility of practical goodness in the natural world, exists only within the free gift of good as opposed to evil, the free offer of free participation in the ultimate option between freedom and . . . nothingness. Good versus bad depends upon good versus evil. This mystery of good and evil "declares the most proper otherness of God, above and beyond every creaturely similitude."[65]

This is the true ontological ground, the ground in human existence in the world, I think, of Przywara's inclination toward the rhetoric of radical otherness, and I believe it is the truth at work in the insistence of the Fourth Lateran Council on the ever-more-radical transcendence of God, and thus the deepest meaning that can connect human existence as humanly accessible with the otherwise unfathomable notion of an ex nihilo creation. The sheer gratuity of creation is the divine correlate of the human experience of radical freedom, the freedom to say yes or no to freedom, the freedom to participate in the ontological burden of freedom. This is the second-order freedom that lies deeper than and inspires and vivifies the freedom to choose the goods of natural fulfillment. We are by grace alone free to choose freedom and eternal life, liberty under God and the laws.

With this understanding of the dependence of naturally choiceworthy goodness on an incalculable divine grace, we see the truth of theological effusions in praise of radical transcendence. At the same time, I beg permission, one last time, to ask whether the circle of meaning must not be completed in the other, descending direction. Can the transcendent glory of infinite grace, the measureless beauty of the free gift of freedom, appear in—or, let us say, leave its trace in—human experience without being implicated in the nobility of natural goodness? Can God's infinite power reach our hearts as love if not accompanied by an ontological confidence in a divine covenant between grace and nature, a trustworthy bond between the mystery of freedom and its incarnation in a natural economy of goodness? Is it necessary, in order to emancipate God from Greek rational necessity, to insist that in his imponderable freedom he might *not* have spread his love abroad through the creation of finite realms of goodness?

The "in-and-above" structure of meaning is present in the most natural and practical grammar of action, and it is insuperable even within the most resolutely transcendent theological speculation. The circle of nature and grace is always already at work *in* whatever is "virtuous, lovely, of good report or praiseworthy," and even the most sublimely transcendent freedom or gratuity must collapse upon itself or dissolve into nothingness if it does find an echo in practical human existence. Transcendence can be *above* (and not simply *radically* other, and therefore finally unspeakable and meaningless) only by embracing the verticality already indicated in actual, practical human existence. Without entangling ourselves in abstractions of absolute necessity and absolute freedom, let us, then, gratefully embrace a creation and an incarnation that was "meant to be." In thus embracing the freedom enacted and revealed by the Son of God's sacrificial atonement, is there any reason to resist gratitude for the fall, the *felix culpa*, that inaugurated this history of freedom as a divine-human partnership?[66] This may be the most fundamental perspective from which to speak about and to act in the world that is ours.

CHAPTER TWELVE

Christianity and the Truth about Man

A debate has recently arisen over the etiology of "woke" political radicalism. To put the matter a little too simply, certain authors (James Lindsay,[1] Christopher Rufo[2]) emphasize the role of "culture" and, therefore, of philosophers or theorists and their ideological systems and academic strategies; others (Christopher Caldwell,[3] Richard Hanania[4]) argue for the decisive influence of the force of law over the persuasion of ideas. For the former, we are victims of a philosophical conspiracy that developed from Hegel through Marx to Neo-Marxism and then to critical race theory. For the latter, the present egalitarian-liberationist madness is a product of the antidiscrimination legal regime rooted in the Civil Rights Acts of the 1960s. This debate is not without interest in discerning the causes of our present malaise, but it must ever remain inconclusive, since ideas and interests, philosophical principles (explicit or implicit), opinions or habits of thought, and the force of law are always bound up together. A political regime is always a melding of answers to the questions "Who rules?" (law and politics) and "To what ends?" (ideas and culture). Every passably legitimate or stable political order depends upon some underlying understanding of our humanity, and every consequential understanding of our humanity must stake some claim to embodiment in a social and political order.

Caldwell himself, who emphasizes our legal regime in explaining where we are today, very perceptively notes that the key shift that, six decades ago, set us on the path to the present eviscerating identity politics was the abandonment of the sobriety of traditional constitutionalism, with its due regard for legitimate material interests within an implicit but broadly shared moral-religious framework. He traces the fall of this traditional constitutionalism of limited government and limited hopes in the political realm to a secular religion of humanity that is in a sense more vaguely and naively "spiritual" (more oblivious to interests and loyalties) than traditional religions and more ideologically secular than the traditional politics of interest-reconciliation.[5] Martin Luther King Jr.'s "rueful and sarcastic address" concerning the Vietnam War at New York's Riverside Church in 1967 proposed "a radical revolution of values" that left behind the project of saving America's soul *as American* in order to adopt the standpoint of "a citizen of the world."[6] And a critical factor in this shift was the complicity of Christians and Christian churches in preferring certain vaguely religious global aspirations of a religion of humanity over a moderate constitutional realism.

Joseph Bottum's *An Anxious Age* similarly traces the collapse of mainstream Protestantism in America into a "social gospel, without the gospel." For postwar American mainline Protestants, Bottum writes, "the sole proof of redemption is the holding of a proper sense of social ills. The only available confidence about their salvation . . . is the self-esteem that comes with feeling that they oppose the social evils of bigotry and power and the groupthink of the mob." This misconceived Christian transcendence of national political identities and interests translates into the ongoing negation of particular, substantive moral contents in the name of the equality or "liberation" of groups deemed to represent "diversity." "Such a social ethics," Bottum observes, "touches only lightly on personal morality, and it does not reach down at all to the old, earthy stuff of life and death that religion once took as its deep concern."[7]

It is sobering and enlightening to recognize that the "woke" ferment that captured so much public attention in the second decade of the twenty-first century, and that I have scrutinized as a way of opening up the most fundamental questions of our age, has conspicuous roots reaching back to the civil rights and countercultural activism of the 1960s as well as to the hollowing out of American Protestantism.

I have argued, moreover, that the patho-psychological elements of the woke dynamic can already be discerned in Tocqueville's probing of the soul of democracy almost two hundred years ago. Tocqueville, for his part, already well understood that the problem of finding ballast for the democratic soul was, at the deepest level, a problem for Christianity. Woke madness is the result of a failure to reconcile a Christian sensibility of equal and universal justice with the inherently "archic" (Manent) or "aristocratic" (Tocqueville) dimension of meaning inherent in practical human existence.

I have proposed that our present confusion, our inability to recognize and resist the drift toward what Tocqueville named "pantheism," is most fundamentally a problem of Christian theology. More precisely, our challenge is to reconcile sound and sober political and moral philosophy, attentive to both the necessities and the nobility of human nature, with an understanding of the truth of biblical humility from the perspective of a God who radically transcends particular, political bonds and who has transvalued natural claims to rule by descending beneath all things. The present tumult concerning "woke" radicalism is only the most immediately visible form of this problem, our moment's manifestation of a moral, spiritual, and intellectual challenge that has always lain at the heart of the Christian and classical roots of Western civilization.[8]

My search for some ballast to steady our civilizational ship, some substance to fill the emptiness of universal humanitarianism on the one hand and boundless liberationism on the other, has led me to consult, most notably, the insights of French (and Roman Catholic) political philosopher Pierre Manent and the teachings of St. Thomas Aquinas as interpreted by certain of his followers. However, it would be more than fair to ask what Thomas Aquinas has to do with us late moderns or postmoderns: What does our contemporary political-theological situation have to do with that of Western Christendom in the thirteenth century? How can an author whose age was defined politically by the power struggle between pope and emperor address the concerns of a generation for whom the exclusive legitimacy of "democracy" is axiomatic? Or, more directly to the point, how can the sainted Angelic Doctor of an ancient faith that is now not only much contested (when not disdainfully dismissed) but also internally divided precisely on moral and political questions—how can a Thomistic theology speak to a humanity that shares no otherworldly commitment and to peoples that are irreversibly pluralistic in religious or moral belief? In a word, how can Christianity speak to the morality and politics of a definitively secular age?

PASCAL AND "THE TRUTH ABOUT MAN"

There can, finally, be only one pertinent answer to such a question—a fragile yet disarmingly simple response: because it is true. To be sure, my effort here has not been to preach the full truth of Christianity or to convert souls. But everything I have said in the end depends upon the proposition that, somehow or in some way, Christianity, as Blaise Pascal wrote, "knows well the truth about man."[9] Whether Pascal's particular perspective on this Christian "truth about man" is one that we can now offer to our fellow citizens as morally and politically sound or plausible is, as we shall see, at least a fair question. A brief engagement with the great Augustinian apologist of the seventeenth century will help to clarify the theological stakes of our more broadly Thomas-friendly or Christian-Aristotelian approach.

Tocqueville memorably and rightly honors Pascal for his extraordinarily disinterested pursuit of truth; the author of *Democracy in America* judges that it was by transcending the ordinary motives of profit and glory that Pascal was "able to assemble . . . all the powers of his intellect in order better to discover the most hidden secrets of the Creator." Tocqueville continues: "When I see him tear his soul in a way from the midst of the cares of life to tie it wholly to that search, prematurely breaking the bonds that hold it to the body, so as to die of old age before forty, I halt in bewilderment and understand that it is no ordinary cause that can produce such extraordinary efforts."[10]

Pascal's perspective on the truth of the human condition was determined by his intention to prove the misery of man without God. Pascal emphasizes that human beings "are in darkness and estranged from God, that He has hidden Himself from their knowledge," and that he presents himself in scripture as *Deus absconditus*, the hidden God (194). When Pascal urges that "religion is not contrary to reason" (187), this seems to have nothing to do with any continuity or analogy between any goods of human nature and divine goodness. Like Tocqueville's democratic individual, Pascal's human being is suspended between two unintelligible infinities, "a mean between nothing and everything," having no natural access to what is truly good, no insight into an intelligible whole that might link natural, practical life with any true purpose of eternal significance.

Pascal's emphasis on human misery and the destitution of human reason as concerns practical guidance in this life sets him in direct opposition to the pride of classical philosophers. This is Pascal's "antiphilosophic intent," as Strauss once observed. The antiphilosophic intent of Pascal's Christian apologetics is bound up with a radical skepticism concerning the intelligibility of the whole, any meaningful order in the world in which human beings find themselves.

> If man made himself the first object of study, he would see how incapable he is of going further. How can a part know the whole? But he may perhaps aspire to know at least the parts to which he bears some proportion. But the parts of the world are all so related and linked to one another, that I believe it impossible to know one without the other and without the whole.
>
> Man, for instance, needs a place wherein to abide, time through which to live, motion in order to live, elements to compose him, warmth and food to nourish him, air to breathe. . . .
>
> Since everything then is cause and effect, dependent and supporting, mediate and immediate, and all is held together by a natural though imperceptible chain, which binds together things most distant and most different, I hold it equally impossible to know the parts without knowing the whole, and to know the whole without knowing the parts in detail. (72)

The impossibility of leveraging our self-understanding as human beings in the search for some understanding of the whole is owing finally to the fundamental dichotomy Pascal assumes between spirit and matter, mind and body. He understands the whole or universe to be determined by a chain of material cause and effect that binds everything together, and he concludes that it is impossible to conceive of matter as being able to know itself. But neither, Pascal thinks, can matter be known by spirit, and so it is a delusion to "speak of material things in spiritual terms." "Who would not think, seeing us compose all things of mind and body, but that this mixture would be quite intelligible to us? Yet, it is the very thing we least understand. Man is to himself the most wonderful object in nature; for he cannot conceive what the body is, still less what the mind is, and least of all how a body should be united to a mind" (72). For Pascal, then, we have no substantial self-knowledge as mixed or composite beings, material and spiritual—no knowledge, that is, that can yield any clue as to the meaning of the whole. The meaning we experience as human beings does not situate us "in between" the beasts and angels in a way that might ground our understanding of an order that would include beasts, angels, and ourselves. Our self-knowledge is thus not like Socrates's self-knowledge, the starting point of an inconclusive yet meaningful reflection on the whole, on an orderly cosmos that would be in some way the home of an orderly human soul. We are a mysterious mixture of matter and spirit, but not a mediating in-between. Insofar as this is the last word of Pascal's anthropology, our self-knowledge can only be knowledge of misery, spiritual knowledge of material meaninglessness, the activity of a "thinking reed" that has nothing to think but the reed's nothingness, and therefore, a thinking that is reducible to a consciousness of nothingness.

A comparison between Pascal and Strauss on the relation of human beings to the whole is instructive. Strauss agrees with Pascal's critique of both philosophical dogmatism and modern dogmatic skepticism, but he draws a very different conclusion from this dual critique. Whereas Pascal gives theoretical or cognitive priority to the whole as a boundless and thus unknowable system of material causality—and thus denies that a part can know the whole—Strauss deliberated takes his bearings from that part that knows itself imperfectly as part of a larger whole:

> Does not the very question of the nature of man point to the question of the nature of the whole, and therewith to one or the other specific cosmology [classical or modern-scientific]? . . . [Socrates's] knowledge of ignorance is not ignorance. It is knowledge of the elusive character of the truth, of the whole. Socrates, then, viewed

man in the light of the mysterious character of the whole. He held, therefore, that we are more familiar with the situation of man as man than with the ultimate causes of that situation.[11]

Pascal at once radicalizes and neuters the mystery of the whole by interpreting it in terms of a modern mathematical science of infinity. Strauss, for his part, proposes a deliberate choice in favor of the superiority of "knowledge of heterogeneity"—that is, "knowledge of the ends of human life," over mathematical formalism/materialism or "knowledge of homogeneity," with its promise of mastery or "charm of competence"—that is, its inherent technological temptation. In this way, Strauss refuses to allow the entire disjunction between theory and practice, between knowledge of the real and fidelity to human meaning, which is fundamental to Pascal: "A pupil of Socrates must be presumed to have believed," Strauss writes of Xenophon, "that nothing which is practically false can be theoretically true."[12] A kind of knowledge of the human soul that begins with a practical awareness of the soul's ends is acknowledged by Strauss to be the key to whatever partial theoretical knowledge of the whole may be possible. "Knowledge of the ends of man implies knowledge of the human soul; and the human soul is the only part of the whole which is open to the whole and therefore more akin to the whole than anything else is." The paradox that arises here—one that is central to the enterprise of this book and that Pascal seems to ignore—is that the "humble" denial of the cosmic significance of heterogeneity, of the human difference, and the consequent reduction of the whole to a homogeneous object of mathematical mastery, is not the opposite but the essential ally of the pride of human mastery, of reason reduced to technology in the service of a flattened, homogeneous humanity. Thus, it is a certain deference to what Pascal would consider the *prideful* illusion of human ends that Strauss associates with "the charm of *humble* awe."[13] Absolute "humility"—the utter deconstruction or evacuation of the "illusion" of natural human ends—subverts itself and becomes the partner of the promise of absolute mastery. In this way, Pascal, by adopting an essentially Cartesian metaphysics, risks abetting Descartes's technological project. Humility as a Christian virtue—that is, a practicable and stable humility—depends upon some minimal residue of the pride essential to human agency, upon a certain confidence in a heterogeneous order of the whole in some way analogous to the substantial heterogeneity of human ends.

As is the case with Descartes's thinking subject, Pascal's "thinking reed" remains a wholly unintelligible exception, a speck of mysterious heterogeneity suspended within an otherwise undifferentiated whole. How, then, does Pascal resist Descartes's conversion of human agency into the infinite project of technological mastery? In his brilliant recent study of Pascal, Manent notes that Pascal takes the side of the new physics but not of the associated technological project—that is, the alliance between science and concupiscence.[14] Manent's Pascal uses modern science to humble humanity, to put human beings in their place, between infinities. We must here ask, however, whether this place is indeed a humanly livable one, one that provides sufficient orientation for human action. Can the order and clarity of geometry be experienced as a good of the human mind without linking this good in some way with the practical good of being human? Can the infinitizing perspective of a modern mathematical perspective be *lived*? Can such an orientation toward the whole, or, rather, toward being, be taken up within human existence without succumbing to the vortex of the modern technological-humanitarian project?

Manent admits concern as to Pascal's radical depreciation of practical reason, the "synoptic" claims of prudence, but he seems satisfied with Pascal's advice to respect the three orders of existence, flesh, mind, and charity in their radical separation, to give each order its due. For Pascal, the order of the intellect is infinitely removed from that of the flesh (politics, economics, society), but then the order of charity or "wisdom" is separated by an "infinitely more infinite" distance from that of the mind.[15] My whole point in this work has been to ask whether we can, in fact, live without effectively ordering these three in some larger whole, however implicit, tentative, and provisional. More particularly, I have asked whether the supernatural virtue of charity must not shelter or make space for the rule of prudence, the "god of this lower world."[16]

I would suggest that what prevents Pascal's Christian consciousness of misery from flipping into the modern subject's consciousness of mastery is not some sheer and unintelligible respect for the infinitely absolute separation of orders, but rather a kind of residual Platonism discernible in Pascal's understanding of being. There is a powerful

Platonic and Augustinian sense of the inherent dignity of thought that survives Pascal's subversion of the prideful illusions of the pagans. Neither Pascal's "humility" as consciousness of nothingness nor his separation of theory (what we know of the whole) from practice (our meaningful existence as human parts) is, after all, absolute. For Pascal, the hole in the fallen soul retains, after all, a certain broadly Platonic shape. Similarly, in the very fragments just cited, while reducing man to the apparently meaningless cipher of a thinking reed, Pascal retains a significant residue of classical Greek anthropology and, therefore, at least a trace of classical cosmology. "Thought constitutes the greatness of man" (346). "All our dignity consists, then, in thought." And this dignity is not finally reducible to a consciousness of nothingness or misery, for the imperative "to think well" is, in fact, "the principle of morality" (347). Although "by space, the universe encompasses and swallows me up like an atom," it remains that "by thought, I comprehend the world." This comprehension is certainly decidedly modest or humble in scope, but the "immateriality of the soul" matters decisively, for anthropology is not without implications for cosmology: "Philosophers who have mastered their passions. What matter could do that?" (349). The dignity of thought is not wholly severed from "the *government* of my thought" (emphasis added). Thus, in Pascal's rigorously humble Christianity, there remains a trace of the proud classical rule of reason.[17]

Our fallen nature retains enough of its original integrity not to achieve satisfaction by the activity of our own reason but still to locate the humanly unreachable end of our souls' desire at the point of the convergence of restful happiness and reason's perfection. Thus, Peter Lawler concludes in his pathbreaking study of Pascal and Tocqueville, "Pascal's identification of human distinctiveness with misery is not consistent or complete. Human happiness exists, after all." We experience ourselves as "deposed kings," which means that we are aware of some "better nature"; we have some inkling of what it means to be a king. The "sublime instincts . . . embedded in nature . . . point toward man's uncorrupted perfection, and to the angels and God."[18]

The universe includes not only beings affected by the mystery of consciousness and thus aware of their misery or destitution in an apparently boundless and meaningless universe but also thinking and moral beings possessing at least a residue of the "government" of thought, of morally meaningful purchase upon a stable reality. As Strauss noted, Pascal understands that we know too little to be dogmatists but too much to be skeptics (in the sense of modern, dogmatic skepticism).

I conclude that we must not let our awareness of the limits of the truth of human pride, of the boastfulness inherent in natural virtue, bring us to deny or dissolve the truth of human distinctiveness or heterogeneity. The Christian radicalization of the philosophic critique of political pride does not necessarily increase the truth of that critique. Christianity must not attempt to secure the absoluteness of its own elevation by subverting the natural basis of our very sense of elevation. As Lawler and his Tocqueville both acknowledge, a certain "Platonism," a prideful belief in the distinctive nonmateriality of the human soul, "must be relied upon to sustain the truth of Christianity over time."[19] Manent, in his *Tocqueville and the Nature of Democracy*, similarly registers the potentially disturbing truth that Christianity itself is subject to the alternative, as much ontological as political, between aristocracy and democracy—that is, in the broadest terms, between Platonism and technology. "Religion itself is available to human beings only in a conventional site, only as it is authorized . . . by certain men or certain institutions."[20] At a certain level, *tertium non datur*: there is no third option, even for a religion of otherworldly orientation; there is no escaping the alternative between aristocracy (particular and partisan) and democracy (universal and empty)—except, that is, by a prudent sustaining of some elements of each. A Christianity that forswears all partnership with classical virtue inevitably tends toward the embrace of a secular-humanitarian and technological perspective on being and on human action.

I am, no less than was Tocqueville, in awe of Pascal's extraordinary hunger and thirst for truth and righteousness. But my diagnosis of the subversion of Christian love by "the idol of our age"—that is, by a new secular religion of humanity—has led me to consider that an extreme separation of divine truth from the soul's natural purpose in governing the body tends to create a vacuum that can be filled only by a radically materialist or reductive understanding of humanity. To sever our understanding of divinity from the goodness and authority inherent in moral and political bonds must end in the subversion of the natural bases of our human confidence in a permanent order of meaning.[21]

CHRISTIAN PURITY AND "LIBERAL COMPETENCE"

Joshua Mitchell's penetrating examination of the tortured post-Christian soul of America's identity politics, *American Awakening*, provides an excellent opportunity to clarify the practical bearing today of my analysis of the problem of Christian transcendence for ethics and politics.

Mitchell's diagnosis of the pathologies of radical identity politics is the deepest we have precisely because he sees clearly and senses vividly the profoundly post-Christian character of this movement and this sensibility. (The post-Christian sensibility is surely much more widespread than the activist movement itself.) Mitchell understands that woke radicalism stems from an obsession with purity or innocence that is unthinkable apart from Christianity. As we have learned from Strauss, the human soul's exquisite concern for the purity of its own motives, the person's openness to a convicting judgment that penetrates beneath the common level of public praise and blame, and beneath even common morality's refined extension in the conversation of virtuous philosophical friends, to the deepest, invisible recesses of the individual heart and mind, is not an attribute of the natural soul as articulated in classical moral and political philosophy. This concern for "purity of heart" becomes possible only with the emergence or revelation of the idea of a transcendent God who searches the individual human heart to its utter depths. For a Christian, there can be no relief from or assurance against an imponderable awareness of sin except in the grace offered through the sacrifice of the divine Son, a sacrificial lamb without blemish. Our modern would-be saints of a purely immanent "social justice" seek some purely secular means to quiet the self's restlessness, an anxiety that arises from our incessant falling away from a residual sense we have of the purity of what is good and true in itself. Thus, Mitchell argues, the awareness of the human stain that Christianity articulates with reference to the fall is projected by today's identity politics radicals upon political scapegoats (most notably white, heterosexual males)[22] designated as the "oppressors" of the holy "victims" designated by leftist ideology. "Though tormented by complicity in the oppression of victims," Mitchell trenchantly observes, "white liberals reliably devise penances that will be performed by other people."[23] He provides this concise history of the rise of this politics obsessed with oppression and victimhood:

> First, the collapse of the mainline Protestant churches shunted the idea of transgression and innocence from religion into politics. Second, the extension of the black American template of innocence to other groups after the civil rights era served a growing class of political brokers, who benefited from speaking on their behalf. Third, the discovery by the academic left in America of European postmodern thought provided a framework more powerful than Marxism for attacking the legitimacy of historical inheritance and for distinguishing who is stained from who is pure.[24]

Thus, Mitchell continues, "Christianity has not disappeared from America; rather, the Christian categories of transgression and innocence have moved into politics—a development Tocqueville thought would lead to the complete paralysis of both politics and religion" (34). To understand and address this migration of a religious sensibility into politics, Mitchell believes, we must confront "the deepest mystery of transgression and innocence" (276). The Christian mystery of the self-sacrifice of God incarnate has been replaced by the "scapegoat identity politics [that] offers up for sacrifice ... the white, heterosexual man. If he is purged, its adherents imagine the world itself, along with the remaining groups in it, will be cleansed of stain." It is "the specter of transgression," the natural, if generally inchoate, awareness of original sin, that underlies the bottomless anxiety that expresses itself in accusatory identity politics.

The result of this secularized quest for redemption and purity is that "an entire generation of young Americans has grown up oscillating back and forth between feelings of extraordinary grandeur and utter impotence" (xxix). This obsession with purity, Mitchell shows, removed from its Christian context, and the attendant projection of guilt upon a designated class of political enemies tend to undermine all experience of practical competence in the real world. His recommendation to overcome this toxic pseudoreligious awakening is a recovery of what he calls "liberal competence": "Liberal competence alone can provide the meal and sate the hunger" (xxxiii). "Liberal competence" for Mitchell includes both economic and political dimensions; it is the ability to work productively and to combine with fellow citizens to "build a world despite our differences" (195). Mitchell's characterization of practical life is thus rather modest, and, we shall see, distinctly Protestant and one might say broadly classical-liberal or Lockean. He speaks of "competence" in meeting needs but never or hardly of virtue; his is essentially an Augustinian politics suspicious of any ends that might seem to be higher than mere compromise with a view to the necessities of mortal existence. Mitchell does not claim that such a minimalist liberal politics is by any means in itself a solution to the problem of anxiety over impurity that drives radical identity politics: "Hide quietly behind your 'identity' if you wish; your anxiety about your own transgressions will not dissipate. Displace your anxiety by relentlessly aiming the arrow of accusation outward at other groups; the haunting specter of transgression will not disappear. Its source is deeper than identity politics comprehends" (xxiv).

Mitchell thus does not contest the psychology of transgression-anxiety, the hunger and thirst for righteousness as *purity*; rather, he argues for redirecting this anxiety or restlessness back toward the authentic Christian longing for an otherworldly redemption:

> Identity politics elicits man's deepest longing for justice in a broken world, the resolution of which was long understood to be so mysterious, so awesome, and so apocalyptic that justice was placed outside of mortal reach. (45)

> It warrants repeating that the notion that inheritance is stained in toto is distinctly Christian and, since Luther and Calvin in the early sixteenth century, decidedly Protestant. . . . Identity politics recapitulates the early Protestant pronouncement about the stain that deforms the world, *and indicts tradition*. (54–55, §36; emphasis added)[25]

It is from this Protestant-liberal perspective that Mitchell criticizes traditionalist-conservative responses to leftist radicalism.

> Here, I think it fair to observe that in response to the relentless attack by identity politics, which declares that tradition is

irredeemably stained, many Republicans have made the opposite claim—namely, that tradition is an unequivocal good. This position is, I think, unsupportable and unhelpful—especially in America, where the legacy of slavery provides clear evidence of the mixed legacy of our traditions. Adopting this position leaves many Republicans unable to treat slavery in America as anything other than an accident that is incidental to the essential goodness of the American Founding, however conceived. Far better, I think, is the position intimated by the parable of the wheat and the tares, which suggests that the redemption of an intermixed world of good and evil is not to be found in the world—as both identity politics and, strangely enough, the Republican conservatism that unequivocally defends the goodness of tradition, suppose. (61)

Here, Mitchell pitches his position rather polemically against some "Republican conservatism" that supposedly embraces "the goodness of tradition" without qualification. Without completely accepting the terms of Mitchell's alternative, I will say that there can be no conservatism—and therefore, in the end, no truly practical liberalism—without the embrace or sponsorship of certain positive understandings of the good of the person and of the common good inherited from the past. Mitchell's politics of "liberal competence" tends to deny all inherited goods as *intrinsic* goods, thus deferring *all* substantive goods in Christian hope to another life. Moreover, since we fallen beings can claim no reliable experience of substantive goods, Mitchell fully embraces the Protestant framing of ultimate meaning in terms of redemption-for-innocence, along with its tendency to reduce salvation to a kind of equal purity with no positive connection to natural and practical virtues. Thus, he speaks of "liberal competence" rather than of virtue or of a morally substantive common good. And surely this practical "competence," stripped of all real moral weight or eternal significance, is itself insufficient to "provide the meal and sate the hunger" of the human soul. This Protestant-classical liberal "competence," unlike a more robust understanding of "virtue," seems too thin a meal even to anticipate or prefigure the soul's eternal fulfillment. Mitchell's alternative to America's obsessive "awakening" thus does not question the ideal of a "purity" utterly beyond practical morality as the ultimate meaning of our humanity but only defers our hope for blessed purity to another world. He thus excludes from his understanding of Christianity anything like a *felix culpa*, a fortunate fall, and with it any positive connection between virtuous action in the natural, political sphere and the meaning of eternity. In a word, he rejects, unsurprisingly, the Catholic principle of an analogy of being, a positive, if somewhat mysterious, linkage between the natural, practical good inherent in human action and divine goodness. In doing so, I would argue, Mitchell risks exposing what Tocqueville calls "moral analogy" to the undertow of reductionism or materialism that I have examined above.

The risk inherent in Mitchell's seemingly absolute deferral of the good to another world becomes apparent as we ask whether our understanding of this deferred spiritual good can remain wholly neutral regarding the natural, political common good in this world below. I have argued that some understanding of the good necessarily circulates between the natural and the supernatural. Some substantive understanding or experience, or, let us say, some inkling of the good, always serves as a kind of touchstone for the hierarchy of the natural and the supernatural. In his resolutely Protestant vision, the practical virtue is reduced to instrumental "competence" and thus provides no inkling of the end of salvation. Mitchell is thus a very thoughtful advocate of saving or somehow restoring the marriage between classical Lockean liberalism and Protestant grace. He effectively neuters the substance of the good, the natural precondition of grace, by reducing the idea of salvation to the negative category of purity as innocence from sin; his effectual good is the negation of the stain of the fall. In this sense, his rigorously Protestant vision fails to challenge the substance of the woke psychology of purity from sin and, thus, the consequent understanding of natural, political existence as wholly and fundamentally sinful. Certainly, it is better to defer our hope for purity-as-innocence to another world than to unleash the passion for secular scapegoats. But how can such an idea of the human person and his or her salvation fail to condition our very sense of meaningful existence and, therefore, our politics here and now?

Mitchell's critique of "woke" or secular awakening thus fails to address at a fundamental level and even, therefore—in theory, at least—reinforces the psychology of anxious dissatisfaction with the practical human condition that underlies the blind activism of much identity politics. We have already seen that, in a sense, the effectual truth of the radical Protestant severing of grace from nature is revealed in the young Heidegger's radicalization of Luther: sin as the irredeemable facticity and "inauthenticity" of human existence. When every last residue of natural potential for good action is eradicated, then, as Manent found in Karl Barth's *Römerbrief*, the category of sin as a moral problem gives way to a purely theoretical or "gnoseological" understanding of conversion, untethered from the practical condition of humanity.

The moral and political risks of Heidegger's reduction of being to time are well known and need not occupy us here. What concerns me is how Mitchell's rigorous Protestant embrace of "purity" as the touchstone of eternal meaning risks an unintended reinforcement of the politics of anxiety, purity, and equality. It is Rousseau's antitelos of a return to a passive natural wholeness, presocial and subrational, that is most relevant to the bottomless longing for purity that defines the deepest stratum of woke psychology. The ontology of innocence, untethered from all traces of substantive practical goodness, can find concrete expression only in an essentially Rousseauian longing to be absolutely "at home" in one's own consciousness. Radical Protestant otherworldliness cannot avoid bearing a moral-political meaning, and Rousseau's equality in purity from the stain of civilization is the shape toward which this truth tends. From this Protestant and Rousseauian point of view, the "gap" that Manent has shown us to be inherent in human action is the source of an unbearable anxiety that must be eliminated in order to liberate the consciousness of pure innocence. Of course, for Mitchell, the only hope for this liberation must be directed finally toward the next life. But, apart from the difficulty of convincing our fellow citizens of this otherworldly hope, the implication of my argument is that there can be no absolute compartmentalization between this world and the next; there must always be "leakage" or circulation between the natural and the supernatural.[26] The idea that the soul's salvation consists essentially in a recovery of innocent purity, untainted by the responsibilities of active virtue, must, in the end, prove stronger than any instrumental "liberal competence."

Action involves initiative (Manent's "archic") and, therefore, difference, heterogeneity, and *inequality*. Virtuous action, one might say, necessarily involves assuming responsibility for a necessarily "impure" intervention in this world. Rousseau's innocence is a pure consciousness—liberated from the responsibilities inherent in the gap of action—that longs for a pure transparency and is essentially passive. (Of course, this longing can drive an ideological activism in view of some impossible social transparency, where all in society or all humanity "see as they are seen," each ratifying the "identity" of all and all of each, without any reservation or competition.) Rousseau's prehuman humanity is defined by its pure exemption from the practical human condition of responsibility for action. Rousseau's longing for a primitive equality and unstained wholeness of consciousness is the effectual truth of Mitchell's absolute deferral of meaning to another world.

Of course, Rousseau's longing for a subrational and subpractical "home" in the innocence of pure, undisturbed, and equal consciousness of existence is very far from Joshua Mitchell's understanding of liberal competence under a Protestant heaven. Let me be clear here that I would be delighted if something like Mitchell's vision of a "middle-class commercial republic," liberal and broadly Protestant, again prevailed in America. The question, though, is whether the liberal Protestant vision is sustainable purely on its own terms. He imagines "liberal competence" to be completely horizontal, without inherited hierarchical priors and/or a trace of aristocratic "honor"—without what Mitchell characterizes as the "stain" of tradition. Thus, he risks contributing to the modern democratic "abolition of moral analogy" that Tocqueville deplored. Can simple "competence," economic, social, and technological, with a view to material necessities,[27] without any trace of relish of salvation *inherent in natural human action itself*, provide adequate meaning to human action? The relish that Mitchell denies to human action—the inherent good of virtue—he locates in a wholly otherworldly purity (whose only effectual translation would tend toward Rousseau's innocent consciousness) or in a providential history that, unlike Manent's, is not a friend of deliberate human action for the good.[28]

Mitchell's perspicacious engagement with the present "awakening" of identity politics provides a valuable case study of Christianity as practical philosophy. I have argued that the rigorously Protestant-classical-liberal approach fails fully to confront the inherent particularity, inequality, and, thus, if you will, the "impurity" of moral agency.

One might thus respond to Mitchell in these terms: all politics and all practical action are in some way and to some degree a politics and action of "identity," of the affirmation of some common good and common goodness, some attachment to the concrete and thus to impure, inherited, and politically mediated elements of patriotism and confidence in tradition. There is no alternative to bottomless victimhood identity but some elevation-identity *that is necessarily inscribed in this (politically articulated) world*. To take our practical bearings *wholly* from anxiety over our impurity is, in effect, to embrace the psychology of passivity and equality. This psychology is bottomless, even when transposed to a Christian (Protestant) framework, since it cannot address the nature of human agency. Purity as innocence, even when understood as deferred mysteriously to another world, cannot supply a foundation for action or an answer to woke madness.[29] Stepping back from our present discontents to a perspective from the standpoint of the deepest questions driving the development and the vicissitudes of the Christian West, we can now say: purity as innocence alone is the wrong conclusion to draw from the rivalry between Jerusalem and Athens.

Conclusion

The pride of virtuous action under a God understood as personal and creative logos is the deepest ground of meaningful human existence and, therefore, of any sustainable liberalism.

TOWARD A PRIDEFUL CHRISTIANITY

My heading is purposely provocative and paradoxical. Pride, after all, is, for a Christian, the fountainhead of sin. Humble obedience before God has always, in Hebrew Scripture as well as in the New Testament, set itself against human pride. I do not by any means propose rejecting biblical teaching regarding humility. However, because the rhetoric of humility has now been allied with humanitarian reductionism and the subversion of virtue, I propose that the one thing needful for Christians and other friends of virtue is the rehabilitation of a certain pride *under God*, a certain confidence in what Tocqueville called liberty under God and the laws. We need to accept and indeed espouse what appears both to the radically Protestant or Augustinian and to the secular-egalitarian mind as the "prideful" character of practical human existence. The Christian warning against the sin of pride or presumption against God must not be interpreted so as to undermine the natural and necessary confidence in the intrinsic goodness of virtue—a confidence that must not be evacuated but rather in a way preserved and transformed in the perspective of a transcendent faith, hope, and charity. To acknowledge the practical truth of this natural pride in virtue, I propose, is, in effect, more truly humble than the misconceived project, at once too spiritual and too materialist, too proud and too humble—of transforming the human condition in view of an idea of purity and innocence alien to the responsibility of active virtue. Pride under God, or *redeemed agency*, is the only alternative to the monstrous power of the incoherent idealistic materialism that Tocqueville already discerned so well: the presumption of gods combined with the abasement of beasts.[1]

In the last pages of *Democracy in America*, Tocqueville restated his humble acceptance of what appeared to him to be the evidence of the work of Providence in the rise of a civilization based on justice as equality. Wrestling with the trade-offs between equality and "elevation," Tocqueville strove "to enter into this point of view of God" and "to judge human things" from this standpoint of equal justice. But in his very next breath, he could not withhold his reservations: "No one on earth can yet assert in an absolute and general manner that the new state of societies is superior to the former state." While recognizing the case for justice as equality, Tocqueville could not help but regret the passing of the pride, the sense of elevation (however often stilted and artificial), that governs aristocratic or traditional societies. Thus, he was driven to hypothesize the existence of "two distinct humanities, each of which has its particular advantages and inconveniences, its goods and evils that are proper to it."[2]

Today, however, we are obliged to recognize that, despite striking differences between dominantly aristocratic and dominantly democratic societies, there are not two humanities.[3] We are faced with the evidence that the attempt to order and enact our humanity on the pure idea of equality alone, or according to the exclusive spiritual ideal of equal purity, is not sustainable. Practical human existence requires a sense of elevation that the movement of democracy necessarily erodes. Democracy is parasitic on aristocracy in the minimalist sense of the residual moral authority of inherited norms instantiated in common institutions. A meaningful human existence cannot renounce all confidence in standing up for some intrinsic good, in action as the freely responsible application of some law understood as higher to some particular social and political context. The archic, initiating, commanding, and thus, in a certain sense, necessarily *prideful*, character of moral agency is essential to our humanity.

If the conclusion Joshua Mitchell draws from his examination of the political problem of Christianity is the wrong one, then it is time to ask directly, What would the right conclusion look like, the right practical disposition in today's world, a disposition governed by a lucid awareness of the competing claims of humble faith and prideful reason? I have already suggested above that Manent's Christian Aristotelianism (or "half-Thomism," as he once humorously ventured[4]) provides a superb example of responsible reasoning in a world that is at once post-Christian and, in a sense, all-too-Christian. Manent rejects all "integralist" or romantic nostalgia for a lost Christendom. I have argued, in fact, that he acknowledges the complicity of a certain hypertrophy of theology in the motivation of the modern rationalist-materialist project. Looking back on the history of modern secularism as it arises from the quandaries of Christian politics, Manent proposes we can now see beyond the rivalry of reason and revelation to an understanding of the common good that has been at work in the "mixed law" that has never been and can never be exhaustively theorized, but that has resulted in practice from this rivalry. In a word, we can be good liberals, in the broadest, practical sense, not by rejecting or even by setting aside our Christian commitments, but precisely in the light of a Christian appreciation of lawful liberty—that is, from the standpoint of a Christian conscience that accepts moral and political responsibility *understood from within the practical frame of our common life*—that is, a responsibility that would be considered "impure" both from the standpoint of a pure liberal-democratic theory and from that of a rigorously Protestant or radically Pascalian theology.[5]

To cap this vitally important point, let me repeat what I wrote above in discussing Manent:

> In the development of the modern liberalism of Europe's Christian nations, natural law has been demonstrated in practice, while obscured by the liberal theory that descends from Machiavelli via Hobbes and Locke. Manent's proposition of natural law is modest

or minimalist theoretically, but practically and spiritually momentous. He invites us to recognize the spiritual good that beckons beyond the visible arena of practical liberalism. He invites the discerning reader, that is, to register the humanity of a liberal natural law "of Christian mark" (that is, indelibly stamped by the spiritual and practical experience of Christian nations). The good of what he names this "mixed law" exceeds both liberal theory and any systematic and, finally, "otherworldly" theology.

Manent's formulation is both liberal and Christian because it posits a real liberty at the heart of creation, the real cooperation of human agency with Providence. The French Catholic political philosopher has consistently, at least since the time of the interviews published as *Seeing Things Politically*, understood human action properly or fully as at once conforming to the "grammar of action" inherent in our natures as rational agents as traced by Aristotle, and at the same time graced by the biblical understanding of Providence as addressing particular human beings each in his or her intimate individuality. Thus, Manent writes, the Greeks "understood everything that was essential to understand of human things, and they said it with incomparable sobriety and force." And yet these Greeks, whether we consider Homer, Plato, or Sophocles, could not give voice to the "inconceivable proximity between human fragility and divine holiness" as expressed, for example, in Psalm 139:15: "My bones were not hidden from you when I was made in secret, skillfully wrought [embroidered] in the depths of the earth."[6] I would add these unforgettable words from Isaiah 49:15–16: "For Can a woman forget her nursing child or show no compassion for the child of her womb? Even these might forget, yet I will not forget you. See, I have inscribed you on the palms of my hands; your walls are continually before me." As Strauss observes in the second-to-last sentence of *Natural Right and History*, "The quarrel between the ancients and the moderns concerns eventually, and perhaps even from the beginning, the status of 'individuality.'"[7] The Christian truth of the mysterious preciousness of every human person lies deeper than—and perversely fuels—the materialistic rationalism of the modern project. The conflagration of the modern project requires that we now learn how to reconcile religious "individuality" with a prudent regard for the natural grammar of action, which must always posit a concrete practical good irreducible to the equality of individuals.

YUVAL LEVIN'S CONSTITUTIONAL POLITICS OF EQUAL DIGNITY

Yuval Levin's eloquent and judicious plea, in *American Covenant: How the Constitution Unified Our Nation—and Could Again*,[8] for a renewal of constitutional politics offers a singular opportunity for clarifying the current political bearing of the "political Thomism" I am here proposing, drawing largely on insights of Pierre Manent. It is precisely because my approach is, in obvious practical respects, so close to Levin's that an engagement emphasizing our differences promises so much clarification on the philosophical-theological level. Even more than in the case of my engagement in the previous chapter with Joshua Mitchell's discerning critique of the perversely Christian character of "woke" psychology and politics, I am willing to risk indulging the "narcissism of small differences" in order to clarify both the philosophical-theological stakes and the contemporary practical bearing of my elaboration (and perhaps extension) of Pierre Manent's Christian-Aristotelian sponsorship of moderate liberalism. More is at stake here, certainly, than in the dispute that Jonathan Swift narrates concerning by which end an egg should be opened.

Levin's admirable book is animated by the same desire as expressed in James Madison's fourteenth Federalist paper, quoted in one of the author's epigraphs, that "the people of America" may yet (or, again) be "knit together . . . by so many cords of affection" and remain "fellow citizens of one great, respectable, and flourishing empire." To promote such togetherness, Levin proposes a refinement of our very understanding of unity: "Unity does not quite mean agreement . . . a more unified society would not always disagree less, but it would disagree better." The problem, Levin proposes, is not that there is much on which we once agreed but now disagree, but that "we have forgotten how to disagree. . . . We have forgotten the practical meaning of unity: in the political life of a free society, unity does not mean thinking alike; unity means acting together" (3). Such statements may seem to suggest a rather thin or instrumental understanding of constitutionalism, but Levin is careful to explain that the Constitution is not to be understood in a way that is "purely procedural or devoid of substantive purpose." Even the negative features of the Constitution—that is, the limits that it defines—"are there for a reason, and that reason is deeply rooted in an understanding of the ends of government" (18). He even goes as far as to describe the Constitution in Aristotelian terms as "the soul of a polity, [which] describes the innermost character of our society" (26). This innermost character is rooted, to take an eminent example, in "the principles articulated in the Declaration of Independence,"[9] understood not so much as a "legal framework" but rather as "a political framework" (28), a framework that "requires . . . a political culture . . . of negotiation and accommodation," one "inclined toward self-help and independent-mindedness" (30). It thus involves an "idea of the human being and citizen that emphasizes our responsibilities to one another and to the common good." This civic culture "counterbalances the liberal ethos because it values not just rights but obligations." A healthy constitutional culture thus combines modern liberalism with classical republicanism and, indeed, with Christian sobriety regarding human nature (269, 275). Levin thus sometimes recognizes that the Constitution cannot by itself produce the culture upon which it depends; the Constitution presupposes nonpolitical institutions "like families, civic and religious groups, and more" to forge politically essential virtues (342).

Still, Levin's strategy for a "renewal and revitalization" of American constitutionalism is not to preach this view of human nature balanced between liberal rights and republican virtue. Instead, he proposes an institutional strategy whereby "unity would have to be at least as much a product as a premise of American politics" (268). He recognizes the mutual causality of beliefs and practices—that is, that "institutions and culture shape each other"—but chooses an institutional strategy because "institutions are much more readily changeable" (296). In fact he hopes to distract us from our ideological or philosophical differences by focusing our attention on the Constitution as a process-defining institution that can teach us through practical experience to "disagree better."

Levin, thus, can hope to revive the educative power of constitutional politics only by drawing our attention away from fundamental differences in belief. He thus concludes his book with a plea that "each party must resist the urge to see the other as the enemy of democracy." And yet it cannot be said that Levin himself completely resists this urge. He cannot, finally, resist a critique, practically a denunciation, of progressivism, which he describes as "essentially integralist" (280)—that is, as fundamentally committed to exploiting or overriding the founders' constitution in view of its idea of "progress." On close inspection, Levin is sometimes willing to blame our current polarization not on a general lapse of reasonableness and moderation but on the fact that "the more progressive vision has been adopted in many arenas of our public life and has pulled our system in its desired direction" (284).[10] For his own part, Levin at least once is ready to confess that he is "a conservative, and not a bashful or halfhearted one," but one whose conservatism "is rooted, first and foremost, not in opposition to progressivism but in a protective disposition toward the best inheritance of our civilization." Now, it would seem that solicitude for "the best inheritance of our civilization" might, in fact, imply "opposition to progressivism," but I can at least sympathize with the author's choice to emphasize the positive. Similarly, he suggests that we attribute our present "problems" not so much to an "excess of liberalism," as "some on the American Right" would have it, but to "a shortage of republicanism" (83). It is easy to imagine a spokesman for this rather casually categorized "American Right" responding that "a shortage of republicanism" would seem to be strictly correlated, if not synonymous, with "an excess of liberalism," but let us defer to Levin's judgment concerning his preferred rhetorical approach. In the end, he judges it best to portray his constitutional revival as nonpartisan, if not quite morally or politically neutral: "This need not be—indeed, cannot be—a partisan enterprise" (286). This practical judgment seems, then, to be the foundation of Levin's rhetorical strategy: while we are relearning the art of productive disagreement, it is best for now to recognize, or to hope, that we can live with "some significant disagreement about exactly what the declaration's principles actually mean regarding the nature of the human person and the proper organization of society" (3).

Just how deeply can we disagree regarding our country's first principles and still share the same Constitution? Levin has once gone as far as to state that our "republican anthropology" (82) must include the idea that "human beings flourish by living in light of the truth" (279). But would it not be hard to deny that the idea that human beings are governed by a truth above or beyond themselves—a passably stable and knowable truth—is contested today and that the division between those who would embrace it and those who would deny it is, to say the least, politically accented? The least one can say is that the very meaning of "truth" has become, alas, a contested political question. How, finally, does Levin understand "truth" as it relates to practical human existence? The author's deepest dive philosophically, or his most strenuous doctrinal effort, comes when he proposes to define the "substantive vision of human flourishing" that supports his "republican liberalism" as a biblical or postbiblical understanding of the human being: "We tolerate people who differ from us because we are confident that every person, including those who are terribly wrong about important questions, is our equal in humanity and dignity and is equally made in a divine image." With this formulation of "truth" Levin seems confident that he has arrived at a deep and consensual premise that lies far beyond politics. In this proposition concerning equal human dignity, the breadth, even the radicality of Yuval Levin's understanding of constitutional tolerance "in the light of truth" is unmistakable. As fellow citizens of a liberal republic, we can engage in constitutional politics in pursuit of the common good even with "those who are terribly wrong about important questions" because we all know or believe that we are all equal in some fundamental if mysterious sense.

At the risk of disturbing this blessed unanimity, a sense of political responsibility compels me to ask: What have we to say to any who might disagree with this very biblical premise? Apparently, any views contrary to Levin's infinitely spiritual premise would not be involved in the process of compromise and adjustment that Levin celebrates, since the process seems to depend on or to be sheltered by this premise. Perhaps dissenters from the deep premise of equal dignity are so few as to be politically and, therefore, morally irrelevant.[11] I trust it is not necessary to stipulate here that I myself am not of a party that would contest the doctrine that our humanity bears the divine image. But is it really safe to assume that no one, or no one that matters, would advance claims that contradict the conviction of equal human dignity? To follow Levin's own advice concerning the emergent truth of constitutional politics: Can we even know what we mean by "equal humanity and dignity," can we discern what is effectively at stake in our practical lives in understanding ourselves as "the divine image," if we cannot even imagine this standpoint being contested—that is, if we "spiritualize" the biblical language to the point of severing it from all concrete moral and political claims?

The real problem is that Levin's deepest premise, his ultimate "light of truth," is now considered at once so mysteriously spiritual and so practically anodyne—that is, so obviously coextensive with an uncontested spirit of democratic openness—that it seems churlish even to wonder aloud about its practical implications. The reader will have understood, however, that to ponder the practical implications of the biblical mystery of individuality has been the whole purpose of this book. How can we live the universal truth of the equal divine image as practical moral and political agents responsible for the goods of finite and particular communities? How can we defend the "light of truth" against the seductive power of materialist and relativist interpretations? How can we resist the reduction in practice of infinite transcendence to the blind process of democratic and humanitarian openness that issues into the vortex what Tocqueville named "pantheism"?

If we cannot give a final and complete answer to this question, we can at least now see that much is at stake when Levin proposes to delve beneath the still politically grounded language of the Declaration of Independence, the perspective of the right to republican self-government, in order to ground American constitutionalism in what is in effect *a proposed synthesis of biblical and modern truth in the idea of equal dignity*.[12] Levin cites Manent's Aristotelian understanding of politics as "the production of the common" in support of the "republican" dimension of his constitutional synthesis (270–71, 279), but he wishes to ground this synthesis in an "equal dignity" quite foreign to Aristotle. But Manent has in fact explicitly warned against the translation of political "rights" into post-Christian and Kantian "dignity":

> In their original source, human rights are the rights *natural* to human beings, those that are inherent in their elementary nature, in their needs and desires and above all their desire for preservation.... Human dignity consists in the fact that human beings can be moved by a motive that is completely independent of nature and superior to it, by a purely spiritual causality. To put it rather bluntly: human rights concern natural freedoms . . . ; human

> dignity is freedom against physical or in general selfish nature, and it is spiritual liberty. . . . The contemporary moral conscience and moral reflection wish to reduce this tension. They seek to maintain the idea of dignity while detaching it from any idea of moral law and spiritual causality, to merge the idea of dignity with the idea of rights. In other words, to absorb, without losing it, the idea of dignity within the idea of rights.[13]

This fusion of rights and dignity, Manent goes on to argue, issues into "a politics of recognition," or the demand that "all life contents, all life choices, all lifestyles must be approved, appreciated, valued, applauded."

Nothing, of course, could be further from Levin's intention than to add fuel to the fire of the politics of recognition. But by leaving largely empty the space between the spiritual doctrine of equal human dignity and the concrete politics of the common good—that is, by seeking a nonpartisan stance with respect to the great moral-political issues of our times—the author of *American Covenant* has effectively preached unilateral moral disarmament to traditionalist lovers of God, family, and country, thus leaving the ideological weapon of mass destruction, the "spiritual" demand for equal recognition of all lifestyles, in the hands of postmodern and post-Christian radicals. To proclaim spiritual equality while keeping all particular beliefs and loyalties[14] at arm's length is effectively to plunge beneath the early modern "state of nature," to dissolve all concrete moral and political questions in the acid of John Rawls's "priority of the self to its ends." The Aristotelian "production of the common good," which the Philosopher understood to be driven by the contest between democratic and aristocratic claims concerning the worth or dignity of alternative contributions to the common good, is impossible if the substantive beliefs of various parties are disqualified or relativized at the outset in the light of that "singular cause of discord,"[15] the supposedly transpartisan claim of equal dignity, that appears at the end of every vista in the groves of our late modern academy. By inviting a politics of pluralism and productive disagreement while neutralizing all serious and concrete propositions about the human and political good, leaving only the elusive principle of equal dignity as a supposed ground of emergent consensus, Levin effectively situates his constitutional politics in a post-Rawlsian frame. The citizens he invokes are discouraged from bringing substantive convictions to the arena of the "production of the common" and thus are effectively invited to start from a place much like Rawls's "original position." Rawls's "priority of the self to its ends" is the effectual truth of "equal dignity" of every individual, the person stripped in advance of any "comprehensive doctrine" regarding life's purpose.

Levin's earnest constitutionalism thus leaves us, certainly despite his best intentions, at the threshold of Justice Anthony Kennedy's exquisitely spiritual hymn to the "heart of liberty" as "the right to define one's own concept of existence, of meaning, of the universe, and of the mystery of human life."[16] This is the powerful tendency of the effort to set Aristotelian pluralism, without due mediation, on the foundation of biblical equal dignity.

GRACE AND NATURE, EXCEPTION AND RULE

It is because of my sense of the responsibility of philosophers and theologians for such mediation between the biblical truth of individuality and the natural claims of virtue's intrinsic good that I have turned here at such length to the work of Manent. Only Manent has, I think, in our times, proposed the indispensable task of reconciling or coordinating Christian anthropology with liberal-republican self-government and its insuperably Aristotelian dimension. Constitutional pragmatics will not produce a working constitutional unity without the sponsorship of philosophers and theologians attuned to the good of freedom understood not in terms of raw "equal dignity" but rather, to repeat Tocqueville's lovely formula, as "liberty under God and the laws." To translate this understanding of political and moral self-government into broadly Thomistic terms, we might propose adapting the principle that grace does not destroy but perfects nature to the problem of liberal democracy today. The result would be something like this: "Dignity does not destroy mediated virtue, it perfects it." More specifically, perhaps, we might venture: infinite dignity does not destroy sturdy Christian and "bourgeois" virtues such as marital fidelity and economic industry and self-reliance. It does not, moreover, limit them, as in Joshua Mitchell's rigorously Protestant liberalism, to a mere instrumental "liberal competence." Instead, I propose, the spiritual idea of equal dignity must preserve a place for the recognition of some true merit, not without eternal significance, in the practical virtues of the soul, as well as in the particular common good of the city.

Manent points the way to such a reconciliation of equal human dignity with a substantial pluralist politics by situating the natural grammar of action, with its element of commanding pride, under a Providence that is a friend of human beings as individual, personal beings of eternal significance. The implication is that nature is open to and ultimately depends upon grace. In a word, Aristotle's articulation of the goodness of action points toward the grounding of this goodness in the love of a personal God, although nature's openness to grace and reason's implication in revelation may be seen only in retrospect from the perspective of revealed finalities.[17] On this view, the natural meaning of action, as limned by Aristotle, cannot finally be supported adequately by the Greek understanding of divinity as a rational impersonal necessity. At the same time, I am ready to propose that the biblical understanding of a personal, loving God cannot finally stand without a complementary understanding of the natural goodness of virtue, a goodness that must not be dissolved by an interpretation of divine freedom as arbitrary will.[18] The mysterious preciousness of every individual must not be severed from the natural structure of the agency of human beings as material, reproductive, and political. One might thus say that the Bible needs Aristotle, or presupposes Aristotle. Or, let us say the Bible is not meant utterly to displace Aristotle; grace is not meant to stand on its own without or apart from nature. I am thus proposing that no truer words can be addressed to the present age than this Thomistic motto: *Grace does not destroy nature, but perfects nature.*

To express the point more prosaically, let me say that the *exception* cannot replace the *rule*. Grace can be considered as an exception to nature, as mercy appears as an exception to justice—a redeeming, fulfilling exception, but still, in a way, an exception. Grace, as an exception, prevents the closure of nature upon itself and grafts an openness to transcendent possibility upon the upward vector of nature itself. The exception checks, interrupts, softens, and may even convict the rule of nature, considered as an autonomous claim. Elevated by grace, virtue rises above mere honor and the boast of self-sufficiency and thus can reach out with compassion to minister to those who are without honor in this world. But the exception that graces the rule also depends upon it.

For us post-Christian liberal democrats today, the exception and the rule have been reversed. Grace has been naturalized, and the celebration of diversity (i.e., of whatever "intersectional" interests can be leveled against any substantial goods and norms that might be held in common) is on the verge of becoming the only politically authorized and culturally affirmed morality. This is not an authentic consequence of Christianity, but it is still the result of a deep impulse abetted by Christianity—that is, of the tendency of an otherworldly religion to undermine all worldly moral authority. Today, the exception—humility, tolerance, self-emptying—would make itself the rule. But when the exception rules, it can no longer function as the exception. If grace displaces nature, it is no longer grace. A Christianity that pretends to be absolutely beyond politics will find itself either utterly irrelevant to practical existence or compelled to be a junior partner in the unnatural politics of empty universalism and humanitarianism. A grace that conceives the ambition to replace nature can only become more naturalistic than nature, more immanent than immanence, more presumptuous than natural pride.

If humility rules, it is no longer humble; if victimhood pays, then we are plainly being played by the "victim."[19] Self-repudiation as a moral weapon and political program is the rankest deception and self-deception. Pretending that the exception can be the rule is a luxury no civilization can long afford.

By contributing to or acceding to the relativizing of all substantial morality, which is always and everywhere morality tainted by particularity and thus by some degree of political closure, Christianity is always at risk of undermining its own moral basis and thus its own practical meaning. For the projection of the possibility of another world necessarily depends upon figures of elevation grounded in this natural, humanly mediated world.

It is no accident that the allied radicalisms of transcendence and of immanence tend to prevail in today's world since their message of the transience or relativity of actual, particular moral-political order, though only a half-truth, is a very apparent and seductive half of the truth, one easy to grasp in its negativity. This half-truth is often productive of short-term material benefits and, moreover, apt to "inspire" or to flatter our pretensions of transcendence in its lofty disdain for common attachments and finite loyalties. The easiest thing to grasp about the City of God is that it is *not* the City of Man—that is to say, that all existing moral-political authority is all-too-human, and that every individual soul is open to some promise, some meaning, some destiny far beyond anything that can be represented in the functionality of an actual political-cultural-economic world.

To counter this ascendant half-truth, we need, now more than ever, confidence in virtue! And if, in the eyes of a Christianity that emphasizes equal fallenness longing for equal innocence, such confidence is equivalent to impurity, then we need impurity!—the impurity and, yes, the inequality inherent in the "archic" character of action itself. To act is to stand up for something, and thus inherently to propose something as good, as better than the alternatives, and to advance one's own claim, however imperfect and fallible, to represent that good.

The practical implications of my view of the interdependence of grace and nature, or, let us say, of the necessary circulation of meaning between "nature" and "grace," could thus not be further from the spirit of what is generally called "political theology." I propose neither to reduce theology to the service of political decisionism through a voluntarist understanding of God (as per Carl Schmitt)[20] nor to deduce a political program from any high-minded but apolitical theological system (according to some "integralism" or "radical orthodoxy").[21] Rather than fusing politics and theology by reducing either one to the other, I propose to *coordinate* the deepest premises of the Christian faith, the foundations of our conviction, whether Christian or post-Christian, of the ultimacy of love, with our most sober moral and political judgments regarding the necessity and beauty of virtue. This coordination necessarily operates in both directions, aligning philosophy and theology with practical goods and supporting practical goods with philosophical and theological reflections. I have striven here to discern the contours of our practical, political nature in order both to give it its due and to point beyond it to a transcending hope and a redeeming God. My theological commitments in this argument are quite simple and general but immense in their implications: I propose that morally and politically responsible human action in this natural world is in some way eternally meaningful; at the same time, I confess that the ultimate end of human action escapes full human understanding and competence. To recall the terms of my introduction, virtue-religion must find its place in a cosmos governed by a creative logos, and the creative logos (or Pope Benedict's "personal logos"), a divinity both fully rational and fully personal, must be understood so as to shelter and cultivate the moderate but confident pride of virtue—a pride tempered by an awareness of human sinfulness and of the dependence of all human things upon a higher power and a transcendent purpose. Faith thus cannot be separated from reason and, in the first instance, from practical reason, nor reason from faith. And this giving to nature its due on the one hand and acknowledging what is beyond nature on the other I have shown to be two sides of *one and the same task*.

My qualified Christian embrace of natural, prideful virtue, in fact, honors the evangelical virtue of humility far better than the pseudo-Christian embrace of relativistic humanitarian compassion. It is because this democratic, post-Christian pseudohumility tends to abet the technological project of mastery of nature from the standpoint of a materialistic understanding of humanity that Christianity must now measure its rhetoric of self-emptying regard for "the other" in order to stand up for the actual humanity of the other human being as a moral and political being called to act responsibly in light of the goods imperfectly represented by its particular political and religious communities. This humility of the practical moral agent under God is a truer and more sustainable humility than the false and incoherent self-repudiation of the extreme Protestant and the democratic humanitarian. The mysterious preciousness of the individual person as loved by a personal Creator must be held together with the integrity of his creation—that is, in particular, with respect for the inherently prideful character of action.

We must learn a humility that loves humanity truly enough to love the confidence and initiative inseparable from purposive action. We have yet to appreciate the profundity of Tocqueville's aristocratic correction of democratizing Christianity: "Far from believing that one must recommend humility to our contemporaries, I should want one to strive to give them a vaster idea of themselves and of their species; humility is not healthy for them; what they lack most, in my opinion, is pride. I would willingly trade several of our small virtues for this vice."[22]

It is time to sacrifice our universalizing and transformative, humanitarian "virtue" in order to recover this "vice" that is inherent in our very humanity and a precondition of true holiness: *pride*.

NOTES

PREFACE

1. A notable recent example of this approach, including a focus on Jean-Jacques Rousseau as the deepest source of the radical ethic of self-expression, is Carl B. Trueman's *The Rise and Triumph of the Modern Self: Cultural Amnesia, Expressive Individualism, and the Road to Sexual Revolution.*

2. See especially Strauss, "Three Waves of Modernity"; Strauss, *Natural Right and History*; Voegelin, *Science, Politics & Gnosticism.*

3. Gallagher, *Enemies of Eros.*

4. The notion of "self-emptying," or kenosis, a subject of much theological reflection, is grounded scripturally especially in Philippians 2:7.

5. Manent, *Tocqueville and the Nature of Democracy*, 132.

6. René Girard's impressive oeuvre argued that victimhood in the form of the sacrifice of the innocent scapegoat is foundational to every civilization. Girard credits Christianity with the revelation of the truth of the innocence of the victim—a truth that haunts Western civilization, which can never fully recognize it. Pierre Manent argues that Girard in a sense proves too much: "I have always found this teaching powerful and impressive; and, at the same time, it has always seemed to me unacceptable and, in fact, particularly dangerous. For one of its consequences . . . is that the human order has no internal consistency and no inherent legitimacy. In any case, political order loses all consistency and legitimacy, because, if the basic truth of civilization, of human society, is undifferentiated violence and that we are all the same . . . there is no reason to distinguish among political societies . . . no reason to recognize that one regime is after all better than another." *Seeing Things Politically*, 72. See also Manent, "René Girard"; Manent, "La leçon de ténèbres." Later in life, Girard came to understand an emerging reign of "victimism, which uses the ideology of concern for victims to gain political or economic or spiritual power," and thus portends what Geoff Shullenberger in "René Girard and the Rise of Victim Power" calls "a genuine and troubling exhaustion of all other sources of authority and legitimacy."

Daniel J. Mahoney reports that "Girard argued at the end of his life [that] untold damage has been done to moral judgment and political prudence by a 'caricatural ultra-Christianity that tries to escape from the Judeo-Christian orbit by radicalizing the concern for victims in an anti-Christian manner.'" "The Delusions of Postcolonial Ideology." This theme is developed, Mahoney tells me, in Girard, *All Desire Is a Desire for Being.*

7. See Levinas, *Éthique comme philosophie première.*

8. Aquinas, *Summa Contra Gentiles* I.5.

INTRODUCTION

1. To be sure, Professor Bloom first got rich from the sales of his book; he had chosen a title that appealed to elites who were sure it applied only to those not so virtuously "open" as themselves. When a few began to discover that the joke was on them—that the "Closing" of the title targeted precisely their dear "openness"— then the reaction against his argument was all the nastier.

2. Bloom, *Closing of the American Mind*, 43.

3. See my engagement with what I call the "High Straussian" philosophical persuasion in *Responsibility of Reason*, 229–39.

4. Tocqueville, *Democracy in America*, 426.

5. Tocqueville, *Democracy in America*, 462.

6. Tocqueville, *Democracy in America*, 426.

7. Mahoney, *Idol of Our Age*, 123. Subsequent citations will be in parentheses in the text.

8. See, more generally, Mahoney's ch. 3, "Soloviev on the Antichrist, or the Humanitarian Falsification of the Good," which draws liberally on Alain Besançon's *The Falsification of the Good.*

9. The song was written by John Lennon, who sings lead on the recording.

10. This famous formulation of Augustine's view of pagan virtue we seem to owe to French philosopher Pierre Bayle (1647–1706). In *City of God* 19.25 (Bettenson, 891) the church father denounces the pride and selfishness of pagan "virtues" and argues that, not being the fruit of faith, they are in fact vices or sins: "Thus the virtues which the mind imagines it possesses, by means of which it rules the body and the vicious elements, are themselves vices rather than virtues, if the mind does not bring them in to relation with God. . . . When they are related only to themselves and are sought for no other end, even then they are puffed up and proud."

11. Remarkably, it is only after a more than respectful consideration of the possibility that the (Platonic) philosopher might reach or at least glimpse the true ground of happiness by his natural powers that Augustine finally defends the Christian proposition of the insufficiency of nature, of even the best natures. Augustine's

very understanding of divinity is certainly much influenced by the Platonist proposition, as he puts it in *City of God* 8.3 (Bettenson, 301–2): "[Socrates] thought that the causation of the universe could be grasped only by a purified intelligence. That is why he thought it essential to insist on the need to cleanse one's life by accepting a high moral standard, so that the soul could be relieved of the weight of the lust that held it down, and then by its natural vigour should rise up to the sphere of the eternal and behold, thanks to its pure intelligence, the essence of the immaterial and unchangeable light where dwell the causes of all created things in undisturbed stability."

12. Augustine, *City of God* 10.32 (Bettenson, 420; emphasis added).

13. Augustine, *City of God* 22.30 (Bettenson, 1088): "Did he [the prophet] not mean, 'I shall be the source of their satisfaction; I shall be everything that men can honourably desire: life, health, food, wealth, glory, honour, peace and every blessing'?"

14. Philippians 4:8.

15. Manent, *City of Man*, 265: "cette notion de loi générale, née de l'action et de l'usure réciproques de la cité et de l'Église" (this notion of general law, born from the reciprocal action and wear of the city and the church).

16. Hancock, *Calvin*.

17. Descartes, *Discourse on the Method*, 119.

18. Besançon, *Falsification of the Good*.

19. To be more precise, for Manent, we modern democrats are too Christian in the sense of an idealization of Christian "values": "The more that modern society effectively barricades itself against the real influence of Christianity, the more it feels itself animated by 'Christian values.'" "Some Remarks," 155.

20. Aquinas, *Summa Theologica* I.1.8 ad 2 (hereafter *ST*).

21. Holland, *Dominion*.

22. Siedentop, *Inventing the Individual*.

CHAPTER 1

1. Tocqueville, *Democracy in America*, 519.

2. Manent, *Natural Law and Human Rights*, 22, 23.

3. Manent, *Natural Law and Human Rights*, 69.

4. Manent, *Natural Law and Human Rights*, 8. Subsequent parenthetical page numbers in this section and the next (on Luther) refer to this text.

5. Strauss, *Natural Right and History*, 177. "It was Machiavelli, that greater Columbus, who had discovered the continent on which Hobbes could erect his structure."

6. We will explore the diverse and interrelated meanings of the "gap" of action further in part 2.

7. "I love my fatherland more than my own soul," Machiavelli wrote to Francisco Vittori on April 16, 1527. One might say that the Reformers, at least in their most radical formulations, chose not the "fatherland" of the world but the promise of the certainty of faith over the practical task of the soul's improvement.

8. Luther, "Appeal to the Ruling Class," 409–10.

9. Luther, *Secular Authority*, 385.

10. Luther, *Secular Authority*, 374 (in part 1), 398 (in part 3).

11. John Calvin distinguishes very sharply—even more radically than Luther—between the spiritual and the temporal, a dichotomy he equates with that between soul and body, or between inner mind and outward behavior. This radical severing of inner spirituality from external works is necessary, Calvin believes, in order to combat the "savage tyranny and butchery" (see the title of chapter 10 in book 4 of the *Institutes* [Battles, 1179]) of popes and priests, who wield power over souls by claiming to know what works are necessary to salvation. Like Luther, he denies freedom of the will. Humans may desire some good, he argues, but this desire is merely instinctive and shared with the brute beasts; it is not a rational choice of some higher good. "The desire for well-being natural to men no more proves freedom of the will than the tendency of metals and stones toward perfection of their essence proves it in them" (*Institutes* 2.2.26 [Battles, 287]). Against the tradition of "the Schoolmen" and even "certain other ancient writers," Calvin vigorously denies that "there is a faculty in the soul voluntarily to aspire to good" (2.2.27 [Battles, 287]). Calvin does not, however, follow Luther's argument that government is necessary only for those who are not true Christians. Rather, he holds that government is directly ordained of God and, in apparent agreement with Aquinas, that it is essential to our humanity (4.20.3 [Battles, 1488–89]). Calvin thus helps to prepare a modern understanding of natural law divorced from a reflection on nature's higher purposes. Precisely because he conceives of godliness as altogether above, or rather beyond, natural human desires, he must conceive reason as governing those desires without reference to anything higher. But this is not to say that Calvin regards natural reason as self-sufficient, even in the secular world to which it is confined. On the contrary, it is precisely because of natural reason's propensity to violate the limitations of preservation, disguising its lust with appeals to some higher purpose, that revealed authority is necessary to the order of society. Apart from the fear of God, human beings do not preserve equity and love among themselves. The rational instinct of self-preservation cannot hold its own against the presumption of reason without the help of revealed authority.

For this reading of Luther and Calvin, see my chapter on the Reformers, "Luther and Calvin." On Calvin, see further my *Calvin and the Foundations of Modern Politics*.

12. The title and all quotations from this essay are my translations from the author's French manuscript, which was later published as "Réflexions de philosophie pratique."

13. Manent, "Réflexions de philosophie pratique," 213.

14. Manent, "Réflexions de philosophie pratique," 213. Subsequent citations of this work and its citation of Barth's *Römerbrief 1922* are in parentheses in the text.

15. "A l'ouverture salutaire de nos yeux pourvoient la souffrance et, se rattachant immédiatement à la donnée limite—*Grenzdatum*—de la souffrance, ce qui dans son essence est une interprétation de cette donnée, à savoir la philosophie lorsqu'elle est digne de son nom" (The salutary opening of our eyes is provided by suffering, and by what joins itself immediately to the givenness at the limit—the *Grenzdatum*—of suffering, which is in its essence an interpretation of this givenness—that is, philosophy when it is worthy of its name). Manent, 222; Barth, 329.

16. Heidegger, *Supplements*. Citations of this source are in parentheses in the text.

17. We might say then that Heidegger uses Luther to deconstruct Aristotle. To round out this sketch of essential sources of the Heideggerian project, we would also have to understand how he uses Aristotle to deconstruct Luther. What this might mean is no doubt clear enough in a basic sense: Aristotle, no more than Heidegger, believes in a transcendent personal divinity, and he takes his bearings from a phenomenology of actual human existence. An Aristotelian method strips Luther of God; Luther strips Aristotle of the good. Thus Heidegger's project represents the most radical case of the production of a modern viewpoint by the mutual erosion of faith and reason. For this mutual erosion, see Manent, *City of Man*.

CHAPTER 2

1. Manent, "Réflexions de philosophie pratique." Subsequent citations are in parentheses in the text. Translations from the French are my own.

2. Manent, *Natural Law and Human Rights*, 33. Similarly, Manent speaks in *Natural Law and Human Rights* of "the indetermination that is specifically characteristic of practice."

3. Manent, *Natural Law and Human Rights*, 48–49.

4. Manent, *Natural Law and Human Rights*, 35. Subsequent citations are in parentheses in the text.

5. See ch. 1, under "Pierre Manent versus Theoretical Hypertrophy."

6. In *The City of Man*, Manent noted that the philosophical tradition explored "so many paths from one to the other"—that is, from practice to theory. And he wrote approvingly of the role of justice and eros in their "continuous nurturing [of the] flame of philosophy" (145). Most significantly, he read Plato and Aristotle as secretly consenting to a certain confusion between law and nature—between practice and theory, we might say. In *Metamorphoses of the City*, Manent declines to follow the classical political philosophers in grafting an idea of final perfection of the soul onto the classical idea of the best city or *regime*, arguing instead that the *inherent* limitation of the classical city gives rise to a rather open-ended "metamorphosis" of political *forms*.

One way of signaling the thesis of the present book (which builds upon Manent's reflection) would be to say that this wholesome confusion, which served to sustain the dignity of practice, can now no longer serve its humane purpose, and that a certain "confusion" between practical and ultimate ends—a "luminous opacity," I will argue—must be made explicit and embraced as such.

CHAPTER 3

1. Tocqueville, *Democracy in America*, 6.
2. The most penetrating analysis I know of the religious diagnosis of the woke is Mitchell, *American Awakening*. I discuss Mitchell's response to this secular "awakening" in ch. 12.
3. The selections date from 1984 to 2021, though all but three of the eighteen pieces were produced in the twenty-first century.
4. Manent, "Christianity and Democracy," 15.
5. And for Charles Péguy, the great patriotic and Christian poet and essayist who died in the early days of the Great War. See the final selection in Manent, *Religion of Humanity*: "An Eminent Predecessor."
6. Manent, "Church between a Real Humanity and a Dreamed-Of 'Humanity,'" 89.
7. Manent, "Political Responsibility," 53.
8. Manent, "Humanitarian Temptation," 36.
9. Manent, "Excerpt from *A World beyond Politics*," 42.
10. Manent, "Excerpt from *A World beyond Politics*," 43.
11. Manent, "Humanitarian Temptation," 37.
12. Manent, "Political Responsibility," 49.
13. Manent, "Political Responsibility," 53.
14. Manent, "Religion of Humanity," 64. Subsequent citations are in parentheses in the text.
15. Lennon, "Imagine."
16. Manent, "Church between a Real Humanity and a Dreamed-Of 'Humanity,'" 96.
17. Manent, "Church between a Real Humanity and a Dreamed-Of 'Humanity,'" 89.
18. Manent, "Who Is 'the Good Samaritan'?," 107. The quotations within the quotations from Manent are from Pope Francis.
19. Emphasis added. Compare this: "[The principle of the Christian word] resides entirely in itself, that is to say, in Jesus Christ, who is its center." Manent, "Migrations and Christianity," 121.
20. Manent, "Who Is 'the Good Samaritan'?," 113.
21. Manent, "Who Is 'the Good Samaritan'?," 107.
22. Manent, "Migrations and Christianity," 121.
23. Manent, "Migrations and Christianity," 122.

24. Manent, "Excerpts from *Beyond Radical Secularism*," 132–34.

25. Manent, "Who Is 'the Good Samaritan'?," 107.

26. Manent, "Church between a Real Humanity and a Dreamed-Of 'Humanity,'" 87.

27. "To describe [the political and spiritual decisions that human communities will take] there is no other lexicon than the catalogue of the cardinal and theological virtues." Manent, "Church between a Real Humanity and a Dreamed-Of 'Humanity,'" 94. The editor notes that these lines were penned in 2012, near the (unforeseen) end of Pope Benedict XVI's pontificate.

28. Mahoney's formulation in fact distills the intention of the second, more constructive part of the present volume.

CHAPTER 4

1. The relation between norms and goods in practical natural law—the entwining of these notions, in fact—will be a theme of part 2.

2. Manent, *Natural Law and Human Rights*, 17. Manent argues in ch. 4 that the illusion of "autonomy" is necessarily accompanied by the purposeless, unanswerable commands of the "machine" of the state.

3. Manent, *Natural Law and Human Rights*, 51.

4. This neglect has more recently been remedied by the work of Eric Gregory and Eric Nelson. See n. 8 below. Citations of *A Theory of Justice* will be given by section number in the main text.

5. For a brief overview of Rawls's career see Peter Berkowitz's respectful but critical memorial of Rawls, which appeared originally in *The Weekly Standard*: https://peterberkowitz.wordpress.com/2002/12/16/the-academic-liberal/. For a profound and full-throated critique there is Allan Bloom's legendarily indignant denunciation, "Justice: John Rawls." A fuller treatment of Rawls's idea of justice than the present would address the shift from a theory of justice (*Theory of Justice*, 1971) to an ostensibly more modest or circumspect political liberalism (*Political Liberalism*, 1993). On this shift let it suffice here to say that Rawls's apparent retreat from all "comprehensive visions" to a "merely" political liberalism cost his theoretical liberalism very little, since this later version, while radicalizing Rawls's retreat from substantive moral and political questions, conceded nothing in terms of authoritative political answers. The realm of politics is presented as philosophically modest, but the assertion of the sovereignty of a certain "liberal" politics over religion and philosophy is in no way compromised.

6. Rawls does nothing to hide this resemblance, which is simply the result of a "reflective equilibrium" that adjusts findings of the theoretical model to what "we" already know is consistent with "justice."

7. Here Rawls is exactly in step with the constructivist foundations of liberalism going back to Thomas Hobbes, and more particularly with J. S. Mill's transformative ambitions as expressed in *Utilitarianism*, ch. 3, "On the Ultimate Sanction

of the Principle of Utility." The ultimate sanction, predictably, is the combined symbolic and material incentives that "society" can bring to bear on the malleable moral psyche of humanity.

8. Eric Gregory's discovery of Rawls's undergraduate thesis at Princeton University confirms the continuity between Rawls's youthful Christian anti-Pelagianism and what I would call his mature anti-Aristotelianism. See Gregory, "Before the Original Position." The common thread in this transition from the concept of divine grace to that of the attribution of all unequal outcomes to accidents of nature and history is the utter rejection of the category of moral merit. Rawls's secularization of radical Protestant grace transfers power from a God beyond all human measure or ken to society (as defined by the imperative of equality and the elusive concept of "reciprocity") as the absolute arbiter of "justice." See also Nelson, *Theology of Liberalism*, 49–72, who shows not only Rawls's affinity with but his debt to Karl Marx in the absolute rejection of unequal moral desert.

9. Rawls, *Political Liberalism*, 456.

10. Siedentop, *Inventing the Individual*, 36. Subsequent citations are in parentheses in the text.

11. Manent, *Metamorphoses of the City*, 99.

12. Hancock, "Les métamorphoses de Pierre Manent."

13. Manent, *Metamorphoses of the City*, 100.

14. See Lilla, "New, Political Saint Paul?"

15. 1 Corinthians 1:21.

16. Badiou, *Saint Paul*, 49.

17. Badiou, *Saint Paul*, 67.

18. Badiou, *Saint Paul*, 92.

19. The brief summary of Kojève's view that follows is drawn from his engagement with Leo Strauss in "Tyranny and Wisdom," an essay by Kojève that Gourevitch and Roth included in their edition of Strauss's *On Tyranny*.

CHAPTER 5

1. Strauss, "Restatement on Xenophon's *Hiero*," 185. Subsequent citations will be in parentheses in the text.

2. Strauss, *Spinoza's Critique of Religion*, 10. Subsequent citations will be in parentheses in the text.

3. The reference to this mean is a very striking echo of Strauss's lecture "German Nihilism," an argument that finally turns as well on the necessity of coercion.

4. The formula "Aristotelian interpretation of Christianity" is too simple and unilateral, to be sure. Certainly Aquinas honored the Platonic-Augustinian vein of Western Christianity as he undertook to appropriate insights from Aristotle. It is not my task here to sort out this question, though my work in parts 2 and 3 of this volume will no doubt bear on it.

5. Strauss, *On Tyranny*, 192.
6. Strauss, *On Tyranny*, 191.
7. Maritain, *Réponse à Jean Cocteau*, 724.

CHAPTER 6

1. Here are the complete lyrics:

> 1. Come, ye children of the Lord, / Let us sing with one accord. / Let us raise a joyful strain / To our Lord who soon will reign / On this earth when it shall be / Cleansed from all iniquity, / When all men from sin will cease, / And will live in love and peace.
> 2. Oh, how joyful it will be / When our Savior we shall see! / When in splendor he'll descend, / Then all wickedness will end. / Oh, what songs we then will sing / To our Savior, Lord, and King! / Oh, what love will then bear sway / When our fears shall flee away!
> 3. All arrayed in spotless white, / We will dwell 'mid truth and light. / We will sing the songs of praise; / We will shout in joyous lays. / Earth shall then be cleansed from sin. / Ev'ry living thing therein / Shall in love and beauty dwell; / Then with joy each heart will swell.

Text: James H. Wallis, 1861–1940. Music: Spanish melody; arr. by Benjamin Carr, 1768–1831.

2. This is the quotation I took for the epigraph to ch. 5, above.
3. Lewis, "Weight of Glory," 15, 14.
4. Tocqueville, *Democracy in America*, xvii. Subsequent citations are in parentheses in the text.
5. This problem is treated more fully in ch. 2 of my *Responsibility of Reason*, "The Crisis of 'Moral Analogy' and the Problem of the Rule of Reason."
6. Pascal, *Pensées*, fragment 72.
7. Tocqueville explores the problem of mediation further throughout part 1 of volume 2 of *Democracy in America*. Chapter 20 shows how democratic historians abandon human agency to "inflexible providence or . . . blind fatality" (471). (The remark concerning providence raises important questions about Tocqueville's own providential rhetoric.) Other chapters in part 1 seem to feature somewhat unrelated and peculiar observations, as are indicated by the following chapter titles: "Why the Americans at the Same Time Raise Such Little and Such Great Monuments" (ch. 12); "Why American Writers and Orators Are Often Bombastic" (ch. 18). But, on closer inspection, these chapters clearly reinforce Tocqueville's teaching concerning the American aversion to mediation—that is, to representations of meaning on a human scale and thus attuned to the nature of moral analogy. Much, if not everything, that Tocqueville then argues in parts 2–4 of volume 2 can be read profitably with this schematic of part 1 of volume 2 in mind; consider, for example, the whole critique of statism in part 4 of volume 2, quite obviously, as well as

the brilliant and far-reaching discussion of "honor" in 2.3.18. But Tocqueville's theorizing about the democratic passion for generalizing abstraction reaches a kind of limit and culmination already in 2.1.7, the powerful and somewhat enigmatic chapter on "pantheism." As argued in our part 1 above, pantheism is the final paroxysm and collapse of democratic universalization, the disastrous triumph of the form of generality or "inclusiveness" over the substance of virtue.

8. Tocqueville, *Old Regime*, 217.

9. I cannot here engage Thomas Aquinas's momentous interpretation of the Creator's self-naming before Moses as the *act* of existence itself. Thomas's interpretation might be understood as an attempt to hold together something essential in the other two readings. See *ST* I.13.11.

10. Mahoney, *Idol of Our Age*, 125. Subsequent citations are in parentheses in the text.

11. Reinsch, introduction, 35, cited in Mahoney, *Idol of Our Age*, 41.

12. Mahoney is discussing Pope Benedict XVI's "The Temptations of Jesus," chapter 2 of volume 1 of *Jesus of Nazareth*.

13. Mahoney is discussing Manent, *Beyond Radical Secularism*.

14. Mahoney is discussing Soloviev, "Nationality from a Moral Point of View."

15. Students of Thomas Aquinas's teaching on natural law will recognize that we are here anticipating an essential feature of this teaching: "Now among all others, the rational creature is subject to divine Providence in the most excellent way, insofar as it partakes of a share of providence, by being provident both for itself and for others." *ST* I-II.91.2 res. See ch. 11 below.

CHAPTER 7

1. Strauss, "What Is Political Philosophy?," 47.
2. Manent, *Natural Law and Human Rights*, 66.
3. Manent, *Natural Law and Human Rights*, 24.
4. Mansfield, introduction, 5.
5. Manent, *Seeing Things Politically*, 160.
6. Mahoney, *Idol of Our Age*, 14. The stability of this divine "image," I would add, depends on interpreting divine kenosis or self-emptying in a way that stops short of emptying our understanding of divinity of all content of nobility as it emerges in practical goods.
7. Manent, *Natural Law and Human Rights*, 101.
8. Manent, *Natural Law and Human Rights*, 101.
9. Manent, *Natural Law and Human Rights*, 111.
10. Manent, *Natural Law and Human Rights*, 110.
11. This teleological project can be considered an understandable but finally ill-considered reaction against modern reductionist materialism and individualism. Both teleological theology and reductionist theory have a certain justification in

their critique of the other. But to define natural law or moral-political deliberation in terms of this opposition tends to blind us to practical goods as such.

12. Manent, "Reason and Faith."

13. Manent, *Natural Law and Human Rights*, 67. Manent here notes that for Aquinas, as for "classical moral philosophy, one could speak of autonomy only with reference to a political body." Manent's relation to Aquinas is an explicit, but still delicately treated, theme in "Recovering Law's Intelligence," the remarks published as an appendix in the English edition of *Natural Law and Human Rights*.

14. Manent, *Natural Law and Human Rights*, 90.

15. Manent, *Natural Law and Human Rights*, 89 (emphasis added). Manent refers to the "knot" that tied together the natural fear of death with fear of a transcendent God. This fearsome knot may be considered the negative image of and alternative to the gap or circle of practical good. If the highest good and ultimate authority is not understood in terms of the practical experience of the just and the noble, then all that remains is a fear and awe that evacuates all good.

16. Manent, *Natural Law and Human Rights*, 90.

17. Manent, *City of Man*, 164.

18. Hancock, *Responsibility of Reason*, 84–87.

19. Manent, *City of Man*, 165, citing Aristotle, *Politics* 1282b14–18, 1284b6. Subsequent citations of *City of Man* are in parentheses in the text.

20. Dates given are for the original French publications.

21. Manent, *Beyond Radical Secularism*, 64 (emphasis added).

22. The case for the deeply political bearing of Thomas's natural law will be made in ch. 11, especially under "Natural Law as Political."

23. Manent, *Beyond Radical Secularism*, 69–70.

24. This is the title of the article, first published in the *Revue Thomiste* (2014), that is included as the appendix to the English edition of *Natural Law and Human Rights*.

25. Manent, *Natural Law and Human Rights*, 128.

CHAPTER 8

1. Manent, *Natural Law and Human Rights*, 66. Subsequent citations are in parentheses in the text.

2. I here adopt Spinoza's term (not Manent's) for the elementary drive or tendency of a being to continue in being.

3. This is the thesis of my *Responsibility of Reason*.

4. The modern craving for interpersonal transparency, and the resulting resort to obsession with the practical obstacle to such transparency, is brilliantly diagnosed in Starobinski, *Jean-Jacques Rousseau*. How to understand the biblical promise that we will finally see "face to face" (1 Corinthians 13), see as we are seen and know as we are known, in the light of the irreducible if luminous opacity of practical

existence may be said to be the ultimate or transultimate question that drives or draws out the present work.

5. Aristotle, *Nicomachean Ethics* 10.
6. Tocqueville, *Democracy in America*, 521.
7. Tocqueville, *Democracy in America*, 521–22.
8. Tocqueville, *Democracy in America*, 518 (emphasis added).
9. This reading of Aristotle is further developed in my *Responsibility of Reason*, 76–87. One can understand the whole project of modern philosophical ethics as an effort to resolve what is for Aristotle this living and irreducible tension between the noble and the just at the heart of human action. There are on the one hand the philosophers of justice, the deontologists, who, with Kant as their captain, strive to vindicate the purity of the just and thus the absolute autonomy of human liberty. At the opposing pole are the utilitarians, who would judge every action in relation to an immanent finality they name utility or the greatest happiness of the greatest number. But these are in both cases ethics of justice (and not of nobility), since the horizon of action is in both cases some pure duty—uncontaminated by any "nonmoral" purpose on earth or in heaven—toward *others*, toward the city of man.

If there is a pure case of the ethics of the noble as emancipated from the just, this would be the Platonizing teaching, not so much of Leo Strauss himself (whose subtle negotiation of the dialectic between the city and the soul admits of no straightforward reduction), but of those I have called the "High Straussians," for whom the summit of philosophy and of human existence is held to be a pure nobility of the soul as achieved only in the absolute elevation of the activity of philosophy itself, which thus finds itself detached in its essence from all but instrumental ties to the practical and affective lives of ordinary (nonphilosophical) human beings.

I will not digress further here to assess such attempts to resolve the Aristotelian tension, except to say that Kantian deontology and utilitarianism are mutually dependent; each ends up falling back on the other: the pure form of autonomy (rational self-legislation) cannot avoid borrowing its practical content from the necessities of the city, and the service of the utility of the greatest number requires an altruistic motive that utilitarian philosophy cannot account for.

As for the High-Straussian solution of pure philosophic satisfaction, one must simply consider for oneself the adequacy of the inhuman goodness of what my late friend Peter Lawler so aptly referred to as "transerotic solitude," praised in particular by Thomas Pangle. Lawler, "America's Cartesian Intellectual Method," 205. (For my critique of the High-Straussian gambit see *Responsibility of Reason*, ch. 5.)

10. Solzhenitsyn, "We Have Ceased to See the Purpose."

CHAPTER 9

1. See Hancock, review of *Political Philosophy*.
2. Pangle, *Political Philosophy*, 62–63.

3. Bloom, *Love and Friendship*, 441.
4. Kass, *Beginning of Wisdom*, 347.
5. Augustine, *City of God* 8.6 (Bettenson, 307).
6. Augustine, *City of God* 8.12.
7. Augustine, *City of God* 10.32 (Bettenson, 420–21).
8. Augustine, *City of God* 10.32 (Bettenson, 424).
9. Augustine, *City of God* 12.18 (Bettenson, 495).
10. Augustine, *City of God* 12.21 (Bettenson, 499).
11. Augustine, *City of God* 12.2.
12. The difficulty of this challenge is immediately apparent in the institution of celibacy as a blessed exception to familial duties of ordinary Christians, even while these duties were held up as central to the Christian vocation for all those who were not covered by the exception. (This perceived inconsistency was of course among the major complaints of the Protestant Reformers.)
13. De Rougemont, *Love in the Western World*, 46.
14. De Rougemont, *Love in the Western World*, 311 (emphasis added).
15. De Rougemont, *Love in the Western World*, 290–91.
16. Robinson, *Gilead*, 57.
17. Robinson, *Gilead*, 147.
18. Homer, *Odyssey* 5.236–43 (page 4 of 8 in bk. 5 of the Page by Page edition of the Butler trans.).
19. For an excellent survey, see Roberts, *Creation and Covenant*.
20. Ratzinger, "Yesterday, Today, and Tomorrow," 11.
21. Ratzinger, "Yesterday, Today, and Tomorrow," 19.
22. Benedict XVI, "Pope's Speech at University of Regensburg."
23. Benedict XVI, "Pope's Speech at University of Regensburg."
24. Strauss, "What Is Political Philosophy?," 38.
25. See ch. 1 under "Pierre Manent versus Theoretical Hypertrophy" and ch. 2 under "Conscience as the Summit and Precipice of Moral Agency."
26. Benedict XVI, *Deus Caritas Est*, 400. Subsequent citations are in parentheses in the text.
27. Pope Benedict XVI thus sees monogamous marriage, a "unique and definitive bond" in "one flesh," as the, or a, proper end of eros, "from the standpoint of creation" and as "the icon of the relationship between God and his people." He notes, too, that "this close connection between eros and marriage in the Bible has practically no equivalent in extrabiblical literature" (404). The eternal status of this privileged expression of the synthesis of eros and agape remains something of a puzzle, however. It is notable that, in the praise of marital love quoted above, Benedict, by placing the word "forever" in quotation marks, qualifies the dimension of eternity in the "definitive" commitment to love a particular human being "forever."

My late friend Peter Lawler, in "The Personal Logos and the Christian Idea of Marriage," an unpublished paper for a conference at Brigham Young University, 2013, showed that Pope Benedict XVI urged the faithful to ground their understanding of personal freedom—that is, of free personality—in the concrete realities of our natural being as embodied, reproductive beings. Our natural affections and dependencies are understood by Benedict, Lawler argued, as a privileged ground for understanding our eternal personhood. Benedict proposes, moreover (as we have seen), that the sacrament of marriage is our highest natural link to the personal knowing that lies at the heart of divinity: it is in the intimate fellowship of true Christian marriage that we come closest to the synthesis of knowing and loving that constitutes the divine Trinity. Still, Lawler explained to the members of the Church of Jesus Christ of Latter-day Saints he was addressing, for Benedict, as for the whole mainstream Christian theological tradition, marriage is for this world only. Referencing Pope John Paul II, Lawler argued that the resurrection closes the historical dimension of marriage and opens up the eternal perspective of communion with all the saints and with God, a communion that excludes all particularized, familial, or marital intimacy. To be sure, as resurrected beings we will remain sexed beings, but there seems to be no eternal meaning that can be ascribed to our eternal differentiation into male and female. Thus, Lawler argued, despite Benedict's emphasis on our sexual differentiation and familial dependencies as figures of our essentially relational and personal being, in the end the Greeks seem to have the last word for the Christians: like Thomas Aquinas before him, Benedict holds that, beyond our sexed and familial natures, it is the mind that most fundamentally defines our eternal being, however "personal." Reproduction, notably, is understood finally as an earthly necessity from which we are ultimately liberated by Christian salvation. Our ultimate end is thus understood as "the loving, relational contemplation of the sexually undifferentiated, personal God" (Lawler, "Personal Logos," 23). A certain tension in Pope Benedict's teaching is well expressed by Lawler: "Our liberation through Christ somehow both is and is not from being a man or a woman. Our liberation both is and is not from being a social (Darwinian, we might say) and political (Aristotelian) being." Thus Lawler argued that, finally, in this Catholic Christian vision, eros is understood to be orientated toward a *contemplative* fulfillment. To be sure, Lawler noted, this idea of "contemplation" departs from pagan philosophy in insisting on the inherently personal, relational quality of divinity. But the meaning of "personal" and "relational," though first grounded in our concrete experience as familial beings, is ultimately untethered from such experiences and directed toward the contemplative love of an immaterial divinity. I have argued, however, that the synthesis of eros and agape embraced by Benedict XVI puts more pressure on the classical concept of "contemplation"—with its ultimate foundation in the same as opposed to the other—than Lawler seemed to allow. A published source for Lawler's discussion of Benedict XVI's understanding of the personal logos is "Defending the Personal Logos Today."

28. In the present volume, see ch. 6, under "Liberty under God and the Laws."

29. Tocqueville, *Democracy in America*, 11. In the present volume, see ch. 6, under "The Democratic-Christian Threat to Moral Analogy."

30. I rely here largely on the admirable treatise of Pierre Aubenque: *Le problème de l'être chez Aristote*.

CHAPTER 10

1. Here I extract some essential insights from Davis's book as a whole. The following words from chapter 1, "The Doubleness of Soul," on Aristotle's *De anima*, seem to me to go to the heart of the problem of the soul's active particularity on the one hand and its dependence on an awareness of the whole on the other: "But how is it possible for a being with a particular disposition or bent to be so self-effacing as to be 'somehow all beings'? Won't the good proper to my nature interfere with the truth of my awareness? Put differently, how is it possible for awareness to be 'mine' and still true?" Davis, *Soul of the Greeks*, 22. Subsequent citations are in parentheses in the text.

2. The deepest truth in Leo Strauss's understanding of the most adequate and permanent human good as openness to the fundamental problems is not, then, the superiority of zetetic Athens over dogmatic Jerusalem, but in fact the very aporia between Athens and Jerusalem, the coprimordiality of the logos and the personal.

3. Taylor, *Sources of the Self*, ch. 9.

4. Tocqueville, *Democracy in America*, 463. Subsequent citations are in parentheses in the text.

5. Leo Strauss's articulation of the project of modern rationalism in three waves (nature as necessity, history as rational, history as nonrational) is an insight of enduring explanatory value. See Strauss, "Three Waves of Modernity."

6. For a thorough consideration of Christianity's implication, according to Tocqueville, in the collapse of the soul into the subject-self, see Hancock, *Responsibility of Reason*, chs. 2 and 6.

7. Levinas, *Éthique comme philosophie première*. Citations are in parentheses in the text, and all translations are mine. The formulation "conscience grounds consciousness" is mine, since "consciousness" and "conscience" cannot be distinguished in the French original.

8. Rolland, "Surenchère de l'éthique," 35.

9. Levinas, *Otherwise than Being*, 77.

10. Levinas, *Otherwise than Being*, 75.

11. Levinas, *De l'existence à l'existant*, 64, 67, 62. Translations are mine.

12. Levinas, *De l'existence à l'existant*, 69.

13. Levinas, "De la phénoménologie," 140.

14. Levinas, *Humanism of the Other*, 28–29.

15. Strauss, *On Tyranny*, 202. "The philosopher's dominating passion is the desire for truth, i.e., for knowledge of the eternal order, or the eternal cause or causes of the whole. As he looks up in search for the eternal order, all human things and all human concerns reveal themselves to him in all clarity as paltry and ephemeral, and no one can find solid happiness in what he knows to be paltry and ephemeral." My interpretation of Strauss's rhetoric of pure philosophic transcendence as inherently practical and aristocratic is developed at greater length in *The Responsibility of Reason*, ch. 5.

CHAPTER 11

1. Aquinas, *Summa Contra Gentiles* I.5. "Any knowledge, however imperfect, of the noblest objects confers a very high perfection on the soul."
2. Tocqueville, *Democracy in America*, 417.
3. The following review of the history of the question of the analogy of being, and particularly of twentieth-century German theologian Erich Przywara's eminent contribution, is heavily indebted to Betz, "After Barth." This excellent chapter appeared in an expanded form as the translator's introduction to Przywara, *Analogia Entis*, 1–115.
4. Betz, "After Barth," 46. It is the analogy of "proportion" that, since Cajetan, has figured most prominently in Thomistic theological discussions.
5. Betz, "After Barth," 48.
6. Betz, "After Barth," 44. Betz here draws upon Clarke, *Explorations in Metaphysics*.
7. Betz, "After Barth," 49.
8. Betz praises Przywara, *Analogia Entis*, as "arguably the most important work of Catholic metaphysics in the twentieth century." "After Barth," 39. See also the superlative testimonials of Christophe Chalamet, Edith Stein, Karl Rahner, and Hans Urs von Balthasar cited by Betz, "After Barth," 40–43.
9. I continue here to follow Betz. Here he quotes Przywara, *Religionsphilosophische Schriften*, 2:7.
10. The full text of Romans 1:20 (NRSV) is as follows: "Ever since the creation of the world God's eternal power and divine nature, invisible though they are, have been seen and understood through the things God has made."
11. Przywara's "in-über" can also be rendered, Betz suggests, "in-over" or "in-and-above." Betz, "After Barth," 53.
12. Betz, "After Barth," 57. The reflection that makes up the rest of this paragraph, while inspired by Betz's Przywara, is my own.
13. See my discussion of Strauss on reason and revelation in *Responsibility of Reason*, 213–21. See also my discussion of Manent's "Reason and Faith" in ch. 7 of the present volume.
14. In his twenties, Przywara worked as a "prefect of music" in Austria and collaborated in the production of a collection of hymns. He acknowledged a significant . . . analogy between his musical and theological sensibilities. "Music as form is the motherland of 'polarity': 'unity-in-tension,' and eventually 'analogy.'" Zeitz, "Erich Przywara," citing Przywara, *In und Gegen*.
15. Betz, "After Barth," 56.
16. Betz, "After Barth," 52, citing Przywara, *Religionsphilosophische Schriften*, 2:7.
17. See discussion of Manent's critical reflection on Barth's *Römerbrief* in ch. 2.
18. Compare Ratzinger in his early *Introduction to Christianity*: "Precisely when we apply the concept of person to God, the difference between our idea of person and the reality of God—as the Fourth Lateran council says about all speech

concerning God—is always infinitely greater than what they have in common." But then Ratzinger goes on to insist, against "mystical" religions, with their "purely negative theology," in which "God's personal nature" is "abandoned outright," that "not only . . . can we experience him, beyond all [earthly] experience, but also that he can express and communicate himself." Ratzinger, excerpt from *Introduction to Christianity*, 9.

19. Betz, "After Barth," 70–72. Przywara cites and embraces the dictum of Lateran IV in *Analogia Entis*, 234.

20. Betz is not unaware of this dialectic: "If one makes God unequivocally 'other,' denying divine immanence (to a real creation), one ends up either with a Gnostic world that is essentially independent of God (paving the way for modern secularism) or, in a second type of Gnosticism, one so devalues the integrity of creation as a natural realm of secondary causes as to absorb the creature (whether inadvertently or not) into the divine life." Betz, "After Barth," 57. The classic exposition in Roman Catholic theology of the collapse of extreme transcendence into secular immanence is Henri de Lubac, *Surnaturel.*

21. Hancock, *Responsibility of Reason*, 76–87.

22. Manent, *La cité de l'homme*, 111. "Tandis que l'orgueilleux philosophe est supérieur aux autres hommes, le modeste sociologue est supérieur à l'humanité même de l'homme."

23. Tocqueville, *Democracy in America*, 519. In the present volume, see ch. 1 under "Pierre Manent versus Theoretical Hypertrophy" and ch. 6 under "The Democratic-Christian Threat to Moral Analogy."

24. For Tocqueville on brutes and gods: Tocqueville, *Democracy in America*, 519. On the case for pride Tocqueville, *Democracy in America*, 604.

25. Here, thanking Betz for the invaluable guidance of his introduction to Przywara, I now venture directly into the text itself of *Analogia Entis*.

26. This characterization of Plotinus, and thus of the Greek understanding of the ontological ground, is painfully simplistic and partial. It is proposed as a clarifying foil to the Christian doctrine of divine freedom and personality. I refer the reader to Schindler's remarkable discussion of Plotinus as a proto-Christian thinker in *Retrieving Freedom*. Schindler shows that an understanding of freedom is already at work in Plotinus's "one": "If Augustine introduces a relatively novel emphasis on the drama of personal choice, Plotinus brings out more clearly the ontological depth from which such a choice is made" (xii). Indeed Schindler suggests that "Plotinus . . . presents in simple outline what later came to be called 'analogy'" (62).

27. Przywara, *Analogia Entis*, 227–28.

28. Przywara, *Analogia Entis*, 228–29.

29. Przywara, *Analogia Entis*, 229–30.

30. Przywara, *Analogia Entis*, 235. Let us note as well, here, that Przywara, along with Aristotle, also sets aside what we may call the broadly Neoplatonic option of mysticism: "The mysticism of rapture is humbled by the distance between Lord and servant."

31. Przywara, *Analogia Entis*, 229. In this densest of passages, Przywara seems to assent to a Heideggerian history of being (and its Nietzschean source) and to situate his philosophy decisively as postmodern: the idea of "fruitful possibility" as a "free gift from above" emerges only in the "twilight of the gods."

32. See ch. 3.

33. Or, I might add, the call of the "other," or the insistence on human "relationality" or even "personhood" understood apart from the question of the right order of the soul.

34. This discussion arises for Przywara in ch. 2 of *Analogia Entis*, "Metaphysical Transcendentalism and Transcendental Metaphysics." The leading question of this chapter concerns the alternative between a "noetic" and an "ontic" approach to the analogy between the human and the divine, that of "a neutral duality between the act of cognition, which questions, and the object of cognition, at which its question is directed" (120; this is in ch. 1). Is analogy concerned, he asks, with a "metaphysical transcendentalism" or with a "transcendental metaphysics"? (130). Przywara observes that for Aristotle the duality is less than fundamental, since for the ancient philosopher both knowledge and being exhibit the "essential liminality of being," the openness of what is to an "ideal unity of essence and existence." Both knowledge and being, for Aristotle, are oriented toward "the true, the good, and the beautiful" (125). This orientation toward the transcendentals has the structure of potency-act (Grk.: *dynamis-energeia*). When the accent is put upon potency or possibility, then the horizon of the liminality is understood to be "something ontically 'purely true'" (125–26). When the accent is on the act, on fulfillment, then "it indicates the realm of virtue [Grk.: *arete*] and so of the good [Grk.: *agathon*]." Finally, when making is distinguished from doing, art from practice, then the transcendental of the beautiful comes to the fore. For Aristotle, then, the noetic/ontic alternative, the question of beginning with what we moderns call the "subjective" or the "objective," is not fundamental, since inquiry is in any case naturally oriented toward what is higher.

35. Przywara, *Analogia Entis*, 127 (emphasis added); see also 129.

36. Przywara, *Analogia Entis*, 130.

37. The fate of the beautiful under the analogia entis is a further question, and of course a very big one. One can easily envision the possibility of an aesthetic regard on the fundamental oscillation or rhythm of analogy. The theme of beauty was central to the aesthetic-dominant theology of Hans Urs von Balthasar, who acknowledged a major debt to Przywara. Graham James McAleer's rich and venturesome *Erich Przywara and Postmodern Natural Law* shows how Przywara's *Analogia Entis* seeks to avoid the oscillating extremes of "angelism" and "vitalism," and McAleer draws out the linkage between embodiment and civilized humanity as expressed in clothing (as per Burke and Merleau-Ponty) and in ritual as indispensable signs of "value tones" that are essential to natural law. In engaging Leon Kass, McAleer is perhaps rather too eager to distinguish the Hebrew emphasis on morality from his own emphasis on "an aesthetic tone." *Erich Przywara*, 84.

But then his linking of Thomas Aquinas to a "long line of thinkers stretching from Plato to Shaftesbury to Kolnai who think in terms of ascending scales of graciousness and participation" seems to invite an association between the beautiful and a broadly aristocratic moral-political order that honors and affirms its own necessarily particular "tone" and civilizational "clothing" (85). But can the veiled liminality of the beautiful, which embodies deference to the "ever greater" transcendence of God (as per Lateran IV), be so closely associated with a politically embodied ascending scale of a concretely pleasing "graciousness," the lovely clothing of a particular civilization, without compromising Przywara's orthodox insistence on radical transcendence? Manent's more Aristotelian articulation of "natural law" would seem to require greater confidence in the good of human action within a particular, political horizon, and less emphasis on the *aesthetic* openness of the embodied to radical transcendence. But perhaps there are two fundamentally different aesthetics, corresponding to the worldviews Tocqueville broadly describes as "aristocratic" and "democratic." An alternative to the noetic-aesthetic alliance suggests itself (as seems to begin to emerge in McAleer's treatment): an alliance between the aesthetic and the moral-political against the overreach of the theoretical or noetic; here the beautiful would retain its ties to the "noble" as displayed in virtuous action. Thomas S. Hibbs's *Virtue's Splendor*, discussed later in the present chapter, can be considered a development of this association of the aesthetically beautiful and the morally-politically noble. Consider also Hibbs on Aquinas on beauty, in *Aquinas, Ethics, and Philosophy of Religion*, 148: "The beautiful should be understood as the way the good manifests itself to the rational creature."

38. Augustine, *Confessions* 3.6.

39. Przywara, *Analogia Entis*, 227.

40. Przywara's references here to the natural "right content" and to the supernatural "correct mode" are to Aquinas's discussion, in *De veritate* q. 14, of the supernatural virtue of charity in relation to the natural purposes of action. The linear economy between means and (natural) ends that Przywara seems here to assume tends to reduce the natural will to determination by naturalistic reason and does not do justice to the complex and subtle interaction between intellect and will that Aquinas is exploring. The possibility of freedom depends on avoiding both the reduction of will to intellect (determinism) and that of intellect to will (voluntarism). Manent's understanding of natural law as the "archic" or initiating enactment of rational principles is thus profoundly consonant with Aquinas's Aristotelian understanding of practical reason. This understanding cannot be sustained if the supernatural end (the beatific vision for which the supernatural virtue of charity forms us) is distinguished absolutely from the natural end of action, or happiness formed by virtue and the common good. Michael S. Sherwin, OP, in his indispensable study of charity in relation to the natural dialectic of will and intellect (*By Knowledge & by Love*), shows that the dilemma of will and intellect (which Thomas fails fully to confront in *De veritate*) is eventually overcome by an understanding of natural action in a way that holds it open to a supernatural

goodness. "To understand how one avoids an infinite regress in the description of practical reasoning, where every cognitive act presupposes a voluntary act and vice versa, St. Thomas appeals to the level of nature and the action of the Author of nature." *By Knowledge & by Love*, 53. The unsurpassable, irreducible content of both reason and will, which prevents their infinite regress, is available to us in nature understood as creation. Both intellect and will must be regarded "as participating in the eternal law of God" and thus "as the twin sources of the natural law" (58). The natural law, the natural good of human action, thus cannot be conceived without an implicit or inchoate reference to the supernatural; the very "psychological foundation of human freedom" thus always already presupposes a "spiritual openness to universal truth and goodness" (59). This openness is, furthermore, as much communal or political as it is psychological, for "the creative character of moral goodness points to the central role of a community in the development of human freedom.... One must be educated in the life of virtue ... as embodied in a particular community." The natural common good is not a closed sphere, much less a "mirrored dome," but an orientation both to and beyond the political common good. It is thus that, Sherwin explains, "the principles of the natural law and the spiritual openness of the intellect and will make freedom possible" (61). Nature rightly understood, it seems, provides the indispensable touchstone for an understanding of the divine synthesis of will and intellect.

41. Such is the profound tendency of John Calvin's radicalizing of Christian transcendence, as I have argued in *Calvin and the Foundations of Modern Politics*. The tendency toward the flattening of the natural moral world is already apparent, for that matter (although with a certain redeeming ambivalence), in St. Augustine's reduction of pagan virtues to "splendid vices" and the consequent interpretation of politics as limited to a necessary compromise of wills regarding material interests. *City of God* 19.17.

42. Let me emphasize that nothing could be further from Przywara's intention than this naturalizing tendency of his "unlimited service to God," when understood as the practical—or, rather, active—conclusion of an analogia entis committed to the ever-greater-God dynamic. And there may be no stable alternative to this tendency in the creedal tradition within which Przywara is working. It may be that from the first theological move by which God's absolute freedom is secured against Platonic emanation by thinking it in terms of nothingness, of a *creatio ex nihilo*, the outcome of the infinite activity of service as opposed to the practical good of virtue is predetermined. An alternative philosophical and theological approach to the meaning of freedom, and thus to the relation between divinity and humanity, seems to me to be proposed by the prodigious investigations and speculations of D. C. Schindler. Schindler is showing the way to rethinking divine freedom as synthesizing (explicitly in the face of Strauss's warnings against such an attempted synthesis) the Jewish understanding of an eternal covenant with a Greek understanding of the priority of the actuality of the good. This thinking requires an excavation beneath Christian Platonism by a return to Plotinus's "freedom as

generative perfection," and thereby to an understanding of "the intrinsic goodness of freedom in itself." Schindler, *Retrieving Freedom*, 61. ("Freedom as Generative Perfection" is the title of ch. 2.) It is worth mentioning here that Aquinas holds a place in Schindler's retrieval of freedom that is at once eminent and imperfect; he is willing to allude to certain "deficiencies in his [Thomas's] thought in relation to this original perfection . . . of the notion of freedom" (45). In his chapter on Aquinas, Schindler brings out from the Angelic Doctor's thought a rich understanding of freedom that is strikingly similar to Manent's: "The fully adequate reason for making a choice comes to be in the *making of the choice*" (256). But finally, Schindler must concede, the absolute priority of the intellect for Aquinas precludes full openness to "the most radical question that can possibly be asked: Does not the supraeternity of God . . . imply that such a reciprocal priority [between love and knowledge, the will and the intellect] would *have* to be the case?" (276). My point in this book is to offer a codicil to Schindler's most radical possible question: Does not moral-political agency—virtuous action or practical "liberty under God and the laws"—provide the only possible touchstone in human experience for this reciprocal priority of love and knowledge?

43. Hibbs, *Aquinas, Ethics*, 8.

44. Hibbs, *Aquinas, Ethics*, 54 (Hibbs does not cite a specific passage from Murdoch). Murdoch's thesis, as cited here by Hibbs, is substantially my own. But Murdoch is more concerned than I with the transcendence of the good and less attentive to the in-and-above dynamic of meaning already at work in practical virtue within a particular political community. She is, accordingly, at least on Hibbs's telling, more inclined, like Alasdair MacIntyre, to scorn liberalism and to sympathize with Marxism as a "grand narrative" of human hope. Hibbs, *Aquinas, Ethics*, 172. The natural correlate of an undue emphasis on radical transcendence, as we have seen, with Tocqueville's help, is a projection of hope upon a future conceived in terms of a material transformation. We saw in the previous chapter how Emmanuel Levinas succumbs to this logic.

45. Hibbs, *Aquinas, Ethics*, 100. See also Hibbs, *Virtue's Splendor*, 22.

46. Hibbs, *Virtue's Splendor*, 23 (Hibbs does not cite a specific passage from Ortega y Gassett). Compare Strauss's subtle endorsement of the pride or self-affirmation of philosophers and his explicit dismissal of the perspective of a God who "searches hearts." See my *Responsibility of Reason*, 207.

47. Hibbs, *Virtue's Splendor*, 177.

48. Hibbs, *Aquinas, Ethics*, 115.

49. Hibbs, *Aquinas, Ethics*, 169. "The articulation of God as utterly transcendent and yet knowing and loving singulars sets aside obstacles to conceiving of God as the Lord of history."

50. The creedal Christian idea of an ex nihilo creation is a strict correlate of the liberation of the idea of God as a personal being (or as a trinity of persons in one God) from the Greek philosophical understanding of divinity as rational-impersonal-necessity. The break with classical necessity motivates the Christian

insistence on the radical contingency of creation. The risk inherent in this repudiation of necessity is, of course, that of emptying the creation of significance by reducing it to what is utterly groundless or arbitrary. "We can say," Hibbs writes, "that Aquinas wants to combat two errors, that of imposing necessity on God, and that of reducing creation to mere chance." The gratuity of creation must somehow avoid both impersonal necessity and pure contingency. To accomplish this, Aquinas writes that God produces creatures not from any need but "because of the love of His own goodness." *ST* I.32.1 ad 3. But any motive we attribute to God may seem simply to reproduce the problem of necessity and freedom: either we have in mind some humanly meaningful quality when we speak of God's "goodness," thus seemingly subordinating God to some essential or necessary good, or our words are strictly meaningless. Hibbs seeks a way through this problem of divine necessity versus arbitrary freedom by focusing on the "striking deployment [in Aquinas] of aesthetic language of appropriateness or suitability." This move clearly would lead us back toward the necessary touchstone of divine creative charity in the human practice of prudence—or, more precisely, the classical, political virtue of prudence as opened up by Christian revelation to the worth of individuals in the creative openness of a divinely guided history. Hibbs notes: "In creating, God acts according to his wisdom, to which we have no independent access except through the order of creation itself." I would only add that, insofar as God blesses us to address him and speak of him from within the order of creation, is it not ungrateful to characterize his wise and good creation as from "nothingness"? Having recognized the inadequacy of the dichotomy of rational necessity and willful freedom for understanding the free goodness of what is, is it necessary to continue the polemic of the freedom of nothingness versus the necessity of reason?

51. Hibbs, *Virtue's Splendor*, 131.

52. Hibbs, *Virtue's Splendor*, 136. For this last point Hibbs cites Aquinas, *ST* I-II.97.3: "Custom has the force of law, abolishes law, and is the interpreter of law."

53. Lanavère, *La loi naturelle*, 17. Translations from Lanavère's French text are mine. Lanavère here cites Aquinas's prologue to the *Sententia libri politicorum*: "It is necessary that this 'whole' that is the city be more 'primary' [*principal, principalius*] than all the other 'wholes' that can be known and constituted by human reason." Lanavère, "La dimension politique," 17. He also references Manent, *Seeing Things Politically* (French original: *Le regard politique*): "The political order is truly what gives human life its form. Political things are the cause of human order or disorder." Consider also Lanavère, "La dimension politique," 135, 139: for Thomas the inclination to know God and to live in society is one single inclination that "expresses itself in two directions." Lanavère thus speaks of a "solidarity that exists [for Thomas] in his doctrine of natural law between metaphysics and politics. . . . By natural law man participates in the orientation towards the common good that is found in eternal law." Cannot one then say that the political (an orientation to the common good) lies at the heart of the religious or spiritual?

54. Lanavère, *La loi naturelle*, 43.

55. Lanavère, "La dimension politique," 120.
56. Lanavère, "La dimension politique," 131, 134.
57. Lanavère, *La loi naturelle*, 87.
58. Lanavère, *La loi naturelle*, 94. Citing Aquinas, *De veritate*, Lanavère adds in his original dissertation: "The only means we have to understanding anything of divine things is by starting with [*prendre appui sur*] our human experience and transposing it analogically." "La dimension politique," 154. Further on in *La loi naturelle*, he will write: "Thomas puts in place a circular relation between divine providence and human prudence: the paradigm of human political prudence allows one to think about divine providence, but divine providence is also the paradigm that makes it possible to understand the full realization of human prudence" (147). Note also that, unlike Hibbs, Lanavère argues that Aquinas finally favors "the paradigm of prudence to that of *ars*" (96, 99). On Aquinas's close association between the point of view of the agent and that of the artisan, see also 209.
59. Lanavère, "La dimension politique," 118–19. Subsequent citations are in parentheses in the text and notes.
60. As befits a Christian, Aquinas extends the virtue of prudence to include those who are governed as well as those who govern, since, as a rational being, even one who is commanded by another is in a certain way an active agent, and so can be considered as practicing the virtue of prudence, albeit in a "derivative" manner (124–25). In this way Thomas means to "defend the compatibility between the dignity of man, as willed by God, and the fact that one man obeys another" (129).
61. Note that the law's application to the slightest detail must be understood with reference to the common good as the end of the law: "From natural law to political laws, it is the 'common' that is singularized" (249). "The capacity to regulate particular actions [is] always with reference to the ordination to the common good" (250). Thus, "Thomas invariably sustains the primacy of the political over the judicial" (264). Thus, contrary to Strauss's argument, Lanavère maintains that "Thomas totally embraces the Aristotelian thesis according to which 'natural right is a part of political right'" (267). "Political justice," moreover, "is relative to the political regime" (275). Nor is Thomas eager to settle the question of the best political regime. Thus he is by no means preoccupied with providing a standard of natural law as superior to human law. Although an occasion may arise in which such a standard may be invoked to disqualify a positive law (284), even in such cases Thomas makes the case for obedience rather than risking political destabilization (287). On the whole, then, the student of Aquinas must recognize "the favorable presumption that positive law enjoys" in his thought. For Thomas, "it is human law that presents itself as the only rule of action, and not natural law, which has as it were 'passed' into human law, which is its concretization" (272).
62. "Don" is an ecclesiastical title of respect; Don Lanavère is a priest in the community of Saint-Martin.
63. The status of human agency in the economy of humanity's ultimate, supernatural purpose is bound up with the question of whether the incarnation is a kind

of backup plan incident to the fall of man or whether the condescension of God in embracing the temporal condition of humanity is inherently appropriate to the self-communicating character of divinity. According to the latter possibility, the grammar of natural purposive agency redeemed by an incalculable supernatural grace—an "in-and-above" structure in which the spark of the "above" is inherent in the "in," and the integrity of the "in" is honored and preserved in the "above"—would appear as the eternal form of redeemed agency, and not merely as an accident of an anomalous fall. The great exponent of Aquinas's theology Jean-Pierre Torrell, while declining to embrace without qualification the terminology of a *felix culpa* or fortunate fall ("which is sometimes hard to separate from a certain anthropomorphism"), shows that Thomas was both deferential to the scriptural teaching that "the reason . . . [for] the Incarnation is the sin of the first man" and open to the possibility that the incarnation was not a backup plan but inherent in God's nature: "It belongs to the Sovereign Good to communicate himself sovereignly to the creature." Torrell, *Saint Thomas Aquinas*, 2:71–73. As has been explained, I think it is a mistake to fashion a theology in polemical reaction to the perceived threat of "anthropomorphism." As Tocqueville already so well understood, the power of dehumanizing secular ideologies by no means lies in their undue respect for human nature but in the dreadful fusion of inhuman pride and inhuman humility. Theologies that fail to honor human nature risk abetting this fusion.

64. Przywara, *Analogia Entis*, 230.

65. An invaluable meditation on the relation between the either/or of faith and the deliberate choice of prudence—between the radically free decision to accept or reject the radically free gift of divine grace on the one hand and the natural freedom of choice with a view to goods that participate in the natural economy of necessity and perfection on the other—is the dense, at times surpassingly beautiful, and without question massively influential work of the French theological philosopher Maurice Blondel (1861–1949). Blondel's first and most fundamental work, *Action*, posits a distinction between the "willing will" (open to a radical and elusive transcendence) and the "willed will," necessarily grounded in concrete action in one's particular world. Anticipating Manent, Blondel sees clearly that "to will what we truly will is to submit to a practical rule"—that is, to "a synthesis of the voluntary and the willed, which is posited as the rule" (133, 135). Action both affirms its own principle and necessarily surpasses itself. Free choice begins with one's family and one's country, but opens up toward a love of humanity (249). But this practical freedom in action presupposes at every moment the fundamental option for a transcendent God, the "yes" to a cosmic freedom from which every practical choice draws its faith, hope, and love. We will not cease to learn from Blondel; we find his markers all along the path we are straining to follow.

66. Compare Schindler, *Retrieving Freedom*, 39: "This redemption [from sin] is then a surprising, novel, even more perfect and fitting following through on what was promised from the beginning. O happy fault!"

CHAPTER 12

1. Lindsay, *Race Marxism*.
2. Rufo, *America's Cultural Revolution*.
3. Caldwell, *Age of Entitlement*.
4. Hanania, *Origins of Woke*.
5. Caldwell, *Age of Entitlement*, 78.
6. Caldwell, *Age of Entitlement*, 27–28.
7. Bottum, *Anxious Age*, 39.
8. Confronting the philosophical and theological challenge of Christian universalism is also essential, I would add, to the articulation of an American conservatism that is American without being abstractly "nationalistic." See Kesler, "National Conservatism vs. American Conservatism," and the excellent symposium on the theme of his essay on the website of *The American Mind*, 3/27/2024, including fine essays by David B. Goldman, Richard Reinsch, and Daniel J. Mahoney.
9. Pascal, *Pensées*, fragment 187 (here, the translation is mine). Subsequent citations are given by fragment number in parentheses in the text.
10. Tocqueville, *Democracy in America*, 435–36.
11. Strauss, "What Is Political Philosophy?," 38–39.
12. Strauss, *On Tyranny*, 99.
13. Strauss, "What Is Political Philosophy?," 39–40 (emphasis added).
14. Manent, *Pascal*, 145. What I have named here "technology" is framed by Pascal, as Manent shows, as the alliance between the concupiscence of the flesh and that of the mind.
15. Pascal, *Pensées*, fragment 792. See Manent, *Pascal*, 129.
16. Burke, "Letter from Edmund Burke." It is in seeking to integrate or at least coordinate the supernatural virtue of charity with the natural virtue of prudence that I risk mobilizing Manent's insights for purposes he may not endorse. To explore this question fully will require a much more substantial engagement with Manent's *Pascal*. For now, let me note that Manent, in response to Daniel Tanguay's important essay on the Pascal book (Tanguay, "Pierre Manent au miroir de son Pascal")—a response, as Manent indicates, that bears on "the whole of his intellectual trajectory [*parcours*]"—rather pointedly sets aside the thought of Thomas Aquinas *considered as a hierarchical system oriented toward a highest good*. What Manent says here of Thomas is consistent with his concession to the founders of modernity that Christianity imposed upon its adepts the affliction of "seeing double," that is, of being bound at once by the supernatural good and by the common good of the city. In the present context, however—that of defending Pascal against Thomism, let us say—Manent does not propose in any way to reconcile Thomism with liberalism or to see liberalism within a context framed by a Christian idea of a covenant and by a friendship between man *as a political being* and God; instead he seems to reconcile himself to a certain "oscillation"

or even "disequilibrium" concerning the claims of Christianity on the one hand and citizenship on the other. "By fixing my attention first on political action for the common good and then on what is specific in the Christian proposition, I have committed myself in two distinct directions of thought and of life, each of which claims us wholly." This candid resignation to the "tensions and sometimes wrenching fractures [*déchirements*]" inherent in the life of the Christian citizen is both illuminating and admirable. Manent, "Individualisme et christianisme."

I remain attracted, however, to a path previously marked out in Manent's thought according to which the silence of the gospel concerning politics is not a mark of "indifference," as Manent proposes here, but rather, as argued above (with the help of interpreters of Thomas Aquinas such as Thomas Hibbs and J.-R. Lanavère), a mark of the high status of human freedom, of active moral agency, in Thomas's understanding of eternal law. And there is no question that Manent has often invited his readers to discern a notable continuity between nature and grace, moral agency and evangelical charity. See my discussions of Manent's lovely Lenten remarks on reason and faith (ch. 7, under "Manent's Political Thomism"), in which he limns a continuous progression from our natural interest in making human bonds sweeter, in serving the common good, to an openness to the greatest possible being, who stands ready to "come towards us." Even more striking is his proposition in *Beyond Radical Secularism* (*Situation de la France*), considered above (ch. 7, under "Providence, Action, and the Nation-State"), that our efforts on behalf of our own *national* common good can be considered in the light of the covenant of friendship between God and human beings: "We address the Most High from the site of our action and for the common good of the city of which we are citizens" (69–70). Without supposing that Manent means to say that we address God *only* from such a political site, we can certainly say that this is an element of profession of faith one cannot imagine in the mouth of Blaise Pascal.

17. To be sure, Pascal immediately counters the ancient philosophers' exaggeration of human virtue, such as the Stoic presumption that "what has been done once can be done always" (350)—that virtue, or reason's government of the soul, can be a secure human attainment. The soul's access to virtuous self-government is best seen not as a secure "throne," but as something attained or glimpsed by an extraordinary "leap" and "merely for an instant" (351). We should not assess human virtue by such a leap, since "the strength of man's virtue must not be measured by his efforts, but by his ordinary life" (352). Still, the decisive point remains that, for Pascal, our "efforts" and our evanescent "leap" have a meaningful direction, however imperfect and obscure, an orientation that confers "dignity" because it is connected at once with the nobility of thought and with our moral self-government.

18. Lawler, *Restless Mind*, 85. Much of my discussion of Pascal here is adapted from my article addressing Lawler's book: "Restless Virtue."

19. Lawler, *Restless Mind*, 156.

20. My translation. The original: "La religion elle-même . . . ne peut se donner aux hommes que dans un site conventionnel, qu'en étant autorisée—au double sens

du terme—par certains hommes ou certaines institutions." Manent, *Tocqueville et la nature*, 144.

21. Pascal himself may not wholly have escaped the secularizing tendencies of an insistence on radical transcendence. Consider Ferreyrolles, "La concupiscence collective." Ferreyrolles shows Pascal's participation, ably seconded by his associate Pierre Nicole, in the modern conception of a state that produces the "effects" of charity in the total absence of the actual virtue of charity (145). This presupposes, of course, that the "good" effects of charity have nothing to do with, or at least are somehow separable from, the goodness of charity itself considered as a virtue of the soul. In a word, there is, for Pascal, no analogy between the "effects" of charity understood in a purely human and political sense and the otherworldly virtue of charity. In his on the whole very appreciative study of Pascal, *Pascal et la proposition chrétienne*, Manent notes that Pierre Nicole "develops *the same argument* to the point where he seems to be satisfied with a world without charity" (189n1; emphasis added). Ferreyrolles mistakenly likens Pascal's approach to that of Thomas Aquinas. The key difference lies in Pascal's separation of the "effects" of order and prosperity from the intrinsic goodness—or analogy to intrinsic goodness—of natural virtue.

22. Mitchell, *American Awakening*, xxi.

23. Mitchell, *American Awakening*, 34.

24. Mitchell, *American Awakening*, 13. Subsequent citations are in parentheses in the text.

25. Compare this: early Protestants understood the brokenness of man and the world; they "labored in competence, and sought the grace of God until he returned and 'saved the world.'" Mitchell, *American Awakening*, 59.

26. Mitchell argues in good Christian fashion that the polarity between "transgression" and "innocence" is a "mortally inaccessible mystery" (131). To be sure, the full meaning of the economy of salvation must remain mysterious to us, but there is no escaping the fact that we must interpret the mystery in some way in relation to our practical existence as a whole (and not only to our religious devotions).

27. Mitchell, *American Awakening*, 21. "Within the liberal politics of competence, citizens need one another; in the identity politics of innocence, they do not."

28. Mitchell, *American Awakening*, 99. "We live, however, in a post-Edenic world, a providential world whose historical unfolding no one can anticipate or arrest. Scientific and technological advances are an ineradicable aspect of that world."

29. In saying this, I must now confess that I am agreeing *up to a point* with the "Alt-Right" position as Mitchell presents it. He refers to the Alt-Right's "breathtaking claim . . . that *the entire configuration of transgression and innocence is responsible for the decay we witness in the West*" (105; emphasis original). My disagreement with the atheistic right lies of course in my conviction that the Christian understanding of the good, natural and supernatural, cannot be reduced to "the entire configuration of transgression and innocence." Without letting down our guard against Nietzsche's extremism, we may acknowledge that he was right about this, which

Mitchell seems to reject, or ignore: a certain "pathos of distance," or, let us say, a respect for a law that is at once "higher" and socially instantiated, is a necessary dimension (the aristocratic dimension) of meaning, albeit one that is rightly countered and modulated by Christian and democratic sensibilities.

CONCLUSION

1. Tocqueville, *Democracy in America*, 519.
2. Tocqueville, *Democracy in America*, 675.
3. Further analysis of Tocqueville's "two humanities" is given in Manent, *Seeing Things Politically*, 103–4. Manent suggests that Tocqueville is perhaps mistaken to posit the eventual erasure of the "aristocratic man" altogether. As he explains, it is unreasonable to "envision the extinction of the higher capacities of the human soul." Nevertheless, Tocqueville rightly shows that equality and "democratic man" ultimately depend upon reference to a more elevated, "aristocratic man."
4. Manent, *Seeing Things Politically*, 118. "I am not saying that there are not admirable things in the Middle Ages—after all, I am still half-Thomist."
5. In case further indications are needed regarding the contemporary political relevance of the perspective of "liberty under God and the law" or "redeemed agency" developed here, let me just say that I trust it is clear that this perspective is as far from any pretension to declare the failure of liberalism and propose some new, illiberal regime as it is from the attempt to articulate a pure liberalism of human autonomy and equality uncontaminated by any elements of religion or tradition. My liberalism, which I intend to be attuned to that expressed by my friends Daniel J. Mahoney and Pierre Manent, espouses and grounds human freedom from a Christian point of view—the most adequate point of view, we think—but without proposing the explicit establishment of any Christian teaching, much less any ecclesiastical hierarchy. In this I mean to join and help renew the efforts of the American Catholic liberal tradition that runs from Orestes Brownson to John Courtney Murray, the tradition that holds that the American founders, in mingling broadly Lockean liberal political strategies with more perennial truths of the human condition, "founded better than they knew." An excellent recent contribution to this tradition is Lawler and Reinsch, *Constitution in Full*. See in this connection Mahoney, "Patrick Deneen's Lost Opportunity" (review of Deneen's *Regime Change*). Also see Reinsch, "Zombie Deneenism." The point of view, or family of points of view, expressed by authors in this "founded better than they knew" tradition of Christian liberalism is as far from theocratic ambition as it is from antitheological ire. The deep source of Christian resistance to illiberalism or integralism must be found, the present work is meant to suggest, in the deep grounding of liberty in natural law and of natural law in eternal law. This moderate Christian liberalism intends to draw from the deep truth of Thomas's teaching that natural law is human *participation* in

eternal law—that is, free, "archic" action for the common good. This is the deepest ground of any viable conservative "fusion" of individual freedom and moral truth.

6. Manent, *Seeing Things Politically*, 63. I should mention here that my own stance in relation to Thomism may not conform exactly to Pierre Manent's. Even if I might also be willing to say of myself that I am a "half-Thomist," I am aware that my half and Manent's are not quite identical. See the too brief discussion of Manent's *Pascal et la proposition Chrétienne* in ch. 12 above.

7. To be sure, the biblical heightening of the dignity of the individual is mediated by the covenant people through whom God prepares to bless all humanity, to fill the earth "with the knowledge of the glory of the LORD, as the waters cover the sea" (Habakkuk 2:14). Isaac was precious to Abraham as a person, as his son, and as the embodiment of the Lord's promise to make Abraham the father of many nations. In Strauss's next sentence, the last of *Natural Right and History*, he continues: "Burke himself was still too deeply imbued with the spirit of 'sound antiquity' to allow the concern with individuality to overpower the concern with virtue." Clearly my present efforts are in a profound sense in continuity with Burke's classical defense of modern liberty, or of liberty in a modern context. Everything, for me, depends on articulating a philosophical and theological space in which a deep, religious sense of the preciousness of the individual can be combined with or coordinated with "the concern with virtue."

8. Citations will be in parentheses in the text.

9. Levin quotes President Calvin Coolidge's famous 1926 speech on the Declaration: "If all men are created equal, that is final. If they are endowed with inalienable rights, that is final. If governments derive their just powers from the consent of the governed, that is final. No advance, no progress can be made beyond these propositions" (272). To quote more from Coolidge's speech would considerably complicate Levin's argument. The only mention of "dignity" in the speech is very concrete and political: "the dignity of a resistance to illegal usurpations." Coolidge sees the Declaration as rooted "in religious convictions," and by this he does not intend simply some universal faith in equal dignity. The president does not shrink from citing the Rev. John Wise's statement circa 1710 that "Democracy is Christ's government in church and state." He credits Americans' freedom and prosperity to the discipline of scriptures "not only in their religious life and educational training, but also in their political thought." Thus he sees Christianity not only as the ground of our belief in human equality but as the source of the "great spiritual development and acquired . . . moral power" that shaped the American character. Rather than granting a priori respect to all expressions of equal dignity, Coolidge warns that "we must not sink into a pagan materialism. We must cultivate the reverence which [the creators of our great heritage] had for the things that are *holy*" (emphasis added). In sum, in Coolidge's political sermon, very much unlike Levin's constitutional pluralism, a concrete, inherited, and institutionally represented idea of "holiness" occupies the fundamental ground where the mystery

of "equal dignity" now stands. I offer this contrast between Coolidge and Levin not at all to suggest that the Republican president's political theology or interpretation of the Declaration should be taken as the final word or that his rhetoric can provide the perfect model for ours today. I mean simply to point out the difference between Levin's attempt to bracket substantive debate by deploying the supposedly consensual rhetoric of post-Christian equal dignity and Coolidge's pointedly substantive propositions. (For a reading of the Declaration in light of our moral and political agency and a certain virtuous pride, see Seaton, "Declaration's Civic Anthropology.")

10. I was reminded of this telling observation of Levin's while reading Jonathan Haidt's important article "Why the Past 10 Years of American Life Have Been Uniquely Stupid." Like Levin, Haidt would like to blame our corrosive polarization processes and manners as if these were unlinked to any ideology, left or right. In his view, the main cause of our "stupidity" is the irresponsible kind of communication facilitated by the new, internet-driven social media. And yet he has to acknowledge a rather flagrant asymmetry in what we might call communicative power: "In the Democratic Party, the struggle between the progressive wing and the more moderate factions is open and ongoing, and often the moderates win. The problem is that the left controls the commanding heights of the culture: universities, news organizations, Hollywood, art museums, advertising, much of Silicon Valley, and the teachers' unions and teaching colleges that shape K–12 education. And in many of those institutions, dissent has been stifled."

11. Machiavelli, *Prince*, ch. 18.

12. We see here once again the pertinence of Strauss's warning against syntheses of Athens and Jerusalem. It seems indeed that Levin's position is at least vulnerable to the call of such a synthesis. I agree with Levin that a defense of American constitutionalism must involve holding together classical republican, modern liberal, and biblical elements. But Levin has failed to guard against the powerful collusion of modern or "Machiavellian skepticism" (275) with biblical universalism.

13. Manent, *World beyond Politics?*, 193.

14. This critique of Levin is unfair insofar as the author of *American Covenant* implicitly embraces the mediation of "America" and of its Constitution. He earnestly desires that Americans remain friends, or perhaps rather that they become friends once again. I share this desire. The whole question is whether this friendship can be conserved or revived without nourishing it more substantially than Levin wishes to do. The problem for Levin's project is that, as soon as we name or give substance to our mysterious "human dignity," it immediately appears less *equal*.

15. Marsilius of Padua, *Defensor pacis*.

16. Planned Parenthood of Southeastern Pa. v. Casey, 505 U.S. 833, 851 (1992), https://supreme.justia.com/cases/federal/us/505/833/#tab-opinion-1959105.

17. See my discussion of Manent's "Reason and Faith" above in ch. 7, under "Manent's Political Thomism." Aristotle's awareness of the dependence of politics

on piety is the theme of Mary P. Nichols's important recent work, *Aristotle's Discovery of the Human*.

18. See my discussion above in ch. 11, under "Pride, Humility, and Service."

19. The exploitation for profit of the posture of victimhood is vividly, even gruesomely portrayed, in a recent novel: Boryga, *Victim*.

20. See Schmitt, *Political Theology*.

21. See Daniel J. Mahoney's judicious remarks distinguishing Manent's approach from that of "political theology" in *Recovering Politics, Civilization, and the Soul*, ch. 10.

22. Tocqueville, *Democracy in America*, 604.

BIBLIOGRAPHY

Aquinas, Thomas. *Summa Contra Gentiles*. Edited by the Aquinas Institute. Green Bay, WI: Emmaus Academic, 2019.

Aquinas, Thomas. *Summa Theologica*. Translated by Fathers of the English Dominican Province. Canton, OH: Pinnacle Press, 2017.

Aubenque, Pierre. *Le problème de l'être chez Aristote: Essai sur la problématique aristotélicienne*. Paris: Presses Universitaires de France, 2013.

Augustine. *The City of God*. Translated by Henry Bettenson. London: Penguin Books, 2004.

Badiou, Alain. *Saint Paul: The Foundation of Universalism*. Translated by Ray Brassier. Stanford, CA: Stanford University Press, 2009.

Barth, Karl. *Der Römerbrief 1922*. Edited by Cornelius van der Kooi and Katja Tostaja. Zürich: TVZ, 2005.

Benedict XVI. *Deus Caritas Est*. [Papal encyclical, 2005.] In Thornton and Varenne, *Essential Pope Benedict XVI*.

Benedict XVI. "Pope's Speech at University of Regensburg (Full Text) September 20, 2006." [Aka "Regensburg Address."] Catholic Culture. https://www.catholicculture.org/news/features/index.cfm?recnum=46474.

Benedict XVI. "The Temptations of Jesus." In vol. 2 of *Jesus of Nazareth*. Translated by Adrian J. Walker. New York: Doubleday, 2007.

Benedict XVI [Joseph Ratzinger]. *Introduction to Christianity*. In Thornton and Varenne, *Essential Pope Benedict XVI*.

Benedict XVI [Joseph Ratzinger]. "Yesterday, Today, and Tomorrow." In Thornton and Varenne, *Essential Pope Benedict XVI*.

Berkowitz, Peter. "The Academic Liberal." Peter Berkowitz website, December 16, 2002. https://peterberkowitz.wordpress.com/2002/12/16/the-academic-liberal/. First published in *The Weekly Standard*.

Besançon, Alain. *The Falsification of the Good*. Translated by Matthew Screech. London: Claridge, 1994.

Betz, John R. "After Barth: A New Introduction to Erich Przywara's Analogia Entis." In *The Analogy of Being: Invention of the Antichrist or Wisdom of God?*, edited by Thomas Joseph White. Cambridge: Eerdmans, 2011.

Betz, John R. Translator's introduction to *Analogia Entis: Metaphysics; Original Structure and Universal Rhythm*, by Erich Przywara, translated by John R. Betz and David Bentley Hart. Grand Rapids, MI: Eerdmans, 2014.

Blondel, Maurice. *Action: Essay on a Critique of Life and a Science of Practice*. First published 1893. Translated by Oliva Blanchette. Notre Dame, IN: University of Notre Dame Press, 1984.

Bloom, Allan David. *The Closing of the American Mind*. New York: Simon & Schuster, 1987.

Bloom, Allan David. "Justice: John Rawls vs. the Tradition of Political Philosophy." *The American Political Science Review* 69, no. 2 (June 1975): 648–62.

Bloom, Allan David. *Love and Friendship*. New York: Simon & Schuster, 1994.

Boryga, Andrew. *Victim*. New York: Doubleday, 2024.

Bottum, Joseph. *An Anxious Age: The Post-Protestant Ethic and the Spirit of America*. New York: Image, 2014.

Burke, Edmund. "A Letter from Edmund Burke: Esq; One of the Representatives in Parliament for the City of Bristol, to John Farr and John Harris, Esqrs. Sheriffs of That City, on the Affairs of America." Available in the Digital Collections of the University of Michigan Library, https://quod.lib.umich.edu/cgi/t/text/text-idx?cc=ecco;c=ecco;idno=004804912.0001.000.

Burke, Edmund. "Letter to the Sheriffs of Bristol." *Selected Letters of Edmund Burke*. Edited by Harvey C. Mansfield. Chicago: University of Chicago Press, 1984.

Caldwell, Christopher. *The Age of Entitlement: America since the Sixties*. New York: Simon & Schuster, 2021.

Calvin, John. *Institutes of the Christian Religion*. Translated by Ford Lewis Battles. Edited by John T. McNeill. Louisville, KY: Westminster John Knox Press, 1960.

Chalamet, Christophe, Andreas Dettwiler, and Sarah Stewart-Kroeker. *Karl Barth's Epistle to the Romans: Retrospect and Prospect*. Berlin: De Gruyter, 2022.

Clarke, W. Norris. *Explorations in Metaphysics*. Notre Dame, IN: University of Notre Dame Press, 1994.

Davis, Michael. *The Soul of the Greeks: An Inquiry*. Chicago: University of Chicago Press, 2011.

de Lubac, Henri. *Surnaturel: Études historiques*. Edited and with a preface by Michel Sales, S.J. Paris: Éditions Desclée de Brouwer, 1991.

de Rougemont, Denis. *Love in the Western World*. Translated by Montgomery Belgion. Princeton: Princeton University Press, 1983.

Descartes, René. *Discourse on the Method of Rightly Conducting the Reason and Seeking for Truth in the Sciences*. In *The Philosophical Works of Descartes*, translated by Elizabeth Sanderson Haldane and G. R. T. Ross. Cambridge: Cambridge University Press, 1983.

Ferreyrolles, Gérard. "La concupiscence collective." Chapter 3 in *Pascal et la raison politique*. Paris: Presses Universitaires de France, 1984.

Gallagher, Maggie. *Enemies of Eros: How the Sexual Revolution Is Killing Family, Marriage, and Sex and What We Can Do about It*. Chicago: Bonus Books, 1989.

Girard, René. *All Desire Is a Desire for Being*. Edited by Cynthia L. Haven. London: Penguin Classics, 2024.

Gregory, Eric. "Before the Original Position: The Neo-orthodox Theology of the Young John Rawls." *Journal of Religious Ethics* 35, no. 2 (2007): 179–202.

Haidt, Jonathan. "Why the Past 10 Years of American Life Have Been Uniquely Stupid." *Atlantic*, November 2024. https://www.theatlantic.com/magazine/archive/2022/05/social-media-democracy-trust-babel/629369/.

Hanania, Richard. *The Origins of Woke: Civil Rights Law, Corporate America, and the Triumph of Identity Politics*. New York: Broadside Books, 2023.

Hancock, Ralph C. *Calvin and the Foundations of Modern Politics*. South Bend, IN: St. Augustine's Press, 2011.

Hancock, Ralph C. "Luther and Calvin." In *An Invitation to Political Thought*, edited by Kenneth L. Deutsch and Joseph R. Fornieri. Belmont, CA: Thomson Wadsworth, 2008.

Hancock, Ralph C. "Les métamorphoses de Pierre Manent: Le prix de la gloire." In *La politique et l'âme: Autour de Pierre Manent*, edited by Giulio De Ligio, Jean-Vincent Holeindre, and Daniel J. Mahoney. Paris: CNRS, 2014.

Hancock, Ralph C. "Le noble et le juste: Les préconditions naturelles de la charité chrétienne." In *Charité et bien commun*, edited by Philippe Bénéton. La Roche-sur-Yon, France: Presses Universitaires de ICES, 2019.

Hancock, Ralph C. *The Responsibility of Reason: Theory and Practice in a Liberal-Democratic Age*. Lanham, MD: Rowman & Littlefield, 2011.

Hancock, Ralph C. "Restless Virtue: Greatness in Lawler, Tocqueville, Pascal." *Perspectives on Political Science* 51, no. 3 (2022): 123–32.

Hancock, Ralph C. Review of *Political Philosophy and the God of Abraham*, by Thomas Pangle. *First Things*, April 1, 2004. https://www.firstthings.com/article/2004/04/political-philosophy-and-the-god-of-abraham.

Heidegger, Martin. *Supplements: From the Earliest Essays to "Being and Time" and Beyond*. Edited by John Van Buren. New York: State University of New York Press, 2002.

Hibbs, Thomas S. *Aquinas, Ethics, and Philosophy of Religion: Metaphysics and Practice*. Bloomington: Indiana University Press, 2007.

Hibbs, Thomas S. *Virtue's Splendor: Wisdom, Prudence, and the Human Good*. New York: Fordham University Press, 2001.

Holland, Tom. *Dominion: How the Christian Revolution Remade the World*. New York: Basic Books, 2019.

Homer. *The Odyssey*. Translated by Samuel Butler. Page by Page Books. https://www.pagebypagebooks.com/Homer_Butler_Tr/The_Odyssey/index.html.

Kass, Leon. *The Beginning of Wisdom: Reading Genesis*. Chicago: University of Chicago Press, 2006.
Kesler, Charles R. "National Conservatism vs. American Conservatism." *The American Mind*, March 27, 2024. https://americanmind.org/features/national-conservatism-vs-american-conservatism/. Excerpted from "National Conservatism vs. American Conservatism." *Claremont Review of Books* 24, no. 1 (Winter 2023/24). https://claremontreviewofbooks.com/national-conservatism-vs-american-conservatism/.
Kojève, Alexandre. "Tyranny and Wisdom." In *On Tyranny*, by Leo Strauss, edited by Victor Gourevitch and Michael Roth. Chicago: University of Chicago Press, 2013.
Lanavère, Jean-Rémi. "La dimension politique de la loi naturelle chez Saint Thomas d'Aquin." Thesis for doctorate in political studies, submitted jointly to l'École des Hautes Études en Sciences Sociales and l'Université Pontificale du Latran, 2015.
Lanavère, Jean-Rémi. *La loi naturelle et politique chez Saint Thomas D'Aquin*. Paris: Bibliothèque Thomiste, 2024.
Lawler, Peter Augustine. "America's Cartesian Intellectual Method." *Society* 53, no. 2 (2016): 204–9
Lawler, Peter Augustine. "Defending the Personal Logos Today." In *Reason, Revelation, and the Civic Order: Political Philosophy and the Claims of Faith*, edited by Paul R. DeHart and Carson Holloway. DeKalb: Northern Illinois University Press, 2014.
Lawler, Peter Augustine. "The Personal Logos and the Christian Idea of Marriage." Paper presented at a conference at Brigham Young University, 2013.
Lawler, Peter Augustine. *The Restless Mind: Alexis de Tocqueville on the Origin and Perpetuation of Human Liberty*. Lanham, MD: Rowman & Littlefield, 1993.
Lawler, Peter Augustine, and Richard M. Reinsch. *A Constitution in Full: Recovering the Unwritten Foundation of American Liberty*. Lawrence: University Press of Kansas, 2019.
Lennon, John. "Imagine." On *Imagine*. Produced by John Lennon, Yoko Ono, and Phil Spector. Apple Records. Released September 9, 1971.
Levin, Yuval. *American Covenant: How the Constitution Unified Our Nation and Could Again*. New York: Basic Books, 2024.
Levinas, Emmanuel. "De la phénoménologie à l'éthique: Entretien avec Levinas." *Esprit*, no. 234 (July 1997): 121–40.
Levinas, Emmanuel. *Éthique comme philosophie première* [Ethics as first philosophy]. Paris: Payot & Rivages, 1998.
Levinas, Emmanuel. *De l'existence à l'existant* [From existence to the existant]. Paris: Vrin, 1990. First published 1947. Translated by Alphonso Lingis as *Existence and Existents* (Pittsburgh: Duquesne University Press, 2001).
Levinas, Emmanuel. *Humanism of the Other*. Urbana: University of Illinois Press, 2006.

Levinas, Emmanuel. *Otherwise than Being, or Beyond Essence*. Pittsburgh: Duquesne University Press, 1998.
Lewis, C. S. "The Weight of Glory." In *The Weight of Glory, and Other Addresses*. New York: Macmillan, 1949.
Lilla, Mark. "A New, Political Saint Paul?" *New York Review of Books*, October 23, 2008.
Lindsay, James. *Race Marxism: The Truth about Critical Race Theory and Praxis*. Orlando, FL: New Discourses, 2022.
Luther, Martin. "An Appeal to the Ruling Class of German Nationality as to the Amelioration of the State of Christendom." In *Martin Luther: Selections from His Writings*, edited and with an introduction by John Dillenberger. Garden City, NY: Doubleday, 1961.
Luther, Martin. *Secular Authority: To What Extent It Should Be Obeyed*. In *Martin Luther: Selections from His Writings*, edited and with an introduction by John Dillenberger. Garden City, NY: Doubleday, 1961.
Machiavelli, Niccolò. *The Prince*. 2nd ed. Translated by Harvey C. Mansfield. Chicago: University of Chicago Press, 1998.
Mahoney, Daniel J. "The Delusions of Postcolonial Ideology." *The American Mind*, January 4, 2024. https://americanmind.org/salvo/the-delusions-of-postcolonial-ideology/.
Mahoney, Daniel J. Foreword to Manent, *Religion of Humanity*.
Mahoney, Daniel J. *The Idol of Our Age: How the Religion of Humanity Subverts Christianity*. New York: Encounter Books, 2018.
Mahoney, Daniel J. "Patrick Deneen's Lost Opportunity." Review of *Regime Change*, by Patrick Deneen. *Law & Liberty*, June 28, 2023. https://lawliberty.org/book-review/patrick-deneens-lost-opportunity/.
Mahoney, Daniel J. *Recovering Politics, Civilization, and the Soul: Essays on Pierre Manent and Roger Scruton*. South Bend, IN: St. Augustine's Press, 2022.
Manent, Pierre. *Beyond Radical Secularism*. Translated by Ralph C. Hancock. Introduction by Daniel J. Mahoney. South Bend, IN: St. Augustine's Press, 2016.
Manent, Pierre. "Christianity and Democracy." In *Religion of Humanity*.
Manent, Pierre. "The Church between a Real Humanity and a Dreamed-Of 'Humanity.'" In *Religion of Humanity*.
Manent, Pierre. *La cité de l'homme*. Paris: Flammarion, 1994.
Manent, Pierre. *The City of Man*. Translated by Marc A. LePain. Princeton: Princeton University Press, 2005.
Manent, Pierre. "An Eminent Predecessor." In *Religion of Humanity*.
Manent, Pierre. "Excerpt from *A World beyond Politics?*" In *Religion of Humanity*.
Manent, Pierre. "Excerpts from *Beyond Radical Secularism*." In *Religion of Humanity*.
Manent, Pierre. "The Humanitarian Temptation." In *Religion of Humanity*.
Manent, Pierre. "Individualisme et christianisme: En réponse à Daniel Tanguay." *Commentaire*, no. 183 (Fall 2023): 555–60.
Manent, Pierre. "La leçon de ténèbres de René Girard." *Commentaire*, no. 19 (Fall 1982): 457–63.

Manent, Pierre. *Metamorphoses of the City: On the Western Dynamic*. Translated by Marc LePain. Cambridge, MA: Harvard University Press, 2013.
Manent, Pierre. "Migrations and Christianity: What Message?" In *Religion of Humanity*.
Manent, Pierre. *Natural Law and Human Rights: Toward a Recovery of Practical Reason*. Translated by Ralph C. Hancock. Notre Dame, IN: University of Notre Dame Press, 2020.
Manent, Pierre. *Pascal et la proposition chrétienne: Essai*. Paris: Bernard Grasset, 2022.
Manent, Pierre. "Political Responsibility and Humanitarian Invention: A Critique of Contemporary Humanitarianism." In *Religion of Humanity*.
Manent, Pierre. "Reason and Faith: A Lenten Reflection." *Modern Age* 50, no. 1 (Winter 2008): 84–87. Available from the Intercollegiate Studies Institute, https://isi.org/reason-and-faith-a-lenten-reflection/.
Manent, Pierre. "Réflexions de philosophie pratique sur la 'foi seule.'" In *Karl Barth's Epistle to the Romans: Retrospect and Prospect*, edited by C. Chalamet, A. Dettwiler, and S. Stewart-Kroeker. Berlin: De Gruyter, 2022.
Manent, Pierre. *The Religion of Humanity: The Illusion of Our Times*. Edited and translated by Paul Seaton. South Bend, IN: St. Augustine's Press, 2022.
Manent, Pierre. "The Religion of Humanity." In *Religion of Humanity*.
Manent, Pierre. "René Girard, la violence et le sacré." Review of *La violence et le sacré*, by René Girard. *Contrepoint*, no. 14 (1974): 44–45.
Manent, Pierre. *Seeing Things Politically: Interviews with Benedicte Delorme-Montini*. Translated by Ralph C. Hancock and Daniel J. Mahoney. South Bend, IN: St. Augustine's Press, 2015.
Manent, Pierre. "Some Remarks on the Notion of 'Secularization.'" In *Religion of Humanity*.
Manent, Pierre. *Tocqueville and the Nature of Democracy*. Translated by John Waggoner. Lanham, MD: Rowman & Littlefield, 1996.
Manent, Pierre. *Tocqueville et la nature de la démocratie*. Paris: Julliard, 1982.
Manent, Pierre. "Who Is 'the Good Samaritan'?" In *Religion of Humanity*.
Manent, Pierre. *A World beyond Politics? A Defense of the Nation-State*. Translated by Marc A. LePain. Princeton: Princeton University Press, 2006.
Mansfield, Harvey C. Introduction to *Selected Letters of Edmund Burke*, edited by Harvey C. Mansfield. Chicago: University of Chicago Press, 1984.
Maritain, Jacques. *Réponse à Jean Cocteau*. In *Oeuvres complètes de Jacques et Raïssa Maritain*, edited by Jacques Maritain, vol. 3. Paris: Éditions St.-Paul, 1985.
Marsilius of Padua. *Defensor pacis*. Translated by Alan Gewirth. New York: Columbia University Press, 2001.
McAleer, Graham James. *Erich Przywara and Postmodern Natural Law*. Notre Dame, IN: University of Notre Dame Press, 2019.
Mitchell, Joshua. *American Awakening: Identity Politics and Other Afflictions of Our Time*. New York: Encounter Books, 2022.
Nelson, Eric. *The Theology of Liberalism: Political Philosophy and the Justice of God*. Cambridge, MA: Harvard University Press, 2019.

Nichols, Mary P. *Aristotle's Discovery of the Human: Piety and Politics in the "Nicomachean Ethics."* Notre Dame, IN: University of Notre Dame Press, 2023.
O'Connor, Flannery. Introduction to *A Memoir of Mary Ann*, by the Dominican Nuns of Our Lady of Perpetual Help Home. New York: Frederic C. Beil, 1961.
Pangle, Thomas L. *Political Philosophy and the God of Abraham*. Baltimore: Johns Hopkins University Press, 2007.
Pascal, Blaise. *Pensées*. Introduction by T. S. Eliot. New York: E. P. Dutton, 1958. Project Gutenberg eBook. https://www.gutenberg.org/files/18269/18269-h/18269-h.htm.
Przywara, Erich. *Analogia Entis: Metaphysics; Original Structure and Universal Rhythm*. Translated by John R. Betz and David Bentley Hart. Grand Rapids, MI: Eerdmans, 2014.
Przywara, Erich. *In und Gegen: Stellungnahmen zur Zeit*. Nuremberg: Glock und Lutz, 1955.
Przywara, Erich. *Religionsphilosophische Schriften*. Einsiedeln: Johannes-Verlag, 1962.
Rawls, John. *Political Liberalism*. New York: Columbia University Press, 2005.
Rawls, John. *A Theory of Justice*. Cambridge, MA: Harvard University Press, 1971.
Reinsch, Richard M. Introduction to *Seeking the Truth: An Orestes Brownson Anthology*, edited by Richard M. Reinsch. Washington, DC: Catholic University of America Press, 2016.
Reinsch, Richard M. "Zombie Deneenism." Review of *Regime Change*, by Patrick Deneen. *Law & Liberty*, June 28, 2023. https://lawliberty.org/book-review/zombie-deneenism/.
Roberts, Christopher Chenault. *Creation and Covenant: The Significance of Sexual Difference in the Moral Theology of Marriage*. London: T&T Clark, 2008.
Robinson, Marilynne. *Gilead: A Novel*. New York: Farrar, Straus and Giroux, 2020. First published 2004.
Rolland, Jacques. "Surenchère de l'éthique." Preface to Levinas, *Éthique comme philosophie première*.
Rufo, Christopher F. *America's Cultural Revolution: How the Radical Left Conquered Everything*. New York: Broadside Books, 2023.
Schindler, D. C. *Retrieving Freedom: The Christian Appropriation of Classical Tradition*. Notre Dame, IN: University of Notre Dame Press, 2022.
Schmitt, Carl. *Political Theology: Four Chapters on the Concept of Sovereignty*. Translated by George Schwab. Chicago: University of Chicago Press, 2005. First published 1922.
Seaton, Paul. "The Declaration's Civic Anthropology." *Law & Liberty*, July 4, 2023. https://lawliberty.org/the-declarations-civic-anthropology/.
Sherwin, Michael S., OP. *By Knowledge & by Love: Charity and Knowledge in the Moral Theology of St. Thomas Aquinas*. Washington, DC: Catholic University of America Press, 2005.
Shullenberger, Geoff. "René Girard and the Rise of Victim Power." *Compact*, December 9, 2022. https://www.compactmag.com/article/rene-girard-and-the-rise-of-victim-power/.

Siedentop, Larry. *Inventing the Individual: The Origins of Western Liberalism*. Cambridge, MA: Belknap, 2017.
Soloviev, Vladimir. "Nationality from a Moral Point of View." In *Politics, Law, and Morality: Essays*, by Vladimir Soloviev, edited by Gary Saul Morson. New Haven: Yale University Press, 2000.
Solzhenitsyn, Aleksandr. "We Have Ceased to See the Purpose." In *We Have Ceased to See the Purpose: Essential Speeches of Aleksandr Solzhenitsyn*, edited by Ignat Solzhenitsyn. Notre Dame, IN: University of Notre Dame Press, 2025.
Starobinski, Jean. *Jean-Jacques Rousseau: La transparence et l'obstacle*. Paris: Gallimard, 1971.
Strauss, Leo. "German Nihilism." *Interpretation* 26, no. 3 (Spring 1999).
Strauss, Leo. *Natural Right and History*. Chicago: University of Chicago Press, 1965.
Strauss, Leo. *On Tyranny*. Edited by Victor Gourevitch and Michael Roth. Chicago: University of Chicago Press, 2013.
Strauss, Leo. "Restatement on Xenophon's *Hiero*." In *On Tyranny*, by Leo Strauss, edited by Victor Gourevitch and Michael Roth. Chicago: University of Chicago Press, 2013.
Strauss, Leo. *Spinoza's Critique of Religion*. Chicago: University of Chicago Press, 1997.
Strauss, Leo. "The Three Waves of Modernity." In *Political Philosophy: Six Essays*, edited by Hilail Gildin. Indianapolis: Pegasus, 1975.
Strauss, Leo. "What Is Political Philosophy?" In *An Introduction to Political Philosophy: Ten Essays by Leo Strauss*, edited by Hilail Gildin. Detroit: Wayne State University Press, 2005.
Tanguay, Daniel. "Pierre Manent au miroir de son Pascal." *Commentaire*, no. 183 (Summer 2023).
Taylor, Charles. *Sources of the Self*. Cambridge, MA: Harvard University Press, 1992.
Thornton, John F., and Susan B. Varenne, eds. *The Essential Pope Benedict XVI: His Central Writings and Speeches*. San Francisco: HarperOne, 2007.
Tocqueville, Alexis de. *Democracy in America*. Translated by Harvey C. Mansfield and Delba Winthrop. Chicago: University of Chicago Press, 2002.
Tocqueville, Alexis de. *The Old Regime and the Revolution*. Edited by François Furet and Françoise Mélonio. Translated by Alan S. Kahan. Chicago: University of Chicago Press, 1998.
Torrell, Jean-Pierre. *Saint Thomas Aquinas*. Vol. 2, *Spiritual Master*. Washington, DC: Catholic University of America Press, 2003.
Trueman, Carl B. *The Rise and Triumph of the Modern Self: Cultural Amnesia, Expressive Individualism, and the Road to Sexual Revolution*. Wheaton, IL: Crossway, 2020.
Voegelin, Eric. *Science, Politics & Gnosticism*. Chicago: Regnery, 1968.
Zeitz, James V. "Erich Przywara on Ultimate Reality and Meaning: *Deus Semper Major* 'God Ever Greater.'" *Ultimate Reality and Meaning* 12, no. 3 (1989): 192–201. https://doi.org//10.3138/uram.12.3.192.

INDEX

A
Abraham (biblical figure), 158–59, 287n.7
action
   Aristotle on, 31, 55, 105, 137, 211, 255
   Manent on, 47–48, 50, 55, 59, 93–94, 105, 120–122, 126–27, 133–47, 171, 182, 199, 222, 241, 247
agape, 162–63, 167–71, 205, 271n.27
agency, 102, 104–5, 110, 137, 183, 201, 223, 245–47, 255, 278–79n.42
   Mahoney on, 115, 118
   Manent on, 42, 46, 50, 55, 66, 121, 124–25, 127–28, 148, 182, 283–84n.16
   Mitchell on, 242–43
   morality and, 24, 26, 32, 45–46, 66, 70, 90, 151–53, 171–72, 199, 242, 287n.9
   Murdoch on 216
   Pascal on, 232–33
   Thomas Aquinas on, 222, 281n.63
Alt-Right, 285n.29
analogia entis, 200–206, 208–9, 240, 276–77n.37, 278n.42
angels, 147–48, 231, 234
animal rights, 55
animals (beasts), 58, 207, 231, 245, 262n.11
   rational, 109, 173

anthropocentrism, 10, 185
apes, 27
aristocracy, 4–5, 242, 246, 253, 276–77n.37, 285n.29
   Christianity and, 67, 73–74, 85, 91, 106, 108, 110, 258
   Manent and, 148, 235, 286n.3
   Strauss and, 78–81, 85–91, 196, 273n.15
   Tocqueville on, 93, 100, 102–3, 106–10, 147, 183–85, 188, 198, 228, 245, 258, 286n.3
Aristotelianism, 157, 202, 217, 221, 229, 249, 253–54, 270n.9
   Heidegger and, 38, 263n.17
   Lanavère on, 281n.61
   Lawler on, 271–72n.27
   Manent and, 36, 44–45, 59, 119, 121–22, 129, 137, 152, 199, 213, 246, 248, 252, 276–77n.37, 277n.40
   Rawls and, 266n.8
   Strauss and, 85, 88
   Thomas Aquinas and, 26, 210–11, 216–17, 221, 266n.4
Aristotle, 43, 50, 94, 158, 170, 179, 201–2, 212–16, 270n.9
   on action, 31, 55, 105, 137, 211, 255
   De anima, 176, 273n.1
   on first philosophy, 173–75, 192
   Heidegger on, 39
   Hibbs on, 215–16, 218–19

Aristotle (*cont.*)
  Manent and, 119, 121–22, 128–29, 133–34, 144–45, 148, 152, 247, 263n.6
  on politics, 13, 26, 49, 129, 131, 133, 252–53, 288n.17
  Przywara and, 275n.30, 276n.34
  Strauss on, 82
  Thomas Aquinas and, 26, 88, 218
  on virtue, 149–51, 206–7
Aron, Raymond, 27
Athens, 13, 75, 81–82, 84–85, 87–88, 91, 113, 166–67, 180, 196, 211, 243, 273n.2, 288n.12
  religion in, 156
Aubenque, Pierre, 272n.30
Augustine of Hippo, 16, 33, 113, 182, 213, 217, 222, 275n.26
  City of God, 15, 159, 208, 260n.10, 278n.41
  Platonism and, 14–15, 159–62, 260nn.10–11
Augustinianism, 14–15, 20, 33, 220, 216, 229, 234, 238, 244, 266n.4
Austen, Jane, 79
Austria, 274n.14

B
Bacon, Francis, 61
Badiou, Alain, 72–74, 76, 83, 89
Balthasar, Hans Urs von, 274n.8, 276n.37
Barth, Karl, 35–37, 40–42, 46, 203, 206, 241
  on grace, 36–37, 51, 121
Bayle, Pierre, 260n.10
Beatles, the, 12
Beethoven, Ludwig van, 98
Benardete, Seth, 178
Benedict XVI (pope), 71, 265n.27, 268n.12, 271n.27, 274n.18
  on Logos, 118, 153, 165–69, 199, 258, 271–72n.27
Berkowitz, Peter, 265
Besançon, Alain, 260n.8 (intro)
Betz, John R., 201–3, 205–6, 274n.3, 274n.9, 274n.11, 275n.20, 275n.25

Bible
  Akedah, 158–59, 287n.7
  Colossians, 159
  1 Corinthians, 11, 155–56, 269n.4
  Exodus, 217
  Gospel of John, 162, 165
  Gospel of Luke, 156
  Habakkuk, 287n.7
  Hebrews, 158
  on humility, 110, 181, 244
  individuality and, 98–99, 252, 254, 287n.7
  Isaiah, 247
  Levin on, 251–52, 254
  on love, 153, 158, 162–63, 167, 271n.27
  Manent and, 137
  New Testament, 71, 220, 244
  Old Testament, 14, 18, 158, 167
  Pangle on, 157–59
  Parable of the Good Samaritan, 57–58
  Paul's letters, 12, 14
  Philippians, 58, 259n.4
  philosophy and, 113, 255
  Psalms, 247
  Romans, 203, 274n.10
  Strauss and, 77, 80, 84–88, 91, 196
  Tocqueville on, 101
  universalism and, 12, 16, 288n.12
Blondel, Maurice, 282n.65
Bloom, Allan, 3–4, 158, 260n.1, 265n.5
Blum, Léon, 194
Boryga, Andrew, 289n.19
Bottum, Joseph, 227
Brague, Rémi, 164
Brigham Young University, 164, 271–72n.27
Brownson, Orestes, 10, 114, 117, 286n.5
Burke, Edmund, 6, 121, 276n.37, 287n.7

C
Cajetan, Thomas, 200–202, 274n.4
Caldwell, Christopher, 226–27
Calvin, John, 238, 262n.11, 278n.41
Calypso, 164
Carr, Benjamin, 267n.1

Catholicism, 86, 88, 119–20, 139, 169–71, 271–72n.27, 274n.8
   Heidegger on, 38
   liberalism and, 286n.5
   Manent and, 36, 43, 46, 53–54, 59, 119, 122, 125, 135, 228, 247
   Protestantism and, 36, 39–40, 43, 59, 171, 203
   theology of, 200–202, 205–6, 209, 240, 275n.20
   See also Christianity
Chalamet, Christophe, 274n.8
charity, 2, 23, 71, 73, 222–23, 233, 279–80n.50, 283n.16
   love and, 11–13, 17–19, 79, 89, 168
   Manent on, 57–60, 122, 283–84n.16
   as virtue, 35, 57–58, 60, 122, 222–23, 233, 245, 277n.40, 285n.21
Christ, 68–72, 83, 86, 97, 166, 211–12, 222–23, 225, 236–37
   Augustine on, 160–61
   God and, 18, 72, 110, 237
   Logos and, 162
   Manent on, 57–58, 264n.19
   Resurrection of, 72, 160, 271–72n.27
   Tocqueville on, 108, 188
   Wise on, 287n.9
Christianity, xi–xii, xvi
   Aristotle and, 26, 85, 88, 119, 121–22, 131, 151–52, 266n.4
   Badiou on, 72–73
   Barth on, 36–37
   charity and, 11–13, 57–58, 60, 223
   communities and, 19–20
   family and, 271n.12, 271–72n.27
   Girard on, 259–60n.6
   Heidegger on, 38–40
   Hibbs on, 215–16, 218
   humanitarianism and, 10–11, 59, 77, 93, 122, 166, 199, 203, 235, 256, 258
   humility and, 244
   identity and, 243
   individuality and, 98–99, 161, 247
   innocence and, 236–37, 239–40, 257, 259n.6, 285n.26, 285n.29
   Logos and, 165–67, 179
   love and, 2–3, 11, 14, 18, 34–35, 79, 97, 100, 137, 153, 162–63, 168–71, 203, 257
   Machiavelli on, 30, 43–45, 48, 61
   Mahoney on, 7, 116–18
   Manent on, 23, 42–47, 50, 52–54, 58–59, 69, 119–20, 123, 128, 131–37, 152, 246, 261n.19, 283n.16
   modernity and, 25, 61–62, 76–77, 88, 95, 108, 177, 247, 261n.19
   Pascal on, 229–30, 233–34
   philosophy and, 37, 47, 50, 62, 68–69, 72, 88–89, 94, 113, 156–62, 165–67, 178–80, 198, 202, 208–11, 235, 242, 260n.10, 271–72n.27, 279n.50
   Plotinus and, 275n.26, 278n.42
   poetry and, 264n.5
   politics and, 4, 32–35, 52–54, 116, 122, 131–33, 219, 236–40, 246–49, 254, 256, 283–84n.16, 286n.5
   Przywara and, 204, 210–13
   Rawls and, 66, 266n.8
   secularism and, 3, 12–13, 16–18, 51, 71–73, 93, 229, 244
   Siedentop on, 67–73
   Strauss on, 23–24, 76–77, 79–80, 82–91, 98, 183, 196
   Tocqueville on, 101–3, 106, 108–10, 188, 258, 273n.6
   transcendence and, 157–59, 178, 209, 211, 227–28, 278n.41
   in the United States, 4–6, 227, 236–37, 287n.9
   universalism and, 12–14, 16, 20–21, 23, 69, 73–74, 85–89, 114, 160, 256, 283n.8
   virtue and, 15, 51, 100, 115, 154, 207, 222, 254, 257–58, 281n.60
   Voegelin on, 96
   See also Catholicism; Protestantism
Churchill, Winston, 116
Church of Jesus Christ of Latter-day Saints, 271–72n.27
Cicero, 172
civil rights, 226–27, 237

Cohen, Hermann, 83
collectivism, 171
Columbus, Christopher, 261n.5
"Come Ye Children of the Lord" (hymn), 97, 267n.1
communism, 72–73
Comte, Auguste, 10–11, 56, 114
conscience, 33, 71, 88, 91, 114, 117–18, 246
   freedom of, 70
   Levinas on, 189–90, 195, 273n.7
   Manent on, 23, 42–44, 46–47, 132, 253
conservatism, 12, 19, 120, 139, 238–39, 250, 283n.8, 286n.5
Coolidge, Calvin, 287n.9
Cooper, Anthony Ashley. *See* Shaftesbury, Third Earl of

D
Darwin, Charles, 271–72n.27
Davis, Michael, 176–81, 183, 189, 273n.1
Declaration of Independence (U.S.), 249–50, 252, 287n.9
De Gaulle, Charles, 116
democracy
   humility and, 258
   Levin and, 249, 252–53
   Manent on, 52–54, 129, 235, 261n.19
   morality and, 73, 103–4, 106, 109, 222, 245–46
   Siedentop on, 76
   Strauss on, 79-80, 86, 91, 198
   Tocqueville on, 5–7, 27, 51, 53, 93, 100–104, 106–12, 184–86, 207, 228, 230, 267n.7 (chap. 6), 276–77n.37
   Wise on, 287n.9
Democratic Party, 288n.10
Deneen, Patrick, 286n.5
deontology, 270n.9
de Rougemont, Denis, 162–63, 169, 171
Derrida, Jacques, 190
Descartes, René, 17, 61, 181, 232–33
Doctors without Borders, 54–55
Dostoyevsky, Fyodor, 79

E
egalitarianism, 4–5, 8, 23, 54, 61, 63–64, 68, 70–71, 226, 244
   Strauss on, 86
   Tocqueville on, 102–3, 108
England, 107
English language, 52, 78, 81, 269n.13, 269n.24
Enlightenment, 6, 102
Epicureanism, 27
Erasmus, 32
eros, 158, 162–63, 167–68, 170, 174, 180, 263n.6, 271n.27
ethics, 172, 227, 236, 270n.9
   Aristotle on, 149–51, 174–75
   Lanavère on, 219
   Levinas on, 183, 188–93
   Murdoch on, 216
   See also morality; virtue
Europe, 29, 48, 53, 71, 102–3, 132–33, 136, 246
   philosophy in, 17, 237
existentialism, 35, 37, 40, 42, 122, 171

F
faith, 16, 23–24, 245–46, 257–58, 262n.7, 283–84n.16
   Augustine on, 14, 161, 260n.10
   Barth on, 35, 37
   Benedict XVI on, 165–66
   Heidegger on, 263n.17
   Luther on, 32–33, 35, 38, 46–47
   Mahoney on, 118
   Manent on, 32, 42–43, 45, 57–59, 124, 133–35, 283–84n.16
   marriage and, 170
   Siedentop on, 68, 70–71
   Strauss on, 83, 89–90
   Thomas Aquinas on, 202
   Tocqueville on, 102
   virtue and, 222
Federalist Papers, 248
Ferreyrolles, Gérard, 285n.21
Fideism, 58–59
Florence, Italy, 48
Fourth Lateran Council, 206, 209, 213, 224, 274n.18, 276–77n.37

France, 54, 103, 132, 164
  philosophy in, 49, 56, 228, 247, 260n.10, 282n.65
  politics of, 53, 63, 107–8, 194
Francis (pope), 10, 57, 264n.18
freedom, 96, 114–15, 209, 223–25, 246, 254, 277n.40, 282n.65, 284n.16
  of conscience, 70
  Levinas on, 191–92
  Mahoney on, 117, 286n.5
  Manent on, 62, 247, 252–53, 279n.42, 282n.65, 286n.5
  Schindler on, 278n.42
  Siedentop on, 68, 70–71
  Strauss on, 77–78, 81
  Tocqueville on, 104, 106, 111–13, 119, 197, 244, 254
  universalism and, 74
French language, 262n.12, 263n.1, 269n.20, 273n.7, 280n.53
French Revolution, 103, 121

G
Germany, 202, 210, 274n.3
Girard, René, 259n.6
Gnosticism, 96, 275n.20
God
  Augustine on, 161–62, 213, 260n.10
  Benedict XVI on, 271n.27, 274n.18
  Bible on, 274n.10
  Blondel on, 282n.65
  Calvin on, 262n.11
  charity and, 57–58, 122
  Christ and, 18, 72, 110, 237
  covenant and, 134, 224, 283n.16, 287n.7
  democracy and, 6
  humans and, 19–21, 38–41, 59, 65, 98–99, 107–14, 122, 132–34, 148, 154, 159–61, 165, 187, 195–201, 206, 209, 217–18, 225, 236, 258, 283–84n.16
  Lanavère on, 220–21
  Lawler on, 234
  Logos and, 165, 169, 178, 199, 244
  love and, 2, 20, 114, 155, 169–70, 180–81, 211, 224, 255
  Luther on, 32–33, 35, 38
  Mahoney on, 114, 117–18, 122
  Manent on, 59, 124, 134, 152, 269n.15, 283n.16
  Marcion on, 14
  nature and, 21, 204, 210, 224
  openness and, 5
  Pascal on, 229
  philosophy and, 68–69, 156–62, 179, 183, 208, 216–17, 279n.50
  Przywara on, 203–5, 209–11, 214–15, 278n.42
  Rawls on, 266n.8
  Sherwin on, 277–78n.40
  Strauss on, 81–83, 87–88, 195, 279n.46
  Thomas Aquinas on, 202, 210, 217, 268n.9 (chap. 6), 280n.53, 281n.58, 281–82n.63
  Tocqueville on, 51, 93, 106–7, 109, 111–12, 186, 197, 200–201, 254
  transcendence and, 9–10, 41, 45, 74, 87, 113, 117, 155–57, 165, 206–11, 213–15, 223, 228, 236, 257, 269n.15, 275n.20, 276–77n.37, 279n.49
Goldman, David B., 283n.8
good, xii–xiii
Gourevitch, Victor, 266n.19
grace, 21, 38, 97, 101, 154, 222–24, 236, 240, 282n.65, 285n.25
  Barth on, 36–37, 51, 121
  Kojève on, 74
  Mahoney on, 117
  Manent on, 32, 36, 41, 44, 121, 124–25, 132, 283–84n.16
  nature and, 1, 16, 19, 44, 51, 59, 73, 82, 85, 88, 110, 124–25, 202–3, 241, 254–57, 283–84n.16
  Przywara on, 214–15
  Rawls on, 266n.8
  Strauss on, 82
  transcendence and, 94, 281–82n.63
Greece, 14, 72, 80, 202, 234, 247, 255, 271–72n.27
  Davis on, 176–77, 180, 183, 189
  philosophy of, 16, 36, 42, 49, 69–70, 87, 113–14, 117, 157–59, 162,

Greece, philosophy of (*cont.*)
    165–66, 208–9, 218, 224, 275n.26, 279n.50
  politics of, 16, 45, 153
  virtue in, 89, 278n.42
Greek language, 167
Gregory, Eric, 265n.4, 266n.8
Gregory the Great (pope), 169

H
Haidt, Jonathan, 288n.10
Hanania, Richard, 226
Hancock, Ralph C.
  Responsibility of Reason, xvii, 273n.6
Harnack, Adolf von, 166
Harvard University, 64
heaven, 64, 102, 155–56, 164, 170, 242, 270n.9
Hebrew language, 98, 113, 244, 276n.37
Hegel, Georg Wilhelm Friedrich, 61, 73–74, 76–77, 86, 108, 226
Heidegger, Martin, 42, 74, 82–83, 171–72, 178, 187, 189
  Levinas and, 191, 193
  Luther and, 23, 37–40, 241, 263n.17
  Przywara on, 211, 276n.31
Heraclitus, 201
Hibbs, Thomas S., 215–19, 276–77n.37, 279n.44, 279n.46, 279nn.49–50, 280n.52, 281n.58, 283–84n.16
Hobbes, Thomas, 27–30, 32, 48, 51, 53, 61, 136, 142, 246
  on desire, 120, 138
  Rawls and, 63, 265n.7
  Strauss on, 261n.5
Holland, Tom, 21
home, xii
Homer, 164–65, 247
honor, 9–10, 15, 100, 144–45, 196, 242, 255, 267n.7 (chap. 6)
  Aristotle on, 150
  Strauss on, 23, 79, 91
Hugo, Victor, 56
humanism, 3, 6, 20, 51, 55, 69, 77, 89, 173

humanitarianism, 1, 5, 9–12, 17, 171, 223, 244, 252
  Christianity and, 10–11, 59, 77, 93, 122, 166, 199, 203, 235, 256, 258
  Mahoney on, 8–9, 114–18
  Manent on, 53–54, 56–59, 110, 122, 211, 228, 233
human rights, 223
  Christianity and, 71
  Manent on, 28, 55, 59, 63, 110, 123, 126, 128–30, 138, 252
humans
  Aristotle on, 94, 149–51, 173–74
  Augustine on, 15, 160
  Badiou on, 72–73
  Benedict XVI on, 271n.27
  Calvin on, 262n.11
  communities of, 19–20, 46, 100–101, 131, 172, 192, 265n.27
  competence and, 239
  covenant and, 134, 224, 284n.16, 287n.7
  Davis on, 178, 181
  Girard on, 259n.6
  God and, 19–21, 38–41, 59, 65, 98–99, 107–14, 122, 132–34, 148, 154, 159–61, 165, 187, 195–201, 206, 209, 217–18, 225, 236, 258, 283–84n.16
  Heidegger on, 38–40
  Hibbs on, 215, 218
  Hobbes on, 27–28
  ideas of nobility, 146–48
  identity of, 21
  individuality of, 1, 8, 62, 76, 83–84, 93, 97–100, 119, 139–40, 153, 161, 255
  institutions and, 10
  Kojève on, 74
  law and, 142, 144, 216, 220–22, 276–77n.37
  Lawler on, 234
  Levinas on, 189–95
  Levin on, 249–51, 253, 288n.14
  Logos and, 166, 244, 258
  love and, 137, 168, 171–72, 282n.65

Machiavelli on, 30, 43
Mahoney on, 115, 118, 122, 199
Manent on, 26-28, 42–47, 51–52, 55,
  58–59, 62–63, 69–70, 93–94,
  124–29, 140–46, 152, 199, 247,
  280n.53
Mitchell on, 240–41
Pascal on, 229–34, 284n.17, 285n.21
philosophy and, 17, 27, 48–49,
  94–95, 121, 160–61, 172–75,
  181, 184
Przywara on, 203–4, 208–10, 212,
  214, 276n.34
Rawls on, 64–66, 266n.8
religion and, 7–9, 11, 23, 33, 54–56,
  184, 187–88, 257–58
Rousseau on, 242
spirituality and, 96, 117, 135
Strauss on, 75–87, 89, 91, 100, 177,
  195–96, 231–32
Thomas Aquinas on, 41, 216–17, 219,
  281n.58, 281n.61, 281–82n.63
Tocqueville on, 93, 101–13, 147–48,
  176, 184–88, 197–98
transcendence and, 155–56, 207, 224,
  276n.34
universalism and, 16, 25, 60, 89, 95,
  160
humility, 16, 18, 54, 116, 151–52, 213,
  228, 232, 234, 256
  Bible on, 110, 181, 244
  democracy and, 258
  Manent on, 50, 121–22
  Strauss on, 91, 196
  Tocqueville on, 110, 207–8,
    281–82n.63
Husserl, Edmund, 189–93, 213
hymns, 97, 267n.1, 274n.14

I
individualism, 8, 76, 119–20, 126–27,
  139, 171, 219, 268n.11 (chap. 7)
  Christianity and, 67, 76, 88, 98
  democracy and, 6, 103
integralism, 246, 250, 257, 286n.5
Iowa, 98

Isaac (biblical figure), 158, 287n.7
Islam, 59, 132–33, 165

J
Jerusalem, 13, 16, 75, 81–82, 84–85,
  87–88, 91, 113, 166–67, 180, 196,
  211, 243, 273n.2, 288n.12
Jesuits, 202
Jesus. *See* Christ
John Paul II (pope), 271–72n.27
Judaism, 13–14, 16, 68–70, 72, 81–87,
  117, 193, 211, 278n.42
  laws of, 13, 42, 70, 84, 86–87, 89,
    91, 188
  scriptures of, 68, 113, 162
justice, 255, 270n.9
  Aristotle on, 149
  Manent on, 42, 55, 129–30, 146,
    148, 228, 263n.6
  Mitchell on, 238
  Rawls on, 63–67, 265nn.5–6, 266n.8
  social, 3–5, 7–8, 91, 236
  Strauss on, 82, 85–88, 91
  Thomas Aquinas on, 220, 281n.60
  Tocqueville on, 100–101, 108, 184,
    228, 245

K
Kant, Immanuel, 63, 83, 115, 129, 252,
  270n.9
Kass, Leon, 159, 162–63, 276n.37
Kennedy, Anthony, 254
kenosis, xii–xiii, 18, 110, 188, 259n.4,
  268n.6
Kesler, Charles R., 283n.8
Kierkegaard, Søren, 85
King, Martin Luther, Jr., 227
Kojève, Alexandre, 73–74, 76–79, 83,
  86, 89, 195–96, 266n.19
Kolnai, Aurel, 10, 116, 276–77n.37
Kosovo, 55–56
Kundera, Milan, 153

L
Lanavère, Jean-Rémi, 219–22, 280n.53,
  281n.58, 281nn.61–62, 283–84n.16

Lawler, Peter, 86, 165, 234–35, 270n.9, 271n.27, 284n.18, 286n.5
leftism, 52, 236, 238
Lennon, John, 56, 260n.9
Lent, 124, 283–84n.16
Levinas, Emmanuel, xvii, 171, 182–83, 188–95, 197, 273n.7, 279n.44
Levin, Yuval, 248–54, 287n.9, 288n.10, 288n.12, 288n.14
Lewis, C. S., 8, 98
liberalism, xvi–xvii, 73, 131, 154, 222–23, 265n.7
   Christianity and, 236, 238, 240, 246, 248, 254, 256, 286n.5
   competence and, 237–40, 242, 254, 285n.27
   Levin on, 249, 251
   love and, 2, 19
   Manent on, 29, 93, 120, 128, 136, 138–39, 247–48, 283n.16, 286n.5
   Rawls on, 63–67, 265n.5
   Siedentop on, 67, 71–72, 76
   Strauss on, 81, 86
   theory and, 29–30
   Tocqueville on, 104
   virtue and, 244
Lincoln, Abraham, 116
Lindsay, James, 226
Locke, John, 48, 63, 136, 238, 240, 246, 286n.5
Logos, 69, 153, 162, 165–69, 179, 181–82, 192, 258, 273n.2
   God and, 165, 169, 178, 199, 244
   Lawler on, 271n.27
   Mahoney on, 118, 199
   Plotinus on, 208
Louis XIV, 53
love, 96–97, 137, 163–65, 170–72, 215, 222–23, 257
   Badiou on, 72
   Benedict XVI on, 165, 167–69, 271n.27
   Blondel on, 282n.65
   charity and, 11–13, 17–19, 79, 89, 168
   Comte on, 56
   definition of, 18–19
   de Rougemont on, 162–63
   of God, 2, 20, 114, 155, 169–70, 180–81, 211, 224, 255
   humanitarianism and, 17, 57, 171, 199, 203, 211, 235
   liberalism and, 2, 19
   Luther on, 34
   Mahoney on, 116
   morality and, 2, 19, 89, 100, 115, 172
   philosophy and, 79–87
   Przywara on, 205
   reason and, 153
   Siedentop on, 71
   universality and, 11–14, 170
Luther, Martin, 46, 142, 238, 262n.11
   Heidegger and, 23, 37-40, 241, 263n.17
   Manent on, 31–32, 34–38, 43, 45, 47–48, 121, 128
   on politics, 32–34
Lutheranism, 34, 39–40, 42, 45

M
Machiavelli, Niccolò, 23, 30–31, 40, 51, 61, 83, 141–42, 262n.7, 288n.12
   Manent on, 27, 30–32, 43–45, 47–48, 128, 136, 246
   Strauss on, 77, 96, 261n.5
MacIntyre, Alasdair, 279n.44
Madison, James, 248
Mahoney, Daniel J., 7–11, 93, 114–18, 259n.6, 265n.28, 289n.21
   on charity, 60, 122
   on freedom, 117, 286n.5
   on love, 116
   on prudence, 60, 117, 199, 259n.6
Manent, Pierre, xv, xviii–xx
   on action, 47–48, 50, 55, 59, 93–94, 105, 120–122, 126–27, 133–47, 171, 182, 199, 222, 241, 247
   on Barth, 35–37, 241
   on charity, 57–60, 122, 283–84n.16
   The City of Man, 26, 128–29, 261n.15, 263n.17, 263n.6 (chap. 2)
   on democracy, 52–54, 129, 235, 261n.19
   on faith, 32, 42–43, 45, 57–59, 124, 133–35, 283–84n.16

on freedom, 62, 247, 252–53,
  278–79n.42, 282n.65, 286n.5
on history, 69, 74, 136, 246–47
on humanitarianism, 53–54, 56–59,
  110, 122, 211, 228, 233
on hypertrophy of theory, 23, 26-28,
  30, 32, 46–48, 62-63, 66, 95,
  120–23, 125, 135–36, 138–39,
  142, 144, 167
on individuality, 99, 119–20, 138–39,
  254
Lanavère and, 280n.53
on law, 261n.15
Levin and, 248, 252
on liberalism, 29, 93, 120, 128, 136,
  138–39, 247–48, 283n.16, 286n.5
on Luther, 31–32, 34–38, 43, 45,
  47–48, 121, 128
on Machiavelli, 27, 30–32, 43–45,
  47–48, 128, 136, 246
Mahoney and, 114, 117, 289n.21
on meaning, 228
on modernity, 18, 29, 62, 119–20, 139
on natural law, 28, 30, 45, 49, 93,
  120, 122–26, 128, 135–36,
  142–45, 152, 198, 213, 246–47,
  276–77n.37, 277n.40
Natural Law and Human Rights,
  26–28, 35, 42–43, 49, 63, 122,
  125–26, 128, 136, 139–40, 263n.2,
  269n.13, 269n.24
on nobility, 143–49
Pascal and, 233, 283n.14, 283n.16,
  285n.21
on philosophy, 42, 44, 47–50, 123,
  128–30, 138–39, 207, 263n.15,
  263n.6 (chap. 2), 269n.13
on politics, 128–35, 254–55
on practice, 41–44, 50–51, 93–94,
  121, 123, 125, 128–29, 144–45
on prudence, 42, 132–33, 199, 222,
  233
Przywara and, 213–14
The Religion of Humanity, 52–59
on secularism, 126–28, 132–33, 246
on theory, 26–30, 41–42, 48, 120–25,
  142–45

Thomas Aquinas and, 41, 43,
  123–25, 128, 132–36, 139, 148,
  269n.13, 283n.16, 286n.4,
  287n.6
Tocqueville and, 26, 286n.3
on transcendence, 155
views of conscience, 23, 42–44,
  46–47, 132, 253
on virtue, 49–51, 59, 94, 110, 134,
  147, 152, 254, 265n.27
Mansfield, Harvey, 101, 121
Marcion, 14
marriage, 2, 8, 18, 163, 254, 271n.27
  Manent on, 28, 62
Marsilius of Padua, xvi
Marxism, 61, 77, 171, 193–94, 226,
  237, 279n.44
Marx, Karl, 58, 194, 226, 266n.8
materialism, 16, 51, 61, 95–96, 173,
  212, 235, 240, 245–47, 252, 258,
  268n.11 (chap. 7)
  Coolidge on, 287n.9
  Manent on, 48, 119–20, 139, 211
  morality and, 11, 28
  in philosophy, 27
  Rawls on, 66
  Strauss on, 232
  Tocqueville on, 100, 104, 245
McAleer, Graham James, 276n.37
McCartney, Paul, 12
mediation, xiv, 2, 9, 35, 70, 93, 116–17,
  171, 187, 196, 288n.14
  Christianity and, 46, 58–59, 102,
    110, 188, 208, 254
  democracy and, 6–7, 102, 110, 186,
    267n.7 (chap. 6)
  institutions and, 6–7, 56
  Lanavère on, 219
  Manent on, 131, 134–35, 254
  subjectivity and, 182–83
Mediterranean Sea, 69
Merleau-Ponty, Maurice, 276n.37
Mill, J. S., 265n.7
Mitchell, Joshua, 154, 236–43, 246,
  248, 254, 264n.2, 285nn.25–29
monotheism, 68, 101
Montaigne, Michel de, 26, 31

morality
  aesthetics and, 276–77n.37
  agency and, 24, 26, 32, 45–46, 66, 70, 90, 151–53, 171–72, 199, 242, 287–88n.9
  Aristotle on, 149–51
  Bottum on, 227
  competence and, 239
  conscience and, 46
  democracy and, 73, 103–4, 106, 109, 222, 245–46
  Hibbs on, 218
  Levinas on, 191
  love and, 2, 19, 89, 100, 115, 172
  Machiavelli on, 30
  Mahoney on, 114, 118
  Manent on, 23, 42, 51, 55, 117, 146, 253, 269n.13
  materialism and, 11, 28
  politics and, 9, 222–23, 227, 229, 241, 257
  practice and, 41, 199
  Rawls on, 64–66, 266n.8
  religion and, 4, 9, 25, 68, 115, 255, 285n.26
  Siedentop on, 70–71
  Strauss on, 85, 87, 211–12
  Thomas Aquinas on, 286n.5
  Tocqueville on, 93, 103–6, 109, 172, 197–201, 223, 242, 267n.7 (chap. 6)
  See also ethics; virtue
Moses (biblical figure), 113, 160, 268n.9 (chap. 6)
Mother Theresa, 116
Muhammad (Islamic prophet), 165
Murdoch, Iris, 216, 279n.44
Murray, John Courtney, 286n.5
music, 97–101, 204–6, 267n.1, 274n.14
Music Man, The, 98–101, 137

N
nationalism, 53, 117, 283n.8
natural law, 265n.1, 268n.11
  Manent on, 28, 30, 45, 49, 93, 120, 122–26, 128, 135–36, 142–45, 152, 198, 213, 246–47, 276–77n.37, 277n.40
  McAleer on, 276n.37
  postmodernism and, 95
  Rawls and, 64–65
  Strauss on, 85, 90
  theory and, 62, 105
  Thomas Aquinas on, 212, 216, 219–21, 268n.15, 269n.22, 280n.53, 281n.61, 286n.5
  Tocqueville on, 113
nature
  agency and, 45–46, 172
  in ancient philosophy, 43–44, 49, 68, 263n.6
  Aristotle on, 150
  Augustine on, 260n.11
  Badiou and, 73
  God and, 21, 204, 210, 224
  grace and, 1, 16, 19, 44, 51, 59, 73, 82, 85, 88, 110, 124–25, 202–3, 241, 254–57, 283–84n.16
  Hobbes on, 28–30, 138
  Levinas on, 191, 193
  Manent on, 46, 49, 62, 124–25, 138–39, 144, 255, 263n.6, 276–77n.37
  Nietzsche on, 91
  philosophy and, 17, 68, 105, 110, 193
  Przywara on, 214–15, 223
  rationalism and, 51
  souls and, 177–78
  Strauss on, 85–86, 90
  Thomas Aquinas on, 19, 82, 85, 88, 124, 202, 216, 222, 255, 277–78n.40
  Tocqueville on, 185–86
Nazism, 194
Nelson, Eric, 265n.4, 266n.8
neoplatonism, 167, 169, 200, 208–9, 275n.30. *See also* Platonism
New York City, 227
Nichols, Mary P., 288n.17
Nicole, Pierre, 285n.21
Nietzsche, Friedrich, 3, 21, 56, 82–83, 129, 181, 276n.31, 285n.29
  on nature, 91
  on truth, 25, 174

nobility, 94, 98, 116, 123, 129, 136, 143–52, 269n.15, 270n.9, 276–77n.37
   freedom and, 111
   Strauss on, 79–82, 86, 89
North Atlantic Treaty Organization (NATO), 55–56
Notre Dame Cathedral, 134

O
O'Connor, Flannery, 86
Odysseus, 164
Odyssey (Homer), 164–65
openness, 2, 4–5, 7, 11, 20, 26, 85, 252, 260n.1, 277–78n.40
   Aristotle and, 276n.34
   Hibbs on, 219, 279–80n.50
   individuality and, 99
   Mahoney on, 117
   Manent on, 146, 276–77n.37, 283–84n.16
   religion and, 45, 47, 59, 82–83, 96, 173, 203, 236, 255
   Strauss on, 273n.2
   as virtue, 3–4
Ortega y Gassett, José, 217

P
paganism, 14, 16, 18, 23, 163, 167–69, 208, 216, 234, 260n.10, 271–72n.27, 278n.41
   Mahoney on, 117
   Manent on, 135, 207
   Siedentop on, 67
   Strauss on, 91, 98, 198
Pangle, Thomas, 157–59, 162, 270n.9
pantheism, 114, 118, 187, 203, 215, 223
   Tocqueville on, 1, 6–7, 9–11, 62, 95, 100, 111, 175–76, 186, 228, 252, 267–68n.7
Parmenides, 201, 203
Pascal, Blaise, 7, 26, 85, 109–10, 188, 229–35, 246
   on knowledge, 184, 235
   Manent and, 233, 283n.14, 283n.16, 285n.21
   on virtue, 154, 284n.17, 285n.21

Paul the Apostle, 12, 14, 16, 67–73, 89, 159
Péguy, Charles, 264n.5
Pelagianism, 210, 266n.8
Penelope (*Odyssey*), 164
phenomenology, 121–22, 189–94, 204, 263n.17
philosophy
   Augustine on, 15, 160–62, 182
   Barth on, 37
   Christianity and, 37, 47, 50, 62, 68–69, 72, 88–89, 94, 113, 156–62, 165–67, 178–80, 198, 202, 208–11, 235, 242, 260n.10, 271–72n.27, 279n.50
   classical, 49, 68–70, 80–82, 85–87, 94, 98, 121, 156–62, 177–83, 189, 207–9, 230, 269n.13
   Hibbs on, 216–17
   history of, 112–13, 226
   humans and, 17, 27, 48–49, 94–95, 121, 160–61, 172–75, 181, 184
   Kojève and, 73
   Levinas on, 189–90, 192–93, 195
   love and, 79–87
   Luther and, 34
   Mahoney on, 116
   Manent on, 42, 44, 47–50, 123, 128–30, 138–39, 207, 263n.15, 263n.6 (chap. 2), 269n.13
   materialist, 27
   modern, 17, 91, 130, 138, 181, 207
   Pascal on, 234, 284n.17
   Przywara and, 213, 276n.31
   Rawls on, 64
   Siedentop on, 68
   Socratic, 44, 80, 172, 174, 201
   Strauss and, 75, 77–91, 181, 195–97, 230–31, 236, 270n.9, 273n.15, 279n.46
   theology and, 94, 105, 113, 120, 125–26, 136, 156–59, 162, 172–74, 197, 201–2, 205, 208–10, 257, 287n.7
Plato, 14, 50, 64, 113, 177, 191, 247, 263n.6, 276–77n.37
   Republic, 67, 156, 158, 201

Platonism, xiii, 14–15, 49, 68, 84, 113, 157–62, 167, 174, 260n.11, 266n.4, 278n.42
   Hibbs on, 216
   Levinas on, 191
   Manent and, 263n.6
   Pascal on, 233–34
   technology and, 235
   See also neoplatonism
Plotinus, 208, 275n.26, 278n.42
poetry, 109–111, 176, 178–79, 183–88, 204, 264n.5
Poland, 202
Popular Front (France), 194
postmaterialism, 212
postmodernism, xv, 21, 80, 86, 95, 125, 228, 237, 253, 276n.31
practice
   action and, 199
   Aristotle on, 215
   Barth on, 36
   Manent on, 41–44, 50–51, 93–94, 121, 123, 125, 128–29, 144–45
   theory and, 26, 41, 104–5, 137, 263n.6
   Thomas Aquinas on, 217
   See also action; theory
pride
   Augustine on, 161–62, 260n.10
   Christianity and, 244–46, 256
   Luther on, 39
   Manent on, 125, 133–34, 143, 152, 255
   Pascal on, 232, 234
   philosophy and, 16, 50, 78–81, 87, 121–22, 125, 151, 181–82, 196, 207–8, 215, 217, 230, 235, 279n.46
   Przywara on, 208, 210, 212–13
   Tocqueville on, 110, 183–84, 197, 207, 235, 245, 275n.24, 281–82n.63
   virtue and, 16, 66, 89, 94, 188, 244–245, 258, 287–88n.9
Princeton University, 266n.8
progressivism, 2–4, 63, 65, 73, 87, 91, 186, 212, 250, 288n.10
   Levinas and, 183, 194–95
   love and, 19
   Manent on, 134
   See also liberalism
Protestantism, 32, 154, 162, 169–71, 203, 206, 227, 244, 258, 271n.12, 285n.25
   Heidegger on, 39–40
   Manent on, 34–35, 37, 42–43, 47–48, 51, 59, 122, 125, 246
   Mitchell on, 237–43, 254
   Rawls and, 63, 65, 266n.8
   universalism and, 16–17
   See also Christianity; Lutheranism; Reformation
providence, 114, 117, 199, 217, 220–22, 268n.15, 281n.58
   faith in, 59
   Hibbs on, 218–19
   Manent on, 128, 132–34, 199, 247, 255
   Tocqueville on, 102–3, 245, 267n.7
prudence, 23, 80, 220–22, 233, 281n.58, 281n.60, 282n.65, 283n.16
   Hibbs on, 217–19, 279–80n.50
   Mahoney on, 60, 117, 199, 259–60n.6
   Manent on, 42, 132–33, 199, 222, 233
Przywara, Erich, 202–6, 208–15, 223–24, 275n.30, 276n.31, 277n.40, 278n.42
   Betz on, 274n.3, 274n.8, 274n.11
   on love, 205
   McAleer on, 276n.37
   on music, 205, 274n.14
   on transcendence, 206, 210, 213, 276n.34
"Pseudo-Dionysius" (theologian), 200

R
Rahner, Karl, 274n.8
rationalism, 95, 103–4, 113, 159, 167, 173, 181, 199, 246–47
   Burke on, 6, 121
   Christianity and, 16, 20, 24, 50–51, 61–62, 67, 73, 76–77, 102
   Levinas and, 188, 195
   love and, 2

Manent on, 48–49, 62–63, 93, 119–20, 123–24, 139, 141
Strauss on, 73, 76–77, 81–82, 84–85, 90, 273n.5
Ratzinger, Joseph. *See* Benedict XVI
Rawls, John, 63–67, 253–54, 265nn.5–7, 266n.8
Reformation, 16–17, 32, 34–35, 48, 51, 166, 262n.7, 271n.12. *See also* Protestantism
Reinsch, Richard, 283n.8, 286n.5
republicanism, 16, 53, 249–52, 254, 288n.12
Republican Party, 239, 287–88n.9
Robinson, Marilynne, 164
Rolland, Jacques, 190–91
Roman Empire, 69, 117, 156
Rosenzweig, Franz, 82–83
Roth, Michael, 266n.19
Rousseau, Jean-Jacques, 53–55, 58, 241–42, 259n.1
Rufo, Christopher, 226

S
Saint-Martin, Community of, 281n.62
same, and other, xiii
Sartre, Jean-Paul, 171
Schindler, D.C., 275n.30, 278n.42, 282n.66
Schmitt, Carl, 257
Scholasticism, 38–39, 123, 200–201
Seaton, Paul, 54, 287–88n.9
secularism
    Christianity and, 3, 12–13, 16–18, 51, 71–73, 93, 229, 244
    humanitarianism and, 11, 17, 212, 227, 235
    Kojève on, 77
    Levinas and, 189, 193
    love and, 18, 56, 89
    Mahoney on, 115, 118
    Manent on, 126–28, 132–33, 246
    Mitchell on, 154, 264n.2
    politics and, 34
    Strauss on, 96
    universalism and, 20, 73, 89
Serbia, 55–56

Shaftesbury, Third Earl of, 276–77n.37
Sherwin, Michael S., 277n.40
Shullenberger, Geoff, 259n.6
Siedentop, Larry, 21, 67–74, 76, 83, 88–89
slavery, 108, 111, 239
social justice, 3–5, 7–8, 91, 236
Socrates, 64, 144, 172, 180–81, 231–32, 260–61n.11
Socratic philosophy, 44, 80, 172, 174, 201
Soloviev, Vladimir, 10–11, 27
Solzhenitsyn, Aleksandr, 10
Sophocles, 247
souls, x, xvi, 177–78, 182–83, 186–88, 198, 205, 241, 255, 270n.9, 273n.1, 276n.33
    Calvin on, 262n.11
    knowledge and, 232, 274n.1
    Socrates on, 260–61n.11
Spain, 267n.1
Spinoza, Baruch, 82–85, 269n.2
Starobinski, Jean, 269n.4
Stein, Edith, 274n.8
Stoics, 284n.17
Strauss, Leo, x, 75, 100, 114, 166, 176–77, 182, 211–12, 273n.2, 288n.12
    Bloom and, 4
    on Christianity, 23–24, 76–77, 79–80, 82–91, 98, 183, 196
    on democracy, 79–80, 86, 91, 198
    on freedom, 77–78, 81
    "German Nihilism," 266n.3
    on individuality, 97–99, 247, 287n.7
    on liberalism, 81, 86
    Kojève and, 73, 77–79, 266n.19
    Lanavère and, 281n.61
    on Machiavelli, 77, 96, 261n.5
    Manent and, 30, 119, 136
    on modernity, 76–78, 80, 83–88, 90–91, 96–98, 119–20, 139, 196–97, 247, 273n.5
    Pascal and, 230–32, 235
    on philosophy, 75, 77–91, 181, 195–97, 230–31, 236, 270n.9, 273n.15, 279n.46

Strauss, Leo (*cont.*)
　on politics, 26–27, 79, 81, 87, 90–91, 136, 189
　on rationalism, 73, 76–77, 81–82, 84–85, 90, 273n.5
　on reason, 23–24, 204
　Siedentop and, 67
Suárez, Francisco, 200

T
Taylor, Charles, 182
theology, 14, 20–21, 110, 165–66, 177, 189–81, 188, 198–202, 204–10, 213, 228–29, 240, 275n.20
　Heidegger on, 38–39
　Hibbs on, 215–18
　Lanavère on, 220
　Manent on, 23, 42, 46–47, 50, 95, 123–24, 128, 132, 139, 142, 246–47
　philosophy and, 94, 105, 113, 120, 125–26, 136, 156–59, 162, 172–74, 197, 201–2, 205, 208–10, 257, 287n.7
　Strauss on, 83
　transcendence and, 95
theory
　action and, 199
　Aristotle on, 215
　Barth and, 36
　hypertrophy of, 23, 26–28, 30, 32, 46–48, 62–63, 66, 95, 120–23, 125, 135–36, 138–39, 142, 144, 167, 199, 213
　Levinas on, 191
　Manent on, 26–30, 41–42, 48, 120–25, 142–45
　O'Connor on, 86
　practice and, 26, 41, 104–5, 137, 263n.6
　Przywara and, 213
　Strauss on, 232
　Thomas Aquinas on, 217
　Tocqueville on, 104–5, 107–9
　See also practice
Thomas Aquinas, xvii, 26, 88, 136, 199–200, 228, 262n.11, 266n.4, 268n.15, 285n.21
　on agency, 222
　on faith, 202
　on God, 202, 210, 217, 268n.9, 280n.53, 281n.58, 281–82n.63
　on grace, 1, 19, 124, 154
　Hibbs on, 215–19, 276–77n.37, 279–80n.50, 280n.52
　on knowledge, 274n.1
　Lanavère on, 219–21, 280n.53, 281n.58, 281n.61
　Manent and, 41, 43, 123–25, 128, 132–36, 139, 148, 269n.13, 283n.16, 286n.4, 287n.6
　on the mind, 271–72n.27
　on natural law, 212, 216, 219–21, 268n.15, 269n.22, 280n.53, 281n.61, 286n.5
　on nature, 19, 82, 85, 88, 124, 202, 216, 222, 255, 277–78n.40
　on politics, 33
　on prudence, 281n.60
　Przywara on, 204, 210, 212, 214, 277n.40
　Schindler on, 278–79n.42
　Summa Theologiae, 41, 217–18
　Torrell on, 281–82n.63
Thomism, xvii, 148, 199, 201, 206, 208–9, 220, 222, 229, 255, 274n.14, 287n.6
　Levin and, 248
　Manent and, 59, 133, 135, 139, 246, 283n.16, 286n.4
　Przywara on, 211, 215
　Strauss and, 82, 85, 88–90
Tocqueville, Alexis de, 21, 54, 147–48, 171, 182–88, 195, 198, 279n.44
　on Christianity, 101–3, 106, 108–10, 188, 258, 273n.6
　on democracy, 5–7, 27, 51, 53, 93, 100–104, 106–12, 184–86, 207, 228, 230, 267n.7 (chap. 6), 276–77n.37
　on freedom, 104, 106, 111–13, 119, 197, 244, 254
　on individualism, 8, 100
　on justice, 100–101, 108, 184, 228, 245
　Manent and, 26, 286n.3

Mitchell and, 237, 240, 242
  on morality, 93, 103–6, 109, 172,
    197–201, 223, 242, 267n.7 (chap. 6)
  on pantheism, 1, 6–7, 9–11, 62, 95,
    100, 111, 175–76, 186, 228, 252,
    267–68n.7
  Pascal and, 229, 235
  scholarship on, 234–35
Torrell, Jean-Pierre, 281–82n.63
totalitarianism, 152, 222
transcendence, 155–59, 224
  Christianity and, 157–59, 178, 209,
    211, 227–28, 278n.41
  God and, 9–10, 41, 45, 74, 87, 113,
    117, 155–57, 165, 206–11, 213–15,
    223, 228, 236, 257, 269n.15,
    275n.20, 276–77n.37, 279n.49
  grace and, 94, 281–82n.63
  humans and, 155–56, 207, 224,
    276n.34
  Przywara on, 206, 210, 213, 276n.34
Trinity, 72, 110, 188, 271–72n.27,
  279n.50
Trueman, Carl B., 259n.1
truth
  Aristotle on, 174
  Levin on, 250–52
  Nietzsche on, 25, 174
  Pascal on, 229
  philosophy and, 172, 175, 182
  Przywara on, 213
  Strauss on, 232, 273n.15

U

United States, 186, 248
  Christianity in, 4–6, 227, 236–37,
    287n.9
  constitution of, 2, 249–52, 288n.12,
    288n.14
  Declaration of Independence, 249–50,
    252, 287n.9
  liberalism in, 63, 286n.5
  politics of, 227, 237–39, 242,
    249–50, 283n.8, 288n.12
  religion in, 53, 227
  Supreme Court of, 2, 8, 254
  Tocqueville on, 5–6, 53, 101, 107,
    111, 267n.7 (chap. 6)

universalism, 15–17, 68–69, 71–74, 95,
  183–84, 283n.8, 288n.12
  Christianity and, 12–14, 16–17,
    20–21, 23, 69, 73–74, 85–89, 114,
    160, 256, 283n.8
  love and, 11–14, 170
  Mahoney on, 114
  Manent on, 28, 93
  of St. Paul, 12, 71–72
  Strauss on, 79, 86–88, 90–91
U.S. Supreme Court, 2, 8, 254
utilitarianism, 270n.9

V

Van Buren, John, 38
victimhood, ix–x, xiv–xvi, 2, 4, 16, 223,
  243, 256
  Christianity and, 18–21, 259n.6
  individuality and, 1, 99
  in literature, 289n.19
  Mitchell on, 154, 236–37
  Rawls on, 64, 67
Vietnam War, 227
virtue
  action and, 105, 116, 147, 214, 223,
    241–42, 277n.40
  aesthetics and, 276–77n.37
  Aristotle on, 149–51, 206–7
  Augustine on, 260n.10, 278n.41
  charity as, 35, 57–58, 60, 122, 222–23,
    233, 245, 277n.40, 285n.21
  in classical philosophy, 49, 89, 98,
    188, 235, 278n.41, 284n.17
  freedom and, 112
  Hibbs on, 217–18
  humility and, 232–33, 235, 258
  Lanavère on, 220, 222
  liberalism and, 244
  love and, 35, 115
  Manent on, 49–51, 59, 94, 110, 134,
    147, 152, 254, 265n.27
  Mitchell on, 154, 239, 242
  openness as, 3–4
  Pascal on, 154, 284n.17, 285n.21
  politics and, 129, 219, 223, 238,
    279n.44
  postmodernism and, 95
  practice and, 213

virtue (*cont.*)
   pride and, 16, 66, 89, 94, 188, 244–45, 258, 287–88n.9
   Rawls on, 65–66
   religion and, 1, 5, 9, 15, 25, 51, 118, 122, 199, 222, 255, 257–58
   secularism and, 4, 51
   Siedentop on, 68
   Strauss on, 76, 84, 89, 91, 98, 100, 287n.7
   Thomas Aquinas on, 281n.60
   transcendence and, 224
   universalism and, 15–16, 197, 267–68n.7
   See also ethics; morality
Vittori, Francisco, 262n.7
Voegelin, Eric, x, 76, 90, 96
voluntarism, 112, 140–41, 166, 199, 257, 277n.40

W
Wallis, James H., 267n.1
Winthrop, Delba, 101
Wise, John, 287n.9
"woke," ix, xv, 226–28
World War I, 264n.5

X
Xenophon, 195, 232

Y
Yale University, xi

RALPH C. HANCOCK
is a professor of political science at Brigham Young University,
where he teaches political philosophy. He has authored,
edited, or translated many books and articles on the interrelation
of religion, morality, and politics, including authoring
The Responsibility of Reason and translating
Pierre Manent's *Natural Law and Human Rights*.

www.ingramcontent.com/pod-product-compliance
Lightning Source LLC
Chambersburg PA
CBHW061426300426
44114CB00014B/1564